DATE DUE

DEMCO 38-296

THE VATICAN AND ZIONISM

STUDIES IN JEWISH HISTORY
Jehuda Reinharz, General Editor

THE VATICAN AND ZIONISM

Conflict in the Holy Land
1895–1925

SERGIO I. MINERBI

Translated by
ARNOLD SCHWARZ

New York   Oxford
OXFORD UNIVERSITY PRESS
1990

Oxford University Press

Oxford   New York   Toronto
Delhi   Bombay   Calcutta   Madras   Karachi
Petaling Jaya   Singapore   Hong Kong   Tokyo
Nairobi   Dar es Salaam   Cape Town
Melbourne   Auckland

and associated companies in
Berlin   Ibadan

Copyright © 1990 by Oxford University Press, Inc.

Published by Oxford University Press, Inc.
200 Madison Avenue, New York, New York 10016

Oxford is a registered trademark of Oxford University Press

Library of Congress Cataloging-in-Publication Data
Minerbi, Sergio I.
[Vatikan, Erets ha-Kodesh veha-Tsiyonut, 1895–1925. English]
The Vatican and Zionism : conflict in the Holy Land,
1895–1925 / Sergio I. Minerbi; translated by Arnold Schwarz
p. cm.   —(Studies in Jewish history)
Translation of: Vatikan, Erets ha-Kodesh veha-Tsiyonut.
Bibliography: Includes index.
ISBN 0-19-505892-5
1. Catholic Church—Relations (diplomatic)—Palestine.
2. Palestine—Foreign relations—Catholic Church.
3. Catholic Church and Zionism.   I. Title.   II. Series.
BX1628.M5613   1990
327.456'3405694—dc20   89-32688

1 3 5 7 9 8 6 4 2

Printed in the United States of America
on acid-free paper

To my wife, Hanna,
and my daughters,
Tamar, Nourit, and Iris

Preface

The subject of this book is the stand of the Holy See toward Zionism from its beginning in the larger context of the Vatican's interests in the Holy Land. The subject, which is complex, is treated concisely, but supplementary sources are suggested to interested readers in case they would like to deepen their knowledge of related themes, such as the structure of the Catholic Church or the relations between Jews and Christians. This book, published in Hebrew in 1985 and in Italian in 1988 (with a preface by Professor Renzo De Felice), is the result of extensive research conducted over many years, which has given as a first fruit an essay.[1]

I do not claim to be absolutely objective on this topic. On the contrary, I feel personally involved for many reasons: I was born in Rome, the cradle of Christianity, and I now live in Jerusalem, the center of Judaism. Moreover, during the Nazi occupation of Rome in 1943 and 1944, I was hidden for seven months in a Catholic college, the San Leone Magno in Rome, and thanks to its director and some of its teachers I was saved. This period gave me a unique opportunity to get a first-hand knowledge of Christianity from the inside, such as I could probably not have received from books alone. At the same time, I am a fervent Zionist and this fact also has some influence on my outlook. Nevertheless, I have tried scrupulously to be as objective as possible, always sticking to all the sources available.

My first academic interest in this subject came from a thesis that I wrote for Professor Meir Vereté in the late 1950s while I was his student at the Hebrew University of Jerusalem. I am deeply grateful to Professor Vereté for his teaching of diplomatic history and its methodology, for his enlightened severity and his brilliant way of enthusiasm for the tiresome research in archives.

Later I gave a lecture on this topic at the World Congress of Jewish Studies, held in Jerusalem in 1981, and taught, as Senior Lecturer at the Hebrew University of Jerusalem, thus receiving the stimulating feedback of my students.

It seems to me that the absence, to the best of my knowledge, of a deep and well-documented investigation of the attitude of the Vatican toward Zionism justifies this book. I used primarily original sources hitherto unpublished, but I have done my best to include available publications.

The most challenging obstacle for anybody working in the Vatican Archives is the availability of documents: those dated before 1922—that is, until the end of the pontificate of Pope Benedict XV—are accessible, but the papers of Cardinal Gasparri were not available because his activity as secretary of state went beyond 1922; moreover, the absence of catalogs and other problems limit the work of the scholar. I therefore could not fulfill my wish to compare the documents in my hands with those of the Vatican and had to look for alternative avenues of investigation. Among the many primary sources examined, the most important were in the Public Record Office in London. Great Britain played a key role in determining the political settlement of Palestine; it is therefore only natural that many important documents are kept in its archives, and most of them were yet unpublished. It was a real pleasure to work at the PRO, and I am very thankful to its director for the help given me.

French, Italian, Belgian, and German diplomats had frequent talks with Cardinal Gasparri, and their reports are credible sources for the views of the cardinal secretary of state. I thank for their courtesy the directors of the archives of the Ministries for Foreign Affairs in Rome, Paris, Brussels, and Bonn and of the Secretariat of State at the Vatican City.

The Central Zionist Archives in Jerusalem and the Weizmann Archives in Rehovot provided me with very useful material about Zionist activity. The Israeli State Archives in Jerusalem were of great help; I am obliged to its director, Dr. Avraham Alsberg, and to Dr. Moshé Mosek for their assistance in obtaining copies of documents from various diplomatic archives.

I wish to thank also the staff of the British Library in London, of the National Library in Jerusalem, of the Franciscan Library at San Salvatore in Jerusalem, and of the Library of Modern and Contemporary History in Rome for their service. I have received precious and learned remarks from Professor Israel Kolat, Professor Dan Segre, and some friends like Hugo Morat and Dr. Yoab Eilon. I thank also Professor Ada Rappaport and Professor Yehuda Reinharz for their support.

Yael Munk typed the first version of the Hebrew manuscript; Dr. Joel Fishmann, Dr. Amedeo Tagliacozzo, Dr. Carmel Shalev, and Nora Gotlib gave me their valuable help at the very beginning of this study. Lotte Forshmit has patiently given her aid in collating and revising the various translations.

I am deeply obliged to the Institute for Contemporary Jewry of the Hebrew University for its financial support, which was indispensable in the first phase of the research. May I thank Professor Moshè Davis, Professor Yehuda Bauer, and Dr. Menahem Kaufmann, of the Institute, for their cooperation and Dr. Lorenzo Jarach of Torino for his constant and brotherly support.

Last but not least is the debt to my family: my wife, Hanna, and my daughters Tamar, Nourit, and Iris, all of whom had to accept the prolonged absence caused by this work. All of them, each in her own way, took some active part in the complex revision process of the text. Nourit and her husband, Michael Padon, dealt also with the first English version of the book, and they deserve special thanks.

Jerusalem   S.I.M.
October 1989

Contents

Introduction

Since biblical times, religion has played a major role in the Holy Land. In the modern era, a number of European powers have tried to exploit religion to promote their national interests in the Holy Land: France, in the sixteenth century, took over Venice's role as protector of Catholics in the Levant, and Russia began at a later date to extend its protectorate to Greek Orthodox adherents. Italy, Germany, and the Austro-Hungarian Empire also used religious institutions to emphasize their presence in Palestine.

Students of the history of Palestine in the modern period then may well ask: What role, if any, did the churches play, especially the Catholic Church, in determining the policy of the Great Powers regarding Palestine? Did the Vatican influence the local population through its representatives more than it was itself influenced by the positions of the Arab population and its leaders, quite a few of whom were themselves Christians? Why did the Vatican from the outset adopt so chilly an attitude toward Zionism? Was this a consequence of immutable theological positions or of a temporary political contingency? Can we draw lessons from this recent past to understand better the Vatican's position today? These are some of the questions I shall try to answer in this book.

The period that I have chosen to discuss, from the beginning of political Zionism to 1922 when the Council of the League of Nations decided to grant Britain the mandate for Palestine and also the period immediately afterward, is important because it largely determined the future of Palestine. I hope one day to continue my research and bring this study up to the present.

My aim was thus to examine the historical roots of the Vatican's position on Zionism and to place it in the context of the period discussed here. It was not my intention to deal with the much wider subject of relations between Christianity and Judaism, or even of the Catholic Church's position on the Jews. Rather, my purpose is to examine the Holy See's policy toward Zionism as a political movement. Accordingly, the method I use is that of diplomatic history, although I also take into account the theological dimension, as the theological and political dimensions are here woven together. For example, the pope is head of both the Catholic Church and the sovereign State of Vatican City. Further, in regard to state policy, the Vatican's theological reasons always predominate. Today, however, the Catholic Church tries to keep its stand toward the Jews separate from its position on Zionism. The reason, I believe, is that the Church does not wish to appear anti-Semitic after the Holocaust, for many feel that the ideology leading to the massacre of the Jews had its roots in traditional Christian anti-Semitism. The Vatican's political position is closely linked to the theology underlying it, but in turn, its theological positions are sometimes dictated by political circumstances. Thus the 1965 declaration on the Jews, *Nostra Aetate,* a purely theological document, was modified in light of the political pressures brought to bear by Arab countries.

In Part I of this book, I describe the complex relations between the Holy See and the Great Powers concerning Palestine, from the end of the nineteenth century to the mid-1920s. The Vatican was disturbed by the far-reaching changes taking place in the Holy Land after the British conquest in 1917 and feared that British rule might impinge on Catholics' rights. In addition, the problem of the Holy Places was on the agenda of all discussions of Palestine's future, either as a pretext for the Great Powers to reinforce their presence in Palestine or as an issue of genuine concern, and it featured centrally in the talks held by the Great Powers during and immediately after World War I. This may explain the great interest in establishing a commission for the Holy Places, which would have examined the contending claims of the various religious communities. But despite the extensive diplomatic efforts invested in this matter, such a commission was never formed.

The end of the capitulations was also supposed to terminate the French protectorate over Catholics in Palestine, an issue that led to a sharp struggle between Italy and France. The Vatican alternately encouraged and discouraged the protectorate, but ultimately it was terminated unequivocally. At the very last moment, the Vatican tried to revive what still remained of it—the liturgical honors accorded to France's representative—but it was too late. The period of the religious protectorate was over, even if France and Italy, despite their opposing stands, had difficulty realizing this.

Part I also deals with internal Church problems, such as the tensions between the Franciscans and the Latin Patriarchate of Jerusalem, and the pressures put on the Vatican to appoint English, French, or Italian priests to the highest ecclesiastical posts in the Holy Land. Today those struggles may appear a bit absurd, but at the time they were felt to have considerable importance.

Just as the mandate was about to be approved by the Council of the League of Nations, the Vatican succeeded in obtaining a postponement, thereby showing its strength. Although the draft mandate was ultimately approved, the Palestinian government was notified that it now had to take into account the Vatican's wishes.

It became evident to me, early in my research, that in order to understand the Vatican's position on Zionism, I had to consider the Vatican's interest in Palestine, especially in the Holy Places. I therefore shall deal first with the various plans for the Holy Places put forward by the Great Powers, then with the French religious protectorate over the Roman Catholics in the East, and finally with the Vatican's intricate relations in those years with Britain, France, Italy, and Belgium. I shall also try to outline the major events in Palestine at that time and the international deliberations about the country's future, for the Vatican in no small measure influenced and was influenced by them.

Part II concerns the Vatican's position on Zionism. A question often arises when talking about the Vatican: "How many divisions does it have?" Although the Vatican of course has no military arm, its influence is often apparent in political decisions related to Palestine. The Great Powers were well aware of this, and therefore each sought to exploit the religious factor for its own benefit and to promote its own political interests; for example, Italy made great efforts to regain the Cenacle, the room of the Last Supper on Mount Zion in Jerusalem.[1]

The first important event that I shall discuss is Pope Pius X's audience with Theodor Herzl in 1904. "Non possumus," the pope told him. These two words, translated as "We cannot [support Zionism]," summarize the Vatican's position on Zionism from the early twentieth century to the present. There may be a more favorable development some day, comparable to or in the wake of what has happened with Church teachings in other areas. In any case, we should not forget that Pius X opposed all forms of modernism and indeed fought those in the Church who believed it possible to come to terms with modern democracy.

Pope Benedict XV, however, was a different sort of man, a refined diplomat and clear thinker. That he received Nahum Sokolow with courtesy in 1917 is not surprising, but I shall try to demonstrate that there was no friendship in his words, and certainly no acceptance of Zionism. The pope, who knew of the existence of the secret Sykes–Picot agreements, was convinced that central Palestine, which included the Holy Places, would be placed under an international regime. On this, then, he had nothing to talk about with Sokolow and said as much. It seems that the pope's comments were not properly understood by Sokolow or the Zionists, who deluded themselves into thinking that they had obtained the Vatican's sympathy, an illusion perhaps based on insufficient acquaintance with the ways and history of the Catholic Church.

From the Vatican's point of view, the situation in Palestine became increasingly worrisome, starting at the end of 1917. News about the Balfour Declaration and the British conquest of Palestine arrived almost at the same time. Pietro Cardinal Gasparri, the Vatican secretary of state and the real éminence grise in the Vatican, received these two news items with deep reservations. "It is hard to take back that part of our heart which has been given over to the Turks in order to give it to the Zionists," he remarked.

Two years later, at the Sanremo Conference, several of the Vatican's ambitions were thwarted. The internationalization that would have given the Catholic countries, especially France and Belgium, predominance in the Holy Places was replaced by exclusive rule by Britain as the mandatory power. And then there was the matter of a commission for the Holy Places, by means of which the Vatican hoped to get the revision of the status quo of the Holy Places that it had not obtained at the Versailles Peace Conference. But again, the commission was never formed, and the Vatican's diplomatic status was weakened by the fact that the pope had not been able to send his representative to the peace conference.

Another result of the Sanremo Conference was the appointment of a Jewish high commissioner for Palestine. Were further proofs needed to confirm that there existed an international plot by Jews and Freemasons conspiring to demolish the Catholic Church? At the same time, an identification of the Zionists with the Bolsheviks began to take hold not only in the Vatican but also in the British press and official circles.

I also note in this book the similarity between the objections of the Arabs in Palestine and those of the Vatican. Despite the various reasons for this, it should be remembered that in the steadily escalating conflict between Jews and Arabs, from the beginning the Vatican took a position that favored only one side.

I

THE VATICAN AND
THE HOLY LAND

1

Tu Es Petrus . . .

The Christian Holy Places

Most of the places holy to Christians are related to the life of Jesus and are concentrated in Palestine. From Jesus's time to our own, these places have experienced many changes, both in intra-Christian terms and with respect to the political regime in Palestine, a land that has changed hands time and again.[1]

In holy places where churches of only one Christian community stand, ownership is usually not a matter of dispute. At other sites, such as that of the Church of the Holy Sepulchre in Jerusalem and the Basilica of the Nativity in Bethlehem, the problem of ownership has been a cause of protracted and bitter conflict among the various Christian denominations. The conflict has been primarily between the Greek Orthodox, who own about two-thirds of these properties, and the Roman Catholics.

The complexity of interchurch relations has been further compounded by international politics. That was so, for example, in 1535 when Francis I, king of France, signed the Capitulations Treaty with Sultan Suleiman the Magnificent, according to which the sultan agreed to grant special rights to French subjects throughout the Ottoman Empire. Consequently, the Catholic Church asked France to defend its (the Church's) interests vis-à-vis the sultan.[2] France fully exploited this religious protectorate on Catholics to further its own political objectives and to facilitate its economic penetration of the Middle East. In the absence of direct diplomatic relations between the Holy See and the Ottoman Empire, the French also served, in effect, as representatives of the Vatican to the empire.

Eventually, Russia accorded its protection to the Greek Orthodox, and thus the powers confronted one another in Palestine, ostensibly to protect the churches' respective interests. The zeal they displayed in purely religious matters to a large extent stemmed from a need to assert their presence and to consolidate their foothold in this part of the world. And indeed, as the Ottoman Empire weakened, the Great Powers' appetite became increasingly voracious.

What is known as "the question of the Holy Places" was above all an internal problem of the various Christian churches concerning the division of ownership of some of the Holy Places in the Holy Land. Although the sultan interceded from time to time and ordered some property to be transferred from one church to another, the main problem continued to be that between the Christian communities themselves. In 1878, the European powers reached agreement at the Congress of Berlin: Article 62 of the Treaty of Berlin recognized France's rights and stipulated that "no alterations can be made in the status quo in the Holy Places." The term "status quo," appearing for the first time in an international convention, referred to the situation prevailing in the Holy Places as of the sultan's final firman (decree) in February 1852. Despite repeated attempts by Catholics and Greek Orthodox to alter the status quo, the firman has been scrupulously preserved to this very day.[3] The Holy See, which had considerable political influence, carefully protected its rights in Palestine, many of which preceded those of the Great Powers and were of special importance in a region where the administration was ineffectual and where for hundreds of years religion and nationality were held to be virtually identical.

The Christian Churches in the East

It would be appropriate at this point to consider the complex nature of the Roman Catholic Church's structure. On the one hand, this church is "the universal society of the faithful" with a defined hierarchy, at whose apex sits the pope. The pope alone is entitled to elect cardinals, and, in turn, only the cardinals can appoint the pope. Some of the cardinals are "curial cardinals," who head the various congregations of the Roman Church. After the cardinals are the bishops, who oversee territorial units, and the priests, who belong to monastic or other orders attached directly to the pope. On the other hand, there is the Holy See, a separate entity and the juridical personification of the Church, which enjoys the right to negotiate international agreements and treaties and to dispatch and receive diplomatic representatives.[4] Finally, the pope is simultaneously the high priest of his church and the head of the Holy See, and today he is also the temporal ruler of the state of the Vatican City.

According to H. E. Cardinale, the term "Holy See" has three meanings. Sometimes it refers to the pope as part of the curia, which consists of the sacred congregations, the tribunals, and other departments. At other times the term refers to the pope in his capacity as head of the Church, and it also denotes the spiritual organization of the papal government. Functioning within the framework of the Holy See is the Secretariat of State, as organized in 1908 by Pope Pius X.[5] The Secretariat of State is headed by the cardinal secretary of state, who is vested with broad powers greater than those of a prime minister. The cardinal secretary of state is the pope's chief aide in all matters related to the conclusion of treaties and the conduct of diplomatic relations with other states.

The Holy See sends to a foreign state an apostolic nuncio, an envoy with ambassador's rank, usually an archbishop who customarily acts as dean of the diplomatic corps in the country where he serves. The nuncio has both a diplomatic and an internal mission: he serves to promote the Holy See's good relations with the

Heads of churches, Jerusalem, 1922. From left to right: superior of the Coptic Convent; Jacobite bishop; Greek Orthodox patriarch; Anglican bishop in Jerusalem; Armenian patriarch; and abbot of the Abyssinian Convent. The Roman Catholic patriarch is missing.

civil government to which he is accredited, and he acts as the pope's representative to the local Catholic Church, and in that capacity he is entitled to intervene in the nomination of bishops and in their decisions. To countries with which the Holy See does not exchange ambassadors, an apostolic delegate is sent. An apostolic delegate does not have official diplomatic status and deals mainly with the local ecclesiastical hierarchy, but de facto, he also maintains friendly relations with the civil authorities.

In the countries of the Middle East, including the Holy Land, the Catholic Church's situation is especially complicated, for there the Church is composed not only of Latins but also of many Eastern churches following different rites and enjoying considerable autonomy, although all are under the pope's authority.[6]

The Eastern churches, or Uniate, include a number of communities worshiping according to the following rites: (1) the Alexandrian rite, to which the Copts and Ethiopians belong; (2) the Antiochene, which includes the Maronites; (3) the Armenian, whose adherents returned to the Catholic Church in the eighteenth century; (4) the Byzantine, which includes the Melkites, or Greek Catholics; and (5) the Chaldean.[7] The Melkites, whose center is in Damascus, are an example. In 1882, a Greek Catholic seminary was opened in St. Anne's Church in Jerusalem but was transferred to Lebanon after the city was reunified in 1967.

The Vatican increased its interest in Palestine in the nineteenth century, in part because of Russia's greater activity on behalf of the Greek Orthodox. In 1843, Russia encouraged the Greek patriarch to reestablish his seat in Jerusalem. Orthodox adherents believe that they belong to the true Church and do not recognize the pope, whom they regard as an apostate. This was the reason for their secession from Catholicism. Today there are a number of local Greek Orthodox churches whose patriarchs enjoy autonomous or "autocephalous" status. In order of primacy, they are the patriarchs of Constantinople, Alexandria, Antioch, and Jerusalem. The patriarch of Constantinople is "first among equals" vis-à-vis the other patriarchs and has the right of initiative in matters common to them. The patriarchate of Alexandria now is greatly diminished in extent, and since 1899 that of Antioch, which is centered in Damascus, consists solely of Arab clergy. The patriarchate of Jerusalem was established in 451 to safeguard the Holy Places and is in the hands of the monastic Brotherhood of the Holy Sepulchre.[8] The upper echelon of the clergy of this patriarchate is Greek, but the local believers and the lower clergy are Arabs, who resent the Greek dominance. Before World War I, about 80 percent of the Christians in Palestine were Greek Orthodox.

Twice, in 1291 and in 1439, attempts were made to reunite these churches with the Catholic Church, but most remained outside its fold, and the few who did return, the Uniate churches, retained their own distinctive rites.[9]

Protestant Christians took an important step in 1841 when Prussia and Great Britain appointed a joint Anglican "bishop in Jerusalem." The appointment stemmed from the Prussian king's aspiration to unify German Calvinists and Lutherans into a single episcopal church, Britain's wish to proclaim its presence as a Christian power vis-à-vis the Sublime Porte, and the Anglican Church's desire to establish relations with the Orthodox patriarchate. A missionary interest in converting Jews to Christianity also played a role.[10]

After a few years, the Catholic Church reacted to the appointment of the joint Protestant bishop and the renewed presence of the Greek patriarch. In 1847, it revived the office of Latin patriarch of Jerusalem, which earlier had been a purely titular position. It also expanded its educational system and opened new seminaries for local Arabs intending to enter the priesthood.

In Jerusalem, the new Latin patriarch encountered another deeply rooted Catholic institution, the Custodia Terrae Sanctae. This is an international body belonging to the Franciscan order, which in 1230 was established in Palestine and in 1342 received papal recognition of the rights to the Holy Places obtained in 1333 from the sultan by Robert of Anjou, king of Naples.[11] The custodia is headed by the custos of the Holy Land, an Italian Franciscan priest, and the leading positions were filled by priests from France, Spain, and Germany, according to a fixed internal rule.[12] The tension that arose between the venerable custos and the newly arrived patriarch was inevitable and left its mark on successors in those positions for many years afterward. The Church has since resolved this problem by introducing a practice whereby the priest appointed as patriarch has twice been the former custos.

At the end of the nineteenth century, the Catholic Church in the Holy Land had founded some thirty orders and associations, as well as twenty convents and monasteries, eighteen hospices, six secondary schools, and five hospitals. This was the fruit of efforts by France, Austria, Spain, Italy, and Germany, all of which wanted to strengthen their presence in Palestine. They supplied financial support, and the Ottoman authorities, who wanted to mitigate complaints about their treatment of the Christian minorities, so as not to provide a pretext for the intervention of Christian governments, offered no objections.[13] From this time to the beginning of the twentieth century, the number of Catholic pilgrims visiting the Holy Land increased; the existing hospices were enlarged; new ones were built; and pilgrims could tour the land proceeding from one Catholic institution to the next.[14] Catholic activity in Jerusalem at the beginning of the twentieth century was mainly philanthropic: building orphanages, nursing homes, institutions for the disabled, and vocational schools and workshops.[15]

Jews have constituted the majority in Jerusalem since 1880, when Jerusalem was still a small city with a population of about 30,000. In that year, the Jews numbered 17,000, compared with 8,000 Muslims and 6,000 Christians.[16] Following the influx of Jews at the beginning of the twentieth century, which led to considerable development in the city, Jerusalem began to attract many Christians, and for the first time Christians outnumbered Muslims. On the eve of World War I, in 1913, Jerusalem had a population of 75,200, of whom 48,400 were Jews, 10,050 were Muslims, and 16,750 were Christians.[17] Then at the beginning of the twentieth century, a new factor came on the scene in Palestine—Zionism.

The Vatican and the Great Powers

On September 3, 1914, a short time after the outbreak of World War I, Giacomo Cardinal Della Chiesa was elected pope and took the name Benedict XV. This pope left his stamp on Vatican policy throughout the war years and during the subsequent peace conference, until his death on January 22, 1922. A contemporary observer wrote the following about Benedict XV:

> Benedict XV is no more impressive to look at than Victor Emmanuel [III]. In his insignificant figure and rather expressionless face there is no majesty, spiritual or secular. . . . He was lost in something impersonal, perpetual, obliterating. It was the Papacy one saw moving in the hush, swallowing up good Popes, bad Popes and indifferent Popes, and surviving them all. . . . One saw him at public functions in the Vatican, drooping under his tiara, dwindling within his embroidered state, plainly bored and burdened by his augustness. . . . He made no appeal to the imagination— a little man, awkward, tired, sallow, one shoulder slightly higher than the other, with no eloquence, no radiance, no personal charm.[18]

Nonetheless, the new pope stirred hopes in France, for he was considered pro-French, and he also named Domenico Cardinal Ferrata, the former nuncio in Paris, as his secretary of state. These hopes were also based on the fact that for many years the new pope had himself served as secretary of state to Pope Leo XIII, in which capacity he promoted a policy favorable to France and Russia. He did so primarily because Italy then belonged to the rival camp—that is, the alliance with Germany and Austria-Hungary. The Vatican had been in sore conflict with Italy ever since the conquest of Rome in 1870, when the pope was forcibly removed from the capital and chose to "imprison" himself in the Vatican. But Italy's departure from the Triple Alliance in the first year of the war, and its declaration of neutrality, led to a change in the Vatican's political orientation. The Italian historian Luigi Salvatorelli wrote on this subject:

> Once the pro-Russian policy of Leo [XIII] ended, the Vatican's traditional support of Austria-Hungary—the biggest Catholic empire in Europe, a barrier against the threat of Orthodox expansion fostered and directed by the czar—regained its importance. German Catholicism with the Center [party] and the network of ecclesiastic and secular organizations represented for the Vatican a major force that would have been extremely dangerous to confront.[19]

Benedict XV took steps to improve the Vatican's relations with Italy, by establishing a permanent "covert tie" through Baron Carlo Monti, his personal friend since childhood who served as director of the Fondo per il Culto (Fund for Religion).[20] In the absence of diplomatic relations between Italy and the Vatican, the link provided by Monti was extremely important, and he in effect acted as Italy's ambassador to the Holy See.

Italy was concerned that its conflict with the Vatican might become an international problem, thus inviting pressures from other countries. When the Italian government learned that the new pope was planning to participate in the future peace conference in order to win international guarantees on behalf of the Holy See, it reacted vigorously. Fearing that papal representation at the peace conference would transplant the Roman Question to the international arena, the Italian government drew up a plan to win French, British, and Russian support for its opposition to papal participation. Italy achieved its objective in negotiations with Britain on entering the war, which culminated in the secret Treaty of London of April 26, 1915, whose Article 15 was drafted according to Italian demands.[21]

The Vatican had broken off diplomatic relations with France, "the elder daughter of the Church," in July 1904, following the visit in April of that year by French President Emile-François Loubet to the king of Italy in Rome. In December 1905, France passed a law separating state and religion, which transferred the titles to many buildings and other Church properties to the French state.[22] Nonetheless, Benedict XV sent a handwritten message to the president of France informing him of his (the pope's) election. And shortly before then, France had appointed author Charles Loiseau to its embassy in Rome, to "discuss with the Vatican matters of interest to our country."[23] Since there were no diplomatic relations at that time between France and the Holy See, Loiseau was in charge of semiofficial relations with the Vatican.

At the end of 1914, after three centuries of no relations, Great Britain sent a temporary diplomatic envoy to the Holy See, the Catholic Sir Henry Howard, as head of the special mission to the Holy See. The temporary British representation became a permanent legation in 1920, but it was not reciprocal, for Britain refused to receive a nuncio in London.[24] In the assessment of Rennell Rodd, the British representative in Rome, the Prussian, Bavarian, and Austro-Hungarian representatives had decisive influence on the Vatican.[25]

After Cardinal Ferrata died, the pope appointed Pietro Cardinal Gasparri to replace him as secretary of state. Pietro Gasparri (1852–1934) was born in Ussita, a small town in the Apennines. From 1880 to 1890, he taught canon law at the Catholic Institute in Paris and in 1904 was assigned by Pope Pius X to direct the codification of all the laws and regulations promulgated by the Church over the centuries. He was made a cardinal in 1907 and from 1914 served as secretary of state under two popes, Benedict XV and his successor, Pius XI. This was quite unusual, as this position is second in importance only to the pope's. Gasparri was a man of simple habits but also an active diplomat who had served as the apostolic delegate in Ecuador, Bolivia, and Peru. Despite the arduousness of his duties as secretary of state, he continued his scholarly work, and in the middle of the war, on May 27, 1917, Pope Benedict XV congratulated him for his accomplishment—the publication of the new *Codex Juris Canonici*. For the first time in its history, the Catholic Church possessed a complete universal code of canon law.[26] Gasparri himself published a sharp reply to the attacks appearing in a French periodical about the purported imbalance in the Holy See's policies toward the belligerent sides.

Gasparri's greatest diplomatic achievement was the conclusion of the concordat with Italy, the agreement signed in 1929 that terminated the unnatural situation that had existed for nearly sixty years—that is, the absence of diplomatic relations between Rome and the Vatican.[27] A British diplomat to the Holy See described Cardinal Gasparri:

> Gasparri came of farmer stock, and sometimes was nicknamed *"Il Contadino."* His dress, in the years when I saw him, showed an unusual indifference to neatness; with his *zucchetto,* or scarlet skull-cap all askew, and the cardinal's robe showing signs of his snuff-taking down its front, he would cause a certain mild surprise or amusement, until you experienced the vigour of his personality. He had humour, geniality and diplomatic adaptability; his scholarship, though in this he was said to be deeply indebted to assistants, was associated with a solid and enduring work, the new Code of Canon Law. Simple though his life was, austere was not the first adjective one would associate with him. Though of marked piety he could obviously relax, enjoy a joke and also make one.[28]

When the Germans violated Belgian neutrality at the beginning of World War I, Britain and France regarded it as an offense against morality and international law and therefore expected that the pope would publicly denounce the Austro-Hungarian and German aggression. But such a denunciation was not forthcoming. The Vatican's silence at the time, which stemmed from the wish above all to safeguard the Church's interests, is somewhat reminiscent of the silence of Pope Pius XII during World War II when the Nazis were murdering the Jews.

Salvatorelli wrote the following about Benedict XV's actions:

> The papacy, before being a court of arbitration, an international high court of justice, and an oracle of morality, is an institution with inner laws of self-preservation and self-development. . . . It was dangerous for the Holy See to try to act as a moral arbiter in the conflict. The Vatican was liable to find itself utterly cut off from one belligerent country or another.[29]

The pope thus refrained from expressing moral condemnation of either side in the war and instead tried to mediate for peace. But his mediation was not successful, in part because Italy's consent would have obliged it to agree to Vatican participation at the peace conference, and Italy wanted to obstruct all access by the Vatican to the international arena as long as the Roman Question was still unresolved.

The Vatican's neutrality was plausible to some British diplomats. J. D. Gregory, who had served as secretary of the British legation at the Holy See from the time of its establishment in 1914 and who was a Catholic, wrote in his memoirs:

> The Vatican could take only neutrality. On one side of the conflict stood the central Empires, representatives of Authority, Order, Law and Stability, involving the Catholic stronghold of Bavaria, the Rhine and Alsace, and the existence of the two remaining Catholic dynasties. On the other side stood Protestant England, Freemason France, Orthodox Russia: a combination of forces that could hardly fail, if victorious, so it was argued, to be inimical to the Church's interests.[30]

The Great Powers and the Future of Palestine

The new pontiff did not at first demonstrate any special concern for Palestine, but the Vatican's traditional interests in the Holy Places were widely known.

The European powers had been occupied with the Eastern Question, the fate of the Ottoman Empire, before the outbreak of World War I. The question of whether to hasten the disintegration of the empire into separate countries—a process that had begun in the nineteenth century—was discussed in foreign offices in many European capitals. Once the war started, it became clear to France and Italy that the inevitable outcome, if their side were victorious, would be the division of the empire, and they therefore began to draw up plans for its future. We shall examine here those plans that pertained to the future of Palestine.

World War I turned Palestine into a battlefield, with all the grave consequences for the civilian population. Church buildings were confiscated by the Turkish army. Many Jews were expelled from the country by the Turkish authorities. Catholic clergy who were not Ottoman subjects were arrested and expelled; the number of Catholics thus dwindled. Although their patriarch was banished, the Greek Orthodox, who were Ottoman subjects, were generally allowed to remain in the country. In the years before the war, it also had been easier for the Greek Orthodox to acquire land and buildings. For centuries, czarist Russia had used its religious protection of the Greek Orthodox to consolidate its presence in Palestine, which was increasingly strengthened by the erection of Russian religious institutions and churches.

Britain, for its part, devoted itself mainly to securing the Suez Canal and a passage to India. On the eve of World War I, oil was discovered in the Middle East, and the region then acquired tremendous strategic importance for the British navy.

World War I heightened the Great Powers' interest in the future of the Ottoman Empire, including Palestine. The boundaries of the country's administrative districts were not clear, and consequently northern and central Palestine were often considered part of Syria, in which France had an acknowledged traditional interest. Furthermore, because of its religious protectorate of the area's Catholics, France could also claim rights in Palestine's Holy Places. In those years this religious protectorate became a point of contention between France and Italy, as Italy also wanted to base its presence in the Holy Land on its activity among the Catholics.[31] At that time, neither Italy nor France maintained normal diplomatic relations with the Vatican. On September 4, 1914, the Allies, Great Britain, France, and Russia, announced in London that they would not conclude separate peace treaties. After Turkey entered the war, in November of that year, this declaration obliged the three powers to hold discussions among themselves about how the Ottoman Empire would be carved up after the war.

Even though the Allies' major interests were military-strategic and economic, they could not ignore the fate of the Holy Places in this region, which had already, for many years, been a subject of international agreements. It is not surprising, therefore, that the problem of the Holy Places was raised at the beginning of the discussions on the future of the Middle East. The Allies' ideas about internationalization, extraterritoriality, an international supervisory commission, and the like had been raised as early as 1915.

Sir Herbert Samuel, "the first member of the Jewish community ever to sit in a British cabinet," began to send memoranda to the cabinet ministers to convince them that the best solution to the problem of Palestine was a British protectorate that would encourage Jewish settlement.[32] Samuel indicated as early as November 1914 that Palestine should remain neutral and that "the free access of Christian pilgrims should be guaranteed."[33] When he discussed his plan for a second time with Foreign Secretary Sir Edward Grey,[34] on February 5, 1915, Grey replied that it might be possible to neutralize Palestine "under international guarantee, and to place the control of the Holy Places in the hands of a Commission in which the European Powers, and the Pope, and perhaps the United States, would be represented."[35] Grey accepted Samuel's principles for an international commission.

In a draft cabinet memorandum written in March 1915, Samuel raised the problem of the Holy Places:

> In order to conciliate the susceptibilities of the Catholic and Greek Churches, it would, no doubt be necessary to accompany British control [over Palestine] by the establishment of an extraterritorial regime for the Christian sacred sites, and to vest their possessions in an international commission in which France (and perhaps the Vatican) on behalf of the Catholic Church and Russia, on behalf of the Greek Church would have leading voices.[36]

The idea of extraterritoriality for the Holy Places—that is, their exclusion from the jurisdiction of the sovereign power in Palestine—was not altogether new. Theodore Herzl had raised the idea in his 1895 book *The Jewish State* and had repeated it at his audience with Pope Pius X.[37] But Samuel's proposal to establish an international commission for the Holy Places seems to have been a new one, and it was intended to thwart the very real opposition of the Catholic Church and to destroy the pretexts of France and Russia, both of which also wanted to gain control over Palestine under the guise of safeguarding the Holy Places. The idea of an international commission was accepted in principle by the British government several years later and went through many transformations until it was incorporated in the text of the mandate. The realization of the project, however, encountered difficulties, and the commission was never established.

In the early stages of World War I, the Vatican was already assured a place in British statesmen's conceptions of future arrangements for the Holy Places. Accordingly, the Vatican may well have been given hints to this effect, thus encouraging the pope to believe that he would play a real part in the control of the Holy Places. How great, then, was his disappointment some years later when it became clear that the Great Powers had left the Vatican no role whatever in the Holy Land. Perhaps here was sown the seed of its opposition to British plans for the region.

Another British cabinet secretary, David Lloyd George,[38] was enthusiastic in his support for the establishment of a Jewish state in Palestine. According to Herbert Asquith,[39] who was then the British prime minister, Lloyd George adopted this position because he thought that it would "be an outrage to let the Holy Places pass into the possession or under the protectorate of 'agnostic, atheistic France.' "[40]

The idea of internationalizing the Holy Places and neutralizing Palestine was raised by other British officials as well. On March 16, 1915, Sir Edmund Barrow, the military secretary of the India Office, wrote that if peace with Turkey were to be achieved, Palestine would have to be neutralized and administered as an autonomous province by an international commission or corporation under the aegis of the Entente. He explained his proposal:

> The abolition of direct Turkish rule in Palestine is also a political consummation which will appeal to many, both Christian and Jew, but which would inevitably create dissension among the Powers unless they were all equally interested in the new dispensation. Any attempt to acquire a special privileged position by one would be resented by the rest of the Powers. . . .[41]

Several days later, on March 27, 1915, Colonial Secretary Lewis Harcourt[42] wrote in a memorandum to the government that it would be "unfortunate if France became the guardian of the Christian Holy Places in Palestine." Harcourt believed that the Holy Places should remain in British hands, and if that were not possible, they should come under the protection of the United States.[43] In the meantime, the Russians had made it clear to Britain that they would insist on internationalizing the Holy Places. A recommendation in that spirit was included in the report of the de Bunsen Committee presented to the British cabinet in June 1915.[44] "We see no reason why the sacred places of Palestine should not be dealt with as a separate question," the report stated. The committee's report proceeded on the assumption that the French demands would be rejected because the forces opposing them were too powerful, and for the very same reason it would "be idle for His Majesty's Government to claim the retention of Palestine in their sphere. Palestine must be recognized as a country whose destiny must be the subject of special negotiations."[45]

The Sykes–Picot Agreement and the Holy Places

Negotiations between Britain and France on the future of the Ottoman Empire, including Palestine, began in September 1915. The British representative to these talks was Sir Mark Sykes, an attaché to the War Office and later, from 1916 to

1919, assistant to the war cabinet secretary.[46] The French representative was François Georges Picot, formerly the French consul general in Beirut. Following the recommendations of the de Bunsen Committee, Britain suddenly put forward a demand at these talks for the internationalization of Palestine.[47] This was the only way to keep the French from gaining exclusive control of the country. Picot replied at the first meeting, on November 23, 1915, that Syria, including Palestine, should be considered French, except for Jerusalem and Bethlehem, which could become a separate enclave under an international regime.

On December 16, Sykes proposed that Britain claim the whole area south of a line reaching the Mediterranean at Acre, not including the Jerusalem enclave, which apparently would not be left to France but would be internationalized.[48] His talks with Picot began later that month. In a joint memorandum by Sykes and Picot in December 1915, the two men designated a "brown" zone around the Holy Places in Jerusalem to be placed under an international administration in order to meet the requirements of Christianity, Judaism, and Islam. They wrote:

> The Latin and Orthodox religions require equal consideration in Palestine. The members of the Jewish community throughout the world have a conscientious and sentimental interest in the future of the country. The mosque of Omar represents, next to Mecca, the most holy and venerable shrine in Islam, and it must be a *sine qua non* that the Mosque of Omar itself should be under the sole control of Moslems.[49]

The British government, however, did not accept Sykes's proposal, which limited internationalization to a small area around Jerusalem, and in the end agreement was reached on the internationalization of all of central Palestine.

On January 16, 1916, Picot suggested to Sykes that Belgium administer the affairs of Palestine as a "trustee" of the Entente powers. This proposal is of special interest, because the "trustee" idea underlay the mandate system developed years later, and Belgium was considered by the Vatican to be the most suitable trustee for Jerusalem and the Holy Places. Sykes seems to have liked Picot's suggestion, and about a month later he wrote to Samuel that "Belgium should assume the administration [over Palestine] as the trustee of the Entente Powers."[50]

At the end of February 1916, a British Foreign Office official viewed the situation in Palestine as follows:

> The Zionists are opposed to an international protectorate and would wish for a British protectorate which seems impracticable. But I understand that the idea has been put forward that there might be an American protectorate. . . . While there would necessarily be an international administration of some kind in Jerusalem itself, it is conceivable that in the rest of Palestine, the Jews could be given special colonizing facilities. . . . Meanwhile, Palestine outside Jerusalem might possibly be left under the administration of some neutral nationality, if the United States will not agree to undertake the administration themselves.[51]

From these remarks by Hugh O'Beirne we learn that the possibility of placing Palestine—with the exception of internationalized Jerusalem—under the protection of the United States or under that of a neutral country, probably Belgium, was being considered at that time. Information about these ideas may also have been leaked to the Vatican.

The Sykes–Picot proposals made no mention of the Jews. On March 11, 1916, however, British Foreign Secretary Grey dispatched a cable to his ambassadors in Paris and St. Petersburg, in which he noted the importance of Jewish support for the war effort and suggested a formula whereby the Jews would be allowed, at some later time, "to take the management of the internal affairs of Palestine (with the exception of Jerusalem and the Holy Places) into their hands."[52] The British ambassador, who conveyed this idea to the Russian foreign minister, Sergei Dimitzievič Sazonov, noted that the British would have to conquer Palestine, and in that case Jerusalem would become international, contrary to the wishes of the Jews.[53]

The Russian foreign minister replied that his government viewed "the proposed settlement of the Jews in Palestine with sympathy, but the Holy Places must be excluded from any such scheme and placed under an international regime ensuring equality of rights for all Christian Churches."[54] In mid-March 1916, Sykes reached an understanding with Picot on a scheme to sign an agreement that would also be satisfactory to Russia and France with regard to the administration and status of the Holy Places. According to this plan, France would act as arbitrator between the administration of the Holy Places and the Palestinian government.[55] It is thus not surprising that several years later France demanded this role of arbitrator, but by that time the understanding between Sykes and Picot on this had been rejected by the British Foreign Office.

A few days later, Sykes again wrote to the Foreign Office in London: "We cannot get them [the Jews] either political control of Jerusalem within the walls of the [old] city nor any scheme tending thereto. I am confident that the French, the Russians, and the Arabs would never agree."[56] Sykes's comment is of great interest, as voices are again being heard today indicating the Vatican's wish to obtain a special status for Jerusalem "within the walls."

The Sykes–Picot agreement, a tripartite agreement among Britain, France, and Russia on the division of the Ottoman Empire, was approved in a letter by Foreign Minister Grey on May 16, 1916. The agreement was kept secret even from the Entente's ally, Italy, but became known to the Vatican at an early stage and seems to have been greeted there with satisfaction.[57] The Vatican regarded internationalization as a sufficient guarantee for safeguarding Catholics' rights. According to the agreement, all the places important to Christians—Jerusalem, Bethlehem, Nazareth, and the shores of Lake Tiberias—were to be included in the international region (the "brown" zone), and the international administration was to be in the hands of the Entente powers only.

The boundaries of the brown zone designated for internationalization[58] were set on the basis of Russia's demands that "not only the Holy Places but, also all towns and localities in which there were religious establishments belonging to the Orthodox Church, should be placed under an international administration, with a guarantee of free access to the Mediterranean coast."[59] As early as February 1915, the Russians made clear to France that they would not tolerate Catholic control over a region that included Jerusalem, Galilee, the Jordan River, and Lake Tiberias.[60] In that way, relying on arguments involving the Holy Places, Britain and Russia pushed France north into Syria and forced it to relinquish its vision of exclusive control of Palestine.

2

Power Struggles
Among the Allies

Lloyd George's Government

For the Allies, 1917 was a decisive year. In December 1916, a new government
had been formed in Britain, headed by David Lloyd George, who since 1915 had
been determined to find a way to defeat the enemy in the Middle East, where it was
weakest. Lord Beaverbrook wrote in about 1917:

> [That year] opened up in disaster for Britain. Germany was the military master of
> Europe. The French nation was exhausted. Russia was staggering to her doom. The
> British people were dispirited and a food shortage threatened the very existence of
> the nation. The Army was stalemated in France and the Navy was unable any longer
> to provide protection for the Mercantile Marine. The sea communications to the East
> and West had been interrupted.[1]

In regard to Palestine, the most important problem still unresolved was the form
of government that would be set up after the British conquest. It was not clear
whether Palestine should be internationalized, be placed under an Anglo-French
condominium, or come under exclusive British control. The British authorities discussed this issue with the French and the Zionists, who had opposing interests. The
French demanded Palestine for themselves, using the pretext of their spiritual mission to defend Catholic interests, and the Zionists objected to a condominium or
any other form of rule that was not exclusively British.[2]

One of the goals of Lloyd George, the new British prime minister, was to obtain
the annexation of Palestine. Sir Mark Sykes, for his part, was fearful of German
ambitions to dominate the Middle East, for if the Germans were to gain control of
Palestine, they would be able to exert pressure on the pope, the Orthodox Church,
and the Zionists. As of January and February 1917, Lloyd George's aim became a
British trusteeship. A condominium with France seemed to the British to be a real
danger, because the principle of an international regime left the door open to Germany.[3]

David Lloyd George (later Earl Lloyd George of Dwyfor), British prime minister, and Winston Churchill, minister of munitions, 1916.

Sykes met with Zionist leaders on February 7, 1917, and told them that British protection would apply to only a Zionist chartered company and in specified areas only. These areas overlapped the region of British influence in Palestine—in the north and south outside the "brown" zone. Galilee, the Hauran region, and the Jerusalem enclave connected to Jaffa by a corridor were to be excluded from the region where the Zionist company would be allowed to operate.[4] Sykes probably offered the Vatican similar explanations when he visited there a month later, and it can be assumed that this was the territorial plan the Vatican knew of when the Zionist leader Nahum Sokolow was received by the pope in April.

On April 19, 1917, Lord Curzon announced in the committee he chaired that "the only safe settlement is that Palestine should be included in a British Protectorate."[5] From that time on, Britain began to press its demand for British rule over Palestine, frequently exploiting Zionist ambitions to advance its own aims.

That same day, the Foreign Affairs Committee of the French parliament reached the unanimous conclusion that except for the Holy Places, which could be placed under Belgian supervision, Palestine must be French. On that same day, too, a tripartite international conference was held in the French town of Saint-Jean-de-Maurienne, with the participation of Britain, France, and Italy, at which Italy won French and British consent in principle to the transfer of the sanjak of Adalia and the vilayet of Aidin (in Asia Minor), with Smyrna as a free harbor, to its rule. Italy also obtained full equality in Palestine in the safeguarding of the Holy Places, over France's objections.[6] But the Saint-Jean-de-Maurienne agreement required Russian consent, which was never received because the Bolsheviks came to power that year and Russia left the war. Thus even though the principle of internationalization, in accord with the Sykes–Picot agreements, was reaffirmed at the conference, six days later the British war cabinet decided that it could not be implemented.[7]

Sykes was sent to Egypt and Palestine, where the British were preparing a new offensive, which later faltered, at the battle of Gaza (1917). It was natural that Sykes, a devout Catholic, would visit the Vatican on his way to the East. At the time, Pope Benedict XV was using all his influence to stop the war and, at the secret consistory[8] of December 1916, stressed that the peace must not be to the benefit of only one of the belligerent sides.[9] Sykes also prepared the visits of the Zionist leader Sokolow in Paris, Rome, and the Vatican (discussed in Part II of this book).

The pro-British stand evinced by senior Vatican officials in talks with Sykes and Sokolow is hard to understand. There was something peculiar about the Vatican's foreign relations, in that Britain was the only Entente power with an official representative at the Holy See. But as is known, the Church views political problems *sub specie aeternitatis* and so does not regard as crucial a dispute spanning only several dozen years. Why, then, was the Vatican positively inclined toward a Protestant power like England?

The most likely answer may be that the Vatican still believed at that time that Palestine would be placed under an international regime in accord with the Sykes–Picot agreements and that British rule, therefore, was no cause for special concern. But later, when British occupation of Palestine became a fact, the Church was compelled to take it into account.

The Vatican's interest in the Eastern Question was also revealed in Pope Benedict XV's initiative on May 1, 1917, to found the Congregatio pro Ecclesia Orientali (Congregation for the Eastern Churches), which he himself headed. In a special *Moto Proprio* published on that occasion, the pope wrote: "When our Eastern Churches will see that the Pope is personally looking after their interests, they will understand that the Holy See cannot express any greater love for them."[10] The Eastern Churches came under the jurisdiction of the new department in May 1917.[11] Although the Vatican does not usually make internal organizational changes under the pressure of events, it created the impression that the founding of the new office during a war that seemed likely to bring about the collapse of the Ottoman Empire was meant to emphasize once again the Vatican's vital interests in the Near East. The establishment of the Pontifico Istituto Orientale (Eastern Papal Institute) in Rome, on October 15, 1917, reinforced that impression.

The Conquest of Jerusalem

Russia's departure from the war after the October revolution led to a turning point on the battlefield. In addition, the St. Jean de Maurienne agreement, which expressly required Russian approval, was nullified. Now that Russia was no longer a combatant and Italy could no longer rely on that agreement, the way was cleared to scrub the internationalization of central Palestine envisioned by the Sykes–Picot agreement.

Two major events at the end of 1917, the Balfour Declaration on November 2 and the conquest of Jerusalem by General E. H. H. Allenby on December 9, called back the attention of the highest ranks of the Vatican to the problems of Palestine.

On December 11, General Allenby proceeded on foot into the Old City of Jerusalem, with a French colonel, Diepape, at his right and an Italian colonel, d'Agostino, at his left. A Franciscan monk read out a British proclamation stressing that "every sacred building, monument, holy spot, shrine, traditional site, endowment, pious bequest or customary place of prayer, of whatsoever form, of the three religions, will be maintained and protected according to the existing customs and beliefs of those to whose faiths they are sacred."[12]

On the next day of Jerusalem's occupation, British Foreign Minister Lord Balfour[13] cabled John de Salis, the British representative to the Holy See, instructing him to assure the Vatican that Britain promised to guarantee order at the Holy Places in Jerusalem. A British colleague wrote the following about Count John de Salis:

> In 1916 Sir Henry Howard was succeeded by a regular diplomat, Count (an hereditary Holy Roman Empire title) John de Salis. He was a shrewd, witty man, with a convenient diplomatic deafness and an unwillingness—from which he derived a certain pleasure—to report always to the Foreign Office just what fitted in with their preconceived ideas.[14]

The Vatican secretary of state, Cardinal Pietro Gasparri, who received a message containing the British promise from de Salis, conveyed the pope's gratitude to the British government. As de Salis noted in the report he filed, *Osservatore Romano,* the semiofficial Vatican newspaper, wrote that the entry into Jerusalem of British troops was greeted with satisfaction by all, especially the Catholics, who could not but rejoice that the rule of Jerusalem had passed into the hands of a Christian power. Furthermore, the paper continued, the British spirit of freedom and justice provided reason to hope that the Catholics' interests and rights would be recognized.[15] Some days later, Gasparri again informed de Salis how pleased the pope was that Jerusalem had been conquered by British forces, and he expressed the pontiff's confidence that the British regime would preserve the Catholics' legitimate rights.

De Salis noted in his report that the Vatican had made no mention of the participation of Italian or French troops in the conquest of Jerusalem and that the anticlerical press in Italy interpreted this omission as indicating hostility.[16] Several days later, de Salis arranged for Cardinal Gasparri to meet with Captain Birch, who had

The official ceremony of Jerusalem's surrender on December 11, 1917. A Franciscan monk reads General Allenby's appeal.

come from Jerusalem after the capture of the city and supplied details about the measures taken by the British military administration to prevent fighting in the vicinity of Jerusalem and to protect the Holy Places. On this occasion too, Gasparri expressed his satisfaction.[17]

Cardinal Gasparri left the British representative with the impression that the British government's words had assured him, but at the same time he put a somewhat different idea before the Belgian representative.

In a talk with the Belgian envoy to the Vatican, Jules Van den Heuvel, on December 12, 1917, Gasparri stated that Britain would probably want to retain control of Palestine, from Gaza to Tyre. The Holy Places would, Gasparri hoped, be under an international regime, a condominium that would belong to all countries with a sizable Christian population. An agreement satisfactory to the Christian countries would have to be reached concerning the appointment of a governor. Gasparri even added, in strictest confidence, that in his view a Belgian candidate would have the best chances, for Belgium would not be suspected of political ambitions.[18] The Belgian foreign minister indicated that he was greatly pleased by the way Gasparri viewed the future of Palestine.[19] The suggestion that Catholic Belgium be assigned a role in the Holy Places had been raised previously in the Sykes–Picot talks and the French parliament. Gasparri supported the idea and subsequently even worked to realize it.

The possibility of giving Belgium the mandate for Palestine was raised at that time in another framework as well. At the end of 1917, Sykes visited Paris, where he met with Jean Goût, the director of the Asia Department in the French Foreign Ministry. Sykes said that some circles were inclined to give the mandate to the United States for a period of twenty-five years, and Goût asked whether Britain might prefer to entrust the international administration of Palestine to a lower-ranking power, such as Belgium. Sykes was somewhat reserved about this proposal.

Goût and Sykes agreed that the Holy Places would be governed by special regulations. They raised the possibility of the Holy Places being controlled by an international commission, similar to the international commission for the Danube. Goût believed, and Sykes concurred, that the commission must be chaired by the French representative, who would also be given the title of governor of Jerusalem.[20]

It appears that France, with the Vatican, tried to persuade a Catholic country like Belgium to accept the mandate for Palestine. Belgium was small enough not to overshadow France and would have been able to ensure the continuation of a French presence in the guise of religious protectorate on Catholics. France wanted to exploit this protectorate to the full and through it obtain the post of governor of Jerusalem. Two years later, several months after the opening of the Paris Peace Conference, this plan was still regarded in Paris as realistic. One wonders whether this dream does not still exist.

Osservatore Romano addressed the issue of Jerusalem several times in that period. On December 15, 1917, the newspaper called the capture of Jerusalem a victory for Christian civilization. An article dated December 23, 1917, under the headline "1854–1917," recalled that in 1854 a coalition of Englishmen, Frenchmen, and Italians had rescued Christian civilization from the threat of the Russian Orthodox. In 1917, the newspaper went on to say, it had been God's wish that Englishmen, Frenchmen, and Italians capture the Holy City, remove it from the hands of infidels, and perhaps eliminate that same danger once and for all. De Salis commented that this semiofficial Vatican newspaper had on a number of occasions taken a clear stand against the Russian Orthodox and the Turks. The Vatican, which maintained neutrality toward the warring blocs, took positions that were either sympathetic or hostile toward countries in both blocs, depending on the Church's special interests.

On December 28, de Salis was received cordially by the pope, who expressed great satisfaction with regard to Jerusalem but asked with "evident anxiety" whether the British government intended to maintain its position there. The pope, while alluding with "expressions of benevolence to the Jews, appeared to fear that H. M. Government might agree to forgo direct control over affairs to the detriment of Christian interests."[21]

While the British representative at the Vatican was reporting the secretary of state's pro-British position, Cardinal Gasparri was employing an altogether different tone in talks with Charles Loiseau.[22]

The conquest of Jerusalem was noted with demonstrations of joy in the Italian churches. All the bells of Rome were rung over and over, save for the bells of St. Peter's in the Vatican, which remained silent. This caused much wonder, and Gasparri talked to Loiseau about it. At first he asked whether the Allies' war objectives bore any relation to those of the Crusades. Loiseau, of course, could not respond affirmatively, and then Gasparri went on to say:

> The Turks are old acquaintances in this house. The same people who blame us that the bells of St. Peter did not ring, are the first to ask us to intervene with the Turks. . . . No day passes without our being asked to intervene for the sake of a prisoner, to save some embassy person or to oppose material destruction. . . . Do you think we should celebrate with special joy the Turkish defeat, when in principle we are above all conflicts, on the excuse that there exists a permanent state of war between Christianity and the Turks? . . . But let us look to the future, what will change? The Holy Places, I hope, when they are under European protection, that is, more orderly protection, will not be a source of any more disputes among Christians, under the distant eye of the Muslims. Even Russia, whose policy provides many occasions for those conflicts, will no longer be able to demand much in Palestine, which was conquered by others. But to present prematurely an operation that was not intended to serve the Church, as a victory for the Catholic Church, is another matter. We have reservations; that is permissible and prudent. On the other hand, do you not already discern Methodist propaganda in Asia Minor? And the perspective of a "national home" that Lord Balfour has just promised the Jews, is that a great consolation for us? It is difficult to take the part of our heart, as small as it may have been, that was in the hands of the Turks, so as to give it to Zionism.[23]

Gasparri thus explained the Vatican's reserve as first of all a function of the need to maintain its neutrality toward all the belligerents, but at the end of his remarks he also alluded to his abhorrence of both Protestantism and Zionism. These were in fact the Vatican's two principal worries at the time. It is of interest, however, to hear another view on this issue expressed in wake of the British conquest of Jerusalem. Professor F. Scaduto, who taught canon law in Italy, declared:

> Unfortunately, the Church is entitled to believe that Muslim rule [over Palestine] is preferable for it to non-Catholic Christian rule, or even Catholic rule. It may fear the propaganda of the non-Catholic Christian, and the Holy See may well prefer Muslim rule and propaganda to Protestant rule. Separatist and agnostic France is no longer the eldest daughter of the Church; Italy still has the unresolved problem of the [Church's] temporal rule. No internationalization under an Anglo-French-Italian protectorate would satisfy the Holy Father. The preference for the Muslim cannot be acknowledged, but it is real. [censored passage] The anxiety over Protestant proselytism seems to be unfounded. The Jews aspire to the reestablishment of their state, as a shelter where they could enjoy full rights and in which they could find refuge. But they probably will remain in the countries where they are, and, therefore, the kingdom of Zion will fail.[24]

This view suggests that apart from the obligations ensuing from its neutrality, the Vatican had difficulty seeing anything positive in the transfer of the Holy Places from familiar Turkish rule to British rule, whose nature was still shrouded in fog. Scaduto appears to have had his finger on the Vatican's pulse, and especially on its fear of Protestant propaganda, which was very real. In talks he held, Cardinal Gasparri did in fact confess a preference for Muslim Turkey, however peculiar that may seem.

The Vatican's Territorial Ambitions

In January 1916, bizarre rumors of German origin were reported in the Italian press, according to which the kaiser had promised the pope to establish a papal state in Palestine with the consent of the Turkish sultan. The sultan would purportedly hand over to the pope the city of Jerusalem, the Holy Places, and a region that would include the port of Jaffa and would be of a size suitable for governing by a cardinal viceroy.[25] We have no confirmation of this rumor from any other source, and so it was probably a fabrication. Nonetheless, the idea of temporal rule in Palestine by the Church, or of a region set aside for the Vatican that would include the Holy Places, was close to Gasparri's heart, as he disclosed a year later in his talk with Nahum Sokolow at the Vatican. On May 1, 1917, Gasparri told the Zionist leader that the Church had claims not only on Jerusalem and Bethlehem but also on Nazareth and its surroundings, Tiberias, and even Jericho.[26]

Temporal rule in Rome was foremost among the pope's demands, for it was considered essential to the Church's freedom of action.[27] When the pope sought to secure the participation of a Vatican representative at the future peace talks, he hoped to achieve two objectives: to internationalize the Roman Question and thereby ensure a solution that would be satisfactory to the Vatican, and at the same time to play the role of supreme mediator among the Great Powers. The possibility cannot be ruled out that in light of the difficulties in resolving the Roman Question, the Vatican began to consider temporal rule in Palestine either as a substitute for the rule it had lost in Rome or as a means to strengthen its claim regarding Rome.

Some support for this conjecture can be found in a strange idea advanced in the nineteenth century about relations between the Vatican and Italy. The idea was put forward in a pamphlet that declared:

> Rome has ceased to be a Christian city. . . . The moment has arrived when the successor of the apostles must leave the Vatican which he had filled with his greatness and saintliness, to make room for a Garibaldi. . . . In the whole of Europe there does not exist one nation where the Holy Father could wear his tiara in security. . . . There is only one city in the world which by its position, its past, its future, its conditions, its memories and by its universal influence, can replace for the Christian world Rome, invaded by the revolution: this is Jerusalem, Cradle and Tomb of Jesus, Mother of all true religions. Jerusalem is the city of God, the Holy City above all.[28]

It is a strange notion, but remnants of it may have persisted into the period around World War I, or it may have been revived because of the war itself. In 1922, Chaim Weizmann, too, feared that the Vatican might have territorial ambitions in Palestine. At the end of 1917, the Soviets published the secret Treaty of London, and the Vatican learned for sure that it would be excluded from participation in the peace conference. Rumors about the treaty had reached the Holy See in January 1916.[29] This may have spurred it to increase its attentiveness to the problem of Palestine, in which it had a distinct interest.

In February 1918, Gasparri spelled out to the Belgian representative Van den Heuvel his position on Palestine:

> In Palestine live Christians, Jews, and Muslims, and freedom of faith for all religions should therefore be guarded and honored. I have heard certain people talking about separating the Holy Places from the rest of the territory and regarding them as a sort of oasis requiring special rule. They would like a dual administration: one ruling the country as a whole and another, independent administration ruling specified regions. This seems to me highly impractical. The most desirable arrangement, in my opinion, would be one that links northern Palestine and Syria to France, and the south to England, to create a defensive disposition for Egypt, whereas the center, from Lake Tiberias in the north to Hebron, would be delivered to a governor. This state would include all the Holy Places, those in Jerusalem, Acre, Bethlehem, Nazareth, Jericho, Bethsaida,[30] and others. . . .
>
> All the great Christian powers should participate. The organization would not be international if only the Entente powers take part and Germany, Austria, and Spain are excluded. The choice of governor will be a matter of very great importance. Some have spoken of rotation among the powers. . . . In my opinion, the simplest solution would be a single Belgian governor. . . . Politically, Belgium is unable to overshadow anybody. Its Christian vitality is expressed religiously in a thousand flourishing institutions.[31]

The words of Cardinal Gasparri may explain the views on the partition of Palestine already expressed some months before in his conversation with Sokolow. Then he was speaking more or less about the same territory slated by the Sykes–Picot agreement to become an international zone, and it appears from these remarks that in February 1918 the Vatican still believed that central Palestine could be internationalized.

At the beginning of 1918, Gasparri's conversations with the Belgian ambassador also reached Denis Cochin, who was then a member of the French parliament and had previously been undersecretary of state for foreign affairs. Cochin reported the idea of entrusting the custody of the Holy Places to Belgium and establishing a "state of the Holy Places"—which would include Jerusalem, Nazareth, and Bethlehem—to a friend in the Foreign Ministry in Paris.[32] Cochin also recommended that the French government not promise to support the candidacy of Belgium as guardian of the Holy Places and, in any case, to reaffirm France's century-old rights of France.[33]

This question continued to hold the attention of the French Foreign Ministry. At the beginning of March, Bruno-François-Marie-Pierre de Margerie, the director general for political affairs, asked the Belgian ambassador about his country's intentions concerning Palestine. The ambassador replied that Belgium did not propose any solution but would agree to appoint the governor of the Holy Places should the Great Powers ask it to do so. De Margerie said that France was not opposed to a Belgian solution of the Palestine problem, and he would even welcome it. France and the Catholic powers would not, however, favor entrusting the custody of the Holy Places to a Protestant power. He added that Cochin's and Gasparri's projects seemed equally impossible to implement.

Cochin held that French honor could be saved by the establishment of an international body similar to that of Shanghai or the consortium of Tangier, with a French chairman acting apart from but closely with a Belgian governor. But this would lead to difficulties. Gasparri's scheme would mean dividing Palestine into three parts: separating a territory in the south to be joined to Sinai and given to Britain, annexing the northern part to Syria and giving it to France, and, finally, creating an enclave between Lake Tiberias and Hebron under the control of an international body headed by a Belgian governor. Why partition Palestine? It would be preferable to keep it unified and appoint a Belgian governor whose responsibilities would extend over the entire country.[34]

This is what we know of de Margerie's ideas, from the report by the Belgian ambassador. They are rather surprising. Perhaps France was already aware that without Russia there was no hope of implementing the Sykes–Picot agreement and was therefore seeking the lesser evil in the appointment of a Belgian governor. Moreover, a Belgian governor might have been the last chance to block exclusive British control of Palestine. In any case, Gasparri's projected establishment of a separate area including the Holy Places was known to France and came up in diplomatic discussions.

Nonetheless, the Vatican, which in February 1918 still believed that Palestine could be internationalized, continued its efforts to include Belgium in its plans for the Holy Land. These efforts, however, were doomed to fail.

The French Religious Protectorate

The history of the religious protectorate of Catholics reaches back to the thirteenth century. In 1258, Venice intervened on behalf of Syrian Christians and pilgrims.[35] After that, other Christian countries, such as Aragon and Naples, intervened on behalf of the Franciscans in the Holy Places, but until the mid-sixteenth century the major protectorate extended was that of Venice.

The French protectorate began after the signing of the Capitulations Treaty between Suleiman the Magnificent and Francis I, king of France, in 1535. This treaty granted to French subjects privileges in regard to personal freedom, commercial rights, and fiscal immunity, in that Ottoman law would not apply to them and they would be subject to French law only. French merchants and their agents, according to Article 6, had the right "to practice their own religion." In 1740, France received the right to extend individual or group protection to all Latin-rite Catholics throughout the empire, regardless of nationality. By custom this protection was broadened to include Eastern-rite Catholics as well.[36]

Furthermore, in the absence of diplomatic relations between the Holy See and the Ottoman Empire, France took upon itself the representation of the Holy See before the Sublime Porte. Not surprisingly, this protectorate accorded France a decided advantage in the East over the other powers. At the Congress of Berlin in 1878, France, contending against England, ultimately succeeded in incorporating an article in the Berlin Treaty (Article 62) that specifically mentioned its rights.[37] The Vatican formally recognized France's rights and in 1888 instructed all priests in the Levant to seek France's protection when needed.

In 1905, France concluded an agreement with Italy whereby Italian religious institutions, or those with an Italian majority, could request to be transferred to Italian protection. This was Italy's attempt to follow in France's footsteps and to use Italian religious establishments as a means to increase the Italian presence in the Holy Land.[38] The breaking down of diplomatic relations between the Holy See and France in 1904 caused France some problems on this issue. The Turkish government, however, abolished the Capitulations after World War I broke out in 1914, and Italy claimed that the Turkish act deprived the French religious protectorate of its legal basis. Italy did not miss a chance to bring about the end of the French protectorate.

The Vatican preferred not to take a clear position between the two Catholic powers, Italy and France, but this was not easy. In June 1917, Cochin, then undersecretary of state for foreign affairs, wrote to Gasparri and asked him whether the Church had in some way revised its position on the French protectorate. Gasparri replied on June 26 somewhat ambiguously that if Turkish rule came to an end or if the abrogation of the Capitulations continued, then the French protectorate would be terminated and would have to be replaced by "something else." In this letter Gasparri noted that the French protectorate in the East rested on a threefold foundation: (1) the Capitulations, (2) the instructions of the Holy See to the orders to seek French protection, and (3) the special liturgical honors deriving from the right of protection granted by the Holy See to the representatives of France.[39]

The priests were obliged to give to the French representative liturgical honors at important religious ceremonies. These honors included singing the hymn "Domine salvam fac Republicam" at the conclusion of the mass at the Church of the Holy Sepulchre in Jerusalem; at ceremonies, a place of honor for the French consul, to the right of the patriarch; the presentation by the patriarch of holy water to the French consul, at the entrance to the Church of the Holy Sepulchre; and the kiss of peace after the reading of the gospel.[40]

The conquest of Jerusalem by the British, with the assistance of French and Italian units, brought the whole problem to the fore once again. The granting of liturgical honors to the French representative at the Church of the Nativity in Bethlehem on Christmas 1917 was the cause of an incident with the Italian commander, D'Agostino.[41] The Franciscans argued at first that the French religious protectorate had been terminated once Turkish rule had come to an end, and instructions in that spirit had been sent to Jerusalem with Gasparri's knowledge and approval.[42] Cardinal Gasparri explained the Holy See's position in one of his talks with the British representative:

> The protectorate had been established a long time ago in order to secure the interests of the Church from the oppression of a hostile and semi-barbaric Government. Various countries had obtained similar rights under Capitulations, but France was best able at the time to give the required protection to religious interests. But now authority in Palestine has passed into the hands of a civilized Government which practiced the rule of justice in its actions. The French protectorate was never intended to apply to such conditions; there was no reason for its continuance, nor was there any right to it, the moment the Turks had left. In a word, the protectorate had gone and there was no reason to revive it.[43]

De Salis noted that to renew French religious protection, the British authorities would have to give France the right to a religious protectorate over all Catholics, a quite unnecessary step.[44]

It can be assumed, then, that the Vatican used this opportunity to free itself from dependence on France and did not conceal its position from the British. In effect, the ball was in the British court. Yet, Cardinal Gasparri surprisingly made a complete about-face on this issue and on March 18, 1918, sent new instructions to the custos, to continue to grant liturgical honors to the French representative until the peace agreement was concluded. That turnabout came after a complaint lodged by the French government with Cardinal Léon Adolphe Amette, the archbishop of Paris.[45] For this reason, even if it is difficult to understand why it was a determinant one, the Vatican was forced to accept the French contention that until the peace treaty was signed, there were no grounds for altering the status quo. At the same time, the Vatican let it be known to the Italians that its basic opposition to a continuation of the French protectorate had not changed. The change was temporary, until the Great Powers could conclude an agreement and a final arrangement for the region was made.[46]

Gasparri wrote in the same spirit to Britain, adding that the Vatican had adopted this course because it wanted to take into account the British position as expressed by General Allenby.[47] Thus the Vatican was able to negotiate a course among France, which clung to its traditional rights, Italy, which wanted the French protectorate immediately terminated, and Britain, which took a dim view of France's intervention in the affairs of Palestine under the cloak of a religious protectorate but preferred that France's special status in the Holy Land be ended by the Vatican.

In the meantime, the war was nearing an end. In September, the British captured the northern half of Palestine and at the end of October 1918 concluded an armistice with Turkey at Mudros. In January 1919, the peace conference opened at Versailles, and the chances increased that Britain would receive the mandate for Palestine. Cardinal Gasparri was critical of the continuation of the French protectorate and told the Belgian representative:

> France is trying to obtain the right not only of a religious protectorate in the Holy Land, as in the past, but also of a civil and political protectorate, which is no different from the annexation of Tunisia. But its plans will not be readily accepted by Italy and Britain.[48]

In the new situation that was created, a position unconditionally opposed to perpetuating the French protectorate crystallized in the British Foreign Office. In March 1919, Cardinal Amette visited the Vatican and was told by Gasparri that the Holy See would accept any arrangement reached by the French and British governments. But to de Salis, Gasparri admitted that it was inconceivable that Britain would recognize the French protectorate.[49]

Cardinal Amette's visit to the Vatican was recalled in a French document, according to which Gasparri reportedly said that Lloyd George and Balfour claimed that they had won agreement from France's Prime Minister Georges Clemenceau for Palestine to remain under a British protectorate. That being the case, the Vatican was reluctant to draw too close to France on an issue from which France itself would soon retreat. When P. Charles-Roux of the French embassy in Rome learned about this, he expressed astonishment, for he apparently was unaware of the secret agreement between France and Britain.

This agreement had been reached at a meeting between Lloyd George and Clemenceau in December 1918, but because no official protocol had been taken, each side interpreted the agreement differently. Lloyd George was convinced that he had obtained France's consent to a British mandate for Palestine, but Charles-Roux remarked that even if such an agreement existed, it was imperative, especially now, for the Holy See and Catholic interests to define the administration of the Holy Places and to give priority in it to a Catholic power—that is, France.

In his conversation with Cardinal Amette, Gasparri stated that he preferred that France and Britain agree on the matter of the religious protectorate and promised to grant France the privileges it claimed in the Holy Places and in the provision of protection to Catholic priests of all nationalities in Palestine. Charles-Roux argued that Britain and the United States were Protestant countries and intimated that they were increasing their activity in Palestine. As an example, he cited the imminent appointment of two Protestant bishops and five American pastors to the Holy Land. Therefore, France alone could offer protection to Catholics. Gasparri seems to have given Amette a satisfactory answer on the issue of the protectorate.[50]

British Foreign Office officials knew quite well that if Britain received the mandate, it would be best to deal with the Vatican directly rather than through France.[51]

At the Council of Four (the Allied prime ministers), which convened in Paris on May 22, 1919, Clemenceau mentioned his talk in London with Lloyd George about Palestine but added that according to the 1916 London agreement (which concluded the Sykes–Picot negotiations), an international regime was to be established there. Lloyd George demanded a British administration with arrangements for the Holy Places, to which Clemenceau replied that he had no objection to such an administration, provided that the Holy Places would be protected.[52]

In July 1919, Gasparri again pointed out to the British chargé d'affaires that the time had come to terminate the French protectorate and stated that he hoped that the British government would take steps in this direction.[53] Everyone, of course, wanted someone else to take the chestnuts out of the fire, but for just that reason Lord Curzon did not wish to add a factor that would be divisive for France and Britain.[54] Gasparri even sent a note to the British legation, in which he asked officially whether Britain agreed that liturgical honors should be offered to the representatives of France.[55]

3

Vision of Peace

The Cardinals Come to Palestine (1919–1920)

The end of World War I in 1918 and the opening of the peace conference at Versailles in January 1919 accelerated the discussions on the future administration of the Holy Places. Britain, which to keep France from gaining total control had initially demanded the internationalization of Palestine, now wanted to bring all of Palestine under its own rule and so began to work against internationalization. Nonetheless, in January 1919 the British still sought a separate solution for the Holy Places. Thus the Italians heard in London that even if Britain got the mandate for Palestine, it would request an extraterritorial regime for and internationalization of the Holy Places, as well as the establishment of a council chaired by a Frenchman or an Italian.[1]

Another source notes that in early 1919 the British were realizing that they would have to ensure "equitable access" to the Holy Places and maintain them under "special authorities constituted for the purpose" and not under the regular administration of Palestine.[2] The British saw a similarity between the problem of the Dardanelles and that of the Holy Places, for in both instances the international interests of many countries had to be guaranteed in advance. A British memorandum on the Near East drawn up in February 1919 for the peace conference stated:

> The international interests in the straits or in the free access to the Holy Places in Palestine for all religions which have a legitimate interest in each of them, are so important, that they should, if necessary, receive priority to the wish of the inhabitants of the areas in which they are located.[3]

The Vatican's diplomatic activity concerning Palestine, which was stepped up markedly in connection with the peace conference, had a number of objectives. Several problems were on the agenda: the future rule of the Holy Places, the continuation of the French protectorate of Catholics, and the place and role of Zionism. To deal with these issues, the Vatican sent a new auxiliary bishop to the Latin patriarchate in Jerusalem Monsignor Luigi Barlassina, and held spirited diplomatic talks with Britain, France, Italy, Belgium, and other countries. After the war, three cardinals visited Palestine: Francis Cardinal Bourne of England, Filippo Cardinal Giustini of Italy, and Louis Cardinal Dubois of France. Their visits appear to have been the result more of initiatives by their respective countries than by the Vatican, but each of the cardinals viewed himself as an emissary of both the pope and his national government.

The visit that most influenced the pope was that by Cardinal Bourne, the first of the cardinals to arrive in Palestine. Bourne, the archbishop of Westminster, was a leading Catholic figure in Britain.[4] He arrived in Jerusalem on January 19, 1919, stopping en route to Palestine in Cairo on an official visit to the British navy. In Jerusalem he refused to be a guest of the custodia but took part in the Franciscan celebrations marking the seven hundredth anniversary of St. Francis's visit to Palestine.[5] The cardinal was struck by what appeared to him to be two serious dangers to Catholic interest: Zionism and the Protestants.

In regard to the Protestants, he was especially fearful of the Interchurch World Movement of America, which represented 19.5 million Americans and was funneling large sums of money to its institutions in Palestine. Bourne noted, for example, that "Palestine girls of good families received full education as boarders at a cost of only five pounds per annum." The American Protestants were using their schools and colleges, at which secondary education was given virtually free, in order to carry out their proselytizing activities, and in consequence, Catholic youth were in danger.[6]

The cardinal's reflections on the dangers facing Catholic educational institutions in Palestine are important to understand the pope's allocution at the secret consistory on March 10, 1919. Pope Benedict XV stated on that occasion that he was concerned by the propaganda of "non-Catholics of great financial means who exploit the poverty of the population to sow their errors."[7] Cardinal Bourne also pointed out that because the Holy Places were the inheritance of the entire Christian world, Christian countries should receive something more than consular representation.[8]

In the view of the Italian representative in Jerusalem, the aims of the cardinal's visit were (1) to underscore the Catholicism of England to Catholics; (2) to examine the possibility of founding an English religious order; (3) to assess the chances of having English bishops appointed to Nazareth and Bethlehem and perhaps also to Transjordan; and (4) to try to get British influence into the patriarchate through the local clergy, as a counterweight to the influence of Italy and France.[9]

The cardinal's visit did, to some extent, serve British interests. It was intended to dispel the Vatican's fears of British rule in Palestine and to reduce the pressure in Ireland, where much of the public was highly sensitive to charges of discrimination against Catholics in Palestine. Cardinal Bourne also seems to have helped persuade Pope Benedict XV to speak out sharply against Zionism, as he did in March 1919. British Foreign Office officials had varying assessments of the Vatican's fears. Some officials were prepared to offer the Vatican far-reaching promises concerning the status of the Holy Places, and others regarded the Vatican's concerns as fully justified. Moreover, the visit to Rome in March 1919 by Léon Adolphe Cardinal Amette of France was seen as related to the problem of the Holy Places, even though the English did not believe that France intended to obtain the mandate for Palestine.[10]

On March 21, a special committee of cardinals, with the pope sitting as chairman, completed its work on the religious and political future of the Holy Places in Palestine.[11]

On April 2, Sir Arthur Balfour, in Paris, cabled the British legation to the Holy See that if Britain were to get the mandate for Palestine, it would be responsible for safeguarding the existing rights in the Holy Places. These places would come under the protection of the mandatory power in the name of the League of Nations, and the protection extended by other countries heretofore would be terminated.[12] De Salis promptly informed the papal secretary of state of the British foreign minister's position. Cardinal Gasparri wished to make it clear that contrary to a recent report in the French newspaper *Petit Parisien,* he did not favor an international regime for the Holy Places. He had said only that such a solution would be preferable to Zionist rule.

De Salis thus concluded that the Vatican would accept fair British rule as the best solution.[13] What served as the basis of his assessment is not at all clear. The Belgian representative heard something similar from Gasparri and added, "Whatever might have been the Holy See's former preferences for an international solution, and even if this is its hidden wish today, the Vatican will not take a stand in the conflict among the powers as long as the Christian interest is preserved."[14]

A few months after Cardinal Bourne's visit to Palestine and after his enlistment in the struggle to safeguard Catholic interests before the British authorities, another visit was made, this time by the Italian cardinal Giustini. The great importance that the Italian foreign ministry attached to this visit was manifested in the fact that it placed a warship, *Il Quarto,* at the cardinal's disposal, on his and the custodia's request. Prime Minister Francesco Saverio Nitti was finally persuaded of the necessity of making the ship available to Giustini, despite the expense involved, for he viewed this voyage as in the Italian national interest. The cardinal reached Jaffa on September 18, 1919, aboard *Il Quarto,* the papal banner flying from its prow and the Italian flag at the stern. The French government accordingly submitted a protest to Gasparri.

Cardinal Giustini came as a special emissary of the pope to the celebrations marking the seven hundredth anniversary of the custodia. A diplomatic incident was created when the French consul and the auxiliary to the patriarch, Luigi Barlassina, wanted the place of honor at the reception for the cardinal to be reserved for the French representative, while the custodia and the Italian consul argued that because the cardinal was Italian, the French protectorate should not be invoked. In the end, there was no way not to accord to France the place of honor at the ceremony held at Jaffa Gate in Jerusalem, but Italian *carabinieri* stood guard at the custodia building throughout the cardinal's visit.

The cardinal was in the country for about a month, during which time he aired his anti-Zionist views (cited and discussed in Part II of this book). Giustini also became convinced that the French protectorate had to come to an end and that the auxiliary to the patriarch, Barlassina, should be recalled to Rome, as the custodia had requested.[15]

At the end of 1919, the French government sent Cardinal Dubois,[16] archbishop of Rouen, on a visit to Palestine. In the Italian consul's view, the purpose of Dubois's visit was to preserve the French character of Catholic religious policy not only for Palestine but for the Levant as a whole. Dubois naturally supported Barlassina against the custodia. In reaction, the Italians protested to Gasparri that "Dubois' journey was undertaken [in the framework of] a clear plan of French policy." Dubois's visit lasted three months, from December 1919 to March 1920, and it took him to Palestine, Syria, and Lebanon.[17]

The Vatican, for its part, bestowed its blessings on each of the cardinals. The Holy See most likely wanted to counterbalance the British cardinal's influence so as to preserve its good relations with France, both because it was interested in renewing diplomatic relations with France and because the problem of the French protectorate of Catholics throughout the Levant had not yet been resolved. Cardinal Dubois subsequently sent a report on his visit to both the pope and the French government.[18]

The British viewed Dubois's visit to Palestine and Constantinople as another attempt by France to force the continuation of its protectorate. But, the pope's representative in Constantinople did not conceal his hope that the French protectorate would end.[19] On his way back to France, Dubois stopped off in Romania, where he said in a newspaper interview that he had discovered that public opinion in Palestine and southern Syria for the most part favored a continuation of the French protectorate.[20] Sir Oswald Arthur Scott, a British Foreign Office official angered by these reports, commented, "I trust the Cardinal was well paid for his opinions."[21]

The Commission on the Holy Places

The proposal that the Holy Places be placed under the supervision of an international commission was put forward once again on August 30, 1919, by the King–Crane Commission of inquiry sent to the Middle East by U.S. President Woodrow Wilson.[22] The commission's report stated:

> There would then be no reason why Palestine could not be included in a united Syrian state just as other portions of the country, the Holy Places being cared for by an international and inter-religious Commission, somewhat as at present, under the oversight and approval of the Mandatory and of the League of Nations. The Jews, of course, would have representation upon this Commission.[23]

In February 1920, the Allied Supreme Council met in London to discuss the future of Turkey and Palestine. Cardinal Gasparri sent an official note to the British legation to the Vatican, in which he demanded the preservation of the rights of Catholics in all buildings owned by the Catholic Church. As for Holy Places whose ownership was disputed, the Vatican wished that an international commission charged with resolving these disputes be established. The Holy See refrained from expressing its view about which powers should be entrusted with protecting the Holy Places, for the political future of Palestine—so Gasparri claimed—was still uncertain.[24] A decision was then reached in London that because the problem of the Holy Places was legal and technical, it would be best to transfer the matter to a special commission to be appointed at a later date.[25] Thus on this point, the British government accepted the view of the Holy See.

The Sanremo Conference and Herbert Samuel's Visit to the Vatican

In April 1920, an international conference was held at the Italian summer resort of Sanremo, at which the Allies decided to grant Britain the mandate for Palestine. The problems of the Holy Places and French religious protectorate came up a number of times at these talks. The proposal to form an international commission for the Holy Places was also raised again. The French delegate declared that France wished to protect the political and civic rights of the non-Jewish communities in Palestine, including the right to vote for the future assembly. Britain undertook to appoint a special commission "in order to study all problems and complaints regarding the different religious communities and to find a settlement." The chairman of this commission was to be named by the Council of the League of Nations.[26]

Following the decision of the Sanremo Conference to grant to Britain the mandate for Palestine, the British government appointed Sir Herbert Samuel to be the first High Commissioner in Palestine. Samuel, a Jew, had held a number of posts as a member of the British cabinet and was generally considered sympathetic to Zionism. The appointment of a Jew to this high office aroused great concern in the Vatican.[27] Samuel therefore decided to visit the Vatican on his way to Palestine, in an attempt to improve the Holy See's attitude toward his appointment and to soften its positions on the problem of the Holy Places.

Samuel was received by Pope Benedict XV and by the secretary of state, Cardinal Gasparri, on June 25. He tried to reassure the pope, as we learn from the report he sent on the following day to British Foreign Secretary Lord Curzon.

> The Pope had read the statement of policy which I had published at the time when my appointment to Palestine was announced, and had read it with much satisfaction: my appointment had caused him some preoccupation but he now felt reassured. I repeated the declaration that an impartial attitude would be observed towards all religions and that there would be complete religious toleration and liberty in Palestine. I recognized to the full the profound interest which the Catholic Church necessarily took in the Holy Land, and that interest would of course be respected.[28]

The pope also spoke about the difficulties that monks and nuns had encountered in obtaining a visa to enter Palestine. Samuel also informed the pope that the peace treaty with Turkey envisioned the establishment of a commission that would deal with the problem of the Holy Places, but its composition had not yet been determined. He, however, thought it probably would be composed of representatives of religious communities, not of states.[29]

More details about Samuel's audience with the pope are included in a report on the conversation in early July between de Salis and Gasparri. According to the cardinal, the pope had been most conciliatory in tone, but he admitted that Samuel's appointment had caused the Holy See great concern. The cardinal said that the high commissioner's task would undoubtedly be a difficult one and that he was glad that the meeting with Samuel had left a positive impression.[30]

The British cabinet had indeed intended to form the Holy Places commission. At the end of July, Sir Hubert Young of the Foreign Office wrote to Robert Vansittart: "We are very anxious to get the Commission on Holy Places set up with the least possible delay. Must we wait the final passing of the Palestine mandate, or can we take action on the Turkish Treaty soon as it is signed?"[31]

The future of Palestine was also discussed in the wider framework of peace negotiations with Turkey. On August 10, 1920, the never-to-be-implemented Treaty of Sèvres, the peace agreement with Turkey, was signed. According to this treaty, Turkey renounced its sovereignty over Palestine, and Article 95 stipulated that the mandatory power appoint "as soon as possible a special Commission to study and regulate all questions and claims relating to the different religious communities. . . ." The chairman of the commission would be appointed by the Council of the League of Nations.[32]

The content of Article 95 is virtually identical to that of the demand, aimed at terminating the French religious protectorate of Catholics in the Levant, which was put forward by the Italians at the Sanremo Conference. The Great Powers also hoped that through such a commission, a fair solution would be found to the conflicting claims to the Holy Places submitted to the peace conference by the Catholics and the Greek Orthodox.

The Franciscans cited their rights in the Holy Places, going back to 1333, and the protection they received from Venice and then from France and recalled the major historical events until the collective demarche in 1850 of France, Spain, Belgium, Sardinia, and Austria. In that joint representation to the Supreme Porte, these countries demanded restoration to the Franciscans of the rights in the Holy Places in Judea held by the order in 1757. The custodia asked the "High Court of the Nations" to examine the controversies among the various Christian communities entitled to officiate in the Holy Places and to check the historical documents of each community so "that each should be put into definite possession of that part to which it is entitled." Appended to this memorandum was a list of places that had always been in the possession of the custodia and those that had once been but had been taken away from it and whose return was now demanded.[33]

The Greek Orthodox replied that they had been the sole owners of the Holy Places since the fourth century, until the Franciscans appeared on the scene and began their struggle against the Greeks with the support of the Western powers. They also argued that the Franciscans were trying "by all means to expel the Greeks from the Holy Places" and that the Franciscans' lists included places that had never been in their exclusive possession. The Greeks also proposed that 1740 not serve as the focal date and suggested instead the status quo recognized at the Congress of Paris (1856) and the Congress of Berlin (1878) as a reference point. The Greek memorandum concluded with the hope that "the Greeks and Franciscans may live together in the Holy Places with mutual esteem and love."[34] The positions of the two Churches were thus opposed, with each side claiming the Holy Places in Judea for itself.

The idea of establishing a special commission for the Holy Places in Palestine, which, as we have seen, was first proposed in 1915, was a subject of extensive diplomatic activity on the part of the Vatican, which hoped to use the commission to tilt in its favor the balance of forces in the Holy Places between Catholics and Greek Orthodox. But the legal situation was such that until the mandate was approved by the Council of the League of Nations, which was responsible for appointing the commission's chairman, it was not possible to appoint members to the commission.[35] We shall discuss later the Vatican's extensive activity on this matter in the early 1920s, for it reflected much of the Vatican's concerns and general ambitions with respect to Palestine.

Relations Between the Custodia and the Latin Patriarch of Jerusalem

From the time that the presence of a Latin patriarch in Jerusalem was renewed, in 1847, relations between the patriarchate and the custodia were tense. The patriarch was convinced that he had been charged with defending Holy Places vis-à-vis the local authorities,[36] and the custodia could not become accustomed to the change in its status, which had consolidated over the centuries. Generally, France and the Vatican sided with the patriarch, and Italy supported the custodia.[37] Although the custodia was an international institution, Italy's influence on it was quite evident.[38] Immediately after the conquest of Jerusalem, the superior general of the Franciscan order in Rome, Father Serafino Cimino, advised the director general for political affairs of the Italian Foreign Ministry to see that Britain did not gain from the Vatican a modification to its advantage in the Franciscan order's rule.[39]

Italy applied pressure behind the scenes on the Vatican to secure the appointment of an Italian priest as custos, and indeed the man named to the post in January 1918 was the Italian priest Federico Diotallevi. At the same time, however, the British wished to have an English priest appointed to a senior position in the custodia.[40] Diotallevi arrived in Jerusalem in February 1918 and claimed that "the other non-Catholic communities and the Zionists are privileged."[41] In his very first talk with General Gilbert Clayton, Diotallevi already suggested abolishing the French protectorate.

The Italian government also tried to obtain from the Vatican the appointment of an Italian priest as the Latin patriarch of Jerusalem. In October 1917, shortly before the British conquest, the Turks deported to the north Patriarch Filippo Camassei, an Italian, who became ill and had to be replaced. This dragged on for months, with the Vatican not deciding to appoint Barlassina as bishop of Capernaum and auxiliary to the Latin patriarch until August 1918.[42]

Barlassina arrived in Jaffa at the end of October aboard an Italian ship that, at Gasparri's request, flew the Vatican flag. Barlassina was received by the Italian representative, Guido Meli Lupi di Soragna. The British government asked the

Vatican to appoint an Englishman to the post of patriarch or auxiliary, but after Camassei returned to Italy in 1919, Barlassina was named patriarch in 1920. He was described in *The Times* on May 31, 1922:

> His Beatitude is a man of distinguished appearance, about sixty years of age, full of vigour and activity, and with a very intellectual countenance. He has a black beard and moustache, which, like his hair, are streaked with white. On his head he wears a skullcap of Pavonazzo (pale purple) silk. He is habited in a long black cassock reaching to his feet. A pectoral cross is suspended from a chain which hangs round his neck. His gestures and eyes are eloquent. In a word, he is a very characteristic Italian prelate well versed in diplomacy.[43]

On November 4, 1918, Pope Benedict XV sent a brief to the custodia in Jerusalem on the occasion of the seven hundredth anniversary of its founding. In this letter the pope recalled the history of the Franciscans, which began in 1230. He repeated and reconfirmed the concession that had been granted to the order as guardian of the Holy Places.[44] The pope also used the opportunity to inform the Franciscans of the impending arrival of the Latin patriarch in Jerusalem and pointed out that they would undoubtedly merit the patriarch's commendation. The pope was apparently trying to appease the Franciscans, who were not happy about the strengthening of the Latin patriarch, for it was he who had deprived them of their virtually monopolistic position among Catholics in the Holy Land. The Franciscans chose to interpret this brief as indicating that the Latin patriarch would have no role in the Holy Places in the future and thus immediately excluded him from their Easter and Christmas celebrations. Camassei, who officially was still patriarch, thereupon turned to the Congregation de Propaganda Fide (for the propagation of the faith) at the Vatican and asked for instructions. In its reply, in June 1920, the congregation stated that the patriarch was the representative of the Holy See and the guardian of the Holy Places.

Ronald Storrs, the British governor of Jerusalem at that time, wrote in his memoirs that the Franciscans and the patriarchate were at odds on almost every issue and were in agreement only with respect to the pro-Italian political stand they shared.[45] This assessment differs from that held by most Italian historians, who view the Latin patriarchate, and especially Barlassina, as decidedly pro-French. The Italian diplomats in Jerusalem in that period also accepted this view, apparently having been influenced by the Franciscans.

A similar opinion was expressed by the British representative to the Vatican. De Salis wrote that Barlassina's candidacy had been supported by six of the seven religious orders represented in Palestine. He presumed that those six orders were more or less under French influence. The Franciscans, however, did not support the appointment.[46] For several months, the British authorities tried to persuade the Vatican to replace Barlassina with someone more suitable. De Salis met with Monsignor Bonaventura Cerretti, one of Gasparri's aides in the Secretariat of State, and suggested that Barlassina's successor be a British subject. Cerretti replied that this would hardly be acceptable to the Vatican, that the Latin patriarchate should be in the hands of an Italian. If an English priest were nominated, the Vatican would be faced with very big claims by the French, which, according to de Salis, "might almost be as great a source of embarrassment to us as to the Holy See."[47]

Sir Oswald A. Scott, of the Foreign Office in London, felt that de Salis should press the question, pointing out that it would be in the patriarchate's interest for the auxiliary bishop to be British, in order to improve relations between the patriarchate and the British administration. D'Arcy Osborne agreed and instructed de Salis to propose Father Paschal Robinson for the post,[48] but the British requests proved to be futile. At the secret consistory of March 8, 1920, Barlassina was named to the post he had filled de facto since his arrival in Palestine and became the new patriarch of Jerusalem. De Salis understood well enough that the new appointment was not a happy one from the British point of view, as Barlassina had shown himself to be "without experience for dealing with our political authorities in the East."[49]

At the end of May, the newly appointed patriarch visited the Foreign Office in London and left a memorandum with Sir John Tilley, in which he spelled out the patriarchate's demands. The patriarch "indulged in a great flow of language" but did not impress Tilley "as being at all a wise or even sensible man."[50] In this four-page memorandum, the patriarch asked to retain all rights in connection with marriage, heredity, and the appointment of guardians for orphan children. He protested the fact that three thousand Jews from Austria could live undisturbed in Jerusalem, while "seven peaceful [German] Benedictines were harshly sent away by the [British] soldiers in the course of twelve hours." The patriarch wanted the British to apply directly to the patriarchate; demanded exemption from taxes, custom duties, and tithes; and asked for representation in the municipality. He underscored the assistance he had given the British administration by forbidding Catholics to participate in political movements, by his efforts to avoid international complications after Indian soldiers had "invaded the enclosure of the Convent of Clarisse," and by teaching English in the patriarchate's mission schools. The patriarch wanted English youth to study at the seminary in Jerusalem, thus hoping that in a few years they would become English priests and would serve in the patriarchate.[51] Samuel read the memorandum and remarked that "we shall take pain to avoid offending religious susceptibilities."[52]

In July 1920, de Salis learned that the pope was about to send Father Robinson to Palestine to report on the situation there. This may have been another step in the Vatican's attempt to keep all bases covered: Father Robinson was an English Franciscan, and sending him on a mission to Palestine was undoubtedly meant to please the British, who did not conceal their displeasure with the plan to hand to France the representation of Catholic interests. De Salis noted that in light of the poor relations between the British authorities and Barlassina, Robinson's appointment was beneficial for British interests. He therefore recommended that the foreign secretary receive him in London for a talk.[53]

The Foreign Office in London took note of the fact that Barlassina had been appointed auxiliary patriarch in Jerusalem in 1918, and by September 1919 it appeared that he would be replaced, as being unsuited for the position. But instead, he was promoted and made the Latin patriarch of Jerusalem. The British government had then proposed Father Robinson as Barlassina's successor as auxiliary patriarch. Nothing had happened since that time, and Father Robinson continued his journeys to Palestine, "which fill Count de Salis with such satisfaction whilst Patriarch Barlassina apparently remains as unsatisfactory in his present exalted posi-

tion as he was previously as an auxiliary."[54] As one Foreign Office official observed, against this background it was hard to follow the Church's maneuverings.
One senses in this observation the Foreign Office's bitterness toward the Vatican
and the realization that Father Robinson's journeys were no match for Barlassina's
unfriendly activities.

The Renewal of Liturgical Honors

The issue of France's protectorate of Catholics in the Levant was raised at the
London Conference in February 1920. The French ambassador in London, Paul
Cambon, claimed that the Holy Places had been in French hands since the fifteenth
century and that the Vatican had always recognized this fact. "Should a mandate
for Palestine be granted to Britain, France would be bound to make certain reservations in regard to the Holy Places." But Lloyd George held that it would be
impossible "to create an empire within an empire."[55] At about the same time, Cardinal Gasparri told de Salis that he had heard of the intention of Britain, France,
and Italy to terminate France's religious protectorate, and he was pleased.[56]

The issue of the religious protectorate also came up for discussion at the Sanremo Conference, at which it was decided to grant the mandate for Palestine to
Britain. On that occasion the Italian prime minister, Francesco Nitti, demanded that
the French protectorate of Catholics in the Levant be terminated, explaining, "The
historical necessity in the past of protecting Christian bodies under the Turkish regime had now come to an end, as the European religious communities were now
represented by a civilized nation which would guarantee to the whole world the
safeguarding of the interests of those communities." It would no longer be possible,
he said, to find fault with a priest for refusing to grant liturgical honors to a country
that might demand them. Nitti was, of course, referring to France. France did not
want to relinquish its traditional rights in the East, but Lloyd George stated that
although the protection France had offered Catholics had been necessary while Palestine had been under Turkish rule, there was no justification for it under the new
circumstances that had been created. He argued that "to continue those conditions
when Great Britain was in charge of the administration of Palestine and to say that
it must be left to France to ensure that her Catholics received fair play under a
British rule, was quite impossible. It would simply lead to a dual administration by
two great European Powers."[57]

The French representative was forced to agree, and a draft resolution presented
to the Allied Supreme Council stated that "question of the religious protectorate of
France . . . had been settled . . . by the undertaking given by the French Government that they recognized this protectorate as being at an end."[58]

Samuel was received at the Vatican by the pope and the secretary of state on
June 25, 1920. When he met with Samuel, Gasparri raised the problem of the
liturgical honors. The cardinal felt that because the French protectorate had been
ended by the Sanremo Conference, the bestowing of liturgical honors should also
cease. "Otherwise, what would happen in the future, when the British high commissioner would be a Catholic and would have to renounce his place of honour in

the church in favour of the French consul?" The cardinal wanted to know the position of the British government on this, and Samuel promised to convey it to him later through de Salis. The cardinal then spoke of the representation of Catholic interests at the Holy Places and assumed that the British would not object if it were given to a representative of France. Samuel replied "The peace treaty with Turkey contemplated the establishment of a commission to deal with these matters; the composition of that commission had not yet been determined but I thought it probable that it would consist of representatives not of nations, but of religious communities as such."[59]

But as had happened many times before, the diplomats of the Holy See told each side what it wanted to hear. Thus the French representative received a different version from Cardinal Gasparri of his meeting with Samuel concerning the liturgical honors. Gasparri told him that he had explained to Samuel two days earlier that representatives of France had been involved for centuries in the defense of Catholic holy places and that French consuls had been the traditional recipients of liturgical honors at religious ceremonies.

Samuel answered that at the Sanremo Conference, France had relinquished its protectorate, and so the Church no longer required defense, as it had during the period of Turkish rule. According to the French version, Gasparri replied that if the capitulations were abolished, Christians would no longer require the protection of a foreign state but would need the defense of an attorney. Samuel expressed his surprise upon hearing this and reminded the cardinal that disputes would be brought before a commission composed not of diplomatic representatives but of emissaries of the various religious communities. Gasparri responded that such a commission was not to his liking, that he did not know how it would be formed, and that even so, the services of an attorney would still be useful.[60]

The French government believed that at the Sanremo Conference it had merely renounced its political protectorate of Catholics in favor of the mandatory government but that it was entitled to demand continuation of the liturgical honors, as they added to France's prestige and were of a religious character.

The British and French representatives had a slightly different understanding of Gasparri's remarks about France's status and the liturgical honors. Samuel understood that Gasparri was interested in having the honors abolished but wanted that to be decided by the British government. At the same time, Gasparri requested that the French continue to represent the Vatican in the Holy Land. The French representative, however, understood Gasparri to be in complete agreement with him and to be interested in preserving France's traditional status as the defender of Catholic interests in the Holy Land.

The differences in the reports of the French and British representatives may have been merely a matter of emphasis and may have reflected Gasparri's need to maintain proper relations with both France and Britain. But the result was quite a few misunderstandings among the Great Powers and flurries of diplomatic activity.

The question of liturgical honors had been raised at the beginning of June, before Samuel's visit to the Vatican, when Italy demanded that Great Britain not recognize any longer French claims about the religious protectorate.[61] The Italian government had approached the British government when it clearly appeared that

France wanted to regain from the Vatican the recognition of its traditional privileged position in matters of liturgical honors and protocol precedence.

Britain and the Vatican each tried to ascertain the position of the other, each of them avoiding the responsibility of decision. The Vatican itself seems to have been divided between its understanding that French protectorate and liturgical honors were now a matter of the past and its desire to preserve for France some vestige of its privileged position. Britain, for its part, contended that the problem was essentially religious and that therefore the Vatican should resolve it. In the middle were the Italians, who wanted France's privileges to be terminated but met with delaying tactics from both sides and failed to obtain satisfaction.

The problem of the liturgical honors was brought before the Vatican Secretariat of State by de Salis, who asked Monsignor Bonaventura Cerretti to give him materials that would enable him to reply to the Italians on the matter of France's demands to retain certain of its privileges in Palestine. This was a rather strange step, since Cardinal Gasparri had asked Samuel about the British government's position on this and then sent de Salis a memorandum of that talk in which he spelled out the problem. In his memorandum, the cardinal noted that at Sanremo the Great Powers had agreed to terminate the French religious protectorate and, by implication, also to terminate the liturgical honors, as they were a corollary to the protectorate. Later in the memorandum, Gasparri brought up the possibility that the Vatican might continue to grant these honors to France. If so, "England, not being a Catholic power, could not of course demand the same honours for her representative in Palestine: but perhaps the representative might be a Catholic." Then Gasparri asked what Britain's position would be if its representative did not receive the honors.[62]

The cardinal returned to the subject in a conversation with de Salis several days later and once again asked for clarification of the British government's position. Another point that the British government had to address was the cardinal's suggestion that France represent Catholic interests in the Holy Places. Thus although on the one hand Gasparri consented to the termination of the French religious protectorate, and even claimed to be pleased about it, on the other hand he wanted a privileged status for France in the Holy Places once again, as the representative of Catholic interests. This twofold position may have reflected the Vatican's desire to find a golden mean among the demands of the various powers—Italy's pressures to end the French religious protectorate and the Vatican's traditional friendship with France, with which it was about to renew diplomatic relations after an interruption of some twenty years.

In his report to the Foreign Office in London, de Salis underscored the talks between France and the Holy See on the resumption of diplomatic relations and indicated that "it would seem clear that the Quai d'Orsay are bringing a good deal of pressure to bear on the Vatican in order to recover indirectly as many as possible of the advantages of the lost protectorate."[63] A number of British Foreign Office officials in London reacted to de Salis's report. Scott commented that the religious protectorate should be ended and de Salis should persuade the Vatican that investing religious protection in any power other than the mandatory power would only lead to political complications. Another official, Sir Hubert Young,[64] suggested that the governments of France and Italy be informed that as soon as the mandate for Palestine were assigned to Britain by the League of Nations, liturgical honors would no longer be granted to the French representative. Another official believed that it was of the utmost importance to force the French government to honor its agreement to terminate its protectorate. In the view of this official, France's demand to retain special ceremonial status was absurd and looked like an effort by France to regain what it had lost. The peoples of the East put much stock in ceremony, and therefore it must be made clear to the Vatican that Britain would not consent to France's retaining ceremonial or any other special privileges. Further, the British government must also oppose the proposal that France represent the interests of the Catholics in the Holy Places. This view was accepted by Foreign Secretary Curzon, who added in his own hand, "I will not move an inch."[65]

De Salis returned to this subject a few days later, to speed up the Foreign Office's reply. It was his view that if the British government continued to stand aside on this issue, the Vatican would be compelled to make concessions to France detrimental to Britain.[66]

The British Foreign Office drafted a reply to de Salis, which stated that the problem of the liturgical honors had to be examined on the basis of two leading considerations: first, the hope that France would continue its activity in Palestine in cooperation with the British government and, second, the "paramount need of a single supreme control" in Palestine, "not only in reality, but also in appearance."[67]

4

An Era of Quest

Britain's Opposition to Continuing the
Religious Protectorate

Referring to the decisions of the Sanremo Conference, the British government informed the Holy See in August 1920 that France's relinquishment of its protectorate of Catholics in the former Ottoman territories was regarded as final and that it viewed with disfavor the representation of Catholic interests in the Holy Places by French representatives.[1] Upon learning of the British government's decision, Cardinal Gasparri expressed his satisfaction.[2]

In November 1920, Gasparri discussed this question once again with the French chargé d'affaires and showed him the British note received in August. It seems that Gasparri had wanted a clear, written response from Britain, behind which he could avoid a confrontation with France. Gasparri maintained that until then he had guarded the tradition but was now unable to ignore the objections of Britain, which was the sovereign power in Palestine. If France wished to challenge that decision, it must inform Britain in writing.

How was it possible, asked the French diplomat, that liturgical honors at a Catholic religious ceremony would be dependent on the goodwill of a Jewish governor? Such a state of affairs seemed to him unacceptable interference. He wrote to his ministry that France should preserve its positions in the Holy Land because the Zionist experiment might fail and the regime in Palestine might yet change.[3] As de Salis noted in his annual report,

> The view taken in London was that the French renunciation of their protectorate over Catholics in territories ceded by Turkey was absolute and complete, and covered all special rights and privileges. The French, on their side, continued to urge the Vatican to give orders for the maintenance of the honours, doubt being thrown on the binding character of the San Remo agreement, which, moreover, to the exclusion of the Vatican, merely concerned France and Great Britain.[4]

The situation was so tense and delicate that even the replacement of one nail in the star in the Grotto of the Nativity in Bethlehem became a diplomatic issue, for the High Commissioner was "particularly anxious" to avoid granting official recognition to the French protectorate of Catholics.[5]

Notwithstanding the satisfaction expressed in August, at the end of November it was clear that Cardinal Gasparri had changed his mind again.

On November 30, H. W. G. A. Ormsby-Gore, then a Conservative member of Parliament, asked the undersecretary of state about Cardinal Gasparri's declaration that the Holy See would recognize the French protectorate of all Roman Catholics in the East and asked whether the British government would accept this. The Foreign Office knew nothing of such a declaration and tried to persuade Ormsby-Gore to postpone his interpellation to a later date, but to no avail.[6]

As de Salis observed,

> The Christmas ceremonies in Bethlehem at the end of the year put the matter to the test, since the French Government, ignoring the negotiations of San Remo, claimed from the Vatican that the *status quo* should be maintained. To this, the Vatican thought they were obliged to assent, especially as they had no official communication of the San Remo agreement, though the Consulta [the Italian Foreign Ministry] had kept them privately informed, at the time, of what was going on.[7]

On December 20, Gasparri suddenly informed de Salis that because the peace treaty with Turkey had not been ratified and the mandate had not been approved, it had been decided that the traditional liturgical honors would be accorded to the French representative in Palestine at the upcoming Christmas religious ceremonies.[8] De Salis's cable on this matter was immediately forwarded to Samuel in Palestine, with the additional comment that Gasparri's position seemed "highly uncooperative and unfriendly," for Britain had in fact already implemented the mandate without any objections from France.[9] The British Foreign Office also instructed its representative to protest to the cardinal secretary of state.[10]

What prompted the Vatican to bring up once again the issue of the liturgical honors? One interpretation is that it was meant as an oblique expression of the Vatican's dissatisfaction over the British government's inactivity with respect to forming the commission for the Holy Places. Some confirmation of this view can be found in the fact that in June 1921, when the commission was discussed in the British Foreign Office, this exchange of letters was reexamined.

At the same time, in Palestine, Luigi Barlassina, the Latin patriarch in Jerusalem, asked Samuel to clarify his position on according liturgical honors to the French representative on Christmas. Samuel replied without hesitation that the British government felt that the granting of honors should be discontinued. In the meantime, however, the patriarch received instructions from the Vatican to continue the former practice.[11] The High Commissioner therefore boycotted the Christmas function in Bethlehem and instructed the members of his staff and the governor of Jerusalem not to attend.[12]

On Christmas Eve, de Salis handed Gasparri a note of protest, which, however, did not explicitly mention the protocol of the Sanremo Conference of April 24,

1920, in which the French government had accepted the termination of its religious protectorate.

De Salis's talks with Monsignor Bonaventura Cerretti, Gasparri's deputy, show that France's President Alexandre Millerand believed that although the Allies refused at Sanremo to recognize the validity of France's rights, it did not mean that those rights had been abrogated. And furthermore, because the problem pertained to religious ceremonies, the only body competent to decide the matter was the Church. The conference's protocol had not been signed by the parties and therefore was not binding. On a previous occasion, Cardinal Gasparri had asked Baron Carlo Monti for the precise wording of the Sanremo Conference's protocol and, on its basis, had refused to restore the liturgical honors as demanded by Marie-Augustin-Jean Doulcet, the French chargé d'affaires. Doulcet, for his part, argued that the demand was based on an agreement between France and the Holy See, which the Vatican was obliged to honor until the mandate was approved.

Gasparri, it seems, did not want France's religious protection to be continued but preferred the discontinuation to come from the British and not from the Vatican, for which the renewal of diplomatic relations with France was a matter of great importance. In the end, Gasparri yielded to the French demand and asked the British government to restore the liturgical honors. He seems to have done so on the understanding that the resumption would be temporary and would be in force only during the transitional period until final approval of the mandate.[13]

In London, Sir Eric Graham Forbes-Adam, a young Foreign Office official, commented that it was hard for him to believe that Doulcet's remarks expressed the position of the French government, as the decisions of the Sanremo Conference were entered into the protocol without the parties' signatures only in deference to Millerand's request, to spare him from having officially to sign the termination of the French protectorate. Forbes-Adams believed that at a suitable opportunity, it would be necessary to obligate the French government to adhere to the letter and spirit of the Sanremo agreement. He saw no need for any further activity at the Vatican in the meantime and drafted instructions for de Salis accordingly.[14]

The Vatican's Objection to Town-planning Schemes

From time to time, the Vatican complained to the British authorities and expressed its fear of any change in Palestine—of the process of modernization itself—that could damage the character of the Holy Land. Thus in October 1920, Cardinal Gasparri complained about an urban-planning program to link the city of Haifa and the mountain by "rail and carriage roads," which he claimed would turn Mount Carmel into a pleasure resort. He was probably referring to Hadar Hacarmel, a new quarter whose construction had begun in that period, and to the plan to build a funicular railway. This project, the cardinal asserted, "would be distasteful to the sentiments of Catholics, who see in Mount Carmel . . . one of the most sacred sanctuaries of the Virgin." He therefore requested the British government to use its influence to have the project abandoned.[15]

Cardinal Gasparri's request was opposed by British Foreign Office officials. Sir Oswald A. Scott remarked that he disagreed in principle with the cardinal. Forbes-Adam held that it should be made clear to the Mandate government in Jerusalem that the cardinal's demand had no support whatever in London but that Samuel should nonetheless supply the material needed to prepare a proper reply. Sir Hubert Young, by contrast, felt that the matter should be submitted to the commission on the Holy Places, and the plan regarding Mount Carmel should be deferred pending the commission's ruling.[16]

In November, the chief secretary to the Palestine government, Sir Wyndham Deeds, replied to Gasparri in the name of the High Commissioner, explaining to him that his apprehensions were groundless and that the plan took into account the religious and historical importance of the site. The cardinal could rest assured, Deeds went on to say, that care will be taken to preserve Mount Carmel's sacred character, holy traditions, and historical interests.[17]

The issue came up again in talks between Gasparri and de Salis, and several months later, at the end of 1920, Gasparri went so far as to offer the Holy See's thanks for the assurances by the British government to preserve the sacred tradition and historical character of Mount Carmel.[18]

But despite all the explanations and assurances, Pope Benedict XV used the Mount Carmel issue for a public airing of the general problem involving the Holy Places. In an allocution to the cardinals entitled *Causa Nobis,* on June 13, 1921, he expressed his great concern over what was occurring in Palestine. Speaking about the Holy Places, the pope pointed out:

> And now, far from diminishing, that anxiety is increasing every day. Indeed, if at that time We lamented the iniquitous activity in Palestine of non-Catholic sects which are pleased to glory in the name of Christian, to-day, too, We must repeat that lament, seeing how they are carrying on that work with even greater activity, themselves possessing abundant means and cleverly profiting by the misery in which the inhabitants of the country were plunged after the war. . . . And again We cannot but deplore the intense activity which is being shown by many to take away the sacred character of the Holy Places, transforming them into pleasure resorts with every worldly attraction. That is worthy of reproof everywhere, but above all in places where at every step the holiest memories of religion are encountered.[19]

Soon after this, another problem related to town planning cropped up, this time in Jerusalem. The Pro-Jerusalem Society proposed that a ramparts walk be built on the walls of the Old City. This proposal caused concern among Catholics, who viewed it as interference in the private domain and as an intrusion into property belonging to the Latin patriarchate and the custodia.[20] This was a somewhat peculiar contention, considering that the membership of the Pro-Jerusalem Society— which had been founded by the governor of Jerusalem, Ronald Storrs—included Catholic priests and Italian architects such as Antonio Barluzzi and Roberto Paribeni. The ramparts walk was intended as the "backbone" of the municipal garden project.[21]

The Renewal of Diplomatic Relations Between
the Vatican and France

Although relations between the Vatican and France had been formally severed, contacts were maintained on a number of levels, for each side had need of the other. France attached great importance to its protectorate of Catholics as a means of shoring up its presence in the East, and by 1917 voices could already be heard advocating the resumption of relations with the Vatican for the sake of recapturing positions in the Levant.[22] Anatole de Monzie, a member of the French parliament, held that to strengthen its influence, France should use the Jews, the Catholics, and the Muslims.[23]

During the war, regular contact between France and the Vatican was maintained by Charles Loiseau, who was received frequently by Cardinal Gasparri. France's struggle to ensure the continuance of the liturgical honors was yet another means to enhance its prestige. In March 1920, the French government appointed Doulcét as chargé d'affaires to the Holy See, with the aim of conducting negotiations for the renewal of diplomatic ties.

The French diplomat's instructions stated that he was to endeavor to be received by Cardinal Gasparri in order to inform him of the French government's wish to renew relations. Should the cardinal prove willing to consider the outstanding problems, the chargé d'affaires would have an opportunity to stress a number of points. First, the accepted principle of reciprocity notwithstanding, the French government felt that it would be undesirable to dispatch a nuncio to Paris right away, for this might stir up harsh internal debate within France. Second, the envoy should confirm his government's wish to continue the traditional policy of granting protection to Catholics in the East and thus to preserve the privileges that French representatives had enjoyed in Palestine, Syria, and Constantinople, and throughout the Levant.[24]

We do not know when the French chargé d'affaires arrived in Rome, nor have we found in British diplomatic correspondence any reactions to his arrival. In November 1920, De Fontarce, a member of the French diplomatic service, was appointed as Monaco's minister to the Holy See, a move that the British representative in Rome viewed as indicative of the French government's desire to "exercise at the Vatican all the influence they can command."[25]

In February 1921, French Prime Minister Aristide Briand[26] spoke with the British ambassador about the possibility of a satisfactory compromise with the British concerning the Treaty of Sèvres. As will be recalled, that treaty, which included Article 95 dealing with the Holy Places, had been signed in August 1920 but had never been implemented. It was therefore necessary to hold additional talks to find solutions to those problems still unresolved. Briand also expressed his intention to maintain, if possible, France's positions in respect to the Holy Places in Palestine.[27]

In May 1921, the Vatican and France renewed diplomatic relations. These relations had been severed in 1904, when the president of France visited the king of Italy in Rome, over the objections of the Vatican, which wanted to prevent recognition of Rome as Italy's capital. The Vatican wanted to reestablish relations with

France, in order to break out of the diplomatic isolation in which it found itself after World War I and to create a common front against the English Protestants, who offered their protection to the Greek Orthodox and the Zionists. France, for its part, was interested in restoring its religious protectorate of Catholics as a way of strengthening its position in the Levant and settling some problems that had arisen with the Church.[28]

Prime Minister Briand appointed Charles Jonnart as ambassador to the Holy See. Jonnart presented his credentials on May 28, 1921, and in his speech raised the problem of the French religious protectorate in the East, but without specifically mentioning Palestine. This, of course, drew the attention of the British representative to the Vatican.[29] According to private information that reached the British representative, the French ambassador declared that with respect to the French religious protectorate in Palestine, his government did not feel itself bound by the Sanremo agreement.[30]

De Salis's cable caused a bit of a stir in the Foreign Office in London. One official even commented that France's relinquishment at Sanremo of the religious protectorate had also been mentioned in the British note of January 19 to the French ambassador in London, in which the British demanded that French military units be withdrawn from Palestine. The French had left about forty soldiers and one officer in Jerusalem who stood guard at several Holy Places. In September 1920, the French told the British that they would agree to withdraw this unit and the other units guarding Holy Places elsewhere in Palestine, on condition that the Italian detachment would also be withdrawn at the same time.[31] In their reply to the British note, the French acceded to the request that they evacuate their soldiers and did not dispute the British assumption that at Sanremo, France had agreed to give up its religious protectorate. Therefore, the official added, "France will now find it difficult to take a position as mentioned in de Salis' cable."[32]

On June 28, 1921, Monsignor Cerretti told de Salis that the French ambassador had declared that the French did not view themselves as bound by the Sanremo agreement and rejected the contention that they had made a commitment. Although the French press had written that in his reply to Jonnart's speech, the pope had expressed his support for the French position, Cerretti said that this was not so. The Vatican's position was that the problem was between England and France, and all the Vatican could do was preserve the status quo until the British mandate for Palestine was approved. In London, Sir Oswald A. Scott remarked that the Vatican was well aware of the British position, and although this was not an opportune moment to take the problem up with the French, it should be suggested to them that this would be the British position as soon as the mandate came into force. Forbes-Adam, however, believed that it would be necessary to wait until the treaty and the mandate went into force, or until the French provided some "tangible evidence that they are trying to withdraw from the Sanremo agreement." It seemed to him "incredible that they should have suggested that the agreement does not bind them."[33]

In any event, the pope's speech in June 1921 caused a great deal of unrest inside the British legation to the Vatican, and most of the diplomats' suspicions were focused on France. It appeared that "the French will attempt to deflect Arab hostility from themselves onto us by stimulating anti-Zionist agitation whilst at the same time endeavouring to regain their religious protectorate."[34]

There were grounds for the British representatives' fears. More than a year before, in March 1920, Colonel Richard Meinertzhagen had reported that there had been protest demonstrations organized by the Muslim–Christian Association in Jerusalem against Zionism and demanding unity with Syria. The French High Commissioner in Jerusalem was set on wrecking the policy of His Majesty's government and appeared to be the source of propaganda in Palestine.[35] The Foreign Office in London was well aware of the situation, as is indicated by the comments on the letter from Cecil Dormer, the British chargé d'affaires to the Holy See.[36]

The problem of the relations between the Vatican and France continued to occupy British diplomats. At the beginning of August, the British ambassador in Paris, Lord Hardinge of Penshurst, forwarded to the Foreign Office in London an article from *Le Temps* about the arrival in Paris of the new nuncio, Monsignor Cerretti.[37]

The author of this article engaged in a polemic with leftist circles in France that viewed the renewal of a dialogue with the Vatican as a threat to secularity. But, the writer continued, the resumption of diplomatic relations with the Vatican stemmed from the foreign policy considerations of the French government. "The experience of the war has brought on us the realization that the Vatican still has a strong influence in international problems, and France could suffer from her withdrawal from this crossroad of international policy, which is useful both for forecasting and for action." The renewal of relations with the Vatican would thus facilitate the search for a solution to critical problems in Alsace-Lorraine and be helpful for renewing French influence in the East.[38] On August 6, 1921, the nuncio presented his credentials to French President Alexandre Millerand,[39] and very cordial speeches were exchanged.[40] The principle of reciprocity was thus preserved, albeit after a delay of about two months.

Forming the Commission for the Holy Places

At an early stage of British civilian rule in Palestine, which started on July 1, 1920, the Catholics complained that they were being treated unfairly, as compared with the Greek Orthodox. In September 1920, Cardinal Gasparri sent the following note to the British envoy at the Holy See:

> In view of the antagonism existing between the Greeks and the Catholics, it would appear that there is considerable danger of the latter being eliminated from the local posts of administration and that thereby the Catholic communities may find themselves deprived of representatives. . . . The Cardinal Secretary of State therefore begs that Your Lordship may give the matter most earnest consideration, urging that the Christians in Palestine may be subdivided into two groups, Catholics and non-Catholics, thereby allowing Catholic communities to have their representatives in local administrative matters.[41]

Despite the efforts of the British government to allay fears concerning the rights of the Catholics in Palestine, the Catholics began to take steps to see that the commission for the Holy Places would be organized so as to ensure acceptance of the Church's demands. Thus in the beginning of November 1920, the Italian Catholic Partido Popolare (Popular party) submitted a memorandum to the parliamentary foreign affairs committee demanding that the Italian government coordinate its activities with the Vatican and France for the protection of Catholic interests in the Holy Places. The objects of this coordinated activity were the nomination of the commission's members and a guarantee that the commission chairman would act impartially and not promote Greek Orthodox interests.[42]

At about that time Sir Herbert Samuel stated his view of the commission for the Holy Places. He said he was "doubtful whether [the] high commissioner should be chairman" of the commission, since its decisions must bring him into conflict with some sections of the population. Samuel preferred that the commission be "in the nature of outside arbitration between local divergent claims" and that it sit as soon as possible after the mandate was approved, and then be summoned only at long intervals.[43]

Samuel elaborated his position one month later, in reply to questions from the Foreign Office. He proposed a commission of thirty-one members: eight Muslims recommended by the grand mufti; three Catholics recommended by the Vatican; three Greek Orthodox; two Armenians; eight Jews; and one each from the Coptic, Abyssinian, and Anglican Churches. Samuel also proposed that the members of the commission not be residents of Palestine "who have been actively engaged in controversies on the Holy Places." In addition, four representatives of the administration should also sit on the commission.[44]

In December 1920, a British interministerial committee, with Samuel's proposals in hand, discussed the establishment of a commission for the Holy Places.[45] Father P. N. Waggett, a Catholic priest who served as adviser to the British government, also took part in the discussion. He asked to reconsider the decision that the third Christian on the commission should be of the Anglican Church; he suggested instead that the third Christian representative "stand for the interests of all the smaller sects, among whom the Armenians were the most important." Waggett also thought that the "different schools" in Judaism should be represented on advisory bodies that could be called in by the main commission to advise, as the need arose. The interministerial committee decided that the commission should consist of six members who would be nominated by the Mandatory government and that the third Christian representative should be chosen from the smaller communities in rotation, beginning with an Armenian. The chairman of the commission would be appointed by the League of Nations on the recommendation of the Mandatory government, and in addition, a group of panels representing each different religious interest would be formed. The committee decided to start an unofficial examination of candidates for membership on the commission, so that immediately after the Council of the League of Nations approved the mandate, the British government could approach the League of Nations and point out that because the guardianship of the Holy Places was a problem of international importance, the salaries of the main commission's members should be paid by the League.[46]

On December 6, 1920, Britain submitted to the League of Nations the first draft of the mandate for Palestine. This draft included Article 13, according to which "all responsibility in connection with the Holy Places . . . including that of preserving existing rights and of securing free access to the Holy Places . . . is assumed by the Mandatory." In its first draft, Article 14, which dealt with the international commission for the Holy Places, stated:

> In accordance with Article 95 of the Treaty of Peace with Turkey, the Mandatory undertakes to appoint as soon as possible a special Commission to study and regulate all questions and claims relating to the different religious communities. In the composition of the Commission the religious interests concerned will be taken into account. The Chairman of the Commission will be appointed by the Council of the League of Nations. It will be the duty of this Commission to ensure that certain Holy Places, religious buildings or sites regarded with special veneration by the adherents of one particular religion will be under the constant supervision of the qualified bodies representing the believers of the concerned religion.

The selection of the Holy Places, religious buildings, or territories to be so protected was to be entrusted to the commission, subject to the approval of the Mandatory government. Nevertheless, in all the cases covered by this article, the rights and duties of the Mandatory government to maintain order and decorum in the specified place would not be infringed, and the buildings and property sites would be subject to those laws concerning the historical sites, as set in Palestine with the agreement of the Mandatory government. The League of Nations would guarantee the right of supervision spelled out in this article.[47]

These two articles of the draft mandate caused a great shock to the Vatican and seemed to have been one factor leading to the pope's allocution on June 13, 1921, mentioned earlier.[48] The Catholics argued that the fact that only the chairman of the commission would be nominated by the Council of the League of Nations—with all other members to be appointed by the Mandatory government—made a mockery of international supervision, for such a commission would prefer not to inconvenience the British High Commissioner.[49]

Discussion of the commission's composition continued in various British forums. On March 24, 1921, a meeting was held on the subject in Jerusalem, at which time the opinion of the British Foreign Office regarding the nomination of the members and payment of the commission's expenses was sought.[50] At one stage Father Waggett was considered a possible candidate for commission secretary.[51] Later, the discussion having gotten down to fine details, it was proposed that the Mandatory government cover no more than the actual travel expenses of the commission members.

In January 1921, the responsibility for Palestine in the British administration, was transferred from the Foreign Office to the Colonial Office.

Sir John Shuckburgh, assistant undersecretary of state in the Colonial Office, wrote to the High Commissioner in Jerusalem on May 20, after having spoken with Father Waggett, and requested that a non-Orthodox Christian be added to the commission. The commission would then be composed as follows: three Christians— one Catholic (French), one Orthodox, and one Armenian; three Muslims—two Sunnis and one non-Sunni; two Jews—one Sephardi (perhaps an Italian from Leghorn) and one Ashkenazi (perhaps Rabbi Stephen Wise of New York). Shuckburgh added: "I am anxious to have all ready by the time the mandate is passed."[52]

On May 21, Winston Churchill, the colonial secretary, asked de Salis to inquire about a suitable French Catholic candidate for the commission. "This would be gratifying to the French Government without serious political disadvantages, provided the individual is chosen more for his learning and ecclesiastical knowledge than for his religious and political views." The idea may have come from consultation with Father Waggett, but it was not well received in the Foreign Office. Lancelot Oliphant doubted that the best way to satisfy the French was to have de Salis look for a suitable candidate at the Vatican. In Oliphant's view, it would be better to explain the matter to Jonnart, the newly appointed French ambassador to the Holy See. "This [is] on the assumption that we want to please the French," an assumption that Oliphant did not share.[53]

The Colonial Office, however, did not want to give the French government any hint of the intended nomination before the suitable candidate was selected, and so the British conducted a covert search for a French Catholic "likely to be acceptable both to the Vatican and to the French Government."[54]

The same exercise was tried, but without success, with respect to the Jewish nominees. Sir Herbert Samuel proposed Cyrus Adler and Stephen Wise from the United States, Rabbi Angelo Raphael Chaim Sacerdoti, the grand rabbi of Rome; Rabbi Badjarano, the acting grand rabbi of Constantinople; and Rabbi Emil Margulies of Florence.[55] Rabbi Badjarano Effendi had arrived in Constantinople as acting grand rabbi in May 1920, after the resignation of Rabbi Haim Nahoum, "whose stormy record as Grand Rabbi is well known." According to the British High Commissioner in Constantinople, Rabbi Nahoum found himself in serious conflict with local Zionists.[56]

The internal discussions continued, but a commission for the Holy Places was not established. This caused considerable anxiety in the Vatican, which apparently was unwilling to understand the reasons preventing Britain from forming the commission before the mandate was approved. The pope's concern for Catholic interests in the Holy Land was expressed publicly in his consistorial address, *Causa Nobis*, on June 13, 1921, mentioned earlier, in which he stated: "However, inasmuch as the situation in Palestine is not yet definitely regulated, We now raise Our voice that, when the time comes to establish these a permanent condition of things, to the Catholic Church and Christians shall be assured the inalienable right, they hold."[57]

De Salis immediately cabled a digest of the pope's speech[58] and later sent the full text and an English translation, Sir Oswald Scott remarked that something more convincing than promises was needed to calm the pope, but the initiative lay with the Colonial Office.[59] It was de Salis's assessment that the pope's real intention had been to protest the delay in the formation of the commission for the Holy Places but chose this as a convenient way to take a swipe at the same time at both the Mandatory and the Zionists.[60]

The pope's speech and de Salis's commentary angered the British Foreign Office. Foreign Secretary Curzon and Colonial Secretary Churchill decided to inform the Vatican, through de Salis, that the British government had no intention of forming the commission before the mandate for Palestine was approved.[61] There was nothing new about that, for the British had informed Father Robinson a year earlier that it was impossible to proceed with the appointment of the commission as long as the mandate had not been approved. The British may have decided to send the Vatican an official note to this effect as a way of expressing their displeasure with the pope's speech and with the Vatican's decision to begin again awarding the liturgical honors to France. It may also have been intended to convey to the Vatican the idea that if the Holy See wanted to speed up the nomination of the commission, the best it could do was withdraw its obstacles to the final approval of the mandate.

Storrs's Mission to the Vatican

The situation in Palestine in 1920, at the beginning of the British mandate, was described by Samuel as follows:

> Palestine had for centuries been almost derelict, politically and materially. We had to build, from the very beginning, a modern state. Further, the country was suffering from the effects of several years of war. Great armies had fought over it; many of its villages had been destroyed; trees cut down wholesale, orange-groves neglected, livestock depleted; there was a general air of poverty and depression. Brigandage was rife in many districts and the Bedu had been raiding across the Eastern border. The capital had lately been the scene of a serious racial riot.[62]

The civil administration in Palestine gradually was established and began dealing with the country's various problems: health, education (especially for Arab children), economic development, and urban planning. But the most difficult problem by far was security, as highlighted by the sudden rioting in Jaffa in May 1921, during which frenzied Arabs attacked Jewish demonstrators and killed nearly fifty of them. As Samuel pointed out, most of the religious communities were disorganized. The Orthodox Church was insolvent; a commission of inquiry was appointed to restore the solvency of the patriarchate; the Supreme Muslim Council was created; and the Advisory Council was established and functioned for two years (1920–1922).

Monsignor Luigi Barlassina, the Latin patriarch of Jerusalem, was a hot-tempered Italian, arrogant and ambitious, who did not find a common language with the British authorities. His public speeches and reports to the pope were replete with complaints about the administration. He also criticized the opening of cinema houses and the presence of about five hundred prostitutes in Jerusalem. The governor of Jerusalem, Sir Ronald Storrs—while in Rome on a private visit to his cousin, de Salis—decided to request an audience with the pope and informed the Colonial Office of his intention. The Colonial Office conveyed word of this to the Foreign Office, which received the idea favorably.[63]

Storrs arrived in Rome on August 23, 1921. On the following day, accompanied by Dormer, the British chargé d'affaires at the Holy See, he visited Gasparri's deputy, Monsignor Francesco Borgongini Duca, who immediately arranged a meeting with Pope Benedict XV for August 25. In Dormer's view, that meeting was of tremendous assistance in dissipating the Holy See's basic fears of British rule in Palestine.[64]

Storrs included in his memoirs an interesting account of his audience with the pope. But he wrote that the conversation took place in 1922 and that he was received by Pope Pius XI, Benedict XV's successor. This is an error, stemming perhaps from the fact that Storrs wrote his memoirs some years after the event. Therefore, the visit can be confidently dated as 1921, on the basis not only of extensive documentation but also of its content. That is, it is highly unlikely that Storrs would have gone on at length about the publication of a speech delivered by the previous pope a year before. Furthermore, the pope referred to the future approval of the mandate, and thus it is clear that the talk must have taken place in 1921, before the mandate was approved, and not in August 1922, a month after it had been approved by the Council of the League of Nations.

Storrs explained:

> His Holiness had evidently been receiving alarmist reports as to the "preponderant influence of Jews" and the partiality of the Palestine Government, and I was able to prove to him by facts and figures that these fears were unfounded. Cinema performances, which had apparently been represented as having been introduced by the British, were common long before the British Occupation: on the one occasion on which the Latin Patriarch had drawn my attention to an undesirable film, I had it suppressed, for which I had received the Patriarch's official thanks. No ball, public or private, was now allowed within the walls of Jerusalem. The Pope seemed mollified, and said that these things proved that *buona volontà* on the part of the authorities was clearly not wanting; but added that he had heard that the Government permitted, without effective opposition, the existence in Jerusalem of many ladies of doubtful reputation. I thanked His Holiness for affording me the opportunity of explaining exactly what had been done to combat these practices. On our entry into Jerusalem, we had found no less than 500 such women living in a special quarter. Of these I had returned as many as possible to their places of origin so soon as possible, and had, more than two years ago, abolished the quarter. There might be still a certain number, but very few indeed when compared with what we had originally found; and I submitted that with the utmost vigilance it was difficult to ensure to any city, however sacred, complete exemption from this particular form of abuse. This was what the British Administration had achieved in two or three years in the Holy City: was the Eternal City after eighteen centuries, wholly immune? His Holiness agreed that such an idea was at present unattainable. I derived from this audience the impression that the Pope had been for some time subjected to very great pressure, which had certainly succeeded in prejudicing him against the Palestine Administration. He remarked, for instance, significantly, that "it would be a great disgrace to any mandatory if, after a certain period the departure of the Turks should be openly regretted."[65]

We also learn of the audience from a detailed report sent by Storrs to Foreign Secretary Curzon right after the meeting.[66]

Regarding the formation of a commission for the Holy Places, Storrs told the pope that the authorities in Palestine were waiting impatiently for its establishment, for it was likely to resolve a number of problems. Responding to Barlassina's protest about the difficulties encountered when trying to publish the pope's June speech, Storrs explained that its publication had been delayed in Jerusalem because it had at first been presented to the censor in a fragmented way, as a separate sentence taken out of context. Had the patriarch informed the authorities that this sentence was the official, authorized expression of the pope's view, it would, of course, have received special attention.

Storrs added that certain facts may have been unintentionally distorted and that he would recommend to the Mandatory government that it send information more frequently to the British legation to the Vatican. The pope expressed his satisfaction and asked whether it was true that the government maintained closer ties with the custos than with the patriarch. Storrs replied that the custos came to see government officials from time to time, whereas the patriarch, unlike his predecessor, tended to send his deputy. The pope remarked that the patriarch was still new in his post and still had some things to learn, but Sir Herbert Samuel had refused to receive him the year before. Storrs explained that a misunderstanding had arisen because the High Commissioner had never received the patriarch's written request, and when Samuel learned of it, he himself went to the patriarch.

Finally, the pope expressed his hope that Storrs would meet with the cardinal secretary of state and stated that he was pleased to discover the existence of goodwill. The pope added that he was glad that the sensitivities of Christians in general, and of Latin Christians in particular, would be taken into consideration in the operation of the mandate, which he presumed would be awarded to the British. Storrs noted that throughout the audience the pope did not in any way raise the matter of the church being built at Gethsemane, or the question of the Cenacolo, the hall of the Last Supper on Mount Zion, still in dispute with Italy and the Franciscans.[67]

5

Vatican Interference

The Problem of the French Protectorate

The pope told Storrs that he hoped he would meet Cardinal Gasparri, and on September 16, 1921, accompanied by Cecil Dormer, Storrs called on the cardinal secretary of state at his home in the village of Ussita in the Marche region. Storrs described the visit in his memoirs:

> We entered the village church, capable of holding perhaps a score, and found the famous prelate celebrating Mass before a dozen worshippers. After the service he took us to breakfast in his cottage. He was good enough to listen attentively to my explanation of various questions that had been raised by the Patriarch or the Press.[1]

The cardinal brought up the problem of the French religious protectorate and commented that it was hard to understand France's position. The Vatican had notified the Holy See in writing that France was giving up the protectorate but not the liturgical honors that the French consul had received under the capitulations. But those honors merely derived from the protectorate and so would be meaningless once the protectorate was over. The Vatican's position was that the problem was a matter to be settled between the British and French governments and that the only solution would be to observe the status quo until the peace treaty was approved and as long as the capitulations were formally still in force.[2]

It was Storrs's impression that the "dignitaries in Rome were genuinely desirous of arriving at the truth, and open to conviction on matters not only of fact but of policy."[3] Seemingly there were no grounds for this impression, apart perhaps from the punctilious observance of protocol in which the Vatican so excels. The fact is that the pope and the cardinal secretary of state did not change their position on Palestine one whit as a consequence of their talks with Storrs.

The death of Pope Benedict XV in January 1922 revived the problem of the French protectorate. At the funeral mass for the pope in Constantinople, the French representative demanded liturgical honors and thereby sparked an incident recorded by the French press.[4]

Italy's opposition to the continuation of the French protectorate being a matter of open record—Italy maintaining that the Sanremo Conference had terminated the protectorate in response to its pressure—the British Foreign Office instructed the British ambassador in Rome to encourage the Italian government to take steps in Paris and in the Vatican, in conjunction with those of Britain, to bring the protec- torate to an end.[5]

The Italian minister of foreign affairs told the British ambassador that he was in perfect agreement with his view. He said that the Italians had informed the Vatican about the Sanremo Conference and had made representations in its spirit to the French government.[6] Italy had raised the problem of the French protectorate several years earlier. The Vatican then decided not to be a party to the dispute and now followed the same policy, thereby trying to avoid having to make a decision.

The British also approached the Vatican through de Salis, their representative at the Holy See. He was told by the Secretariat of State that the Vatican had not yet been officially informed of the Sanremo agreement of April 24, 1920, according to which France relinquished its religious protectorate in the Levant and, with Britain and Italy, agreed that none of these countries would enact such a protectorate in the future. The British Foreign Office therefore decided that it would formally inform the Vatican of the agreement and would request that Catholic clergy in the East be instructed to prevent a recurrence of such regrettable incidents in the future. The British also made representations to the French government on this matter.[7]

One of the aims of the Vatican's stalling tactic was probably the preservation of good relations with France. In any event, the British representative was unable to obtain the decision that his government wanted from the Vatican on the termination of the French protectorate, for the cardinals were in conclave to choose a new pope. Cardinal Gasparri was himself a candidate for the high office.[8]

The Vatican had already unofficially received the protocol of the Sanremo Conference from the Italian government but apparently wanted to press home to Britain, as it had already done in 1920, that the Vatican's diplomatic isolation and its exclusion from international conferences also created confusion and caused inconvenience for Britain itself.

The Vatican, it seems, had learned from the French that there was no formal, written agreement on the termination of the protectorate and that it was only an understanding implied from the talks as recorded in the conference's protocol. Charles Jonnart, the French ambassador to the Vatican, heard of the British de- marche and spoke to Gasparri about it. The cardinal said that he intended to explain to the British that the Holy See had not participated in the Sanremo Conference, nor had it received any announcement from the concerned governments about a change in the traditional arrangements. It therefore could not take the requested action.[9]

About a year later, a new crisis erupted in French-Vatican relations when it was reported in the press that the Vatican intended to appoint a nuncio to Constantinople to oversee all Catholics in the Levant. The French press, which viewed the appointment as an attempt to replace the French protectorate with the protection of the nuncio, went so far as to recommend retaliatory measures against the Vatican.[10] But the French protests were of no avail.

The ado over the liturgical honors lasted for several more years. On April 10, 1924, Cardinal Gasparri sent the Latin patriarch in Jerusalem a cable instructing him to cease granting the honors. France refused to accept this. In 1926 an agreement was concluded in Paris between the Holy See and France, according to which the liturgical honors would be renewed in countries that had previously been part of the Ottoman Empire if the local ruling power consented.[11] This put the problem back in the British court; although France obtained in principle what it wanted from the Vatican, it was unable to implement the agreement in Palestine because of British objections, and this diplomatic exercise ultimately altered nothing. The era of the religious protectorate and liturgical honors was over for good, despite France's difficulties in accepting the loss of this traditional source of prestige. The question, of course, is whether the religious protectorate and honors were still an asset. Although today we can answer this question in the negative, at the time the French and the Italians still believed they could promote their political interests in the Levant by means of the Catholic religion.

Ecclesiastical Appointments in Palestine

In October 1920, Father Paschal Robinson was made special envoy of the Holy See, with the title of apostolic visitor, and was sent to the Holy Land to try to conciliate the custodia and the patriarchate. An Italian newspaper remarked that the appointment was related to Vatican foreign policy,[12] and this aroused the curiosity of the French Foreign Ministry.[13]

Cardinal Gasparri, whose sympathies were with the patriarchate,[14] told the French chargé d'affaires, Marie-Augustin-Jean Doulcet, that Father Robinson had been appointed by the Congregation de Propaganda Fide (for the propagation of the faith), that he himself had no hand in it, and that in his view the appointment should have been put off to some later date. Gasparri's statement is surprising, for it is hard to imagine that the Congregation de Propaganda Fide would not have asked the secretary of state's opinion before deciding on Robinson's appointment, but it may point to the existence of divergent views within the top echelons of the Vatican. Gasparri supported Luigi Barlassina and was aware that sending Robinson, a Franciscan, in response to British pressure was liable to be interpreted as an expression of no confidence in the Latin patriarch of Jerusalem.

Doulcet dispatched another letter with more details about Father Robinson. He had taught at the Catholic University in Washington, D.C., and had been sent to the Holy Land for the first time in 1919 on behalf of the Secretariat of State. This time he had been sent to investigate the dispute between the custodia and the patriarchate. Barlassina, the patriarch, who was known to have a certain fierceness of character, had recently lashed out against both Zionism and the High Commissioner. Father Robinson was interested in problems of education and tried to prevent "English" from being almost automatically identified in Palestine with "Protestant." He therefore wanted to establish English Catholic schools or to have English taught in the custodia schools. To the French chargé d'affaires, this seemed to be compatible with French interests, for emphasis on the international character of the custodia would keep it from becoming an Italian institution. The future thus looked promising to the French, and the situation in Palestine, in their view, was still fluid.[15]

Meanwhile, relations between the Latin patriarch in Jerusalem and the Mandatory government continued to worsen. Barlassina did not find a common language with the British, and to improve communications with the patriarchate, the authorities thought the Vatican should be persuaded to appoint an auxiliary bishop whose native tongue was English as assistant to the patriarch. Once again, Robinson's name came up. He had just left the country after a stay of several months, and Samuel wrote to the Foreign Office that his visit had been of great value. Robinson had done much to improve relations between the Latin patriarchate and the Mandatory government and had himself suggested that an English-speaking priest be appointed as auxiliary to the patriarch.[16]

It was Storrs's general impression after his visit to the Vatican in August and September 1921 that the Vatican was not altogether unfriendly to the administration in Palestine but was keeping a close watch on developments there. The Vatican did not put much stock in Barlassina's diplomatic skills but regarded him as honest and dedicated and had no intention of replacing him.[17] In Rome, Storrs also met Monsignor Biasotti, who unofficially represented Barlassina in Rome. Storrs's impression after talking with Biasotti was that "some of the difficulties caused by the Patriarch's personality are well realised" and that Barlassina "had been recommended to adopt a more friendly tone and attitude towards the British authorities." Biasotti had also intimated that "we might before long expect to see an English ecclesiastic attached to the Patriarchate as a liaison officer with members of the administration."[18]

But Robinson told Storrs that the French were pressing heavily for the appointment of a French ecclesiastic as auxiliary bishop to the patriarch in Jerusalem, and in his view the British government should act officially and directly vis-à-vis the Vatican, which never leaned in any direction except in response to forceful pressure.[19]

Storrs's Vatican trip aroused the interest of the Italian consul general in Jerusalem even before his departure. At the end of August, Consul General Villarey reported that Storrs was intending to visit Rome, apparently for the purpose of persuading the Vatican to recall Barlassina, "whose position becomes very difficult." The custodia feared that under combined pressure from the British and French governments, a new patriarch hostile to Italy would be selected, and in that case it would be best if Barlassina were kept on. If the patriarch were returned to Rome, the custodia would propose Monsignor Ruggero Rossetti, canon of San Giovanni in Laterano, as his replacement. Villarey argued that the quarrel between the custos and the patriarch, which the Italians viewed as against their interests, thus would come to an end.[20]

The problem was sufficiently important to the Italian foreign minister, Pietro

Tomasi della Torretta, for him to dispatch an urgent letter on the matter to Baron Carlo Monti, who represented his country's interests at the Holy See. Della Torretta asked Monti to obtain information on the subject as soon as possible,

> trying, in the eventual appointment of a new Patriarch, to employ cautious and wary action as may be possible on this delicate matter, in order to obtain that due account be taken of our interests. Since the important questions of the abolition of the honors to France and the disputes on the Holy Places should be solved in the near future, it is clear that the presence of a Patriarch not exclusively linked to France or to England is for us of the utmost interest.[21]

Monti replied that Barlassina's removal from Jerusalem was not even being considered.[22]

Sir Herbert Samuel wrote to Colonial Secretary Winston Churchill that the appointment of a British cleric as auxiliary bishop would not by itself effect a substantial change in Barlassina's attitude and that the appointment of a British private secretary to Barlassina was likely to be almost as efficacious. All the same, and although the most that could possibly be obtained was the appointment of a British private secretary, Samuel proposed pressing for the appointment of a British auxiliary bishop, if only to have the British request on record.[23]

The British government continued thus to press for the appointment of a British ecclesiastic as auxiliary bishop to the patriarch in Jerusalem. The Vatican was mindful of Britain's intentions but also was fearful of France's opposition to such an appointment. It proposed instead that a British priest be named private secretary to the Latin patriarch and held that this position would be as influential as that of auxiliary bishop, whereas the appointment was not likely to arouse opposition from France. Because this proposal accorded with British expectations and ambitions, Dormer suggested that for the time being the Foreign Office relax its pressure on the Vatican.[24]

At the Foreign Office in London, in response to Dormer, Lancelot Oliphant remarked that it was hard to recall any instance of the Vatican's proving its good intentions. He went on to say that if a British secretary were appointed, the Vatican would later claim that he was not in a proper position to be named auxiliary bishop or, alternatively, that because there already was a British secretary, it would have to nominate as auxiliary bishop a priest of a different nationality. Oliphant therefore suggested asking the Colonial Office whether it was prepared to be satisfied with the appointment of a secretary alone.[25] The Colonial Office wondered whether it should add anything to Samuel's opinion of October.[26]

The Vatican, fully aware of the tense relations between Barlassina and the Mandatory government, returned to an idea that had been raised two years earlier—to have Father Robinson act as a liaison in Palestine between the British administration and Latin Church authorities. De Salis again recommended accepting Gasparri's offer, on the grounds that Robinson enjoyed the administration's trust.[27]

The fine points of the Vatican's maneuvers may be perplexing to the outside observer, but they were transparent to Barlassina, and the impression is that he dutifully followed the instructions he received from the Vatican, even if in doing so he gave them his own personal coloring. The Vatican, though, was prepared to send Father Robinson again, but not as auxiliary bishop, as the British demanded, thus making it clear that his role would be temporary and of little importance.

The problem was not resolved, and months later, in September 1922, the British were still pressing for the appointment of an auxiliary bishop, and the Vatican was still playing for time, claiming that the secretary of state was absent from Rome.[28]

That relations between Barlassina and the British authorities in Palestine were tense was widely known. Romolo Tritonj, the Italian consul general, wrote about this in November 1921 in a top-secret report to the Italian foreign minister, referring to a conversation with Monsignor Biasotti:

> But I wish to make clear that it appears logical and natural that the Latin patriarchate, in face of the clear preference of the English authorities for the Zionists and the Orthodox, finds itself pushed to adopt a posture of resistance and opposition and to insist on the existing rights of Catholicism. Therefore, even if the personal relations between the patriarch and the governor [Storrs] are improving, one cannot but expect that this attitude [of the patriarchate] will continue in the future.[29]

Tritonj had a favorable impression of Barlassina's intelligence and energy and did not believe that he was hostile to Italy, as the previous consul general in Jerusalem had thought. His was truly a delicate situation in relation to France, which continued to play the role of the protector of Catholics, in disregard of the Sanremo agreement. Monsignor Biasotti, who was visiting Palestine at the time, told Tritonj that Reis, the French consul general, had complained sharply about both Barlassina's and the custodia's pro-Italian leanings and claimed that more Italian than French was being taught in the patriarchate's and the Franciscans' schools. Tritonj felt that from Italy's point of view, it was best that Barlassina not be replaced. He did not imagine that Biasotti may have been passing on information that, though pleasing to hear, was perhaps less than precise.

Before returning to Rome, Biasotti again told Tritonj that Reis had been expressly hostile to all Italian activity in Palestine. Tritonj could not understand why the activities of Italian religious institutes should damage France, as it was the legitimate and natural expression of a predominantly Catholic country's spiritual interest in Palestine.

France wanted to monopolize Catholicism at the expense of Italian Catholics but was remissive or uncaring vis-à-vis the Orthodox. According to Biasotti, the French consul had sent a formal protest to the Vatican regarding Barlassina because two hundred orphans from Palestine had been placed by the patriarchate in Italian educational institutions. Biasotti claimed that the pope himself wanted the orphans to become good farmers; the patriarchate put at their disposal a farm in Rafat (near Jerusalem) where a new agricultural school belonging to the Salesian order was established. "In this way," concluded Tritonj, "parallel to the agricultural rebirth of the land in which the Zionists are active, a similar activity will be conducted by the Catholics for the undoubted benefit of the Holy Land."[30]

This is one of many examples of the wish of Catholics and Arabs to copy the Zionists' methods, as if these held the secret of success. Moreover, the Salesian order was well known for its vocational schools, and it was natural that the patriarchate would want to use them to equip the Arab population with vocational skills that could help it overcome the difficulties of adjusting to a modern society.

The Commission for the Holy Places and the League of Nations (1922)

The approval of the mandate by the League of Nations was delayed for some time, because of both reservations by the United States, which demanded adequate guarantees for the rights of Americans in Palestine, and resistance by France, which did not want the Palestine mandate approved before its mandate for Syria was confirmed. At the same time, approval of the Syrian mandate was being held up by negotiations between Italy and France on the safeguarding of Italian interests in Syria.

Sir Herbert Samuel was anxious to publicize the fact that the British government intended to set up a commission on the Holy Places, and on October 1, 1921, he proposed addressing and making public the following communiqué to the Council of the League of Nations: "To the effect that the Council not having found it possible to approve the Mandate for Palestine at the present meeting, His Majesty's Government feel that further delay in the appointment of the Commission provided for in Article 95 of the Treaty of Sèvres is highly undesirable." The announcement was also to state that the British government had so far refrained from approaching candidates for membership on the commission, "as they feel that until the Council has had an opportunity of expressing an opinion on the appointment of the Chairman, it would be undesirable for the Mandatory Power to proceed with the appointment of other members." Samuel referred to the fact that "considerable apprehensions have been aroused in Catholic circles by the delay of the appointment of the Commission" and hoped to silence hostile criticism by publicizing the statement to the Council.[31]

Foreign Secretary Lord Curzon's response was chilly. He saw nothing to justify giving public opinion in France and Italy special consideration by attempting to create the commission before the mandate went into effect, especially as the delay in implementing the peace treaty with Turkey had to a large extent been caused by France and Italy. All the same, Curzon suggested that the announcement refer to Article 14 of the draft mandate.[32]

On November 15, 1921, Churchill, who at the beginning of 1921 had become colonial secretary, thereby receiving full responsibility for the administration of Palestine, sent the British government a draft of an announcement to the Council, mentioning Article 95 of the Treaty of Sèvres, Article 14 of the draft mandate, and the fact that the committee headed by Samuel had met in Jerusalem on March 29 and had recommended the following:

1. That the post of Chairman would most suitably be filled by an Englishman of judicial experience, and, so far as possible, worldwide reputation.
2. That the other members of the Commission should include two Christians

(one Catholic and one Orthodox), two Muslims (both Sunnis) and two Jews (one Sephardi and one Ashkenazi).

3. That the Palestine Administration should be represented by a Vice-Chairman, who would act in a dual capacity as a member of the Commission and representative of the Administration. Father Waggett was recommended for this appointment.[33]

In December 1921, James Eric Drummond, the secretary general of the League of Nations, visited the Vatican with the aim of promoting approval of the mandate and assured Gasparri that the British government would examine the Vatican's proposals with great care.[34] We do not know what these proposals were.

At the beginning of 1922, the British government decided to renew its efforts to get the mandate approved as soon as possible. One obstacle was the appointment of a commission for the Holy Places. The cabinet secretariat sent a letter to the secretary general of the League of Nations stating that it would be highly desirable for the chairman of the commission to be appointed without delay and adding that it would please the British government if the Council of the League of Nations appointed the chairman in accord with Article 14 of the draft mandate. The British government intended to appoint a vice-chairman and to invite distinguished Christians, Muslims, and Jews to join the commission but had so far refrained from approaching anyone, for in its view, it was not desirable for the Mandatory power to appoint the members of the commission before the Council of the League of Nations had expressed its opinion on the appointment of the chairman.[35]

At the same time it began to occur to the British Colonial Office that it might be best not to press for the appointment of a British chairman. More important, in its view, was to demonstrate to the world that Britain had acted fairly and honestly and was not to be held responsible for the fact that the commission had not yet been formed.[36]

Before the Council meeting of January 14, 1922, Edmund Cecil Harmsworth, the British representative at the League of Nations, tried to determine the positions of the other representatives. Guglielmo Imperiali di Francavilla, the Italian ambassador, informed him that he had received explicit instructions from his government not to agree to any proposal having to do with the future of Palestine, as long as the peace treaty with Turkey had not been implemented. The French representative said privately that he sympathized with the wish of the British government to establish the commission but that he had explicit instructions to propose that its formation be postponed . He added that he was prepared to cable Paris for new instructions, but in the absence of a foreign minister—following the fall of the French government—he feared nothing would come of it. It was thus clear to the British representative that he would not be able to obtain a unanimous decision from the Council. He thus preferred that his remarks be entered into the protocol and asked that the debate be postponed to the next meeting of the Council, in April. He also informed his government that in his view "difficulty will also be encountered in persuading the Council to appoint a British subject as Chairman of a Commission all the other members of which are to be nominated by His Majesty's Government."[37]

In another letter, from the Foreign Office to Colonial Secretary Churchill, it was said that Imperiali, the Italian ambassador, had told Harmsworth in a private conversation that the best way to solve the problem would be to persuade a Swiss Calvinist to accept the appointment, for that would prevent conflict between the Catholics and the Greek Orthodox. It is not clear whether this was Imperiali's personal view or whether he was hinting at a rather improbable position held by his government.[38]

The New Pope, Pius XI

Pope Benedict XV died on January 22, 1922. He had been a great statesman who greatly expanded the Vatican's involvement in international problems. He increased the number of countries with which the Vatican maintained diplomatic relations, from fourteen at the time of his predecessor, Pius X, to twenty-seven, including Great Britain (as of 1915) and France (as of 1920). Benedict XV might also have succeeded in reestablishing relations with Italy had the Nitti government not fallen, and therefore the Roman Question remained unsettled.

> His ardent desire to call back to the mother Church the separated brothers and his predilection for the Uniate Churches of the East, was proved by the autonomy given to the special Congregation [of the Eastern Churches] and the establishment of a Pontifical Institute [for Eastern Affairs] upon which he decided to "wake personally."

In June 1919 he made Achille Ratti, who later succeeded him as pope, a cardinal.[39]

Benedict XV dreamed of a papal presidency of a universal state and in 1920, in his encyclical *Pacem Dei,* totally disregarded the existence of the League of Nations when he called for the establishment of "a league of nations based on Christian law." With his openness to innovations, sensitivity to social problems, and keen awareness of international affairs, he was a pope of exceptional stature.

Benedict XV's successor, Cardinal Ratti, who took the name Pius XI, ascended to the papal throne after extended service in the Vatican archives and library. His diplomatic experience was limited to a brief stint as nuncio in Poland, and he had served as archbishop of Milan for an even shorter time.[40] The Vatican's foreign policy did not change substantially under him, especially because Gasparri continued to serve as secretary of state.

At the same time, the date set for the debate in the Council of the League of Nations on the draft mandate prepared by the British was drawing near. The British government and the Zionist Executive began to work with redoubled vigor to overcome the obstacles to approval. Opposite them stood the Catholic Church, which was applying pressure on the British directly and was working indirectly by mobilizing Catholic powers for the Vatican position and encouraging them to worsen their relations with the Mandate government in Palestine. There were rumors to the effect that the Vatican was even supporting Arab ferment against the Jews and British rule. In any case, the Vatican focused its concern on the Holy Places in

Pope Pius XI.

Palestine, and because the commission for the Holy Places had not yet been formed, it became increasingly nervous as the date neared for the mandate's approval.

In early April 1922, the Zionist Organization sent Chaim Weizmann to Rome to soften the Vatican's position.[41] In his talks with Weizmann, Gasparri again mentioned his dissatisfaction regarding the place on the commission for the Holy Places allotted to representatives of the Catholic Church. Weizmann replied that the Zionist Organization was not a party in the control of the Holy Places and was prepared to welcome any agreement among the Churches in Palestine that would contribute to lasting peace.[42]

The establishment of a commission for the Holy Places encountered innumerable difficulties as the international rivalry associated with it continued. In an eleventh-hour effort to block the mandate, the Vatican launched a new round of diplomatic activity. Weizmann's explanations apparently did not satisfy Gasparri, as he sent a note to de Salis on April 6, 1922, spelling out the Vatican's position.

In addition to repeating the Vatican's opposition to Jews' being granted a privileged and preponderant position in Palestine, the cardinal raised the problem of Article 14 of the draft mandate, according to which a "special Commission to study and regulate all questions and claims relating to the different religious communities" was to be set up. Britain was to appoint the commission, and the Council of the League of Nations was to choose its president. The draft mandate did not state how many members it was to consist of or in what proportions the various religions were to be represented.

"The Holy See," the cardinal wrote, "cannot agree that Catholic interests would be dealt with by representatives chosen not by the competent hierarchical authorities, but by England." He stated further that the draft did not say what would be done "regarding those places which are regarded with special veneration by the adherents of different religions (e.g., Catholics and schismatics). . . . It is only too probable that in the Commission itself, composed of representatives of all religions, a fierce conflict may arise . . . thus hindering any possibility of calm judgment." The cardinal therefore submitted that some modifications were necessary in the next draft of the mandate.[43] Gasparri refrained at this stage from offering clear counterproposals but said he would do so later in a memorandum he would submit to the League of Nations.[44] Meanwhile, Gasparri sent to all the cardinals the draft of Article 14 proposed by the British and asked for their comments.[45]

Although Gasparri did not put forward counterproposals, the view of Catholic circles was known, for a year earlier a memorandum had been sent to the Council of the League of Nations by the Union Catholique d'Études Internationales, which had its seat in Fribourg, Switzerland. This memorandum raised objections to Articles 8, 12, 13, 14, and 15 of the draft mandate. In the view of its authors, who called themselves "a group of Catholic professors and writers," the powers granted to the mandatory in the places sacred to Christians in Palestine, and especially in Jerusalem and Bethlehem—where rights of consular protection in the spirit of the capitulations had existed—went far beyond the stipulations of Article 22 of the League of Nations Covenant, which had established the mandate system.

The French protectorate had been expanded to most Catholic institutions, even those that were not French, by wish of the Holy See. Furthermore, the Catholics in Palestine were organized under the aegis of the Latin Patriarchate of Jerusalem and possessed legal and administrative autonomy that should be respected. But the British authorities had introduced changes and had seriously upset traditional educational arrangements, even though freedom of education was supposed to be preserved. The special role of the power extending protection to the Holy Places should be continued: "The general control of Christian affairs in Palestine could be entrusted to a permanent international Commission, consisting of the consuls-general of four or five Powers from Europe or America, whose subjects in Jerusalem and in Palestine include large numbers of Christians."[46] The writers of this memorandum wholly ignored the abrogation of the capitulations and the termination of the *millet* system of the Ottoman period. On the matter of the religious protectorate, they were closer to the French than to the Vatican position, but the idea of an international commission composed of consuls was acceptable to Gasparri.

The British foreign secretary, Lord Curzon, reacted sharply to Gasparri's letter and sent the following cable to his representative at the Holy See:

> I am at a loss to understand in what manner Vatican can regard itself as being entitled to interfere in the matter in this way, except in so far as it may reasonably expect to

be consulted about selection of the Roman Catholic representative on the Commission on the Holy Places. . . . It appears to me that memorandum from Cardinal Secretary of State of 6th March enclosed in your despatch no. 58 amounts to nothing less than protest against whole policy which H.M.G. has been commissioned by the Powers and the League of Nations to carry out in Palestine.[47]

The Appointment of the Commission Chairman

The British government pressed the League of Nations to accelerate the appointment of the president of the commission on the Holy Places. On the other side were the Catholic powers and the Vatican, which sought to postpone the nomination as long as the commission was not constituted to their liking. In late April 1922, Cardinal Gasparri drafted a message to the representative of a Catholic power in the League of Nations. The message was delivered on May 5, 1922, by the nuncio in Bern, Monsignor Luigi Maglione, who then served as liaison between the Vatican and the League of Nations and later became the cardinal secretary of state.

The appointment of the president of the commission was on the agenda of the meeting on May 11, 1922, of the Council of the League of Nations, and Gasparri expressed his astonishment at the haste with which the Council wanted to name the president. In his message, Gasparri suggested that the decision be postponed in order to allow the Council time to study the problems of the mandate, and especially the articles dealing with the Holy Places. If a postponement were not possible, the Vatican proposed that a Catholic be named president, as it was clear that the Catholics' rights in the Holy Places were above those of the other religious denominations. Gasparri suggested that the president be a Belgian Catholic, as Belgium had no national interests in Palestine.[48] Thus Gasparri's old plan for Belgian involvement in the affairs of the Holy Land was resurrected. The nuncios in Paris and Brussels urged the governments of France and Belgium to support either the immediate appointment of a Belgian president or the postponement of the debate.[49]

The secretary general of the League of Nations, Drummond, began assembling information about the Belgian who was being proposed to preside over the commission. The Spanish representative on the Council intervened with the secretary general as early as May 2 in an attempt to postpone the appointment.

France and Italy also worked to delay the appointment of the commission. Italy argued that the subject should not be brought up for debate at the League of Nations before the Treaty of Sèvres was replaced by a new peace treaty with Turkey.[50] The French government, which had also been asked by the Vatican to seek a postponement of the appointment of the commission president, claimed that the nomination should not be taken up before the League of Nations confirmed the British mandate for Palestine and the Treaty of Sèvres.[51] The Vatican's maneuver was designed to block the formation of the commission as long as its demands for radically modifying Article 14 of the draft mandate were not satisfied. But the main reason for the Holy See's demand to postpone the debate was its fear that the question of the mandate for Palestine would be settled without the participation of its representative. That is why Gasparri demanded that the debate be postponed until the Holy

See's memorandum was received, and he sent a cable to the Secretariat of the League of Nations to this effect.[52]

At the meeting of the Council on May 13, as a consequence of the pressure applied to the Catholic countries, the Vatican obtained a postponement of the debate to a later session, not before July, Lord Balfour agreed to the postponement but emphasized the need for a speedy decision. Britain, for its part, softened its position on the composition of the commission.[53]

6

The Struggle to Block
Approval of the Mandate

Barlassina's Visit to Europe

As the date drew near for the debate in the Council of the League of Nations on approval of the British mandate for Palestine, the Vatican increased its opposition to the draft mandate and intensified its fight to block its approval by the League of Nations. The Vatican was unhappy about Britain's proposals for the composition of the commission for the Holy Places, the privileged status that in its view the mandate would confer on the Jews, and the modernization introduced in Palestine by the British administration. In advance of the upcoming debate in the Council of the League of Nations, which was set for May 13, 1922, the Vatican summoned Barlassina to Europe, where he was to voice, with his characteristic vehemence, the Catholic arguments against the danger of a Jewish-Orthodox-Protestant takeover of the Holy Land. Barlassina had been known for some time to hold extreme views. In November 1921, several months before Barlassina's arrival in Rome, Cecil Dormer, the British chargé d'affaires at the Vatican, wrote about him: "The fact that Msgr. Barlassina lacked those traits which would have made him more suitable for his post as Latin Patriarch of Jerusalem, is now quite clear to the Holy See, as is the fact that his formal relations with the administration are far from cordial."[1]

On May 11, before being sent to London, Barlassina delivered a lecture in Rome in which he scathingly attacked both Zionism and the British administration in Palestine. The lecture was delivered at the Istituto di San Giuseppe, which was under French influence, and the audience included three cardinals. De Salis chose not to attend, relied in his account on press reports, and enclosed a clipping from the newspaper *L'Italie*.[2]

In his talk, Barlassina called for a vigorous defense of the rights of Catholics in the Holy Land and for aid to Catholic schools. He maintained that England had tried to divide the Christians in Palestine by favoring over the Catholics the Churches not aligned with Rome.[3] Britain's military conquest of Palestine and its receipt of the mandate gave rise to fears in the Vatican of a possible Anglican–

Orthodox alliance and to a suspicion that Britain was perhaps interested in replacing Russia as protector of the Orthodox.[4] Another view held that Britain intended to undermine Italian and French influence in the Middle East with the help of the Greek Orthodox clergy.[5]

As will be recalled, Pope Benedict XV had on several occasions warned against Protestant propaganda in Palestine. In an allocution on June 13, 1921, for example, he pointed out:

> And now, far from diminishing, that anxiety is increasing every day. Indeed, if at that time We lamented the iniquitous activity in Palestine of non-Catholic sects which are pleased to glory in the name of Christian, to-day, too, we must repeat that lament, seeing how they are carrying on that work with even greater activity, themselves possessing abundant means and cleverly profiting by the misery in which the inhabitants of the country were plunged after the war.[6]

When Ronald Storrs, the governor of Jerusalem, was received by Pope Benedict XV on September 20, 1919, he tried to convince the pontiff that the British military government had never exploited its position to promote Anglican propaganda. The pope agreed but added that he had good reason to believe that others had taken advantage of this position.[7] The notion that the British authorities in Palestine were acting to promote the Anglican religion and that Protestant propaganda had substantial financial backing, had firm roots in the Vatican.

Barlassina concluded his lecture with these fervent words: "We must have those people feel that Catholics throughout the world are standing vigilant and are working effectively for the preservation of their rights in the land that was sanctified by the blood of Christ."[8]

De Salis sent someone on whom he could rely to hear the lecture and was told that its tone was far from moderate. He brought this up with Gasparri, saying that the style was extreme and adding that Barlassina indeed could have opinions of his own but that it was regrettable that the man whose duty was to work in perfect understanding with the High Commissioner and the British authorities behaved in such a fashion. The cardinal gave indications of being displeased and promised to look into the matter.[9]

Barlassina's remarks evoked an official denial by the British government. Replying to a question in Parliament, Edward Wood Halifax, the colonial undersecretary, declared that the claim that the rights Catholics had previously enjoyed in Palestine had been suspended or violated was utterly unfounded. The accusation that the judiciary was biased was also utterly false.[10]

Barlassina went to London toward the end of May, apparently on a mission for the pope, to meet with British government representatives. According to a newspaper that based its report on "official Vatican circles," the decision to send Barlassina was reached after Balfour asked the Council of the League of Nations to speed up the debate on the mandate for Palestine following the agreement that had been reached on it between the Foreign Office and the United States government. The newspaper added that the Vatican's anxieties had been increased under Pius XI by Chaim Weizmann's recent declarations.[11]

In London, Barlassina met with a member of the Italian embassy, who reported that the patriarch was imbued with an anti-Zionist and anti-British fighting spirit. The patriarch said privately that his action would be made easier if the Italian embassy were to mention his presence to the Foreign Office and suggest that the British government hear his view.[12]

The Italian foreign minister, Carlo Schanzer, immediately sent a reply to the embassy in London, instructing it to act with extreme caution on matters related to Palestine and to let Barlassina operate in official British circles and with the local press as he wanted, but not to allow any suspicions to arise of an agreed collaboration between the Italian government and the Vatican, especially because such a collaboration did not exist. The Italian foreign minister requested that the embassy refrain as much as possible from personal contacts with Barlassina and in no way interfere between the patriarch and the Foreign Office.[13]

Bearing in mind the continual friction between the patriarch and the British administration and their mutual accusations, we can readily appreciate that Barlassina was not the most suitable envoy for convincing the British government of the justice of the Vatican's arguments. Nonetheless, the pope sent him to London, probably to stir up public opinion there against the British government and its policy in Palestine.

As early as May 18, Joseph Cowen, the former president of the British Zionist Federation, could inform the Zionist Executive in London that Sir John Shuckburgh, assistant undersecretary of state at the Colonial Office, had said that Barlassina had not come to London on any mission and would not be received by the authorities.[14] Foreign Secretary Balfour and Colonial Secretary Churchill did in fact refuse to see him. H. Eugene Bovis claimed that this refusal forced the Vatican to put its arguments into writing in a letter sent by Gasparri to the secretary general of the League of Nations on May 15, 1922.[15] But as we mentioned, Gasparri had sent a note with similar arguments to the British representative several weeks earlier. Moreover, Barlassina had arrived in London at the end of May, and on the day Gasparri's letter was sent, he still hoped to be received by British government representatives.

The Vatican's Proposals

On May 15, 1922, Gasparri sent a note to the League of Nations, which for many years afterward served as the basis for the Vatican's policy on Palestine. The note dealt with the preferential rights that had allegedly been granted to the Jews and with the proposed commission for the Holy Places. This note is not identical with the memorandum of June 4, 1922, covering the same issues, which was also sent, but not signed, by Gasparri. This needs to be emphasized because even experts such as Bernardin Collin and Walter Zander tend to confuse these two documents.

In his first note, Gasparri stated that Article 14 proposed that all religions be represented on the commission for the Holy Places but did not say in what proportions. He continued:

> Clearly the Holy See cannot agree that the interests of Catholics be handled by representatives who were not chosen by the proper authorities. . . . This article [14]

is formulated so vaguely that it gives rise to many difficulties. Indeed, no definition of how the proper bodies representing the various religions would be composed has been suggested. . . . Since we are dealing with places holy to several religions we can anticipate, unfortunately, an all-out struggle inside the Commission. . . . For all these reasons, Article 14 seems unacceptable. The Holy See would like to propose that the members of the Commission should be the Consuls in the Holy Land of those powers, which are members of the Council [of the League of Nations].[16]

Gasparri later felt it necessary to introduce some changes in the May 15 note and on June 14 sent a new aide-mémoire, which began by stating that the Holy See did not object to the mandate for Palestine being granted to Britain:

The Holy See does not at all object to the decision already taken by the League of Nations, i.e., the bestowal of the mandate for Palestine on Britain, since it has often praised the spirit of justice and impartiality of this nation. Nonetheless, the Holy See feels obliged to ask for changes in a few articles of the Balfour proposal, keeping in mind the interest of the noble British Nation, which should desire that the mandate received on Palestine should be handled peacefully, and not lead to disturbances of the local population's religious feelings.

But the most important changes had to do with the commission for the Holy Places, about which the memorandum said:

The Holy See states once and for all that it could never admit that such a commission should claim the right to put under discussion the ownership of the Sanctuaries, almost every one of which has been for many centuries, even under the Turkish domination, in the peaceful possession of Catholics.

In the aide-mémoire Gasparri suggested that the commission for the Holy Places be composed of the consuls in the Holy Land of the powers that were members of the Council of the League of Nations; in that case, the decisions of the commission would be reached impartially and would be accepted more readily by all sides. "The Holy See," Gasparri wrote, "does not oppose the representatives of the various religious denominations taking part in the commission as long as their vote is only consultative." Gasparri's note to the secretary general of the League of Nations was made public and received wide publicity.[17]

As Zander pointed out, the Vatican was proposing that only Catholics have a voting voice and that controversies between Latins and Greek Orthodox be investigated and decided by Catholics alone.

After he sent the note to the League of Nations, Gasparri rejected the contention that the Holy See meant to call into doubt the British mandate for Palestine. The cardinal "believed it to be an act of straightforwardness and courtesy to communicate these observations to the British Government and it has therefore been not a little surprised that they should have given an unfavourable reception to a note drawn up with that intention."[18]

In Paris, members of the Zionist Political Committee, Senator Anatole de Monzie and parliamentary deputies Marius Moutet and Léon Blum, had a talk with French Prime Minister Raymond Poincaré, who had sent new instructions to the French delegation at Geneva, according to which France would withdraw its opposition to approval of the mandate if a Frenchman were appointed chairman of the commission for the Holy Places.[19] De Monzie also met with Weizmann and pointed out to him repeatedly that he had obtained a definite promise from Sokolow that the president of that commission would be French. Weizmann did all he could to explain to him that the only thing that Sokolow could promise was his help and cooperation in this matter and had loyally abided by that; the Zionist Organization was not in a position to give such promises, that could only in a small way offer its good offices.[20]

The Vatican also approached the Brazilian government, asking for its support for the nomination of a Belgian Catholic, Jules Van den Heuvel, as chairman of the commission. But the British maintained that the chairman "ought to be a person of judicial character, of wide outlook and not in any sense a partisan of any one particular faith."[21]

In London, the Foreign Office decided to "await consultations with the C[olonial] O[ffice] after the general question of the line to be taken with the Vatican has been discussed with Count de Salis" and until then sought to postpone communications to representatives of Italy and other countries, on the Vatican's opposition.[22]

In an attempt to overcome the Holy See's hostility, Sir Eric Drummond, the secretary general of the League of Nations, tried to obtain new proposals related to the Holy Places. On June 9, 1922, he circulated two such proposals, the second of which had been drafted by the French office for the League of Nations. Drummond believed that "the more moderate Vatican circles did not expect any change" concerning the establishment of a Jewish national home and that the demand for this change in the status of the Jews and the Holy Places was put forward in order to have something to bargain with in regard to the Holy Places, to which the Vatican, and Catholic opinion generally, attached the greatest importance.

The first proposal would have had the Council of the League of Nations appoint countries, not persons, with only the commission chairman to be appointed directly by the Council. According to the second scheme, the commission was to be composed of six Christian members nominated by the governments of Britain, Italy, the United States, Holland, Spain, Romania, and Greece, and two Muslim members nominated by Egypt and Morocco.[23]

A New British Draft of Article 14

On June 14 an interministerial meeting was held in London, in Sir Cecil Hurst's room, on the Vatican's opposition to the mandate for Palestine. Sir Eric Drummond explained that the Vatican's opposition was prompted by the fear that the Zionist commission might obtain complete control of the administration and eventually of the Holy Places commission. The Vatican's objections to the Zionist portion of the mandate would disappear once it was satisfied in regard to the Holy Places. De Salis took generally the same view but said that he would like to have some material to answer the Vatican regarding Britain's Zionist policy. The Colonial Office was ready to meet the Vatican's fears regarding the Holy Places commission, provided that it kept some control over its appointment.

At the end of the meeting, a new draft Article 14 was composed, which Drummond and de Salis thought might satisfy the Vatican. The draft article was designed to give the Council as well as the Mandatory government a say in the appointment of the commission. The commission's main duty would be investigating and deciding existing claims on the Holy Places, and the right of appeal to the Council of the League of Nations would be retained. Furthermore, to meet the Vatican's demands, it was also decided that the representatives of the religious communities "would be less responsible people to sit on the Commission than the representatives of the Powers," and among the Great Powers to be represented were the United States, Britain, France, and Italy. De Salis was to return as soon as possible to Rome and sound out the Vatican regarding the acceptance of the article, while at the same time the United States, France, Italy, Belgium, and Brazil were to be notified of it. Lancelot Oliphant, of the British Foreign Office, remarked that "if we can overcome Vatican opposition by amending non-vital points, so much the better."[24]

Gasparri met with the British chargé d'affaires, Cecil Dormer, and told him that the French government had suggested to the nuncio in Paris that the commission be composed of representatives from France, Britain, Italy, Spain, and perhaps Belgium and that the chairman be a French Catholic. In that case, the French government would insist that the chairman be accorded the liturgical honors. The nuncio reacted with astonishment and mentioned the Sanremo agreements, which had ended the religious protectorate. The cardinal believed that the representatives of all these countries should serve as chairman in rotation. In any event, Belgium should be represented. The Vatican would not oppose the granting of liturgical honors, provided, of course, that they were given only to a Catholic. Dormer replied that the suggested composition of the commission differed from that proposed in Article 14 and that he had not heard of any French suggestion, and he doubted that it would be accepted. Nor did he understand how the liturgical honors had found their way into this issue.[25]

After the interministerial discussions in London, and as a last effort to appease the Vatican, the British government prepared an alternative draft of Article 14, according to which the commission's reports would be laid before the Council for confirmation. Britain included the new proposal in a reply to Gasparri's letter of May 15, which was sent to the secretary general of the League of Nations on July 1, 1922. In their note, the British rejected Gasparri's allegations regarding the Jews' privileged position.

Responding to Gasparri's observations concerning Article 14, the British agreed that the delicate task of determining the existing rights in the Holy Places should be entrusted to a body of whose impartiality there could be no question, and they suggested that not only the composition of the commission be subject to the approval of the Council of the League of Nations but also that any report made by them be laid before the Council for confirmation. As a further means to ensure absolute impartiality, His Majesty's Government would be prepared to select nominees for the commission from a panel selected under some international procedure, whether by the Assembly or the Council of the League of Nations, or by the president of the International Court of Justice. The panel should be composed of persons of worldwide reputation to be selected in such a way that none of the Great Powers interested in Palestine and none of the three confessions would be without representation on it. His Majesty's Government would also invite the Council of the League to appoint one of the members of the commission as its first chairman. The British would no longer try to determine the precise number of commission members and stressed that they should not be persons who might be regarded as agents of a particular power or community, since the appointment of the commission should be subject to the approval of the Council. Religious interests would be equally well protected by the provisions that the commission would consult with representatives of the denominations concerned and that any religious confession could appeal to the Council of the League of Nations, which might require the mandatory to reassemble the commission. A new draft Article 14 was attached to the British note.[26]

Gasparri was shown in advance by de Salis the new draft Article 14 and the British note. The cardinal expressed his appreciation of the British proposals on a matter that was of the deepest concern to the Holy See. The goal of establishing an independent and impartial authority for the Holy Places was satisfactory and in accord with the Vatican's wishes. De Salis drew attention particularly to the sections dealing with the composition of the commission, and Gasparri again expressed his satisfaction.[27]

Another attempt to dispel the Vatican's fears and remove its opposition to approval of the mandate was made by Sir Herbert Samuel, who arrived unexpectedly in Rome on July 4. The High Commissioner was received by the new pope on July 6, and afterward, with de Salis, by Gasparri. Pope Pius XI "maintained a very friendly attitude and said he had no doubt [that] the British administration would overcome any difficulties in Palestine." He had read the British reply to Cardinal Gasparri and regarded it as satisfactory on the whole. There were some details still to be discussed, but the reply was reassuring. The pope also spoke of the Jews.

Samuel stated that the Palestine Administration recognized the profound interest that the Christian world took in the Sacred Sites, that it fully respected this interest and would maintain an attitude of absolute impartiality and justice toward such matters. Monsignor Barlassina was alone in failing to acknowledge the impartiality of the British position. Samuel feared that the information given to the Holy See by Barlassina was not always correct, and he also mentioned the lecture that Barlassina had delivered in Rome. The pope said that he had heard of the speech and would take up the matter very soon in a conversation with the patriarch.

To Gasparri, Samuel explained the principles of the mandatory system, which was not equivalent to annexation but contemplated a gradual progress toward autonomy. The legislative assembly would unite the representatives of the mandatory power and the people of Palestine; the various sections of the population would be represented in proportion to their number. Gasparri thought that the new form of Article 14 was a great improvement on the whole but was obscure in some particulars.[28]

Weizmann, for his part, hoped that he could campaign for de Monzie; the British supported the candidacy of de Monzie, a pro-Zionist Frenchman whom France's prime minister, Poincaré, wanted as the commission's first chairman. In Weizmann's view, with the new Article 14 the British were mainly endeavoring to satisfy the Vatican, and the Council of the League of Nations was to discuss the issue at its meeting in London on July 17.[29]

Weizmann, who tried to rally all possible support for approval of the mandate, wrote to Shuckburgh of the Colonial Office that if the French obtained the presidency of the Holy Places commission, Poincaré would not insist on the simultaneous passing of both mandates, for Palestine and Syria. He had received this information from three French politicians friendly to Zionism, including Senator de Monzie, who had recently met with Prime Minister Poincaré.[30] Weizmann wrote to his wife: "We could achieve everything here if only the British would agree to let the French have control of the Holy Places. This will have to be done."[31]

As Weizmann had been told, France demanded the chairmanship of the commission for itself but did not stop at that. In a note written by the French ambassador in London on July 13, the French also spelled out a number of fundamental objections to Article 14. In their view, the article did not take into account the existing rights and traditional regime of the Holy Places. The new commission would thus have to resolve a number of problems that had heretofore been within the purview of the French consul, but nowhere was it stated that the commission would have to abolish the traditional regime. The French ambassador stressed that there were some Holy Places with a clear juridical status about which there was no dispute: sacred Muslim sites, Jewish holy places (the Western Wall was not mentioned), and Christian holy sites that belonged to one country or one Church. Hence, these were outside the commission's responsibility. Conflicts might arise in places held in common by several Christian communities, such as the Church of the Holy Sepulchre in Jerusalem or the Basilica and the Grotto of the Nativity in Bethlehem. These places were exterritorial and not national. "They are in Palestine, but are not quite Palestinian." Their traditional status could not be modified without the consent of all concerned parties, and therefore it could be said that they did not fall within the scope of Article 85 of the Treaty of Sèvres, for the article was to deal with people, not places. The commission was meant to function as an arbitrator, to preserve and interpret the existing practices and traditions called the status quo. It therefore had to be a permanent body that would convene annually around the time of the high Christian holidays. France demanded that the commission be composed of a French chairman and six members—one each proposed by Italy, Spain, Greece, and Ethiopia, and two by Britain.[32]

Such was the content of the French note. It is of interest both in the principles it put forward and as a practical proposal. Legally it was extremely difficult to prove that certain places should come under an extraterritorial regime, but the very proposal to set up an international commission was proof of an intention to introduce international supervision in such a sensitive realm, instead of exclusive British jurisdiction. France tried, first, to exclude from the commission's jurisdiction those churches, institutions, and Holy Places whose ownership was not disputed. It hoped then to play a decisive role, through the French commission chairman, with respect to the remaining places.

The Colonial Office in London began to form the opinion that its only option was to try to win approval for the mandate from the League of Nations, except for Article 14, which would remain open to further discussions in the future.[33]

Daily ceremony of opening the gates of the Holy Sepulchre in Jerusalem. The religious community asking for the opening calls on the Moslem guardian of the key and passes him a ladder, since the keyhole is high up on the door. Three bells behind the door signal the opening: the first chime is that of the community that requests the opening; the other two are those of the other communities, as a sign of approval.

The Mandate's Approval

The Council of the League of Nations convened in London on July 17. The Spanish delegate, José Maria Quiñones de León, who was presiding, announced that the nuncio in Paris, Monsignor Bonaventura Cerretti, had come to London to explain to the Council the Vatican's position. Cerretti was not invited to testify, but the ambassadors of France, René-Raphaël Viviani, and of Italy, Guglielmo Imperiali di Francavilla, brought up the problem of Article 14.

According to the official transcript of the meeting, Viviani observed, the continuation of the discussion would show whether it was necessary to hear the nuncio, but it should be realized that there were other interested parties who might also ask to be heard. Lord Balfour began by saying that the fate of the mandate for Syria was bound up with that of the mandate for Palestine. Because the agreement on the mandate for Palestine appeared to be complete except for Article 14, the Council might perhaps discuss that article. Viviani supported this proposal and stated that there were two objections to Article 14. First, it was necessary to determine how the majority on the commission should be composed. Should it be Catholic or not? Second, there was the question of the commission's responsibility, because as he (Viviani) understood the British proposal, the commission's duty would be to substitute a new regime for the status quo. Article 13 asserted the principle of the sovereignty of the mandatory power, which was entrusted with maintaining order and assumed entire responsibility for the Holy Places; it was therefore for the Sanctuaries of Jerusalem and Bethlehem alone that it had been necessary to draft Article 14.

Evident in Viviani's remarks was France's apprehension that the new commission might be empowered to alter the status quo in the Holy Places to the detriment of Catholics. According to the *Daily Telegraph*, France feared that a Jewish state would be formed after the termination of the British mandate and that the control of the Holy Places would pass into the hands of just one nation, which moreover would not be Christian. In France's view, it was thus necessary to ensure that the commission would not be able to alter the status quo of 1852 and that it would be required to preserve its permanent international character.[34] Balfour replied that it had never been the intention of the British government to substitute an entirely new regime for the status quo. The commission's decisions would be concerned only with current issues, but it was desirable not to appoint a permanent commission that would create a kind of executive power by the side of the mandatory power, which must be sovereign.

The Italian delegate, Marquis Imperiali, said that the commission should be composed of representatives of the powers that had the most interest in the country, most of which were Catholic. Balfour drew attention to Britain's note to the secretary general of July 1, in which it stated that none of the Great Powers with interests in Palestine, and none of the three confessions, would be without representation. Balfour also pointed out that the Council might decide to approve the mandates for Syria and Palestine, stipulating that they should enter into force simultaneously, reserving Article 14 for a later stage. Viviani was ready to accept the proposal, but pending the drafting of the text of Article 14, the status quo in regard to the Holy Places would persist. Imperiali, however, doubted whether it was possible to adopt the Palestine mandate if Article 14 remained unresolved.

At the meeting on July 22, Imperiali again said that if Article 14 were reserved, he would find it difficult to approve the mandate. A revised version of Article 14 was therefore drafted, which stated that the method of nomination, the composition, and the functions of this commission would be submitted to the Council for its approval. The commission would not be appointed or begin operation until approved by the Council. The Council endorsed the revised draft of Article 14 and on July 22 approved the mandate in its entirety.

The representatives of Spain, France, Italy, and Belgium all stated that they considered the presence of one of their nationals on the commission as indispensable. The Spanish representative, in particular, reiterated his country's special position in the Holy Land. At the public meeting on July 24, Balfour explained that the Palestine mandate consisted of two parts: one was concerned with Palestine and its inhabitants; and the other was concerned with the Holy Places, about which there would be further discussion.[35]

The Vatican tried to influence the debate in the Council of the League of Nations up to the last moment. On July 22, Gasparri received de Salis and told him that

> it was even proposed that Article 14 should be suppressed altogether and the Holy Places separated entirely from the mandatory regime of Palestine, given an international status in which they might possibly be placed, for the direct representation of the Holy See. The Italian government were in favour of this idea though opposed to the French pretension to a right of appointing the President of any such international body.

Gasparri was thus still hoping for an international regime in which the Vatican would have direct representation, and there seem to be echoes here of the Vatican's territorial ambitions in Palestine, or at least in part of Jerusalem. The cardinal informed de Salis that he had sent instructions to Monsignor Cerretti to go to London and do his best. He also expressed his approval of the revised British version of Article 14, which in his opinion contained features of value to the Holy See. De Salis wrote:

> I gather that this is especially the case as regards the idea that the Holy See should be able to appoint its own representative for the defence of its positions. . . . By the revised article Great Britain was pledged to the maintenance of order and decorum in the Holy Places. What would happen under the auspices of a really international regime?

Gasparri knew that this duty would be conscientiously performed by any British force. He would therefore telegraph Cerretti to be careful. "Internationalism in such matters would be intolerable," the cardinal concluded."[36]

What Gasparri actually wanted is hard to determine from this dispatch by de Salis. On the one hand, he may still have been toying with the long-term hope of internationalization, but on the other hand, he was interested in seeing to it that Britain did not shirk its immediate responsibility to maintain order at the Holy Places. Perhaps he understood that the British were in Palestine to stay and that the dream of internationalization could not be realized in the near future.

The Council reached a decision on that day, July 22, and approved an abbreviated version of Article 14, which left the method of appointment, the composition, and functioning of the commission for the Holy Places to future deliberation and approval by the Council.

At the very last minute, Cerretti again tried to postpone the approval of the mandate to allow the Vatican to submit an important document. Weizmann recalled that he was sitting in the London hotel room of the French delegate, Viviani, when Cerretti entered and asked for Viviani's help in obtaining the postponement. The French ambassador replied that it was for Weizmann to decide, and Cerretti "bounced from the room in high dudgeon."[37]

The Council approved the mandates for Palestine and Syria on July 24. Because the composition of the commission for the Holy Places had not been fixed, extensive diplomatic activity concerning its determination continued. On August 3, in an internal memorandum, the British Foreign Office proposed that each religion be represented by two representatives, and if necessary, the number of Catholic representatives could be increased to three or four, provided that the representation of the Greek Orthodox, the Jews, and the Muslims be increased to the same number.[38] De Salis reported his conversation with Gasparri, at which he read out the British explanations. Gasparri again mentioned Van den Heuvel of Belgium as a person of international reputation and good independent judgment. The cardinal also repeated his original proposal: a commission chosen from the consuls of the various powers in Jerusalem.[39]

7

The Impossibility
of Implementation

New British Proposals for the Commission

Balfour did not leave the French note unanswered and on August 5 sent a detailed reply. He pointed out, first, that the new text of Article 14 stipulated that the method of nomination, the composition, and the functions of the commission for the Holy Places were to be submitted to the Council of the League of Nations for approval. The chairmanship of the commission should be held in rotation by its member, in order to avoid jealousy and friction. His Majesty's Government had "at first considered the appointment of a judicial commission composed of experts in the ecclesiastical law of the three great religions" but was later convinced that it would be better to establish a commission "upon which not only the great Powers interested in Palestine, but especially the three great religions concerned, should not be without representation."

Balfour then went on to refute almost all the points raised by France. In his view, the term "Holy Places" in Article 13 could not be regarded as synonymous with the three Christian Holy Places. It would thus be for the commission to define the rights of worship in the three Christian Holy Places, as they would define the rights in any other Holy Place, religious building, or site in Palestine, whether Christian, Muslim, or Jewish. Balfour wrote further that "His Majesty's Government regret that they cannot recognise the claims of the French Government or their representative in Palestine either to continue to protect the Custodia or to receive honours or a ceremonial or liturgical precedence as part of such protection." France's renunciation of the protectorate at the Sanremo Conference had "definitely modified the traditional regime of the three Christian Holy Places so far as such a regime involved the position of the French Government." The British government "could not recognise the French Government's suggestion that a French national should obtain the permanent presidency of the commission." Nor could the British government accept that these three Christian Holy Places be defined as extraterritorial. Balfour reminded the French government that

even under the Turkish regime, Turkish troops were responsible for the actual maintenance of order in the precincts of the Holy Places, and such foreign intervention
as the Turkish Government admitted derived from the capitulatory regime, . . .
which under Article 8 of the mandate are no longer applicable in Palestine. In any
case, under Article 13 of the mandate, H. M. Government as mandatory assumes a
responsibility for the preservation of the existing rights and the maintenance of order
which they could not transfer to the representative of any foreign Government or
any international commission.[1]

Several days later, the British Foreign Office decided to comply with the French
demand that a Frenchman serve as chairman of the commission, provided that the
commission be composed of a seven-member Christian subcommission, a three-
member Muslim subcommission, and a three-member Jewish subcommission. In
that case, all the work would be carried out within the framework of the subcommissions, and the chairman's role would be wholly honorary.

Sir Cecil Hurst reported on this same occasion on his talk with the French representative, Henri Fromageot, from which he understood that difficulties could be
expected from the French government on the issue of the commission's appointment. The French regarded the British proposal requiring all the commission's reports to be submitted for approval to the Council of the League of Nations as a
stratagem to enable the British to veto any suggestion not to their liking. The two
delegates thus concluded jointly that the commission should not be vested with
administrative powers and that its role should be limited to restoring rights on the
basis of the status quo that prevailed before the war.[2]

But Cardinal Gasparri did not accept the British proposals and on August 15
sent a memorandum with counterproposals that focused on three main points:

1. The commission should be permanent (an idea first raised by France and
   rejected by Britain because of fear that this would produce a body with powers paralleling those of the Mandate government).
2. The principal Catholic nations should be represented, notably Belgium,
   France, Italy, Spain, and Brazil; the Catholics had to be a majority on the
   commission.
3. The members should reside in Palestine. The commission might be be composed of the consuls of the powers represented on the Council, but whatever
   the composition, points 1 and 2 should be kept in mind. The commission
   should be under an international organization such as the Council of the
   League of Nations and should not be allowed to discuss rights already acquired by Catholics that have been peacefully enjoyed even under the Turks.[3]

During the procedural debate on the commission's composition—that is, on the
meaning of Article 14—the important problem of sovereignty over the Holy Places
came up again. The British government stood by the draft of Article 13 as approved
by the Council of the League of Nations, by which the mandatory government
would be responsible for maintaining order in the Holy Places as well and could
not transfer this responsibility to any foreign government or international commission.

In his letter to Count Charles de Saint-Aulaire, Balfour reaffirmed this as the

British government's position.[4] This is of special interest in light of the fact that Theodor Herzl had expressed the idea of the extraterritoriality of the Christian Holy Places and had discussed it with Pope Pius X as early as 1904. Years later, in 1947, a short time before the termination of the British mandate, the United Nations Special Committee on Palestine (UNSCOP) proposed establishing a *corpus separatum* for all of Jerusalem and its surroundings, with the aim of protecting the Holy Places. The position of the state of Israel after 1967 was that the Holy Places should be placed under the supervision of the religious bodies with which they were associated, an idea quite close to extraterritoriality.[5]

The relations between the Vatican and the Catholic powers were such that it is not always easy to determine which side activated which. That is, to what extent did the Vatican want to involve the Catholic nations in the problems of the Holy Places so as to gain their support, and to what extent were these nations themselves interested in becoming involved in religious matters so as to assert their presence in Palestine? In this context, we might recall Italy's efforts against the French religious protectorate, or France's stubborn insistence on the continuation of liturgical honors.

Another example was Spain's behavior. Its representative on the Council of the League of Nations, Quiñones de León, declared that the Spanish government "felt obliged to emphasize the rights and privileges granted to her by consequence of the special situation in Palestine." He therefore requested that a place on the commission for the Holy Places be reserved for a Spanish subject.[6] Spain even took exception to the proposed draft of Article 14, sparking angry responses in the British government. The Colonial and Foreign Offices decided to ask the Spanish ambassador for clarification, for the special status of the Spanish that accorded them a right to object to any article of the mandate was not at all evident to the British.[7]

On August 27, 1922, the Colonial and Foreign Offices submitted a joint memorandum to the British cabinet with new proposals for the commission's composition.[8] This memorandum was subsequently presented by Balfour to the Council of the League of Nations, which convened in Geneva on August 31. The innovation in the British proposal was the division of the commission into three subcommissions. The chairmanship of the Christian subcommission would be reserved for a French national, and this subcommission would have three other Catholic representatives (an Italian, a Spaniard, and a Belgian), three Orthodox representatives (a Russian, a Greek, and a Romanian), an Ethiopian, an Armenian, and a Copt. The chairman of the plenary commission would be an American Protestant. He and the chairmen of the subcommissions would be appointed by the mandatory power, subject to approval by the Council of the League of Nations.[9]

Balfour's new plan provoked misgivings at the Vatican. According to *Osservatore Romano* on September 6, the Catholic Church would find itself in a disadvantaged position:

> After having held the quasi totality of the Sanctuaries in the Holy Land in their possession for centuries, they would now have in the subcommission only a tiny minority (four against ten) against a majority which, as one can foresee, could be too easily united against them, since this majority consists of elements which for centuries have been at the root of the continued strife against the Catholic Church.

> It must be noted that since unanimity is required for each decision, and such unanimity cannot be achieved in a Sub-Commission which is formed by so incongruous and opposite elements, the final decision will practically rest with the President of the plenary Chairman of the Commission, in other words, a Protestant, and this is simply preposterous.[10]

Balfour's proposal also received a cool reception from the Italians, who feared that the recommended appointment of a Frenchman as chairman of the Christian subcommission might indicate a change for the worse in the British position on French religious protection of Catholics in Palestine.[11]

Gasparri was absent from the Vatican at the time, and de Salis communicated Balfour's proposals to Monsignor Francesco Borgongini Duca. According to de Salis, the proposal seemed likely to encounter opposition from the Vatican, but not having received an official reaction, he sent to London the article from *Osservatore Romano* just quoted, which beyond doubt represented the views of the Secretariat of State.[12]

The Italians did not stand idly by but put forward a proposal of their own on the commission's composition: seven Catholics—including representatives of Italy, France, Belgium, Spain, Britain, and the Holy See—and five Orthodox; the chairman of the commission would be the representative of the Holy See, and his deputy would be the British Catholic representative.[13] With this proposal, granting a Vatican representative an official standing in the international arena but only insofar as the Holy Places were concerned, the Italians may have sought to improve their relations with the Vatican without conceding anything on the Roman Question.

On September 19, the British chargé d'affaires at the Vatican was received by Pope Pius XI. At the audience, the pope "insisted on the fact that most of the Holy Places were beyond dispute the possession of the Catholic Church, which would find itself outvoted in the commission in matters which concerned interests to which the highest importance was attached." The pope added that he "did not wish to make a public protest but was afraid he might find himself obliged to do so." Gasparri, for his part, thought of "making an appeal to the justice of the British Government, who hardly seemed to realize the importance which the Catholic Church attached to the rights it had enjoyed for so many centuries, even under the rule of the Turks."[14] The cardinal secretary of state's nostalgia for Turkish rule was not surprising, considering that by applying pressure on the crumbling Ottoman Empire, the Vatican had been able to obtain what it wanted. The pope's words threatened a public protest that the British government definitely wanted to avoid.

Dormer forwarded Gasparri's letter of September 21 to the British prime minister, David Lloyd George. In this letter, Gasparri repeated the Vatican's by-now familiar arguments against Lord Balfour's proposed composition of the commission for the Holy Places: the Catholics, who had almost all the Palestinian sanctuaries, would find themselves in a striking minority on the Christian subcommission. Gasparri continued:

> This injustice is aggravated by the fact that no decision can be come to by this sub-Commission except by unanimous vote and failing such unanimity the final decision is to be deferred to the President of the Plenary Commission who is an American

Protestant. . . . It follows that the interests and the rights of Catholics will be in the hands of a Protestant, always arbiter of the situation.

Gasparri conveyed to Lloyd George the pope's appeal to prevent a serious injustice to Catholics.[15]

Several days later, Borgongini Duca told Dormer that the Vatican would have much more confidence in a British court of justice than in the commission proposed by the British Government, as

> the ownership of the Holy Places was a purely judicial question, and instead of being submitted to an independent tribunal of magistrates, before whom the conflicting parties could plead through their own advocates, it was under the British proposal to be dealt with by a mixed religious commission, the members of which were all interested parties.

As far as the Vatican was concerned, it "would be far preferable to maintain the *status quo* of the Turkish regime, i.e., if any claims as to ownership were to be raised, let them be dealt with by the British tribunals."[16] The Foreign Office reacted with some surprise:

> The Vatican seems to be climbing down. The Colonial Office would be perfectly content that there should be no commission. But it was the Vatican themselves who, a short time ago, were asking that the consuls of the Powers interested in Jerusalem should form the desired commission—hardly the juridical body they now desire to secure.[17]

Somewhat surprisingly, the Italian proposal was favorably received by the British Foreign Office. Assistant Secretary Lancelot Oliphant informed the Colonial Office that Foreign Secretary Lord Curzon did not object to granting the Catholics a majority on the Christian subcommission, for the Italian proposal also required that all decisions be reached unanimously. That would allow the Orthodox representatives to veto any decision opposed to their interests. The British government should, however, insist on its proposal that the chairman of the plenary commission be an American Protestant. The British Foreign Office thought that the Christian subcommission could be composed of six Catholics and five Orthodox, one of the Catholic representatives being the Vatican's representative.

One of the aims of the Italian proposal was to block the appointment of a Frenchman as chairman of the Christian subcommission, but the British preferred that the Italian and French governments reach an agreement on this between themselves, which they were prepared to honor.[18] Dormer commented that the Italian proposal would not, however, satisfy the Vatican, which would not "abandon this attitude unless they are given a real concession."[19]

The British Foreign Office asked Colonial Secretary Winston Churchill to propose a draft for the prime minister's reply to Gasparri's letter of September 21.[20] The Colonial Office stressed that the arrangements originally contemplated should satisfy the demands of both the Vatican and Italy. In any event, the findings should be subject to the ultimate confirmation of the Council of the League of Nations, on which Catholic countries were not without strong representation, while there was not one representative on the Council who could speak in the name of the Orthodox or non-Orthodox Eastern churches.[21]

A New Round of Debate on the Commission

At a meeting of the Council of the League of Nations on October 4, Balfour formally withdrew the proposals that he said were prepared by the British Colonial Office, which he had submitted at the previous meeting, on August 31. He said that the prejudice against his scheme was based on a misunderstanding:

> There was a very strong feeling throughout the Catholic world that to put a Protestant in that position was, as it were, to outrage the spirit of history and to offend a great many very strong susceptibilities. To put a Protestant in a position in which he could offer an opinion upon Catholic dogma or Catholic ritual or Catholic ecclesiastical practice or Catholic ecclesiastical law would have been a gross impertinence. . . . But of course, that was not what the Protestant Chairman of this Commission was ever intended to do. He was only intended to act as a Court of Appeal in a dispute between one Christian denomination and another, and not in matters which concerned Catholic opinion as such. There is obviously some advantage in having as a judge a man who widely sympathizes with the religious sentiments of all those concerned and is himself wholly unconnected either with one party to the litigation or with the other. Under the old system, Mohammedans had for more than a thousand years acted as a Court of Appeal. We thought that to substitute an American judge for a Mohammedan judge was an action for which perhaps some gratitude would be due to us. . . . We chose a Court of Appeal from among the citizens of a country which is not the Mandatory Power, which is wholly unconnected with the actual subject in dispute, and entirely disinterested in the local politics and the local interests of Palestine.

Balfour also noted the difficulties that resulted from the disagreement between France and Italy and from the rivalry among the Christian churches. "It is its [the mandatory's] business also to see that justice is done as between Catholics and Orthodox, Orthodox and Jews, Orthodox and Armenians. . . . Next to the great Catholic body in the world stands the Orthodox. It is not very strongly in the League of Nations."[22]

The Council of the League of Nations, before which a French proposal was also placed, decided to return the matter for further examination to the governments concerned. In addition, France and Italy would have to reach an agreement within a year, for the Council wanted to conclude the debate on the mandate and begin its operation in 1923.[23]

On October 13, Lloyd George drafted a reply to Gasparri but did not sign it, for in the meantime he had tendered his resignation; the letter was thus delivered without his signature. The British prime minister stated that his government's proposals were intended to ensure that the claims and rights of the three great religions in Palestine would be impartially examined and determined in a spirit of even-handed justice. Gasparri's primary objection, which pertained to the powers of the proposed American president of the main commission, appeared to rest on some misapprehension. There were obvious advantages in having as a judge a man who widely sympathized with the religious sentiments of all those concerned; his findings should be subject to the ultimate confirmation of the Council of the League, on which the Catholic countries were strongly represented.

The British government was prepared to consider any reasonable and agreed procedure to settle those cases for which unanimity was not achieved in the subcommissions. For the British, the chief stumbling block to agreement appears to have been the presidency of the Christian subcommission (an allusion to the differences between France and Italy). The British government had spared no pains to bring the discussions of the Council to a successful conclusion, and the fault did not lie with the government if such an agreement on the commission had not yet been found. "The sole desire of H. M. Government throughout these proceedings has been to find, as quickly as possible, some impartial arrangement which might reach with the ready assent of all parties concerned, not least with that of the Great Church of which Your Eminence is so distinguished a representative," Lloyd George concluded.[24]

The Latin Patriarchate and the Custodia

After the mandate was approved by the Council of the League of Nations, the expectation was that relations would calm down, but this did not happen. Barlassina continued to rankle the British authorities in Palestine. The British legation at the Holy See was convinced that the Vatican realized that the patriarch was wholly unsuited to his post, but the difficulty was how to dispose of him. The British legation thought that he would be removed as soon as a post could be found for him, but it is not clear on what ground this belief was founded. In any event, Barlassina continued as the Latin patriarch of Jerusalem for many more years, and we may suppose, therefore, that the Vatican did not dissociate itself from him. This seems to me an example of the tendency of some diplomats to base their reports on their own wishful thinking rather than on the facts.

The British wanted to secure the appointment of an English auxiliary bishop or, failing that, of an English secretary to the patriarchate. The obvious candidate for this position was Father Paschal Robinson, but the fact that Robinson was a Franciscan was an insuperable obstacle, because his appointment would have involved difficulties with other religious orders. Francis Aidan Cardinal Gasquet, a British subject who had been appointed chief librarian of the Church in Rome, was asked by the pope if he knew of another English priest who would be acceptable to the British government. He recommended Father Godric Keane, who was made secretary to the patriarch.[25]

When Agostino Cardinal Richèlmy died in Turin, the British government hoped that Barlassina would be named to replace him, thus giving Robinson, the eternal British candidate, the chance to be made patriarch. This appointment would be welcomed by the British government and acquiesced to by the French government, while the British would then not object to the appointment of a French priest as

Heads of the Franciscan Custodia Terrae Sanctae in Jerusalem.

auxiliary bishop. But Gasparri said there was no likelihood of either appointment, and Barlassina remained in his post.

In 1923 Barlassina did not attend the service in the Anglican Cathedral of St. George in Jerusalem on the occasion of the British king's birthday and apparently persuaded the Catholic consuls in the city to adopt a similar attitude and to stay home as well. Lord Curzon took so serious view of this incident that the British legation was instructed to make a strong representation to the Vatican and to add that unless satisfactory assurances were given, the British mission would have to be withdrawn. Gasparri immediately expressed his regret at Barlassina's interference in the actions of foreign representatives and gave implicit assurances as to his future conduct; these regrets were expressed in an official note.

The Franciscans were "somewhat alarmed" by the intention to appoint Father Keane, whom they regarded as reinforcement for the patriarchate by a priest who would have easy access to the administration, but they were assured by the British that Keane would not act as an intermediary in any question affecting the Holy Places.[26] The mills of the Vatican grind slowly, but finally, in 1924—to the disappointment of the Arabs and the French—Keane was appointed auxiliary bishop to the Latin patriarch, as the British had wanted.[27]

But as might have been expected, Keane's appointment did not solve the problem of the impaired relations between Barlassina and the mandatory administration, especially because the patriarch regarded himself as the official representative of the Holy See in Palestine. Still, the Vatican did not want to give up the services of Barlassina, who did express the official policy of the Holy See, if perhaps with excessive zeal.

To improve the Vatican's formal relations with the British administration in Palestine without changing its basic positions, the pope decided to appoint a "permanent apostolic visitor." The British learned that Father Robinson would most likely be named to that position and might later be made an apostolic delegate.[28] That would take from Barlassina any pretensions of being the representative of the Holy See. Robinson thus was sent to Jerusalem as apostolic visitor and received instructions stating that the Latin patriarch served only as bishop and did not represent the Vatican in any diplomatic manner whatever.[29]

That seemed to bring a long story to an end: the Latin patriarch was restored to a purely religious role after eight years of actively interfering in the government of Palestine and working against the British administration and Zionism. But a somewhat different view was presented by Salim Sayegh, a priest who himself had been associated with the patriarchate. He mentioned the 1923 arrangement regarding the division of responsibilities between the patriarch and the custos and contended that the patriarch continued to act as a liaison with the civilian authorities in matters related to the status quo in the Holy Places even after the establishment of the apostolic delegation in Palestine in 1929. His version, however, is not compatible with the contents of a letter written by Gasparri, also quoted by Sayegh, which declared that the apostolic delegate would deal with the High Commissioner and the authorities as the representative of the pope, as was customary in countries in which there was no nuncio.[30]

The Great Powers and the Composition of the Commission

Apart from the Vatican's religious interest in the scrupulous safeguarding of its rights of ownership in the Holy Places were the problems surrounding the composition of the commission for the Holy Places as well as the interests of the various countries. Italy waged a stubborn fight against France to keep it from extending its protectorate over Catholics and from obtaining the liturgical honors and the chairmanship of the Christian subcommission. These efforts, however, were massed against an illusory objective, for during the British mandatory rule over Palestine, the religious trappings of France's glorious past in the Levant no longer had any meaning. But the Italians persisted in their struggle, mindless of the consequences of the war, which included the abrogation of the capitulations in Palestine.

The capitulations of 1535 (see Chapter 1) gave France "complete preeminence over other European powers, who might only trade with Turkey in ships bearing the French flag, and whose European residents depended for their protection on the French consuls" and ultimately included all Catholics throughout the empire. The capitulations agreement was unilaterally rescinded by Turkey in 1914, and its abrogation was subsequently recognized by the Great Powers in the Treaty of Sèvres and in the mandate for Palestine.

France was in fact occupied with much more tangible questions, for its presence in the Levant was now based on the mandates for Syria and Lebanon. The territory ruled by France was smaller than that under the British mandate, and France tried constantly to undermine the British in Palestine. Still, France was more powerful than Italy, which lost out on all issues after the program for internationalizing Palestine was shelved.

Spain also demanded a share in Palestine, based on its special status in the Franciscan order according to its ancient internal rule. On October 11, 1922, an article appeared in the Spanish newspaper *Sol*, which attributed the absence of Nuncio Monsignor Federico Tedeschini from Madrid to disagreement between the Spanish government and the Vatican regarding the Holy Places. The dispute concerned Spain's protection of a number of Catholic institutions in Palestine, including the Franciscan monastery attached to the Church of the Holy Sepulchre.[31] *Osservatore Romano* vigorously denied the rumors of differences between the Vatican and Spain,[32] but the matter concerned the British Foreign Office, and on November 8 the embassy in Madrid reported the return of the nuncio to the Spanish capital. Upon his return, the nuncio published an announcement denying *Sol's* allegation that the Vatican had tried to turn Spain out of the Holy Land.[33]

At the end of October, Borgongini Duca, who had in the meantime replaced Cerretti as secretary for extraordinary ecclesiastical affairs, repeated his earlier suggestion that there should be no commission for the Holy Places and that if any claims were raised regarding the Holy Places, they should be dealt with by ordinary British tribunals. The more he thought about the matter, said Borgongini Duca, the more he was convinced that "they offered the best solution of the difficulty."[34]

Britain then proposed a third draft Article 14, which was accepted by the Council of the League of Nations in November 1922. It read:

> A special Commission shall be appointed by the Mandatory to study, define, and determine the rights and claims in connection with the Holy Places, and the rights and claims relating to the different religious communities in Palestine. The method of nomination, the composition and the functions of this Commission shall be submitted to the Council of the League for its approval, and the Commission shall not be appointed or enter upon its functions without the approval of the Council.[35]

It was already evident to everyone that formation of the commission was doomed. Nonetheless, the Belgian government, in reply to Balfour's request of November 4, promised to continue to work for a suitable solution.[36] The Belgian ambassador in Madrid then proposed that Belgium mediate among France, Italy, and Spain.[37] The Vatican, for its part, took no stand, favoring neither the French nor the Italian proposals, which, according to the Catholic writer Bernardin Collin, were influenced more by their national interests than by a desire to defend the Church's interests.[38]

Pope Pius XI brought up the problem again in his consistorial address on December 11, 1922, *Vehementer Gratum*. He mentioned the speech by his predecessor on the same subject on June 13, 1921, and expressed his agreement with what was said on that occasion. He repeated the request to safeguard the interests of the Catholics and all Christianity in Palestine when the time came to decide the future of this land. The pope stressed that these rights must be honored and protected not only against the Jews and unbelievers but also against the non-Catholic sects of any nationality or race.[39] In December 1922, after the pope's speech, and possibly in reaction to it, the British government decided to circulate to the members of the Council of the League of Nations that year's correspondence between the former prime minister, Lloyd George, and Cardinal Gasparri.[40]

In May 1924, the Colonial Office decided that no steps should be taken to establish the commission and proposed that the Foreign Office agree that the courts of law in Palestine adjudicate the cases included in Article 14, provided that the court be composed solely of British judges and that there be right of appeal to the Court of King's Bench.[41] Indeed, the first annual report submitted by the Mandate government to the League of Nations stated that the administration of Palestine had assumed responsibility for the Holy Places and for strictly maintaining the status quo in them. On July 25, 1924, an Order in Council was issued providing that "no cause or matter in connection with the Holy Places or religious buildings or sites in Palestine shall be heard or determined by any court in Palestine." Such cases were to be referred to the High Commissioner himself, who had to make the final decision.[42]

The End of Internationalization

Thus ended a controversy that had occupied the European powers and the Vatican for a number of years. According to de Salis, Pope Benedict XV's allocution in June 1921 was prompted by his desire to express his dissatisfaction over the delay in the formation of a commission for the Holy Places. This explanation is interesting because it reveals the British representative's interpretation that the commission, and not Zionism, was foremost among the Vatican's concerns. If this assessment is accepted, then an internal contradiction is revealed in the pope's position, as follows: several months earlier, in December 1920, Gasparri used the fact that the mandate had not yet been approved to restore the French religious protectorate. At that time, many thought that the Vatican had been pro-German at the beginning of World War I and then became pro-French again after it. In 1921 the pope complained that the commission, whose formation depended above all on the mandate's approval, had not yet been established. Yet, as we saw, the Vatican did all it could to postpone approval of the mandate when it came up for debate at the Council of the League of Nations.

It may well be that the Vatican had initially hoped to obtain a redistribution of the Holy Places between Catholics and Greek Orthodox more favorable than that of the 1852 status quo, thereby restoring the privileged situation that had prevailed in the eighteenth century. The Vatican therefore sought the prompt establishment of a commission with a Catholic majority. Vatican diplomacy was enlisted to accelerate the formation of this commission, but when it became clear to the pope and the cardinal secretary of state that they would not be able to secure a Catholic majority on the commission, they preferred to defeat the whole plan. In the event of a dispute over the Holy Places, they would be satisfied with recourse to the British courts. They knew that they could rely on the British judiciary, which in any event was the lesser of the two evils for the Vatican.

France had wanted to perpetuate its privileged status, based on the protectorate over Catholics, through the appointment of a Frenchman as chairman of a permanent commission. Italy, which insisted on the abolition of the French religious protectorate, was opposed to the French ambition for the very same reason.

Britain, which feared the interference in Palestinian affairs of an international commission that might become permanent, did not in the end oppose the indefinite postponement of the commission's establishment. The idea of the commission had first been put forward merely to appease the Vatican and as a way of preventing it from impeding approval of the mandate. Once the mandate was approved, and the Vatican itself no longer showed any interest in such a commission, the British had no reason to try to insist on it. Nonetheless, the British government knew how to shift responsibility for failure to those that proved unable to reach an understanding on the presidency of the Christian subcommission—that is, Italy and France—and even announced formally that it was ready to accept any equitable scheme acceptable to all other members of the Council of the League of Nations.

Thus the plans for the internationalization, extraterritoriality, or international supervision of the Holy Places in Palestine were shelved for a number of years, although they did not vanish. The *corpus separatum,* an international enclave of Jerusalem and its surroundings, of the 1947 United Nations partition plan was the last vestige of those earlier plans. And today, too, the Vatican would still like to see a "special statute internationally guaranteed" for Jerusalem, a city considered holy to the three monotheistic religions.

II

THE VATICAN AND
POLITICAL ZIONISM

8

The Dawn of Zionism

The Catholic Church and the Jews

Part I discussed the Vatican's religious and political interests in the Holy Land to help explain its attitude toward Zionism, which Part II will describe at length.

As I have already indicated, the Holy See's policy toward political Zionism is inseparable from the Catholic Church's religious stand regarding the Jews. From the beginning, its attitude toward the Jews was scored by a deep internal contradiction: On the one hand, Christianity did not deny its Jewish origins, but on the other hand, it attacked and defamed Judaism in order to assert its own independent identity. Thus over the centuries, Judaism came under severe attack, and many Jews met their death for no reason other than their loyalty to their faith.

But beyond physical persecution, Christianity sought to separate the Jewish people from their spiritual roots. Thus the Jewish Bible became the Old Testament, a preface or forerunner of the New Testament to be interpreted exclusively in the light of Christian faith, with emphasis on the prophecies of the advent of Christ and the transference of the divine promise from Israel to God's Church—that is, the Catholic Church.

For hundreds of years, the Catholic Church has taken the theological position that the Church is the "true Israel" and the exclusive heir of the Bible. According to St. Augustine, the Jews are a "witness people" against their own will, for they preserve the Holy Scriptures, which are testimony that the Christians did not fabricate the prophecies related to Jesus. To serve as witnesses, the Jews were dispersed among the nations, to all places where the Church of God had come. The Jews, therefore, are both ostracized and witnesses to the "truth" of Christianity. They must suffer, but they should not be exterminated, for they must fulfill their role as witnesses, and at the last judgment they all will become Christians. Many Catholics regard the Jews as an obstinate people who refuse to recognize the divinity of Jesus, a people guilty of the crime of deicide and therefore an accursed people whose exile is clear proof of God's punishment. This "teaching of contempt," as

Jules Isaac termed it, is what the Church has taught its flock for nearly two thousand years.[1]

The result was inevitable. The Jews suffered in Christian lands from discriminatory laws, banishment, degradations, and murderous persecution. There were, moreover, forced conversions to Christianity, accusations of defaming Christianity, alleged profanation of the host, and blood libels, depending on the time and place. Anti-Jewish arguments and stereotypes became deeply ingrained features of the Western European culture, absorbed even by anti-Catholic writers and thinkers.

Here we shall deal with only part of the complex of relations that developed between the Catholic Church and Judaism and that have been the subject of many valuable studies.[2] Our examination is limited to the political and diplomatic aspects of the Vatican's activities regarding political Zionism. The Vatican's policy was certainly influenced by the Church's theological position, for the Holy See is but the government of the Church. Indeed, in September 1987, an official joint communiqué of the Holy See and a Jewish delegation stated that "representatives of the Holy See declared that there exist no theological reasons in Catholic doctrine that would inhibit such relations [with the state of Israel]."[3] But at the same time, the Vatican operates in the international arena in ways not dissimilar to those of other countries, and so we shall examine its attitude toward Zionism in the context of its stand on Palestine and the Holy Places there.

The Zionist movement entered the Vatican's field of concern when the Holy See began to fear that the Zionists posed a threat to Catholic interests in Palestine. The period covered in our study extends from the birth of Theodor Herzl's political Zionism to the mid-1920s, a period that was extremely important to both the determination of Palestine's political future and the consolidation of Zionism.

Herzl and Christianity

Theodor Herzl, the founder of political Zionism, initially advocated total assimilation as the solution for the Jewish "problem." Around 1893 he considered the idea of obtaining an audience with the pope, to tell him: "Help us against the anti-Semites and I will lead a great movement for the free and honorable conversion of Jews to Christianity." He even envisioned, somewhat theatrically, how this mass conversion would be carried out: "In broad daylight, on twelve o'clock of a Sunday, in St. Stephen's Cathedral, with solemn parade and the peal of bells." The leaders of the movement, Herzl among them, would remain Jews but would be the "final generation." He imagined himself standing before the pope, who regrets that Herzl himself is not converting to Christianity.[4]

Nothing remains of this fanciful plan, but for years Herzl yearned to meet the pope in order to win his goodwill toward the Jews. As a result of his assimilationist past and his involvement in Western culture, Herzl had a better appreciation than did many other Zionist leaders of the Vatican's importance and influence among many of the world's political rulers. He was aware of the numerous Christian claims to Jerusalem and therefore thought it vital to find a solution for the problem of the Holy Places that would be satisfactory to the Church.

Herzl's solution was intended to dispel the fears of the Christian world and to demonstrate that the Jews in no way constituted a threat, as they would not at all interfere in the Holy Places of either Christianity or Islam. Herzl apparently had in mind the exclusion of certain buildings and sites from civil jurisdiction; he might have been inspired by the special extraterrritorial status enjoyed by Great Britain in China following the treaties of 1842 to 1844. In regard to the concept of extraterritoriality, Sir Francis Piggot wrote:

> Extraterritoriality is in essence the extension of jurisdiction beyond the borders of the state. It embodies certain rights, principles and immunities which are enjoyed by the citizens, subjects or protégés of one state within the boundaries of another, and which exempt them from local territorial jurisdiction and place them under the laws and judicial administration of their own state. Extraterritoriality is often confused with exterritoriality, but the latter refers only to the immunities accorded a diplomatic envoy and his suite in accordance with international law, while the former may be said to involve the establishment of an international servitude by elevating the nationality principle of jurisdiction over the territorial principle.[5]

This approach differed altogether from that of the Great Powers and the Vatican, which used the term "Holy Places" in a much broader sense that included all of Jerusalem and sometimes much more.

In his book *The Jewish State,* written in 1895, Herzl touched on the problem of the Holy Places:

> The sanctuaries of Christendom would be safeguarded by assigning to them an extraterritorial status such as is well known to the law of nations. We should form a guard of honour about those sanctuaries answering for the fulfillment of this duty with our existence. This guard of honor would be the great symbol of the solution of the Jewish Question, after eighteen centuries of Jewish suffering.[6]

In 1896, in the midst of wide-ranging political activity for the Zionist idea, Herzl again proposed his plan for the Holy Places. When Philip Michael de Newlinsky, an Austrian journalist, told him that the sultan would never hand over Jerusalem, because the Mosque of Omar must remain forever in the hands of Islam, Herzl replied: "We can get around that difficulty. We shall extraterritorialize Jerusalem, so that it will belong to nobody and yet everybody; and with it the Holy Places become the joint possession of all believers—a great condominium of culture and morality."[7]

On May 19, 1896, Herzl was received by the nuncio in Vienna, Antonio Agliardi. "He is tall, slender, well-bred, and stiff," Herzl wrote in his diaries, "exactly as I had envisaged a papal diplomat." Agliardi asked a number of questions, and then the following discussion, as recorded by Herzl, ensued:

> "We are not contemplating a monarchy [said Herzl] but an aristocratic republic. We require only the consent of the Great Powers, and in particular that of His Holiness the Pope; then we shall establish it ourselves—with the extraterritorialization of Jerusalem understood. As to the Sultan, we shall reorganize his finances." Agliardi smiled: "He will be highly pleased. You propose, then, to exclude Jerusalem, Bethlehem and Nazareth, and set up the capital, I take it more to the north?" "Yes," I said. . . . Result of the conversation: I believe Rome will be against us, because she

does not consider the solution of the Jewish Question in a Jewish state, and perhaps even fears it.[8]

The problem of Jerusalem thus came up at this first meeting with a papal representative; the Vatican wanted Jerusalem, Bethlehem, and Nazareth to remain outside the Jewish state if such a state should be created. This territorial conception would continue for many years as a basis of Vatican policy toward Palestine. Herzl realized, however, that this approach was at odds with his extraterritorial plan and that apart from its show of formal courtesy, the Vatican was opposed to a Jewish state.

The First Contacts Between Zionism and the Vatican

One of the first references to Zionism in a Catholic periodical was in 1897, the year of the First Zionist Congress in Basel. About four months before the congress, the Jesuit journal *Civiltà Cattolica,* known for its anti-Semitic tenor, published an article that reflected an abhorrence of Zionism:

> 1827 years have passed since the prediction of Jesus of Nazareth was fulfilled, namely that is that Jerusalem would be destroyed . . . that the Jews would be led away to be slaves among all the nations, and that they would remain in the dispersion till the end of the world. . . . According to the Sacred Scriptures, the Jewish people must always live dispersed and wandering among the other nations, so that they may render witness to Christ not only by the Scriptures . . . but by their very existence. As for a rebuilt Jerusalem, which could become the center of a reconstituted state of Israel, we must add that this is contrary to the prediction of Christ Himself.[9]

This article clearly states the theological grounds for the Catholic opposition to Zionism.

Several days after the First Zionist Congress, Herzl received Italian and French newspapers reporting that the pope had issued a circular letter protesting the projected occupation of the Holy Places by the Jews.[10] According to the *Daily News,* the apostolic delegate in Constantinople, Monsignor Bonetti, was called to Rome by the pope for consultations "on measures to be taken against the Zionist movement." It was said that the pope had also turned to France, as the protector of the Catholics in the Levant, and the French Foreign Ministry opposed any change in the existing situation of the Holy Land. Earlier, the Italian press had quoted an item from *Osservatore Romano,* according to which the Vatican intended to protest the occupation of Palestine by Jews.[11]

Herzl immediately wrote to the new nuncio in Vienna, Monsignor Egidio Taliani, and asked for an audience to talk about Zionism. Taliani at first refused to see Herzl separately, while the Vatican issued a denial in the *Politische Korrespondenz* stating that "the Curia has taken no diplomatic action concerning the Zionist Congress, nor shall it do so in the future."[12]

The *Jewish Chronicle,* borrowing from *L'Italie,* reported that the pope thought it right to take all possible measures to prevent the restoration of the Jewish nation in Jerusalem. A special papal envoy was therefore sent to Constantinople with a message for the sultan underscoring the pope's admonition not to deliver Palestine to the Jews.[13]

About a year and a half later, in February 1899, Herzl was finally received by the nuncio in Vienna, Taliani, to whom he stressed that no takeover of the control of the Holy Places was ever intended. Jerusalem and Bethlehem would be given extraterritorial status, and the capital of the Jewish nation would be located elsewhere. Recording the conversation in his diary, Herzl added:

> He gave me a very friendly reception, saying that he personally was not unfavorably inclined toward the [Zionist] matter. . . . Incidentally, the Holy See had always been well disposed towards the Jews. If they were locked up in the ghetto, it was only to protect them from the mob. "There have also been interruptions in this benevolent tradition," I remarked.[14]

In his opening address at the Second Zionist Congress, in August 1898, Herzl pointed out the relationship between the Jewish Question and world politics. He emphasized the importance of Palestine as a passageway to Asia and added:

> Now when the most modern monarch of the inhabited earth [the German Kaiser] plans a voyage to the Holy Places, public opinion of all countries echoes with hidden anxiety, at times to the point of pure hatred. This land cannot be, and indeed never shall be, the possession of one great Power. The return of the Jews to Palestine would solve this question for the world and for the Turks.[15]

A similar idea was expressed a year later in the British *Daily Mail*, following a discussion of the problem of the Holy Places. It would be worthwhile, the newspaper said, to consider seriously whether the Zionist movement might well prove the solution that would avert the threatening conflict.[16] But this idea did not gain wide acceptance, and certainly not within the Catholic Church.

The absence of any mention of Jerusalem at the Third Zionist Congress, in 1899, led *Civiltà Cattolica* to comment:

> What sort of Zionism is this, that from the start renounces Jerusalem and the ancient kingdom of Palestine? Does this not prove that they are betraying themselves and confessing that their intentions were utopian? Why not then completely give up the name Zionism? A race of murderers of God, even if supported by all the anti-Christian sects, feels itself beaten before the fight even begins, beaten by Jesus.[17]

This attack is somewhat surprising, for the concern of Catholic circles stemmed, among other things, from a fear of possible Jewish rule over Jerusalem. Therefore, if Zionism were to give up Jerusalem, this Jesuit organ should have been pleased, instead of turning it into a pretext for yet another anti-Semitic attack.

On December 28, 1899, in Vienna, Herzl met with Oscar Straus, the American ambassador in Constantinople, who "considered Palestine impossible to attain." Herzl recorded the conversation in his diary:

> The Greek and Roman Catholic Churches would not let the Jews have it. I told him, that I considered only Rome to be a serious opponent. I forgot to give him my deeper reason: that only Roman Catholicism is as ecumenical as Judaism. Rome is the rich brother who hates the poor brother; the other Churches are national, and can therefore dispense with Jerusalem as an Archimedean point of leverage.[18]

This comment reveals Herzl's understanding of the real reasons underlying the Catholic Church's hostility toward Zionism. He harbored no illusions about the Vatican but correctly identified the Catholic Church as the chief opponent of his vision and appreciated the crucial importance the Church attached to Jerusalem and to Catholic predominance in the city.

Herzl's Audience with Pope Pius X

For some time, Herzl tried to obtain an audience with the pope in the Vatican. As early as 1903, he asked Felice Ravenna, the chairman of the Zionist Federation in Italy, to arrange an audience for him. On that occasion, he reiterated his view that the Holy Places in Palestine should be extraterritorial, "res sacra extra commercium du droit des gens," a holy matter outside the nations' jurisdiction. He hoped that the pope would support his suggestion.[19]

Finally, a few months before his death, Herzl obtained an interview with the pope, thanks to a painter, Count B. De Lippay, whom he had met by chance in Venice. On January 22, 1904, he was received by the secretary of state, Rafael Cardinal Merry del Val, who was then thirty-eight years old, tall, slender, a Spanish nobleman. "Fine, large, brown, serious, inquiring yet not unreligious eyes in a still young, but already grave face." Herzl told him he wanted the goodwill of the Holy See for his cause:

> THE CARDINAL: I do not quite see how we can take any initiative in this matter. As long as the Jews deny the divinity of Christ, we certainly cannot make a declaration in their favor. Not that we have any ill will toward them. On the contrary, the Church has always protected them. To us they are the indispensable witnesses to the phenomenon of God's term on earth. But they deny the divine nature of Christ. How then can we, without abandoning our own highest principles, agree to their being given possession of the Holy Land again?
>
> HERZL: We are asking only for the profane earth; the Holy Places are to be extraterritorialized.
>
> THE CARDINAL: Oh, but it won't do to imagine them in an enclave of that sort.
>
> HERZL: But is the present state of things more satisfactory to Christendom, Eminence?
>
> THE CARDINAL: The College of Cardinals has never taken up this question. Of course the existence of such a movement is known through the newspapers; but the College as such could not go into the matter in detail unless a memorandum were submitted to it.
>
> HERZL: It would be in consonance with the great policy of the Church, Your Eminence, if the Holy See declared itself in our favor—or, let us say, as not against us. . . .
>
> THE CARDINAL: Certainly, a Jew who has himself baptized out of conviction is for me ideal. . . . But in order for us to come out for the Jewish People in the way you desire, they would first have to be converted. . . . Still, I see no possibility of our assuming the initiative.
>
> HERZL: No one is asking you, Your Eminence! The initiative will be taken by one of the Great Powers. You are simply to give your approval.[20]

The secretary of state expressed the Church's basic attitude toward Zionism with surprising candor. The Church, he indicated, was prepared to offer the Jews "pro-

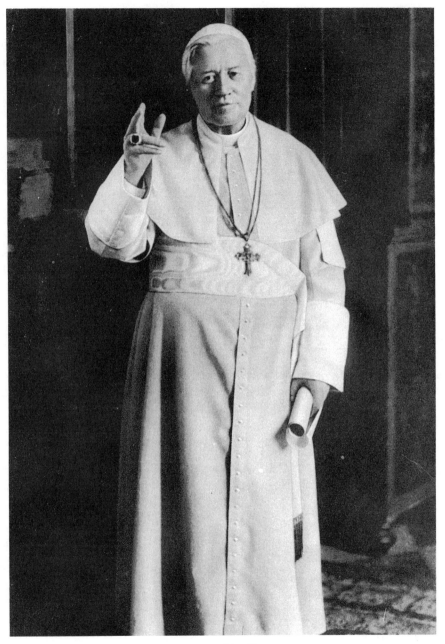

Pope Pius X.

tection"; that is, it would help them stay alive as sufferers, for they are indispensable to the Church as witnesses of divine punishment. But the Church could not agree that the Jews would again rule Palestine. The problem was thus both theological and political, and the gap between the Zionist positions and the Church's approach could be bridged only by a change in the Vatican's stand.

The cardinal secretary of state nonetheless arranged for Herzl to be received by Pope Pius X on January 25, 1904. The pope, who looked to Herzl like a "good, coarse-grained village priest," did not take refuge behind vague diplomatic formulas and spoke sternly and categorically. This conversation too was conducted with frankness.

> THE POPE: We cannot encourage this movement. We cannot prevent the Jews from going to Jerusalem—but we could never sanction it. The ground of Jerusalem, even if it were not always sacred, has been sanctified by the life of Jesus Christ. As the head of the Church I cannot tell you otherwise. The Jews have not recognized our Lord, therefore we cannot recognize the Jewish people.[21]

Recording the conversation in his diary, Herzl observed at this point that

> the conflict between Rome represented by him and Jerusalem represented by me was once again opened up. At the outset, I tried to be conciliatory. I recited my little piece about extraterritorialization, *res sacrae extra commercium gentium*. It did not greatly impress him. *Gerusalemme* was not to get into the hands of the Jews.

Herzl then asked about Jerusalem's current status:

> THE POPE: I know, it is not pleasant to see the Turks in possession of our Holy Places. We simply have to put up with that. But to support the Jews in the acquisition of the Holy Places, that we cannot do.

"I said," Herzl continued, "that our point of departure had been solely the distress of the Jews and that we desired to avoid the religious issues."

> THE POPE: Yes, but we, and I as head of the Catholic Church, cannot do this. There are two possibilities. Either the Jews will retain their ancient faith . . . in that case they are denying the divinity of Jesus and we cannot help them. Or else they will go there without any religion, and then we can be even less favorable to them. The Jewish religion was the foundation of our own, but it was superseded by the teachings of Christ, and we cannot concede it any further validity. The Jews who ought to have been the first to acknowledge Jesus Christ have not done so to this day.

Herzl then tried to appeal to the pope's sense of charity: "But, Holy Father, the Jews are in a terrible plight. I do not know if Your Holiness is aware of the full extent of their tragedy. We need a land for these harried people."

> THE POPE: Must it be *Gerusalemme?*
> HERZL: We are not asking for Jerusalem, but for Palestine—only the secular land.
> THE POPE: We cannot be in favor of it.
> HERZL: Does Your Holiness know the situation of the Jews?
> THE POPE: Yes, from my days in Mantua, where there are Jews. I have always been in friendly relations with Jews. Only the other evening two Jews were here to see me. There are other bonds than those of religion: courtesy, for example, and philan-

thropy. Such bonds we do not refuse to maintain with the Jews. Indeed we also pray for them, that their spirit see the light.[22] This very day the Church is celebrating the feast of an unbeliever who became converted to the true faith in a miraculous manner—on the road to Damascus. And so, if you come to Palestine and settle your people there, we will be ready with churches and priests to baptize all of you.[23]

Thus ended the talk lasting twenty-five minutes between Herzl and the pope. As Herzl later recalled, the pope also spoke of the Temple in Jerusalem, which had been destroyed forever, and asked whether any thought were being given to rebuild it and to renew the sacrificial services in the ancient way.[24] Both Pope Pius X and the cardinal secretary of state frankly presented Herzl with a position based on theological grounds, one that, at the least, clearly reflected the Church's view. The pope's question concerning the rebuilding of the Jewish Temple in Jerusalem proves that this issue also worried the pope.

The Vatican was consistent in its policy toward Zionism for many years to come, despite the seemingly positive exchange in 1917 between Pope Benedict XV and Nahum Sokolow. Several months after Herzl's Vatican visit, Cardinal Merry del Val said in an interview to *Die Welt:*

How can we deliver up the country of our Redeemer to a people of a different faith? Whenever a bad book appears or an ugly picture which mocks us, or a newspaper which defames us—then . . . we find the Israelite behind it. . . . Yet the Church would do nothing to impede the Zionists' effort to obtain, "a home in Palestine secured by public law. . . ." For that is quite another matter. . . . If the Jews believe that they can ease their lot in the land of their fathers, that is a humanitarian question in our view. The foundation of the Holy See is apostolic; it will never oppose an undertaking that alleviates human misery.[25]

The Vatican stand, based on humanitarian considerations, did not change for years; in 1917, at the time of Sokolow's talks at the Vatican, the cardinal secretary of state and the pope both vigorously opposed Jewish rule in Palestine and feared the damage it would cause to the Holy Places, or, to be more precise, to the status of the Catholics at these sites. Both the pope and the cardinal were ready to offer humanitarian support to the Jews, in keeping with Christian tradition, but in no event was this support to be political.

Politically, Zionism posed a greater threat to the Holy Places in Jerusalem than did the Islamic regime there. On this point centers the main problem of the Vatican's attitude toward Zionism, for the Catholic Church saw itself as the only one possible truth. After a struggle of hundreds of years for the safeguarding of Catholic rights in the Holy Places against other Christian communities and against the Ottoman regime, the Vatican was now confronting a new element: Zionism.

In attempting to gain the pope's backing, Herzl differed from later Zionist leaders, who concentrated their diplomatic efforts on trying to obtain the support of the Great Powers. As early as the beginning of the century, Herzl as a good political animal already understood that the Vatican would have political importance in any debate of the Palestine problem, stemming from its influence on some of the Great Powers of that period: Austria-Hungary, France, Italy, and Germany. Although the Vatican's diplomatic relations with Italy and France had been severed, the population of these two countries were largely Catholic; they had a Catholic press with a large circulation; and their governments wanted to avoid clashes with the Vatican. Furthermore, they viewed the Catholic religious factor as a convenient instrument for extending their penetration of the Middle East and maintaining a presence there. That was the source of the dispute between Italy and France, each of which wanted to ensure for itself the protectorate of the Catholics in Palestine and throughout the Ottoman Empire.

The extent to which Herzl pierced the veil of diplomatic protocol and formal courtesy and perceived the Vatican's true intentions is astonishing. Sokolow, by contrast, fell captive to several fine phrases uttered by the pope as part of normal diplomatic etiquette. Even worse, Sokolow failed to understand that the pope's readiness to support humanitarian actions on behalf of Jews whose lives were in danger, whether in czarist Russia or under the Ottoman yoke in Palestine, was itself a total rejection of Zionism. To try to save lives with nice words—yes; but to support the idea of a Jewish state—no! Sokolow may have lacked the deep acquaintance with Christian culture that Herzl had gained. Sokolow may also have been so imbued with a Jewish spirit, and so concerned by the dramatic situation of Jews in whatever country they were endangered, that he implicitly assumed that whoever wanted to help save Jewish lives also supported the Jewish national cause. But Herzl realized that the very opposite was sometimes true and, in any event, correctly perceived the equivocal and nebulous language of the Holy See's diplomacy better than Sokolow did. Chaim Weizmann, for his part, never had any illusions about the Vatican's hostile policy. Rather, he hoped to find breaches in the wall of enmity, an approach that perhaps was not given an adequate chance.

The Vatican's Humanitarian Efforts

As a result of World War I, the center of the Zionist Organization in Berlin was cut off from the rest of the movement, and tension developed within the movement between the pro-German Zionists and those, like Weizmann, who regarded Britain as the only hope for furthering the Zionist cause. The problem was augmented by the fact that Russia was Britain's and France's ally, whereas many Jews hoped that Russia's military defeat would lead to the Jews' liberation from the agonies they had suffered under the czarist regime.

Leonard Stein remarked that once the Holy Synod of the Russian Orthodox Church had taken an active part in instigating the persecution of the Jews in czarist Russia, the Jews could therefore be supposed to have a common interest with the Roman Catholics in undermining the position of the Orthodox Church. And in fact, Cardinal Gasparri reminded Sokolow that Catholics and Jews alike had suffered under the czarist regime.[26]

In December 1914, to keep the Zionist movement neutral, a bureau was opened in Copenhagen to maintain contact with Zionist organizations in both warring camps. Sokolow moved from Berlin to London to carry on his political activity; subsequently, after the Balfour Declaration was issued, London became the center of the World Zionist Organization.[27]

At the beginning of the war, a strange proposal was made in London to a Jewish leader. Stein reported that in the summer of 1915 the Frenchman François Deloncle, a former member of the Chamber of Deputies, called in London on Lucien Wolf, of the Conjoint Foreign Committee then active in favor of Russian Jews.[28] Isaiah Friedman related that Deloncle had been received twice by the pope, in May and in June 1915, and that His Holiness was prepared to issue an encyclical on the suffering of the Jews in Russia if the Jews would cooperate with him.[29]

Deloncle proposed that British Jews use their influence to secure the Holy See's admission to the peace conference, as representing the neutral states and the cause of religious liberty, especially the emancipation of the Jews and other oppressed dissenters in the Russian Empire. The Jews should also support a proposal that the pope be permitted to accredit a special diplomatic mission to Britain and the Russians be advised to receive a similar mission. Deloncle even told Wolf that Jews and Catholics had a common interest "in desiring to preserve Palestine from Russian domination." The Conjoint Committee of British Jews did not, however, take Deloncle's proposals seriously and rejected them. The American Jewish Committee, by contrast, showed a keen interest in them.

The Vatican's obvious eagerness to participate in the peace conference was expressed on several occasions during World War I, and Deloncle may have been acting on behalf of the Holy See, which was seeking a new avenue of influence on the governments of Britain and the United States. The statement about a common interest in Palestine is somewhat harder to understand. If indeed there was someone in the Vatican who held that view, this was no longer the case two years later. Nonetheless, the well-known Jewish feelings opposing Orthodox Russia may have prompted this move.

In the winter of 1915, Deloncle returned to Rome and was again received by the pope. On this visit, he was accompanied by Herman Bernstein, an American-Jewish journalist and former secretary of the American Jewish Committee. On this occasion, Benedict XV expressed a position that appeared quite sympathetic to Zionism. To Bernstein's question about his attitude toward the establishment of a Jewish national home in Palestine, the pope replied: "I have full sympathy for the national plan of the Jews in Palestine. We want freedom and justice and that is what the Jews are seeking everywhere."

Rabbi Zvi Peretz Chayes, who quoted this in a 1925 lecture on Zionist foreign policy, noted that the pope had been certain his remarks would be published. Chayes also said that it is not clear what happened subsequently to lead to the Vatican's negative position. He conjectured that the pope's sympathy may have been for Zionism as a utopian idea rather than for a living movement; thus when Zionism became a reality, the Vatican began to oppose it.[30]

The American Jewish Committee presented the pope with a petition drawing attention to the cruelties Jews were being subjected to in the eastern war zone and appealed on humanitarian grounds to the Holy See to intervene. The pope responded sympathetically. Later, Deloncle produced a document according to which the Jews of the world would work under the auspices of the Roman Catholic Church for the independence of Poland, but the Jews of England and the United States rejected the suggestion, thus ending this peculiar French Catholic initiative for political cooperation with the Jews. According to an entry in Vera Weizmann's diary of March 25, 1916, on that occasion it was proposed "as regards Palestine, that it should be neutralized, with the Pope's representative in the Government." The Zionists thought that "if the Pope got the upper hand in Palestine, it would be unacceptable."[31]

The Zionists and the Sykes–Picot Agreement

In 1916, as described earlier, Sykes and Picot reached an agreement according to which the central part of Palestine would be placed under international administration. On February 7, 1917, Sykes met with Zionist leaders in London, and even though he kept secret his agreement with Picot, he stressed that the Zionist chartered company to be established would operate only in certain parts of Palestine. Galilee and the Hauran, as well as the Jerusalem enclave—connected with Jaffa by a corridor along the railway line—were to be excluded from the sphere where the company could operate under British protection. The Zionists maintained that Jerusalem was a Jewish city and that internationalization therefore should be limited to the actual sites of the Holy Places.

On February 8, Sokolow met Picot in Sykes's presence and told him that the Zionists had resolved not to interfere in the Holy Places:

> There was not the remotest danger that the Holy Places would suffer at the hands of the Jews. As to the Christian sects, Mr. Sokolow expounded the view that only when the Jews were in Palestine, could there be a real religious peace in the world. Only on the soil of Palestine, in proximity to the places whence the Christian dispute and differences originate, could these differences be resolved. There was no reason to fear that any possession of the Christians in Palestine would be disturbed or harmed by the Jewish population of Palestine.[32]

The idea was conceived that for the common interest of Zionism and Britain, Sokolow should visit Paris and Rome to try to convince the two countries' governments to consent to the Zionist demands. At the beginning of April, Sokolow held an important talk in the French Foreign Ministry. He told Sykes in Paris about the meeting, and they talked about the center of the future Jewish autonomous area. Sokolow wrote to Weizmann:

> It can be assumed that it is the ancient part of Jerusalem, particularly the area within the walls, that falls within the religious sphere meant to be set apart in one way or another. But since we need a center, the "*baal habayit*" [landlord, that is, Sykes] pressed us to accept Haifa as one, for such various reasons as the advantage of a harbour, its proximity to Acre, the importance of Galilee, etc. I answered him that it was too early to settle this question, and that we would consider the situation, and offer a national solution in good time.[33]

There is no direct reference in Sokolow's letter to the idea that Jerusalem would be included in a Vatican-ruled enclave, as one source indicates. The mention of the Old City within the walls as a separate entity is interesting, for, as already noted,

Sir Mark Sykes at the time of the signature of the Sykes–Picot agreement, 1916.

the Vatican has recently tried to revive plans of this sort. Later in this letter, Sokolow wrote:

> I only noted that we need a center among our major colonies in Judea. . . . We must
> concentrate in Judea-Haifa, for if ancient Jerusalem belongs to the religious sphere,
> we could set up a center in the new Jerusalem. And if we meet for the time being
> with objection to that as well, we shall set up a temporary center elsewhere in Judea.
> Thus we shall secure both Judea and Galilee (while a center in Haifa will weaken
> the Galilee colonies).

Sykes and Sokolow at the Vatican

Sokolow arrived in Rome at the end of April 1917 for a series of talks with Italian
government officials on Palestine and Zionism. The source of the idea that while
in Rome Sokolow should also visit the Vatican is not clear. Weizmann, who was in
London, urged him to return immediately, but Sokolow, wanting to underscore the
importance of his Rome visit, wrote back to Weizmann: "It never crossed my mind
before that I should approach the Vatican. I was not prepared for the Vatican pour-
parlers . . . but I had no choice . . . I had before me a fait accompli."[34]

A few days earlier, James A. Malcolm, who was the president of the Armenian
National Committee in London and had accompanied Sokolow to Paris, told Weiz-

Nahum Sokolow, one of the leaders of the Zionist Organization in London.

mann that Sokolow had been asked by the French government to go to Rome. The government had two reasons, Malcolm said: to encourage Italian involvement and to awaken the pope's interest, with the hope that he would support a French protectorate or supervision (while excluding the British) as a way to win back France's loyalty.[35]

It thus appears that while he was still in Paris, Sokolow already knew he would be meeting the pope. But he may have preferred to explain that he had no choice, after Weizmann became concerned that his negotiations were liable to be interpreted as a Zionist acceptance of a French protectorate or of an Anglo-French condominium in Palestine.

Sokolow arrived in Rome on April 23 and met the British ambassador, who handed him a note from Sykes on his meeting with the pope. Sykes had prepared the ground for Sokolow's Vatican visit, having met several days earlier with Monsignor Eugenio Pacelli, Cardinal Gasparri, and the pontiff himself.[36] Pacelli was then secretary for extraordinary ecclesiastical affairs in the Secretariat of State. Twenty years later, he became Pope Pius XII.

Meeting with Sykes and de Salis, Pacelli remarked that the high office the British government had given to Sykes, a Catholic, "was a signal example of the toleration which existed in that country." Sykes spoke of the "immense difficulties which surrounded the question of Jerusalem, . . . and the conflicting interests of the Latin and Greeks, besides the aspirations of the various Powers." He mentioned the possibility of the Orthodox regaining strength in Russia, despite the Menshevik revolution, and, in consequence, the possibility of renewing the ancient conflict between Russia and France over the Holy Places. Pacelli hinted that the idea of a British patronage of the Holy Places was not distasteful to Vatican policy. The French certainly did not seem ideal in any way. Sykes then raised the subject of Zionism, explained its purposes and ideals, and proposed that Sokolow be given an audience. "Of course," wrote Sykes, "one couldn't expect the Vatican to be enthusiastic about this movement, but [Pacelli] was most interested, and expressed a wish to see Sokolow." As for the Holy Places, Sykes promised that "the Zionists had no aspirations in that direction."[37]

Later, on April 13, Sykes was received by Pope Benedict XV for a brief interview that lasted only ten to twelve minutes. Sykes, however, considered this audience to be of great value, "as we shall have to deal not only with the Latin Patriarch but also with the Custodian of the Holy Places." The interview might also serve to pacify the Vatican in the eventuality that the British would be forced to expel German priests. This was certainly clear foresight on Sykes's part.

On April 14, 1917, Sykes wrote Sokolow the following letter:

> My Dear Mr. Sokolow,
>   I visited Msgr. Pacelli, and was received in audience by His Holiness. On both occasions I [stressed] the intensity of Zionist feeling and the objects of Zionism. I was careful to impress that the main object of Zionism was to evolve a self-supporting Jewish community . . . which should . . . be a proof to the non-Jewish people of the world for the capacity of Jews to produce a virtuous and simple population. . . . I further pointed out that Zionist aims in no way clashed with Christian desiderata in general, and Catholic desiderata in particular, in regard to the Holy Places. I should strongly advise you to visit Msgr. Pacelli, and if you see fit an audience with His Holiness. Count de Salis . . . can arrange this if you will kindly show him this letter.
>
> Yours sincerely,
Mark Sykes[38]

Sokolow willingly accepted Sykes's advice and had time to prepare himself mentally for the course, similar to Sykes's, that he would follow in Vatican City. A series of letters to Weizmann in Russian sent by Sokolow from Rome—all of which have not yet been published—reveal details about Sokolow's thoughts both before and after his talks in the Vatican. He used a kind of code, as if he were writing about commercial matters, but it is easy to decipher:

> He [the British Ambassador] had your *baal habayit*'s [landlord's, that is, Sykes's] letter and handed it to me personally. The landlord met with the local rebbe's chief *gabbai* [head of synagogue, that is, Pacelli], and with the *rebbe* himself [the pope]. He did a fine job recommending our firm, and tried to remove certain well-known prejudices. He [Sykes] is pleased with the outcome, and insists that I meet them. That's no easy matter. It will take lots of time and running around, but he is sure of success. I am, of course, working on it, and will give you a full report.[39]

Sokolow was received by Monsignor Pacelli at the Secretariat of State on April 29, 1917, and afterward wrote to Weizmann: "Today I was received by the *gabbai* who takes care of foreign affairs [Pacelli]." Pacelli heard Sokolow's explanations of the goals of Zionism and commented:

> That is not enough. Borders must be determined, what the Holy Places are must be defined, for on this there are differences of view: some hold that they mean all the country, others—that they are only a few isolated sites. We must know in advance what you demand, in order to avoid conflicts and competition between us.

Sokolow remarked that despite Pacelli's extraordinary courtesy, the meeting was somewhat strenuous for him.[40]

Sokolow seems to have been unprepared for the Vatican's demands, despite his preliminary talks with the British representative to the Holy See, who undoubtedly told him what to expect. It also emerges from Sokolow's detailed letter that although Pacelli wanted to hear precise facts about the Zionist movement from its representative, Sokolow tried to refer him to published pamphlets on the subject. Nor did Sokolow bring a new formula for the Holy Places but merely repeated what Herzl had said some years earlier in the same place—that the Zionists wanted only the secular lands.

But the misunderstanding was profound, for despite the hints Sokolow had received about the contents of the Sykes–Picot agreement while still in London—before setting out on this journey—he seems not to have understood Pacelli's remarks about the definition of the Holy Places. Pacelli wanted clear geographical bounds acceptable to the Vatican to be demarcated, whereas Sokolow seems not to have grasped that the Vatican's demands went far beyond a few buildings or sites scattered around the country. Indeed, Pacelli told Sokolow expressly: "In addition to the existing property, there is also a peripheral area which we shall require."[41]

Two days later, on May 1, 1917, Sokolow was received by the secretary of state, Cardinal Gasparri. Regarding this talk, too, we have only one source—the letter Sokolow sent to Weizmann immediately after the interview. A number of topics came up in this conversation, which was held privately: the situation of the Jews in general and why they needed Palestine, the situation of the Jews in Russia, political arrangements for Palestine, the Holy Places and the Church's stand regarding them, and the Church's attitude toward Zionist aspirations.

> Gasparri at first tried to convince Sokolow: Those who attribute medieval tendencies to the Church in its attitude to the Jews are mistaken. The Church only condemns anti-Catholic instigation and if it is done by Jews this evokes indignation. But as long as Judaism tends to its own affairs, it can rest assured that it will be fully respected. And if some clerical group or another in various countries comes out with anti-Jewish tendencies, the Church denounces it and if there are complaints they can always be referred to the Church center.

The previous secretary of state, Merry del Val, had also mentioned anti-Catholic incitement on the part of Jews, perhaps because the Church was still waging a battle against the Freemasons, who were often fought jointly with the Jews.

The conversation then moved on to the situation of the Jews in Russia. Gasparri expressed shock and sympathy but added that Catholic believers also were perse-cuted there. It seems to me that then, as today, the Church tended to deny the unique character of Jewish persecutions. Sokolow rightly replied that the situation of the two groups was not comparable, for the Catholics had a "powerful center which protected them," whereas no one helped the Jews and they had no center. The cardinal thought this was a reproach and excused himself, said that the Vatican was unable to protect the Jews, and asked: "If the other countries were not able to help you, how can we?"

Sokolow remarked that the Church's word had tremendous influence in the Catholic world and expressed his appreciation of the papal bull that had been pub-lished at the time of the Beilis trial.[42]

Gasparri replied: "We are glad it made a good impression. We could not but intervene. In fact, at a certain stage we received a report on the persecutions from the Jews of the United States and extended our sympathies. Not only do we not condone these persecutions, we condemn them in the sharpest terms." (It should be noted that in March 1916, in reply to the American Jewish Committee in New York, which had asked Gasparri to intervene to help ease the suffering of the Jews of Eastern Europe, he expressed his sympathy and said that "the Jews have the right to exist.")[43]

The conversation then moved to the subject of Palestine. Sokolow expounded on the British interest as the chief factor and also spoke of the French interest. Gasparri asked about the Russian position, and Sokolow answered that Russia had no interest in Palestine and that the new regime in Russia was likely to demand guarantees only for its religious interests. That, Gasparri replied, was only natural, but Sokolow's impression was that he was not convinced and remained quite skep-tical. He asked about Italy's position, and Sokolow stated that it did not have im-portant interests in Palestine. Gasparri thought otherwise: "Here you are mistaken. They do have, no less than France. They have schools, institutions, and the like."

Sokolow, who seems to have been wholly unaware of the Italian claims, re-torted: "These may be religious interests, but this is a question I shall not enter. It is a realm that does not concern us; our settlement is outside that realm. I believe Britain and France take a much greater interest in this subject, especially the for-mer." The cardinal also believed that this was above all a matter for the British, and Sokolow even received the impression that Gasparri tended to favor the British.

"The moment he mentioned the [holy] places," wrote Sokolow, "I repeated our statement concerning the inviolability of the holy places, and spoke of our loy-alty. . . ." Then Sokolow stated: "We do not deal with this question. We are sure you have a fine plan that includes involvement of one or two countries who will take care of this as should be. I surmise your center will play an important role in this matter."

Gasparri replied: "We still have no plan and I do not know how this will be settled. We will have to manage somehow. The center will of course be in Jerusa-lem, branching from there to Bethlehem and Jericho, and we have demands regard-ing Tiberias, Nazareth, and possibly also Tabor-Nazareth."

At this point, Sokolow felt a chill in his bones. Perhaps for the first time in his life, he began to grasp the scope of the Vatican's territorial demands and expressed the hope that historical memories referred only to certain places. The conversation continued as follows:

> GASPARRI: That is a question now being discussed.
> SOKOLOW: I hope the discussion is accompanied by sympathy for our cause.

Here Gasparri became extremely courteous: "Naturally we are sympathetic to it. It is absolutely just. You must do this and we will be extremely glad if you succeed in establishing the Kingdom of Israel."

> SOKOLOW: We do not intend to establish a kingdom, just an autonomous home.
> GASPARRI: Don't worry. I used the term only as a figure of speech. Call it what you will. I assure you that from Church you will have no opposition. On the contrary, you may count on our sympathy. We shall be glad to see the land of Israel. . . . You will certainly need priority in acquiring lands and for the immigrants. . . . I wish you full success.

Finally, Gasparri told Sokolow he must see the pope and again wished him success.[44]

This translation, based on the Russian original, differs slightly from Leonard Stein's, which conveys the general spirit of the talk. Notably, I found no mention in Gasparri's remarks of a "reserved area" for the Vatican, as Stein mentioned, nor did Gasparri make his wishes for the Zionists' success conditional on the satisfaction of the Church's demands. But these are perhaps details of secondary importance. Sokolow could have concluded from this conversation that the problem of the Holy Places and the Vatican's demands were serious matters. Sokolow also could have concluded that the cardinal expressed sympathy for Zionism. This sympathy, if in fact it was expressed in those terms, was short-lived, lasting only until the Balfour Declaration. The cardinal may have envisaged Zionism as a movement trying to solve the problem of the pogroms by establishing a few agricultural villages outside the area that interested him. Nevertheless, this goodwill is surprising and does not show up in the talks Gasparri held at the time with foreign diplomats. The cardinal's sympathy for Britain, which Sokolow believed he favored more than France, was also somewhat new. Gasparri may have been thinking of a power that would provide protection.

As mentioned earlier, several days before, in a talk with Sykes, Pacelli had hinted that the Vatican did not oppose the idea of a British protectorate of the Holy Places and did not consider France the ideal choice for that role.[45] The Vatican archives relating to this period do not contain any documents on these conversations, and as a result we are forced to rely solely on Sokolow's account of his talks at the Vatican. These reports are necessarily subjective and more than once contradict the policy adopted by the Holy See. It is not unlikely that on occasion Sokolow heard what he wanted to hear.

Gasparri did not conceal the Vatican's territorial ambitions for the central region of Palestine, an area that was slated by the Sykes–Picot agreement to be international and that included the Holy Places. Gasparri expressed a similar idea several months later to the Belgian representative at the Vatican.[46] The cardinal's sympathy for the Jews was essentially humanitarian and was directed to the Jews of Russia; in fact, the Church had condemned the persecution of Jews in Russia.

Sokolow's Meeting with Benedict XV

On May 4, 1917,[47] Sokolow was received by Pope Benedict XV, the conversation between them lasting three-quarters of an hour, longer than the usual papal audience. We have two different reports of this important talk, one in French and the other in Italian, both by Sokolow. I prefer to rely on the French-language account, both because the conversation was probably held in that language and because this report was written in Sokolow's own hand right after the interview. The other account, which for some reason is better known, was typewritten in Italian several days after the audience.

What follows is the content of the conversation as recorded by Sokolow himself:

HIS HOLINESS: I am sure you did not come only as a matter of ceremony but as a representative of the Zionist idea. That has great significance. It refers to the rebuilding of Judea by the Jewish people—is that not so? What a historical turnabout. Nineteen hundred years ago Rome destroyed your country, and now, wanting to rebuild it, you come to Rome.

SOKOLOW: I am deeply moved by these historical memories, which are so apt. Allow me the liberty to add that the Rome that destroyed Judea was duly punished. It vanished, whereas not only do the Jewish people live on, they still have sufficient vitality to reclaim their land.

HIS HOLINESS: Yes, yes, it is providential; God has willed it.

SOKOLOW: The new Rome and all those who will help us rebuild Palestine shall not be destroyed but shall be strengthened. I dare hope that H[is] H[oliness] in his wisdom will accept this idea. That is why I have come. Loyal to the states, with a perfect solidarity with the people among whom they live, they [Jews] are everywhere and therefore should everywhere be treated with the same justice that is allowed to any other man or citizen. For us it is a question of the survival of historical Jewry, concentrated within itself, and existing by virtue of its spirituality and the forces of its land that embody the genius of our race, biblical traditions in their purity and to which one could not question their liberty and independent character. It matters not whether this Jewry is large in number or small; this shall be a Jewry dwelling in its home, working, acting for its project, developing all its traits, and granting refuge to those of its sons who will be in need of it, and in any case inspiring all of Jewry by the example of its idealism.

HIS HOLINESS: That is a fine idea. Great Britain is the greatest and most experienced colonizing power in the world. That is a good school for settlement. . . . But the problem of the [H]oly P[laces] is for us of utmost importance. The sacred rights must be preserved. We shall arrange this between the Church and the Great Powers. You must honor these rights to their full extent. . . . These are rights hundreds of years old, guaranteed and preserved by all the governments. With a new order in the country—if the situation so dictates—all these problems will be discussed and will have to be resolved with utmost consideration for [Catholic] religious feeling. As a man of high culture, which I believe you are, you are well aware of this great problem, are you not?

> SOKOLOW: Yes, H[is] H[oliness]. Our people are sage and cautious; they will not be
> sacrilegious or blaspheme the religions of their neighbors. I can assure H[is]
> H[oliness] in good conscience that we shall not touch the H[oly] P[laces] and shall
> respect with the greatest consideration the arrangement that will be reached on this
> matter. We ask that His Holiness give us his moral support.

The pope concluded by saying: "Yes, yes, I think we shall be good neighbors."
He repeated the sentence several times.[48]

The Italian version, translated and published by Sokolow's son Florian, differs
slightly. First, in the Italian report, dictated six days after the audience, Sokolow
seems to have added details that were absent from the first report and to have
touched up his own remarks, giving them a more distinctly Zionist flavor. Thus
only in the second report does Sokolow mention his demand to build a national
home for the Jews in Palestine and his insistence on the right of the Jews to "a
place of their own under the sun." The impression from the first report and from
the letters on his talks with Pacelli and Gasparri is that Sokolow was more apologetic in tone, or at least tried to avoid sharp polemics with the Church. But this is
not the case in the second report, in which, for example, Sokolow stated:

> Above all, we mean the creation of the possibility that the Jewish people may attain
> its historic homeland. Mighty is our desire to harness all our strength to establish a
> home of our own for those of the Jewish people who will seek refuge and to inspire
> by the power of our idea the entire Jewish Diaspora.

According to this second report, the pope asked about the number of Jews in
Palestine, what the Jewish Holy Places were, and whether large numbers of Jews
would settle in Palestine.[49]

After the audience, Sokolow cabled Weizmann:

> The pope granted me a special audience, lasting forty-five minutes. The pope lis-
> tened to me attentively and remarked that although he had received a report from
> Cardinal Gasparri, he welcomed the opportunity to hear further details. The pope
> spoke very sympathetically of the Jews' effort to establish a national home in Pal-
> estine. As for his religious interests, which refer only to the Holy Places, he sees no
> objection whatever and is quite sure that these places will be guaranteed under a
> special arrangement. I declared that we, the Jews, will be most scrupulous in our
> respect for Christian religious property and feelings. He answered that he accepts
> the declaration on trust and wishes the fulfillment of our plan. His declaration cul-
> minated with him saying repeatedly: "We shall be good neighbors." He also spoke
> most sympathetically of Great Britain's intentions. That I was honored with a long
> audience and the spirit of the talk itself indicate a most positive approach.[50]

The first draft of Sokolow's telegram makes no mention of a national home, but
only of the Jews' efforts to settle in Palestine, to which the pope was sympathetic.[51]
The talk with Benedict XV was uncustomarily cordial and lasted longer than was
usual, evidence of the pope's recognition that even though Zionism was still in its
infancy, it would become an important factor in the region.

Stein cited several reasons for Sokolow's positive reception at the Vatican: (1)
the Vatican's wish to demonstrate goodwill toward Great Britain, whose view it
already knew would carry weight and might be decisive for the future of Palestine;

(2) its assumption that the Jews could have a common interest with the Roman Catholics in undermining the position of the Orthodox Church in Eastern Europe and Palestine; (3) its hope that the Jews would work for Vatican participation in the future peace conference (from which it was excluded by Article 15 of the Treaty of London, on Italy's insistence) and for the acceptance of a Vatican special mission in both Britain and Russia, for which in return the pope promised to publish an encyclical against the persecution of Jews in Russia; and (4) its wish to enlist world Jewry on behalf of Poland's independence.[52]

Stein's assumption about possible Jewish activity for Vatican participation in the peace conference receives some support from a rather strange report from the United States vice-consul in Geneva. He claimed that there was a secret understanding with the Vatican: "In return for the Catholic adhesion to the Jewish program in Palestine, the Jews were to use all their financial and political influence to have the Vatican represented in the forthcoming Peace Conference."[53] But such an agreement was hardly possible, for the Zionists were in no position to promise action on an international issue of such importance. Nonetheless, Deloncle's mission to England, as we mentioned, was also related to the future peace conference.

Another of Stein's suppositions, concerning Polish independence, is not compatible with Charles Loiseau's comment that in November 1916 Gasparri was very skeptical about the possibility of reestablishing an independent Poland.[54]

As I see it, the pope's short-lived sympathy for Zionism had three sources: the utopian aura that still clung to Zionism, humanitarian feelings toward the Russian Jews during the war, and knowledge of the Sykes–Picot agreement. Friedman believes that the pope and Gasparri intended their remarks as a broad hint to Sokolow and on a political level, there was some common ground between the Catholic Church and the Jews.[55] I disagree. On that level, the Vatican was interested in dealing only with the Great Powers; the Zionists had to remain outside the central region, which included the Holy Places, and not interfere in the rights of the Catholics there.

The pope, though, was ready to respond to the humanitarian aspect of the Jewish problem, in both czarist Russia and Palestine. By mentioning the pope's sympathetic reply to the petition about the Russian Jews, Gasparri wanted to emphasize that in regard to humanitarian issues, common ground could be found. The Church was prepared to defend the Jews where that was necessary, but it was not prepared to see them assuming equal status in the Holy Land. Friedman was certainly correct in stating that the Vatican had territorial ambitions in Palestine, but to achieve them it did not need the Zionists and was not especially anxious to secure their goodwill.

The sentence repeated several times by the pope, "We shall be good neighbors," should also be understood in light of the Sykes–Picot agreement, the substance of which was known to the Vatican. "Neighbors," the pope said, knowing that the Vatican would have a presence in the central region, which was to be internationalized, whereas the Zionists would remain in regions bordering it but outside it. Friedman shares this view and writes: "The Pope's assurances of good neighborliness to Sokolow must therefore be read not in the spiritual but in the geographical context."[56]

It is hard to fathom why this sentence uttered by the pope caused such enthusiasm in Zionist circles, an enthusiasm that four years later still echoed in a political report to the Zionist Conference in London:

> Mr. Sokolow spoke in Rome with several Cardinals, including Cardinal Gasparri, the Papal Secretary of State. He was finally received in private audience by the Pope who after receiving satisfactory assurances about the Jewish attitude towards the Holy Places, expressed himself in favor of Zionism and closed the interview by saying that Jews and Catholics would be good neighbors in Palestine.[57]

Humanitarian feelings were, as we said, a second component in the overall sympathy for Zionist aspirations. We find such sentiments expressed by both Benedict XV and Gasparri, as Sokolow reported. They both referred to the suffering of the Russian Jews and to the Church's activity to alleviate it.[58]

At the same time, because it had accurate information,[59] the Vatican properly assessed the special status that Britain would have in Palestine. Nonetheless, despite the cordial reception it accorded Sokolow, the Vatican clearly stated its position on the Holy Places, while excluding the issue from discourse with the Zionists; that was a problem the Church intended to discuss directly with the Great Powers. The Jews did not have to be a party to a possible agreement on the Holy Places; they merely had to honor it.

Weizmann was severely annoyed by Sokolow's having taken upon himself this diplomatic mission. He was very much afraid that policy makers in Washington and Moscow might think that Sokolow considered it possible to advocate a French protectorate or Anglo-French control for Palestine. As far as Weizmann was concerned, Sokolow had simply to inform the French and the Italians about Zionism, but under no circumstances was he to embark upon negotiations about the fate of Palestine.[60]

Weizmann thus took issue with Sokolow concerning the Vatican's stand and, in a letter to him on May 1, 1917, wrote:

> I am not at all hopeful that you will really find genuine support in the Vatican circles. The Vatican press at various times has expressed itself in favor of internationalization of Palestine and naturally it would be unreasonable to expect another attitude from the Vatican. Whether it expressed platonic sympathy with the Zionist demands or not is quite indifferent to us, and I would certainly not waste time and energy on that score.[61]

On May 3, Weizmann received a letter from Felix Pinkus, one of the leaders of the Zionist Federation in Switzerland, who spoke of a great danger looming on the horizon. The Vatican, he said, was organizing all the Catholics in the world against a Jewish Palestine under British protection. A meeting on the subject was recently held in Chur, Switzerland, attended by the bishop of Chur, high-ranking Italians and Austrians, Reichstag member Matias Erzberger, and the Jesuit general. It was decided at that meeting to organize the Catholics in all countries, and especially in the United States, to bring about the internationalization of Palestine under the protection of the pope and to oppose British protection for Palestine by all means.[62]

Chur was the residence of the head of the Jesuit order, then considered a great enemy of Zionism.[63] Henry Wickham Stead, foreign editor of *The Times,* had told Weizmann that the Zionists had three great enemies: the Jewish plutocracy, the

Bund, and the Jesuits. "The Pope may support you," he said, "but the Jesuits never will."[64]

At about the same time, a Swiss newspaper, *Journal de Genève,* published an article on the Vatican and Palestine that observed:

> The matter preoccupying Vatican policy at present is that the Zionist dream should not be realized, and that instead of becoming a Jewish kingdom, Palestine, will remain a permanent possession of the Christian powers. . . . It already seems almost certain that the Holy Land will be proclaimed international.[65]

The article caught the attention of Felix Pinkus, who sent it to Weizmann with his own comments. He wrote that he had reason to believe that the Vatican would do its utmost to bring about the internationalization of Palestine. Weizmann showed the letter to Sir Ronald Graham of the Foreign Office in London, who was infuriated by it.[66]

Weizmann was right in believing that the Vatican's objective was the internationalization of Palestine, and it appears that Sokolow chose not to raise this controversial subject at all. Weizmann himself, however, as we shall see, hurried to establish contact with the Vatican in 1922, when the approval of the mandate was at stake, and even tried, though unsuccessfully, to obtain an audience with the pope. In reply to Weizmann, Sokolow said that he had to go to Rome because the French government advised it and so did Sykes and that he was sure his talks at the Vatican "had been useful to ascertain that no insurmountable opposition was to be expected from that quarter."[67]

On May 6, 1917, a few days before he left Rome, Sokolow received a telegram from Weizmann with details about the expulsion of Jews from Jaffa and Jerusalem at the end of March.[68] When he received another cable through the British representative,[69] Sokolow asked de Salis to bring its content to the attention of the Vatican. De Salis agreed to do so and discussed the matter with Gasparri. Several days later, Gasparri replied in a note to the British legation to the Holy See that the ambassadors of Germany, Austria, Spain, and Holland were convinced, on the basis of reports they had received from their consuls there, that the persecution, murders, and looting of Jewish homes supposedly committed by the Turks had never taken place. The Turkish foreign minister himself reported that there had been no persecution and that the expulsions were carried out only in Jaffa, and those for military reasons.

De Salis did not let Gasparri's note go unanswered, because it sought to refute charges that had never been raised. Weizmann's telegram spoke clearly of the expulsion of eight thousand Jews from Jaffa and three hundred from Jerusalem but made no mention of murder. It should be noted that we have no facts to support the claim made by Sokolow's son, that the Vatican's intervention "saved Tel Aviv from destruction."[70]

From the talks he held in the Foreign Ministries in Italy and France, Sokolow could have discerned that the problem of the Holy Places interested the Italians and French greatly and that they were well aware of the Vatican's attitude toward Zionism. Thus, for example, the secretary general of the Italian Foreign Ministry, Giacomo De Martino, expressed joy when Sokolow told him that the pope had consented to the Zionist solution.[71] The Italians' apprehension about exacerbating their relations with the Vatican (after they succeeded in excluding the Vatican from the future peace conference) was so great that Foreign Minister Sidney Sonnino preferred not to receive Sokolow at all, so as not to upset the Vatican.[72] Moreover, Italy needed the Vatican to end the French religious protectorate, and just several days earlier, at the Saint-Jean-de-Maurienne conference, Sonnino had presented Italy's view of the problem of the Holy Places. Italy's Prime Minister Paolo Boselli, told Sokolow that the Holy Places would be under an international regime.[73]

It is somewhat surprising that at no time during World War I did the Zionist leaders take any account of what Pope Pius X had said to Herzl. Although Herzl's diaries, on which we relied in recounting his meeting with the pope, were first published in 1922,[74] it is safe to assume that the substance of the conversation was known to his intimates, including Joseph Cowen. Cowen himself kept various documents that belonged to Herzl in a safe-deposit box in the Anglo-Palestine Bank in London. He continued his Zionist activity after Herzl's death, was chairman of the Zionist Federation in Britain in 1909, and joined the Zionist Executive in 1921.[75]

9

Growing Opposition
to Zionism

The Conquest of Jerusalem and the Balfour Declaration

The situation was radically changed at the end of 1917 by the Balfour Declaration and the British conquest of Jerusalem. As stated earlier, Cardinal Gasparri gave the British representative at the Vatican the impression that the British government's explanations were satisfactory. He adopted another tone, however, with the French semiofficial representative, Charles Loiseau. The day after the British conquest of Jerusalem, Gasparri told Loiseau that the Turks had been the most faithful custodians of the Holy Places and that their departure was liable to be a source of problems. The Zionists, to whom Balfour had presented Palestine as a gift, were likely to cause new strife.[1] On that occasion the cardinal also observed: "The bells of the Vatican do not chime over the conquest of Jerusalem. It is difficult to take back a part of our heart that we have given to the Turks, in order to hand it over to the Zionists."[2]

Isaiah Friedman wrote that on December 13, 1917, the *Osservatore Romano* ascribed to Gasparri a statement in favor of the British occupation of the Holy Land. Friedman added that the "Papal Curia was also in sympathy with the creation of a legally based homeland for the Jews."[3] But a check of the *Osservatore Romano* on that date reveals no such statement. The newspaper did, however, publish a statement by the cardinal vicar of Rome, Basilio Pompili. He announced to the people of Rome the liberation of Jerusalem and expressed his joy that the Church of the Holy Sepulchre was once again in Christian hands. "Let your prayer express thanksgiving to the Lord, for now the Christians in the whole world will again be able to feel at home in the Holy Places."[4] This statement may have reached the German government in distorted form. Friedman noted that Chancellor Georg von Hertling told Eugenio Pacelli, nuncio in Munich since May 1917, that the Vatican appeared sympathetic to the Entente and that Germany could not accept this.

On December 14, the *Jewish Chronicle,* quoting the Central News Agency, wrote that the proposal to reestablish a Jewish state in Palestine had sparked con-

Arthur James Balfour (later First Earl Balfour), British foreign secretary (December 1916–
October 1919).

siderable debate in Vatican circles.[5] The pope had had a number of talks on the subject with cardinals and bishops and would soon publish a statement setting forth his views on the plan. The *Jewish Chronicle* article also quoted *The Times,* which wrote: "The Sultan will reign over the Holy Places no more; the scattered Jews will have a prospect of returning as a free people to their national home . . . if the tyranny of the Turks is doomed."[6] But the pope refrained from issuing an immediate reaction to the Balfour Declaration, for the situation was exceedingly complex and delicate, and he avoided taking a public stand before examining all aspects of the issue.

The Balfour Declaration certainly aroused great concern in the Vatican, which returned to its traditional position of coldness toward Zionism. The Vatican apparently assumed that the Jewish "home" would not include Jerusalem and the other Holy Places, though there was nothing in the latest developments to support such an assumption. On December 15, the clerical daily published in Rome, *Il Tempo,* noted that the news about the Zionist movement, which until then had been regarded with indifference by Christians and Vatican authorities, had in the meantime become a cause of serious concern. The paper added:

The undefined formula of "home" referred so far only to the southern portion of Palestine, which is also the most fertile part. Jerusalem and the Holy Places thus were not included, which explains the equanimity with which the Catholics and the Vatican followed the new projects. But now news has arrived of an enlargement of the movement being planned by pro-Zionist circles in Italy and France. The undefined British "home" is to become a political and independent state. The southern portion of Palestine is expanding northward so as to include Jerusalem and the Christian Sanctuaries.[7]

The article concluded by suggesting that the plan for a Jewish state, with Jerusalem as its capital, was supported by the Freemasons in France and Italy. It should be recalled that at the time the Catholic Church was waging a struggle against the Freemasons and had often expressed the fear that a worldwide conspiracy against the Church was being plotted jointly by Jews and Freemasons, with the aim of fighting Christianity and conquering the world. These fears had served as a pretext for an anti-Semitic crusade in the Catholic press at the end of the nineteenth century.[8]

The Vatican's understanding of the division of Palestine into districts was probably based on the information it had about the Sykes–Picot agreements. At the end of 1917 and in early 1918, this understanding engendered a number of moves and was reflected in the series of talks between the Belgian minister at the Holy See, Jules Van Den Heuvel, and Gasparri. Also evident in these talks was Gasparri's anti-Zionist approach. On December 18, 1917, he told Van Den Heuvel:

> Rumor has it that wealthy Jewish financiers have a plan to set up an autonomous Jewish state. I do not know if this group of moneyed people is strong or has support, but the transformation of Palestine into a Jewish state would not only endanger the Holy Places and damage the feelings of all Christians, it would also be very harmful for the country itself.[9]

On December 26, Pacelli, then the nuncio in Munich, sought to lessen the importance of the statement attributed in the *Osservatore Romano* to Gasparri. He wrote to the chancellor of Germany that the remark had in fact been made by Cardinal Pompili. But the matter came to the attention of the kaiser himself, who commented on an article in another paper:

> To the joy of the Pope, who is Christ's representative on earth, Jerusalem is taken away from the Mohammedans by heathen Indians, in order to hand it over to the Jews who crucified Christ! And about this Benedict XV is enthusiastic! In such an incomprehensible muddle I shall take no part.[10]

The kaiser's comment was typical of an attitude that apparently was widespread in that period. Thus, for example, United States Secretary of State Robert Lansing wrote to President Woodrow Wilson on December 13 suggesting that formal consent to the Balfour Declaration be postponed. He offered the following reasons:

> First, we are not at war with Turkey, and therefore should avoid any appearance of favoring taking territory from that Empire by force. Second, the Jews are by no means a unit in the desire to reestablish their race as an independent people. . . . Third, many Christian sects and individuals would undoubtedly resent turning the Holy Land over to the absolute control of the race credited with the death of Christ.[11]

And in the British government at that time, George Curzon, then a member of the inner war cabinet, maintained that "under no circumstances could the Jews be allowed control over Jerusalem with its Holy Places."[12] It is hardly surprising, then, that the pope expressed his fear to the British representative that Great Britain "might agree to forgo direct control over affairs [in Palestine], and hand it over to the Jews to the detriment of the Christian interests."[13]

The pope's main concern in December 1917 was the fear that the Jews might succeed in establishing autonomous rule in Palestine that would not be subject to effective British supervision. From this time on, the Vatican policy toward Zionism was once again hostile, as it had been in the days of Pope Pius X. To understand the sudden switch in the Vatican's position, we shall take another look at Sokolow's talks with Pacelli and Gasparri a few months earlier, at which time the Zionists were told they must remain outside the area that included the Holy Places.

In France, the Catholic newspaper *La Croix* wrote that the pope could not be excluded from the negotiations on Palestine. France, the paper said, could agree to the Jews' building a homeland for themselves in Palestine but could never tolerate Jewish rule over the Holy Places. Monsignor Henri-Marie-Alfred Baudrillart, who was close to Gasparri and subsequently became a cardinal, agreed that the Jews could go to the Holy Land but vigorously opposed granting them privileges greater than those of the Muslims.[14]

In June 1918, the Italian government sent Captain Guido Meli Lupi di Soragna to Jerusalem, to represent Italian interests in the transitional period during which it was still not possible to reopen the consulate general in Jerusalem. The newspaper *Il Resto del Carlino* noted on that occasion that the representation would be especially desirable for the Vatican because of its anti-Zionist character.[15]

The Zionist Position on the Holy Places

As we have seen, Herzl had proposed extraterritoriality for the Holy Places back in 1895. In 1917, Sokolow declared that the Jews would not interfere with the Holy Places. The Zionist leaders were thus aware from the very beginning of the great sensitivity of this issue but naively hoped the problem could be resolved by mere declarations of "noninterference." A short time after Sokolow's audience with the pope, the British Zionist Federation held its annual conference in London, and on May 20, 1917, Weizmann proclaimed:

> One of the most important problems to be considered in connection with the future settlement of Palestine is the delicate question of the Holy Places. It is not for us to discuss how this complicated question, which forms an important point in international relations, is to be settled. We trust in the fairness and justice of the nations who are going to build up a better world after this catastrophe, that they will see to it that the arrangements made are fair and satisfactory to everyone.[16]

A few months later, at the end of 1917, Sokolow spoke on the religious question in a speech delivered in Manchester. He recalled his talk with the pope and stated:

> We don't like mere toleration by non-Jews and we don't want them to be tolerated. We know that Palestine is full of sanctuaries and Holy Places, holy to the Christian

world, holy to Islam, holy to ourselves. Are we blind not to see that there are these places of worship and of veneration? Palestine is the very place where religious conflicts should disappear. There we should meet as brothers, and there we should learn to love others, not merely to tolerate each other. I declared this to the representatives of the great Churches, and I can repeat it here.[17]

In Jerusalem itself, Weizmann, who had arrived there with the Zionist Commission, made another statement on April 27, 1918:

The city of Jerusalem was for Jews a holy shrine. For that reason, if for that alone, the Jews were able to respect the sentiment of others for whom Jerusalem was sacred. They wished to interfere in no way with the Holy Places to which the hearts of Moslems and Christians turned with reverence.[18]

The pope had earlier told Sokolow that the question of the Holy Places had to be resolved by the Vatican with the Great Powers, and not in negotiations with the Zionists. The Zionist leaders themselves consequently had no intention whatsoever of interfering in the Holy Places or of trying to resolve this complex problem, which "is not for us to discuss." Ostensibly, then, there was no conflict between the two positions, but in fact the pope and the Zionist leaders differed greatly on the concept of the Holy Places. When they spoke of them, the Zionists meant the church buildings and places of worship of each of the Churches. The pope and the papal secretary of state, however, used the vague term "Holy Place" to refer to a considerable part of the territory of Palestine. The Zionists viewed this as solely a religious problem, whereas the pope had in mind political aspects as well. This was perhaps the root of the misunderstanding, which deepened with time, between the Vatican and Zionism.

Toward the Peace Conference

World War I had ended. At the same time, the Vatican's opposition to Zionism had intensified, as Sykes felt markedly during his visit to Rome in December 1918. Gasparri's hostility toward Zionism was pronounced, although his deputy, Monsignor Bonaventura Cerretti, was found by Sykes to hold a more sympathetic position and was even able to understand that "the aims of Zionism are pure, natural, inevitable and anti-materialist."[19]

The Peace Conference opened in Versailles in January 1919. The tension at the Vatican rose, both because it had been excluded from participation in the conference and because the news arriving from the Holy Land increased the fears of a Zionist takeover there. When Sykes arrived at the Paris Peace Conference in the beginning of 1919, after returning from a visit to Palestine, he said that he was convinced that an estrangement between the Zionists and the Catholic Church would mean that "two moral forces, pivoted on the same center, instead of radiating outwards will consume their strength inwardly."[20]

At the beginning of December 1918, Soragna cabled from Jerusalem that the declarations by James Cardinal Gibbons in the United States, to the effect that the pope supported the rights of the Jews in Palestine, had made a bad impression on the local Christians. He also expressed the wish of Barlassina, the Latin patriarch, that the Vatican be mindful of the interpretation the Zionists were offering, according to which the pope supported "political rule by their nation" over all of Palestine.[21]

Cardinal Gibbons, who had always been sympathetic to the Jews, had in fact responded to an appeal by the Zionist Organization in the United States as follows: "It is with pleasure that I learn of the approval accorded by His Holiness, Benedict XV, to the plan providing a homeland in Palestine to the members of the Jewish race."[22] As formulated, his reply was somewhat qualified in that it was conditioned by the pope's position, which in fact differed from what the Zionist Federation had claimed it was and probably was based on Sokolow's talks.

Gasparri did not conceal his anti-Zionist views. In December 1918, he told the Belgian representative:

> There is talk of a Jewish State. I do not believe that the big Jewish bankers of England and of the United States will be so unaware of the opinions of many of their faith as to support this plan. Do we not see the Jews at the head of the revolutionary movements in Russia and in Poland?[23]

Not long after that, in January 1919, Gasparri repeated his worries about the Jews in Palestine to the new Belgian representative:

> Britain has apparently assumed an obligation towards the Jews, to whom they will hand over part of the administration of Palestine. Influenced by the big Jewish bankers of England and the United States, the British politicians do not sufficiently take into account the deep difference which exists between them and the Jewish people. It seems the British politicians fail to appreciate the dangers of this solution for Christian interests in the Holy Land.

Gasparri's concern was shared by the pope, but the Belgian representative also conveyed the view of official British circles, which held that they had no intention at all of handing over the administration of Palestine to the Jews, because of Germany's influence on the Jewish masses.[24] In that period, some British still feared that Germany retained a great influence among the Jews that could be damaging to British interests.

Cardinal Bourne and the Pope

We have already spoken of the visit to Palestine by Francis Cardinal Bourne between December 1918 and March 1919. There is no doubt that the reports he sent greatly worried the pope. Bourne, the archbishop of Westminster, had set out on his journey fully aware that the pope was anxious about Palestine's future. According to Bourne's biographer, the Holy See had fears about Zionism, and while in the Balkans, Bourne received a message to the effect that Lloyd George, then prime minister, "did not go as far as Mr. Balfour on Zionism."[25] At the end of January 1919, he sent a letter to the British prime minister and the foreign secretary, in which he wrote:

The Zionists here claim that the Jews are to have the domination of the Holy Land under a British protectorate; in other words, they are going to force their rule on an unwilling people of whom they form only 10%. They are already asserting themselves in every way, claiming official posts for their nominees, and generally interfering. This has resulted already in a great lessening of the welcome, which, at the outset, was given wholeheartedly to the British. . . . The Zionists too claimed that they had obtained the approval of the Holy City [See]. . . . There is no foundation for this claim. The whole movement appears to be quite contrary to Christian sentiment and tradition. Let Jews live here by all means, if they like, and enjoy the same liberties as other people; but that they should ever again dominate and rule the country would be an outrage to Christianity and its Divine founder. It would mean, moreover, most certainly, the controlling influence of Jewish, which is German finance. Is this really what England desires after recent experiences?[26]

Balfour replied to the prime minister: "I suspect that the motive of most of them [Catholics] is not so much anxiety for the Holy Places as hatred of the Jews."[27]

Some years later, Cardinal Bourne recalled his visit to Palestine:

When I visited it [the Holy Land] in 1919, the situation was distinctly menacing. There was a tendency on the part of certain immigrant Jews to claim and assert a domination in no way in harmony with the Balfour Declaration. This naturally aroused a fierce resistance on the part of the indigenous native Arab population, both Moslem and Christian.[28]

Convinced that the Balfour Declaration had complicated the problem of Palestine, the cardinal felt obliged to act:

Men of every class come to me with a loud and emphatic protest against Mr. Balfour's promises and against the projects of the Zionists. . . . These projects went far beyond the mere establishment of a home for nationless Jews. . . . Able to borrow money at 3% while Christians or Moslems pay 10% and more, Zionists were acquiring Palestine's not very extensive land at alarming speed. Through their new University they hoped that Jews would soon fill every lucrative and influential position in the country.[29]

In his letters and declarations, the cardinal expressed all the familiar Catholic objections to a Jewish state in Palestine. He claimed he was speaking in the name of the entire non-Jewish population, Muslim and Christian alike, a claim also made from time to time by Barlassina. Bourne also feared that the Jews would try to occupy all the important official posts, a fear later repeated by the pope himself. Interesting in this context is the attack on the Hebrew University, which may explain, at least in part, the hostility toward the university later evinced by Gasparri. Bourne appears in this way to have prepared the ground for the pope's address in 1919, in which some of the same arguments against the privileged position of the Jews in Palestine were restated. If this in fact was so, it would seem that the pope was greatly influenced by the reports sent from the Holy Land by Custos Federico Diotallevi and Latin Patriarch Luigi Barlassina.

Father Federico Diotallevi, custos of Terra Sancta in Jerusalem since 1918.

The Muslim–Christian Associations

Cardinal Bourne was probably influenced by the growing opposition to Zionist aspirations of the Arab population, both Muslim and Christian. By November 1918,
Muslim–Christian associations, in which Christians were disproportionately represented, had already been founded in a number of cities, with the aim of opposing
Zionism.[30] These associations seem to have been formed by anti-Zionist officers in
the British military administration and in early 1919 were united into one nation-
wide organization centered in Jerusalem. General Gilbert Clayton, the chief politi-

cal officer, reported that "Jewish predominance in Palestine would be a nightmare for both the Muslims and Christians."[31]

In protest notes and memoranda sent to the British authorities, the Arabs claimed that it was absurd to give such a small minority, the Jews, power over the great majority of the population. They also stated that Jerusalem was holy to three religions and that the religious link of the Jews to Palestine did not differ from that of the Muslims and Christians. To foreigners they also used the argument that it was forbidden "to deliver Jerusalem into the hands of the crucifiers of the Messiah."[32] Other arguments were that the Jews spoke German, had pro-German leanings, and were bringing Bolshevism into the country and into the Middle East as a whole. It should be noted also that British intelligence failed to distinguish between the Zionist left and Communism.[33]

Another set of arguments concerned the disruption of the traditional way of life caused by the new Jewish immigrants. "The civilization which the Jews are bringing to and spreading in Palestine is nothing but anarchy, Communism and the destruction of family life."[34] The Turks told the Arabs that Britain had sold out to the Zionists for money,[35] that a large proportion of Palestinian Jews were hostile to Zionism,[36] that there was not enough land to enable the realization of Zionism,[37] that Jewish immigration would cause the Arabs to emigrate from Palestine,[38] and that the Jews were members of a universal religion and not a people in need of a country of its own.[39]

Among the initiators of the Muslim–Christian associations, the Greek Catholic bishop of Haifa, Youssuf Gregorius Hajjar, was particularly active. He was the only Christian clergyman who participated actively in the Arab Palestinian movement in those years. In January 1919, he tried to sow mistrust of British intentions regarding the Zionist problem and to encourage reliance on the French forces in Syria. He also tried to bring around Orthodox Arabs to his views.[40]

The Vatican had undoubtedly absorbed these anti-Zionist arguments. Barlassina, the Latin patriarch of Jerusalem, came into contact with the Arab members of his church, heard and was receptive to their arguments, and apparently passed them on to the Vatican, where they found a receptive audience. Barlassina's main objective was, of course, to win converts to Catholicism in the Holy Land. To that end he resolved to be as Arab as the Arabs, who then made up 90 percent of the country's population, to support their national aspirations, and to serve as a spokesman for their claims before the authorities. This, in Barlassina's view, was the only way to guarantee that long-standing and recently established Catholic institutions in the Holy Land would be filled with large numbers of believers. A hint to this effect may be found in an article by one of Barlassina's followers extolling his activity in the Holy Land.[41]

An interesting explanation for the anti-Zionism of Christian Arabs in Palestine is found in the memoirs of Justice Gad Frumkin:

> They were well aware of their numerical inferiority and knew that if a Muslim–Jewish alliance were created, they would become an insignificant minority in the country. On the other hand, they also understood that despite their small numbers, they in fact were the most highly educated Arabs and were confident that in a Muslim–Christian alliance, they would have the upper hand. Their aspiration was clear: to forestall Muslim–Jewish concord, to establish a Christian–Muslim alliance,

to head it, and thus to become spokesmen for the Arabs of Palestine to the British authorities, with whom they shared the kinship of Christianity.[42]

This idea of Muslim–Christian unity against the Jews is also found in the French Catholic newspaper *La Croix*: "The Arabs and the Christians do not look favorably upon the establishment of a Jewish state in Palestine and fear that the arrival of those 'hornets' will upset the unity and activity of the beehive."[43]

Catholic Activity Against Zionism

The opening of the Peace Conference in Paris in January 1919 occasioned a series of Catholic actions against Zionism. In January 1919, the Franciscans in Jerusalem, along with some members of Agudat Israel, American Protestant missionaries, and the American consul in Jerusalem, Reverend Otis A. Glazebrook, drafted a strongly anti-Zionist memorandum. This memorandum stated that Russian Jews would bring Bolshevism to Palestine, that Yiddish-speaking Jews would be under German influence, and that the Vatican would be unhappy if the Jews ruled the Holy Places. It also stressed that it was not fair for one religion to dominate the other two, that a Jewish state would lead to a revival of anti-Semitism, and that the Zionists were Godless.[44]

The *Jewish Chronicle* reported an interview given to *Le Matin* in Paris by Monsignor Baudrillart, rector of the Catholic Institute:

> I have been represented as an enemy of Zionism. Why, I do not know. My opinions have always been based on the advantages to the Jews themselves and the peace of the world. I desire the welfare of the Jews in this material world. . . . I see no objection to their establishing a home in Palestine. But a Jewish State is something quite different. This would be unfavorable to the Jews, and lacking sufficient legal foundation. The Jews are a religion and a race. If they become a nation, they would be foreigners everywhere. They cannot aspire to two nationalities. It is not for us to dictate to the Governments a line of conduct as to the future of Palestine. . . . The re-established Cross ought to reign in the city [of Jerusalem].[45]

This interview is of particular interest, first, because Monsignor Baudrillart was a close friend of Gasparri's and many of his arguments were used by the secretary of state in his own talks. Furthermore, Baudrillart's comments were reported in an English Jewish weekly, and therefore the Zionist leaders could not possibly ignore them. Moreover, that same issue of the *Jewish Chronicle* also reported another anti-Zionist attack, by the Catholic newspaper *The Tablet*, which denied the story being circulated that the Holy Father was a supporter of Zionism:

> The story is quite untrue and has been denied. Some time ago an attempt was made to gain from the Holy See a formal expression of approval for Zionism as a sort of Jewish state, an expression of purely political opinion, in which the Holy Father would not indulge, confining himself to good wishes to any who desired to take part in the formation of a Jewish "home" in Palestine. Cardinal Bourne's visit should help in dispelling this and other unfounded stories. . . .[46] He [the pope] had offered his good wishes to any who desired to take part in the formation of a Jewish "home"

in Palestine . . . but there could be no question of approval of a "sort of a Jewish state."[47]

The *Jewish Chronicle* noted that the pastoral of Cardinal Bourne, which was read in Westminster Cathedral, was the first in centuries to carry the phrase "Given in Jerusalem." "And we fear it spells trouble!" observed the paper justly.

The explanation of the pope's audience with Sokolow, offered by an important Catholic weekly such as *The Tablet,* should have roused doubts among Zionist leaders, but it did not. In any case, several days later, similar remarks were made by the pope himself.

Gasparri Versus the Zionist "Threat"

Gasparri's anti-Zionist feelings are more pronounced in French than in British reports. Although the cardinal may have adopted a slightly different tone, depending on the identity of his interviewer, it is equally possible that the French were more receptive to expressions of anti-Zionism, for such expressions conformed to their policy of competition with Britain for the rule of Palestine.

At the beginning of March 1919, Léon Adolphe Cardinal Amette arrived in Rome and met with Gasparri. The details of their talk were later conveyed to Charles-Roux of the French embassy in Rome, for at that time France's diplomatic relations with the Vatican had not been renewed. Charles-Roux's report is dated March 7, and thus the conversation presumably took place a few days before that date. According to the report, Gasparri said:

> We are very worried about Palestine. Zionism is threatening to invade every place, to take everything, actually to buy up Palestine. Foreign newspapers, among them American ones, have published that the Holy See consents to the Zionists plans for Palestine. This is a falsification. Not only does the Holy See not consent to those plans, it is also greatly worried by them. I have written to Balfour about this and await his reply. Balfour's speech the day after the conquest of Jerusalem has worried us, and it is easy to understand why we cannot be too happy about that conquest.
>
> Undoubtedly, the Holy See will not object to the Jews' being received in Palestine, as in any other country, with full equality. This is natural. But it protests the preferred status the Jews want to acquire when they claim or purchase Palestine for themselves. An English colonel told me [today] that the Jews want to bring to Palestine annually a sizable quota of Jews, who will be taken from all countries. Who is unacquainted with their invading spirit? A man from Hungary told me that in his country the Jews made up one-fifth of the population but held 80 percent of the liberal professions.
>
> I will try in a roundabout way to warn Orlando [the Italian prime minister] before he returns to Paris, for, we are told, Zionism is gaining victories every day at the [Peace] Conference. Yet the Zionist plans are not to the liking of all the Jews.[48]

Some of the arguments put forward here had already been aired on other occasions: the denial of the Holy See's alleged support of Zionism appeared in the letter just mentioned, sent by Cardinal Bourne to Balfour in January 1919. Bourne had issued that denial on instructions from Gasparri. The Jews' being awarded a privileged position in Palestine became the central issue raised by Pope Benedict XV a few days later. And even the example of the Jews in Hungary reappeared in Gasparri's remarks to Ronald Storrs some two years later! Especially interesting is Gasparri's admission of having put anti-Zionist pressures on the Italian prime minister. At the time of the mandate's approval in 1922, the Zionist leaders, particularly Weizmann, feared the Vatican's negative influence on Italy but of course did not have such clear proof of it.

The idea that not all the Jews supported the "excessive plans" of the Zionism also appeared on other occasions, and the anti-Semitic tone of Gasparri's remarks about the Jews of Hungary was reechoed several months later in the French Jesuit journal *Etudes,* which published a series of articles on the "Jewish invasion of Hungary."[49]

10

The Pope's Outcry

Pope Benedict XV's 1919 Speech

Gasparri again expressed his concern about the future of Palestine, and especially about Zionist demands, in a talk with the British representative, de Salis.[1] As we have seen, this concern also stemmed from the news brought by Cardinal Bourne, who upon his return from Palestine told the pope that the Zionists definitely wanted to achieve a political takeover. The pope had also received reports from Barlassina, who claimed that atheism, Communism, and immorality were rampant among the new Jewish immigrants.[2] According to de Salis, the Vatican considered Sokolow a moderate, which was why it received him cordially, but Weizmann's plans caused it great anxiety. De Salis also reported that the Vatican took a favorable view of the British conquest of Palestine but feared it might again require the help of other governments, in a revived form of the religious protectorate. If the British government accepted the Jewish demands without any consideration for the Vatican's view, this could lead to a justified claim of the Vatican and would oblige it to turn to another party to obtain protection of its former rights.[3]

Gasparri's remarks implied a threat by the Vatican: if Britain acceded to Zionist demands, the Vatican would turn again to France and Italy and renew the religious protectorate. Gasparri was well aware that Italy and France disliked British policy in Palestine and used this knowledge in an abortive attempt to exploit the still-unresolved problem of the religious protectorate to persuade the British to abandon the Zionists.

The British Foreign Office, however, suggested that the Vatican's fears could be allayed by promising that control of the Holy Places in every instance would be retained by the Christians, and Balfour accepted this.[4] Thus to appease the pope, the British Foreign Office cabled reassurances to de Salis, informing him that Sokolow was one of the representatives of the Zionist Organization who had appeared before the Paris Peace Conference on February 27.[5] But by the time the Foreign Office's promises reached Rome,[6] it was too late; the pope had already delivered

Pope Benedict XV.

his consistorial allocution. We may assume, therefore, that Gasparri's remarks to the British representative were meant to prepare the ground for the pope's speech, about which the British had not received any advance word.

In his speech on March 10, Benedict XV stated that the Eastern Church had always been an object of special attention of the Roman pontiffs. Mindful of the ancient glory of this Church, his predecessors not only saw to the preservation of the Eastern customs and traditions but also held their rites in great honor. The pope added:

> We founded first of all a special congregation destined exclusively for the Oriental Church, and then an institute of higher studies. . . . But there is one matter on which We are most specially anxious, and that is the fate of the Holy Places, on account of the special dignity and importance for which they are so venerated by every Christian. Who can ever tell the full story of all the efforts of Our predecessors to free them from the dominion of infidels, the heroic deeds and the blood shed by the Christians of the West through the centuries? And now that, amid the rejoicing of all good men, they have finally returned into the hands of the Christians, Our anxiety is most keen as to the decisions which the Peace Congress at Paris is soon to take concerning them. For surely it would be a terrible grief for Us and for all the Christians faithful if infidels were placed in a privileged and prominent position; much more if those most holy sanctuaries of the Christian religion were given into the charge of non-Christians.
>
> We learn, too, that non-Catholic foreigners, furnished with abundant means and profiting by the great misery and ruin that the war has brought on Palestine, are there spreading their errors. Truly harrowing indeed is the thought that souls should be losing their faith and hastening to damnation on that very spot where Jesus Christ Our Lord gained for them life eternal at the cost of His Blood. Helpless, deprived of all they have, those poor souls are stretching out to us suppliant arms imploring not only food and clothing but the rebuilding of their churches, the re-opening of their schools, the restoration of their missions. To this end We have for Our part already set aside a certain sum, and most willingly would We give more if the present poverty of the Holy See allowed. But it is our intention to excite the interests of the Bishops of the whole Catholic world that they may take to heart such a noble and holy case, arousing among all the faithful that sense of active charity which their ancestors always showed towards their brethren of the Orient.[7]

The next day, the pope sent a letter to the Catholic missionaries in the Holy Land, in which he mentioned his speech to the cardinals and called on bishops around the world to help the Catholic missionaries in the Holy Land, who were receiving no aid and were vulnerable to threats from non-Catholics.[8]

A few days later, Cardinal Gasparri explained the pope's remarks to the Belgian representative:

> The danger we most fear is the establishment of a Jewish state in Palestine. We would have found nothing wrong in Jews entering that country, and setting up agricultural colonies. But that they be given the rule over the Holy Places is intolerable for Christians. Balfour's reply to Lord Rothschild unfortunately gives us reason to fear that the British government supports the Zionist claims. A high-ranking British officer has recently confirmed our fears, and explained the steps being prepared in London and in Paris. These measures can be explained by the influence the Jewish

element has on the leading Allied statesmen. Sonnino is a Protestant but is of Jewish origins; the private secretaries of President Wilson, Clemenceau, and Lloyd George are Jews. Add to this the activity of Jewish banking and you will understand the causes of our concern. The Holy See must speak up, because of the rumor that has been spread that it supports the Zionist claims.[9]

Cardinal Bourne told the Belgian plenipotentiary minister to the Holy See that the Zionists had tried to spread the news that the Vatican approved of their plans. But Cardinal Gibbons, who was more cautious, had said only that if the pope supported the Zionists, he too could do as much. Bourne stated further that the British government had no intention of giving the rule of Palestine to the Jews. That is, the British could not view with equanimity the front line of Egypt falling into Jewish hands, knowing as it did that the Germans still exercised a decisive influence on them.[10] The Jews of Palestine made up only one-tenth of the population, and not all of them were Zionists; most of whom were nonbelievers and secular, whereas the local Jews were mostly religious.[11]

From the Belgian representative's report, therefore—which no doubt echoed the Vatican's stand—it is clear that Zionism stood little chance of winning over Cardinal Gasparri.

Press Reactions to the Pope's Address

The pope's address provoked many comments in the general press and, of course, in the Jewish press as well. The *Jewish Chronicle* published a letter entitled "The Pope and Palestine":

> We have read with great regret the recent allocution delivered by the pope. . . . The apparent reference to Jews as "infidels" we cannot let pass without the most earnest protest. . . . There is not . . . the remotest intention on the part of the Jews in any way to interfere with the Holy Places. On the contrary . . . the utmost respect will be accorded to them, and indeed no Jewish policy could hope, or would desire, to exist for twenty-four hours, which acted otherwise. We do not follow his Holiness in the further remark that non-Catholics are disseminating their doctrine.[12]

The *Jewish Chronicle* understood this last remark by the pope as aimed against the Hebrew University, whose cornerstone had been laid the year before, although by "non-Catholics" the pope probably meant Protestants, not Jews. Nonetheless, in 1922 Gasparri did tell Weizmann: "It is your university that I fear." The *Jewish Chronicle* seems to have had amazing insight.

On March 17, the *Osservatore Romano* charged that commentators who saw only a political motive in the pope's remarks were short-sighted.[13] Two days later, the Vatican newspaper wrote:

> Is the pope's heartfelt cry that the Holy Places may fall into the hands of non-Christians, after having been released from their control, truly political? How can the pope not take an interest in the policies of the nations when these do not refrain from imposing a partial, or even an absolute, restriction on the rights of Catholics?[14]

The Jesuit organ *Civiltà Cattolica* pointed out that the enthusiasm generated by the liberation of the Holy Places by General Edmund Allenby at the end of World War I had quickly subsided, for Allenby's intentions had not been to promote Christian interests, and certainly not Catholic interests, but to support the Jews and the Anglo-Saxon Protestants, who wanted to found a Jewish republic in Palestine. The pope could thus no longer remain silent but had to speak out for the sake of Christians. The Holy Places were in danger of falling into the hands of the enemies of Christian civilization. It would be criminal to allow non-Christians to gain a privileged position in Palestine, especially if the Holy Places were to be entrusted to their safekeeping.[15]

The authorized Catholic responses all note the seeming danger of handing the Holy Places to the Jews, but the real fear was of the foundation of a Jewish republic in Palestine, and the Holy Places argument was employed primarily to engage religious sensibilities and to mobilize the Catholics.

The Italian newspaper *Il Giornale d'Italia,* by contrast, wrote that the pope's speech reflected an exaggerated fear of the Zionist movement and that his allocution was influenced by the Vatican's long-standing dispute with the non-Catholic Churches. After analyzing Vatican policy in the East—which the paper claimed was dictated by the fear that Greek Orthodox Christians might be granted preferred status—the article concluded:

> All that remains is to examine the Vatican's thoughts on the Jewish problem. It may safely be assumed that on this matter it will not be difficult for common sense to prevail. For the establishment of Jewish cultural centers or Jewish agricultural colonies in Judea—and the aspirations of this people, which has been cradle for the Church and has given humanity its most noble figures, seem to be restricted to these two goals alone—harbors no danger for the future of Christianity.[16]

The pope's speech and letter were timed for what seemed to be the most opportune moment for influencing the course of events at the Paris Peace Conference, to which they made explicit reference. It is thus not surprising that the diplomatic missions followed these pronouncements with interest.[17] On March 12, de Salis cabled a résumé of the pope's speech to the Foreign Office in London. In London it was assumed that the pope's anti-Zionist position was affected to some extent by the reports of Cardinal Bourne, who had returned only a short while earlier from his visit to Palestine.[18]

The Italians, too, knew of Bourne's influence, as is evident from a report by Baron Carlo Monti, who at that time maintained semiofficial contacts between the Italian government and the Vatican. On March 19, 1919, he wrote to Foreign Minister Sidney Sonnino:

> The Holy See is quite certain that Cardinal Bourne did not act in Palestine in any way contrary to our interests. He went there primarily to further the interests of Christianity and Catholicism, and to see the magnitude of the grave problem of Zionism at close hand. I have learned that he sent a report on this problem to Foreign Secretary Balfour, which sought to prevent what the Holy See regards as a most serious danger not only to the Church but also to all of Christianity. . . . The Holy

See is understandably worried about such a possibility, and the pope's speech at the last consistory is the religious proof of this profound concern.[19]

British Reactions

De Salis reported that great anxiety had been aroused in the Vatican by proposals according to which the Zionists would be given a privileged position at the expense of Christians and noted that such a position could readily be exploited by elements opposed to British policy in the East, be they French or Italian. In London, this report reinforced the view that the Vatican's worries were based for the most part on the letters sent to the pope by Cardinal Bourne, which were similar to those he had sent to Prime Minister Lloyd George. The pope's fears about Zionism's extreme intentions were also shared by some senior officials in the Foreign Office. As evidence is the following comment penned in the margins of de Salis's cable:

> This is only the sorrowful beginning of our troubles in Palestine, once we are with the mandate, and I share the pope's anxiety regarding the most extreme intentions of the Zionists. He must be thinking of something more vague and frightening than merely earthly aspirations; he foresees a spiritual campaign against Christianity. Is the anti-Christ not a Jew according to the Roman tradition? Judaism, under the cover of Bolshevism, has already destroyed the Orthodox Church; could Bolshevism not do the same to Rome? The reference to Zionism is important because Sonnino is of course a Jew. . . .[20]

The Italian foreign minister was sometimes thought to be a Jew, because of his surname but was actually a Protestant, like his mother; his father was Jewish.

About ten days later, de Salis sent another cable in which he stated that the Vatican was especially worried by the prospect that the Zionists would be granted privileged status, as compared with that of the Christians. The Vatican appealed to the Italian prime minister for support on this matter. Léon Adolphe Cardinal Amette, the archbishop of Paris, also came to the Vatican, and according to de Salis, he too would be taking on that issue.[21]

De Salis's cable produced some interesting comments in the British Foreign Office. One official wrote:

> This matter has gone direct to Paris and can only be dealt with there. But it should surely be possible to give the Vatican some assurances that, if we are the mandatories for Palestine (1) they shall be given a hearing as regards the disposal of the Holy Places; (2) our policy in Palestine will not any more than in any other part of the Empire be directed towards [giving] any one religion a preferential position over others.[22]

Another official observed:

> The preoccupation of the Vatican with the idea that Zionists are to be placed in a privileged position as regards Christians, is amply justified by the resolution of the Zionist Conference here, e.g., that all educational establishment in Palestine should be under Zionist supervision and that Hebrew should be the principal language of instruction.

This official then recalled that Italian clerics in the Holy Land worked for Italian nationalism and, commenting on Cardinal Amette's hasty visit to Rome, said that "France will make all possible capital out of the British difficult position there."[23]

It is astonishing that someone in the Foreign Office could have regarded the Zionist demand that Hebrew be the principal language of instruction in Jewish schools as justifying the Vatican's anxiety about a Jewish "privileged position." Also discernible in these remarks is the close link in the minds of these officials between Jewish privileges and the future of the Holy Places. This may have been another source of misunderstanding between the British government and the Vatican; that is, Britain was using legal terms to reassure the Vatican, and the latter was resorting to emotional arguments about privileges being given to the Jews to safeguard its overall position in Palestine and to protect itself from Zionism, which the Vatican perceived as a new threat.

A few days later, in an interview Gasparri gave to the French newspaper *Petit Parisien,* he was reported to have said that he supported the internationalization of Jerusalem. Gasparri explained his remark in a conversation with the Belgian representative: "I expressed the fears Zionist aspirations arouse in me and said I prefer the internationalization of the Holy Places to seeing Jerusalem in Jewish hands." It was the view of the Belgian representative that the Vatican would refrain from taking sides in the dispute among the Great Powers, provided that Christian interests were safeguarded. The mention of the danger posed by Zionism was meant as a warning to Britain, which the Vatican suspected of having made a commitment of the Zionists.[24]

De Salis heard a similar explanation from Gasparri, who said that he had not expressed his support for an international regime for the Holy Places; he preferred internationalization rather than Zionist rule, which he opposed not only concerning specific places but in general for the Church's interests in Palestine.[25]

The King–Crane Commission

At the end of August 1919, the King–Crane Commission, sent to the Middle East by U.S. President Woodrow Wilson to "find out the will of the people," completed its report. Crane was a Catholic, who later worked to form an alliance with the Muslim world against a Jewish takeover in Palestine. He was probably influenced to a great extent by the views prevailing among the Catholic clergy in Palestine.[26] Among the commission's conclusions is the following:

> There is a further consideration that cannot justly be ignored, if the world is to look forward to Palestine becoming a definitely Jewish state, however gradually that may take place. That consideration grows out of the fact that Palestine is "the Holy Land" for Jews, Christians and Moslems alike. . . . With the best possible intentions it may be doubted whether the Jews could possibly seem to either Christians or Moslems proper guardians of the Holy Places, or custodians of the Holy Land as a whole. The reason is this: the places which are most sacred to Christians—those having to do with Jesus—and which are also sacred to Moslems, are not only not sacred to Jews, but abhorrent to them. . . . In fact, from this point of view, the Moslems, just

because the sacred places of all three religions are sacred to them, have made naturally much more satisfactory custodians of the Holy Places than the Jews. . . . In
view of all these considerations, and with a deep sense of sympathy for the Jewish
cause, the commissioners feel bound to recommend that only a greatly reduced Zionist program be attempted by the Peace Conference. . . . This would have to mean
that Jewish immigration should be definitely limited, and that the project for making
Palestine distinctly a Jewish commonwealth should be given up.[27]

The commission's arguments concerning the Holy Places clearly reflected the
kinds of fears that were also widespread in Vatican circles. Some are even trum-
peted to this day by Arab propaganda. For centuries, the Vatican had accepted in
relative quiet the Muslim Ottoman rule of the region where the Holy Places were
situated and now was not about to accept Jewish rule of that region. In addition,
the King–Crane Commission used the religious factor—custody of the Holy
Places—to promote the Arabs' political demands for restrictions of Jewish immigration and for renunciation of the plan to establish a Jewish national home.

In any case, the Vatican's opposition to Zionism was being revealed at that time
even more clearly. Its position apparently stemmed from a convergence of a number
of factors: fear that the Zionists might destroy the positions the Catholics had
achieved in Palestine over the centuries; fear, which was also then taking root
among some British and Italian government officials, that Zionism might also bring
Bolshevism in its train; and dislike of some Zionist leaders who were thought to be
too extreme. And in the background was the theological opposition to the return of
the Jews to the Holy Land.

This theological reason had been expressed, as noted earlier, in the talk between
Pope Pius X and Theodor Herzl and reappeared in April 1919 in an article in *Osservatore Romano*. Opposing what was called the "Zionist illusion," the article
stated that the Jews had been dispersed by divine decree and would return to Palestine only after they had converted to Christianity. The author of this article went
on to assert: "The salvation of Israel will arrive when all the nations open their
souls to the hope of the Kingdom of God." And he concluded by observing: "Even
when East and West fully join the Catholic Church and the Jews accept Christianity,
there will still be no assurance that the Jewish nation will arise again."[28]

The Visits of Cardinals Giustini and Dubois

The visit to Palestine by Filippo Cardinal Giustini in October 1919, mentioned
earlier, gave the Vatican another opportunity to express its stand on Zionism. The
cardinal cabled the pope from Jerusalem and asked for his intervention in order "to
prevent the re-establishment of Zionist Israel in Palestine." The pope replied:

The Holy Father thanks His Eminence for the information he has sent, and reminding
him of what he has already said in his consistorial allocution of March 10, he repeats
his wishes for the future of Palestine and wishes that Zionist rule, which has already
been denounced by him, will not come to damage Christian conscience.[29]

During his visit in Palestine, Cardinal Giustini was the guest of Custos Federico
Diotallevi, and his anti-Zionist position very likely reflects his host's opinions.

Giustini arrived aboard the Italian ship *Il Quarto,* whose captain sent a report to his superiors about the Custos's views:

> [Diotallevi] is clearly opposed to Zionism, and stresses that the Christians are of one mind with the Moslems in this deep hostility, and are even prepared to slaughter the Jews. In his opinion, Zionism is only a pretext for establishing Jewish rule at the gates of Europe, for the absolute benefit of the Jews, who are already all-powerful in the old continent [Europe] and the new [America]. . . . According to Diotallevi, the British government approves of the Zionist movement.[30]

In Jerusalem, Giustini met with Muslims who warned him of the dangers that could be expected to ensue from the establishment of Zionist rule in Palestine. Lazzaro Negrotto Cambiaso, the Italian representative in Cairo, wrote that Giustini "was impressed [by these conversations] and intended to report on them to the pope, so that he [the pope] would make an explicit proclamation of the Church's views on the Zionist problem when the cardinals convene."[31]

One cardinal's visit to Palestine was followed by another. After the British Cardinal Bourne and the Italian Cardinal Giustini, came the French Cardinal Louis Ernest Dubois. A statement attributed to Dubois—which he is alleged to have made at the end of 1919 in Haifa—is somewhat surprising, and we cannot be sure that he actually made it. According to our source, Dubois insisted that the Entente powers were victorious in part because of the Jews and remarked: "We cannot fail to be grateful to the Jewish people, which has contributed so much. Furthermore, the problem of Palestine has emerged from the historical phase, and today the idea that it will belong to the Jewish people is already an established fact."[32] But another press interview has that same Cardinal Dubois taking an altogether different line. In the *Journal des Débats* of March 20, 1920, he is reported to have said upon his return from Palestine that Jewish immigration to Palestine and the establishment of a Zionist state should not be permitted.[33] The newspaper also spoke of the anticipated arrival in Paris of a Christian–Muslim delegation, which the French may well have had a hand in organizing.

About two months later, Cardinal Dubois again spoke out on the Palestine problems: "The Jewish Home the British wish to found is a dangerous step and is full of threats for the future." He warned of a civil war and the danger of Pan-Islamism.[34] Cardinal Dubois also stated that the Muslim–Christian Association had demanded that Syria and Palestine be united and that it felt friendly toward France.[35] It should be noted that at that time France was distributing large sums of money among the Arabs of Palestine to encourage them to demand the annexation of Palestine to Syria.[36] The French hoped in this way to gain control over both Syria and Palestine, but their fanning of nationalist sentiments in the end came back to haunt them.

At the beginning of 1920, articles appeared in the Catholic press, especially in France, on the severe problems that Jewish immigration to Palestine was supposedly causing. One such article stated:

> The Jews will become the owners of vast lands in all of Palestine. . . . Every day, commerce is falling into the hands of the Jews, who are known for their commercial skill. . . . But most shameful for Christianity will be to see the Holy Places occupied by the Jews, and perhaps even under their political yoke.

The author of the article went on to say that public opinion must be aroused and that agreement must be reached with the missionaries of other Christian communities and with Muslim religious officials, to persuade the *fellahin* not to sell their lands to the Jews, explaining to them that if they held out, they would be able to obtain a much higher price of their lands at a later date.[37]

On the same question, *Suria Al Jenuvia* reported that Catholic and Orthodox patriarchs ordered their monks and priests to warn the Christians during prayer not to sell land to the Jews.[38]

The French Catholic newspaper *La Croix* claimed that this danger must be made clear to the Arabs. According to this paper, non-Jewish natives of the Holy Land would be no more than strangers, more or less tolerated at first, but afterward oppressed, tortured, and robbed with each new wave of Jewish immigration. The British were giving the Jews an additional homeland, apart from the one in which they were born.[39]

Sir Herbert Samuel at the Vatican (1920)

When the decision was reached at the Sanremo Conference in April 1920 to grant Great Britain the mandate to administer Palestine, the Reuters news agency reported that the Holy See was worried that the Jews might be granted a predominant position in Palestine and that it wished to see the Zionist movement confined "within a framework of just boundaries." The editor of the Italian-Jewish weekly *Israel* wondered what the Vatican considered a "just framework," as compared with the position of the Zionists, who called for freedom for all religions and international protection for the Holy Places.[40]

After the Sanremo Conference, the British government appointed Sir Herbert Samuel as the first High Commissioner in Palestine. Before assuming the position, Samuel visited Rome and on June 25 was received by the pope.[41] Despite this courtesy call, Samuel, a Jew, was accused of being unsympathetic to the Catholic Church.

After Samuel arrived in Rome, Gasparri told de Salis frankly that Samuel's appointment was troubling to the Holy See.[42] Surprisingly, de Salis, a Catholic, did see fit to inform the cardinal that the British government did not discriminate against Jews in its appointments. His own views may have been close to those of the Vatican, and it is possible that he believed deep in his heart that a Jew should not have been appointed to so high and delicate a post.

In his report to London, Samuel made no mention of the problem of the Jews or of Zionism. But two days after the visit, the French representative at the Vatican heard from Gasparri that Samuel had made it clear that he was setting out for Palestine for the sole purpose of supporting Zionism and that his appointment was itself a step in fulfilling Balfour's promise. According to the French report, Gasparri retorted that the Jews had seized all the posts and that non-English pilgrims and missionaries were encountering difficulty entering Palestine. Samuel promised that all this would change.[43] Gasparri's views seem to be accurately reported here, although there is no certainty that he said all this to Samuel as well, and if he did, it is curious that Samuel did not mention it in his report. The cardinal also called Samuel's attention to the article by the Frenchman Roger Lambelin, which had appeared on May 25, 1920, in *Le Correspondant*.

Many articles by Lambelin, all with a distinctly anti-Zionist tenor, were translated and published in the *Osservatore Romano*. The article mentioned here also appeared in the Vatican newspaper at a later date, on June 16, 1920, under the title "Palestine and Zionism." Lambelin wrote that historically, geographically, and economically, Palestine belonged to Syria, even though the British had received the mandate. He also quoted the British General Louis Bols, who had been chief administrator in Palestine until Samuel's arrival. According to Bols, a number of administrative and political measures that had been taken in Palestine facilitated the fulfillment of the Jews' plans. In light of Samuel's appointment, the obstacles in the way of Catholic missionaries who wanted to enter Palestine, and, by contrast, the ease with which the Jews could enter, it was not surprising that the hope had been planted in the Jews' hearts that their dream would be realized. The article also described the protests and demonstrations of the Arab population and the bloodshed that followed: "Christians and Moslems in Palestine are united today against the common danger and for the common salvation."[44]

In the *Osservatore Romano*, Lambelin also mentioned an article that appeared in the *Spectator* in England that supposedly demonstrated that the realization of Zionism would be detrimental: because Palestine could support a population of no more than 1.5 million people, it would be necessary to expel all the Arabs, and according to the paper, these were the efforts of Lieutenant Colonel J. H. Patterson, the commander of the Jewish battalion. Lambelin concluded that it was unthinkable that Palestine would be liberated from the Turks only to be abandoned into the hands of Zionism, the "birthplace of Bolshevism and anarchy." It was inconceivable as well that Jewish soldiers would stand guard at the Holy Sepulchre. Britain must therefore oppose Zionism for the sake of peace in the Middle East.[45]

Lambelin, a monarchist activist, subsequently moved toward the extreme right-wing, nationalist, and anti-Semitic camp of Action Française and saw to the publication in France in 1921 of the well-known anti-Semitic book *The Protocols of the Elders of Zion*,[46] parts of which had already appeared in June 1920 in his newspaper, *Le Correspondant*.

In his first talk with Samuel, Gasparri relied heavily on Lambelin, an indication that he regarded Lambelin's article as credible. Furthermore, the fact that the Vatican paper, *Osservatore Romano*, had reprinted Lambelin's article a few days before Gasparri's talk gives further reason to suppose that it was published as a result of Gasparri's direct intervention. The publication of others' arguments was a Vatican method of presenting, while concealing, its own official position, for the selection of the material published was itself an expression of the viewpoint of the editor of the Vatican's newspaper.

That same right-wing French newspaper, *Le Correspondant*, had in the past served as a publication vehicle for an article by Gasparri. This was so, for example, at the end of 1918 or the beginning of 1919, when Gasparri replied to Camille Barrère, the French ambassador in Rome, who had contended that the Vatican had sided with the two central empires in World War I against the Entente powers.[47] *Le*

Correspondant was thus not only a source on which the Vatican newspaper could draw for anti-Zionist material but also an organ for the Holy See's views, a fact indicative of the newspaper's ideological affinity.

A few days after these articles appeared, the Vatican newspaper published another fierce attack on Zionism. Because the points raised were so similar to those that Gasparri had set out to Samuel, it is more than likely that they were suggested to the paper by the secretary of state.

The *Osservatore Romano* wrote that Jews were seizing most of the posts in the mandatory administration, because their commission supplemented their wages, whereas Christians and Muslims were being forced to leave these jobs because of the low salaries. Jews were also buying land and homes, exploiting the poverty of the non-Jewish inhabitants. Immigration permits were easily granted to Jews, whereas French nuns had to wait months for entry visas. Missionaries were donning French military uniforms to enter Palestine, and German scholars of Christian archaeology were barred altogether from entering the Holy Land. The Jews wanted to assert their hegemony over the Holy City in the spiritual realm as well, a possibility that all the world found odious.[48]

Samuel's stop at the Vatican on his way to Palestine also provoked a number of anti-Zionist reactions in the Italian press, for example, the following:

> The Holy See has for some time revealed its view of Zionism. It views as intolerable the possibility that the Jews will receive a position of power in Palestine, to the disadvantage of the existing religious communities there. The Holy See believes that the establishment of a national home as first planned could be viewed without excessive concern, but this is utterly different from the Jews' dominating the other races, as seems to be happening today.[49]

The Jewish weekly *Israel*, which published this item, quoted extensively from *Il Tempo*, a newspaper that often aired the views of the Vatican secretary of state. *Il Tempo* appealed to the descendants of the Crusaders and to the hundreds of millions of believers to oppose the shrewd and unrelenting activity of the Jews, the allies of British imperialism. The paper believed that the Jews had a plan to expel the natives of Palestine, buying them out by means of money, and that they exploited the general destruction caused by the war to purchase whatever could be purchased, even at extravagant prices. The paper further charged the Jews of having begun to uproot the natives by force. In its view, the Jews should be a religion and a faith, not a nation in the full sense of the term. The aspiration to return to the promised land and the demand of the Jews to be more than a religion were theoretical extremes damaging even to a just struggle. "Among those things which are just," the newspaper continued, "we may include the search for a territory for those Jews who are without a homeland where they live."[50]

The weekly *Israel* commented on this: "To find a territory yes, but not in Palestine. Does the author of the article believe it right, to quiet his conscience, that Jews should die in Europe while Palestine remains empty and barren? For whom? Not for Christianity, not even for Islam."[51]

Meanwhile, the Italian diplomatic representative in Damascus, Gaetano Paternò di Manchi di Bilici, reported on the "joint protest of the Greek Orthodox and the

Moslems for the rebirth of the Arab people." Catholics were also said to be cooperating in the activity against Zionism, for they too were worried by the decisions on Palestine reached at the Sanremo Conference. The Zionist movement had thus unified the different peoples of the Levant in an effort to prevent the establishment of a Zionist state. The Christians in particular felt vulnerable, reported Paternò, for unlike the Arabs they could not always rely on the willingness of local governments to assist them. Their hopes were pinned primarily on the Holy See, but they were disappointed by the indifference of the Christian powers and by the clearly pro-Zionist position of the Anglo-Saxon powers. They were also frustrated by the lack of interest demonstrated by the Vatican.

Paternò went on to claim that affluent Jewish organizations were gaining control of commerce and were undermining the property of Christians and Arabs, in order to force them to emigrate. He recommended that the Italian government show indifference to the Zionist problem but demonstrate some sympathy to the struggle of the Christian Arabs in Palestine. The response to this in the Foreign Ministry in Rome was that it was best to show indifference to both sides.[52]

Barlassina's Arguments

When he arrived in Palestine, Sir Herbert Samuel visited the Church of the Holy Sepulchre, which until then no Jew had been allowed to enter. The Catholics were furious, and a short time afterward, Luigi Barlassina, the Latin patriarch of Jerusalem, sent a pastoral letter strongly protesting the Great Powers' decision to establish a Jewish national home in Palestine.[53] In this letter, dated July 20, 1920, Barlassina recalled the goodwill with which he had been received by the British representative on his arrival at Lydda. He then went on to say:

> Yes, we are all very concerned by the change which—it is said—is contemplated for Palestine. This is the object of our most serious anxiety, and the subject of our interest. Not only Catholics [are worried by this], so are all the other peoples of the country that this problem concerns, and we will remember very well that when a commission was sent last year by President Wilson, to learn the public opinion of the whole country, if there was difference of opinion on some points, yet on the question we are now dealing with, all answered in one unanimous voice: "Let Palestine be internationalized rather than someday be the servant of Zionism." Our existence, from which a former yoke has been lifted, cannot endure a new subjugation worse than the former, of which the aim would be, according to some of the interested parties, to eliminate everything that is not Jewish in order to establish an autocratic Zionist domination.

Barlassina went on to recall his "most explicit declarations" in London, which exposed the "dangers of social strangulation." After returning from Rome, he visited the High Commissioner, not only for the sake of Catholics, but also for the sake of all non-Jews, and in his pastoral letter wrote:

> His Excellency the British High Commissioner received us with great courtesy and honor. He repeatedly made the most explicit declarations, and assured us that all the

rights of the religious creeds will be safeguarded, and that no injury would be made to the welfare of all in general and of each one in particular.

Barlassina asked his followers to refrain from violence should the declaration of the High Commissioner not be fulfilled, because "our action ought not to be aggressive but limited to defending our rights alone." No one should act on his own initiative, for "you have a pastor"—Barlassina himself.[54] The pastoral letter was sent a short time after the decisions of the Supreme Council at Sanremo in April 1920 conferring the mandate on Great Britain and a few days after the arrival of the newly appointed High Commissioner.

Barlassina also mentioned the King–Crane Commission, which, as we have seen, recommended the unification of Palestine and Syria. He emphasized the danger of "autocratic Zionist domination" that sought "to eliminate all that is not Jewish." His style in these remarks was especially caustic and extreme, and one can only wonder why the Zionist leaders did not react. Barlassina wanted to speak not only in the name of the Catholics—which was natural, although his base was too narrow—but also in the name of the entire non-Jewish population. No one had given him such a mandate, and it seems that to win de facto recognition for this claim, he had to be more extreme than the most fanatic local Muslim Arabs. His words even carry a veiled threat, that if the assurances given by the High Commissioner were not implemented, "Chief Pastor" Barlassina would intervene again. Against the background of the first pogrom in Jerusalem a few months earlier, Barlassina's letter could be seen as encouraging violence, even though he did pay lip service to the principles of nonviolence.

The Italian consul general in Jerusalem, Alberto Tuozzi, had a clear opinion of Barlassina, whose personality he described thus:

> He is a man of great initiative and great dignity but has an exaggerated estimation of the importance of his role and person. Today he is engaged in the mission of defending Catholics here and fighting Zionism, a program which no one can criticize, but which must be implemented with tact, [a quality] that the patriarch wholly lacks.
>
> Relations between him and Sir Samuel are already tense, and will get even worse in the future; in the not distant future, the Catholic Church will find itself in open and declared war with the local administration in Palestine, a fact which will have grave consequences, since the solution to this situation might be to bring a patriarch of British nationality here, that is, a man more flexible to accept the directives of the British administration. In the meantime, Catholic interests will suffer.[55]

This report by the Italian consul general, who was an avowed anti-Zionist, attests to the poor relations between Barlassina and the British authorities, which were due not so much to political reasons as to the patriarch's personality.

The Vatican's concern about the spread of Zionism was expressed again in an interview with Nathan Strauss published in the *Osservatore Romano*. This article claimed that the Zionist plan was to get hold of land to build settlements in which only Jewish workers would be employed, to induce a "delicate" expulsion of the Arabs, and to encourage the intellectual and technological development of the Jews, all with the aim of achieving the ultimate goal, which was to unite all the religions under a Jewish common denominator. Another view expressed was that Britain did not intend to retain its rule over Palestine. The paper warned that "if the Jewish minority eventually receives absolute rule, hard days will lie ahead for Christianity in the Holy Places."[56]

Anti-Zionist arguments were expressed once again by British Cardinal Bourne in an article from Paris. In his view, all the inhabitants of Palestine, including the Jews, were opposed to Zionism and among the new immigrants were extremists who "want to destroy the Holy Places," as well as many Bolshevik Jews. It should be noted that the identification of Jews with Bolsheviks was widespread in that period in Church circles and, at times, even in the British administration. Thus, for example, the important Catholic biweekly *Civiltà Cattolica* published a series of articles on Jewish bandits plundering the Ukraine in an alliance with the Bolshe-viks,[57] on a Jewish Bolshevik commissar of exceptional cruelty,[58] and on blood-thirsty Jews among the Bolsheviks.[59] Cardinal Bourne added that the Jews wanted more land and intended to confiscate it from the local people. These remarks were cited by Roger Lambelin, who also noted that French influence over the Holy Places was being weakened.[60]

The fact that the Vatican newspaper was conducting a campaign against Zionism on instructions from above was confirmed by the press survey of the Italian Foreign Ministry, according to which the Vatican was extremely worried by the expansion of the Zionist movement in Palestine, and the *Osservatore Romano* had already taken a negative stand and "was to continue its campaign against Zionist expansion in the Holy Land."[61]

The London Treaty of 1915 prevented the Vatican from participating in the Peace Conference, and at first it acted behind the scenes in the usual diplomatic manner. Later, it took a public stand against Zionism. The three cardinals who visited Palestine in 1919 and 1920 competed among themselves in the display of anti-Zionist sentiments, and quite conceivably their reports, in addition to those sent by Custos Diotallevi and Patriarch Barlassina, influenced the Vatican's policy and strengthened its opposition to Zionism. It may be said, therefore, that apart from the meeting between Pope Benedict XV and Sokolow, the Vatican position against Zionism was continuous and consistent for the first two decades of the twentieth century.

Yet despite the pope's speech in March 1919 and the many articles in the Cath-olic press, the Zionists continued to refer to the pope's remarks to Sokolow in 1917 as if they still reflected the Vatican stand on Zionism. The following, for example, is what the *Zionist Review* wrote in that period:

> It has always been Zionism's consistent policy to honor the legitimate interests and feelings of the Catholic Church and all other religions. The Zionists gladly accepted the Pope's personal promise to Sokolow, His Holiness expressing his wish that "we should be good neighbors." However, one cannot deny that not always did great Catholic personages show the same goodwill, as the Pope did, towards the aspira-tions of the Jewish People to resettle in its land. . . . In some cases, as for example, in the latest declarations of that enlightened Prince of the Church, Cardinal Bourne,

we can only attribute the hostility towards Zionism to a misunderstanding of its aims. For if there is any domain in the Holy Land where no Zionist aspirations exist, it is precisely that of religious rule.[62]

The Zionist Organization continued to attend to developments in the Vatican's position, and a few days after the Sanremo Conference, on May 7, 1920, at a meeting of the Zionist Executive in London, Sokolow raised the subject of the pope's position and the demands regarding the Holy Places made by the Franciscans.[63]

11

Christian–Muslim Cooperation

Anti-Semitism in Europe

In 1920, Europe was washed by a wave of anti-Semitism. In the summer of that year, the *Morning Post* in London published an eighteen-part series on the conspiracy against Christianity purportedly being plotted by Jews, Freemasons, and Bolsheviks, the so-called Jewish–Freemason danger. The first edition of *The Protocols of the Elders of Zion* appeared in England in January of that year, and *The Times* published a summary of it on May 8. In the United States, automobile magnate Henry Ford made sure that this heinous work received wide distribution. In Germany, after its defeat in World War I, the ground was fertile for anti-Semitic propaganda attributing all the world's woes to an international Jewish–Freemason plot, and in 1920 alone *The Protocols* was published in five German editions. In Italy, the banner of anti-Semitism was carried by an ex-priest, Giovanni Preziosi, who in August 1920 published an article on the "Jewish international" and in 1921 published an Italian translation of *The Protocols*. Preziosi was the leading ideologue of Italian anti-Semitism, and many of his arguments were subsequently adopted by Catholic and Fascist newspapers.[1]

The Protocols also found its way into the *Osservatore Romano*. In October 1920, the Vatican daily ran an article from the French Catholic newspaper *La Croix* on the "Jewish peril," asserting that the Jews were behind the British policy and were among the leaders of the Bolshevik Revolution. Most Jews, according to this article, were divided between those who lived "in good faith" in their centuries-old mistakes and those who worshipped Satan.[2] The danger lay in their hatred of Christ and the Christian nations. The article went on to review *The Jewish Peril,* an English translation of *The Protocols*. Although the article questioned the book's credibility, it concluded that the danger it described was real, that the Jews had carried out in Russia the plan set forth in the book, and that they had stirred up the miners' strikes in England as well.[3] The *Osservatore Romano* returned to the subject of *The Protocols* in May of the following year and again quoted *La Croix,* which declared that even if the book was not to be believed, the Jews' plan certainly was. In Paris, the article continued, not only were warnings being issued about the Jewish peril, but prayers were being offered for the conversion of the Jews to Christianity.[4]

The Catholic press, especially in France, continued to publish anti-Zionist articles. In October 1920, a Jesuit priest wrote:

> The fact that Palestine was conquered by the English, and is closed [to us], causes us, the French Catholics, great sorrow. Zionism is receiving official sanction and its implementation has begun. . . . When the Jews have a nation, it will be normal and national to consider them everywhere else as foreigners and to treat them without cruelty, but also with no privileges, as if they were resident aliens. But this they do not want. . . . They want to preserve their parasitic nature, which lets them live at the expense of others.[5]

This argument about the status of Jews elsewhere in the world after the establishment of the Jewish national home in Palestine had wide circulation in those days, and it was what non-Zionist Jews—those who regarded the establishment of a Jewish national home as unwise—most feared. One of the most prominent such Jews was Edwin Montagu, the British secretary of state for India in 1917, under whose influence a clause was added to the Balfour Declaration to the effect that the declaration would not prejudice "the rights and political status enjoyed by Jews in any other country."

The anti-Zionist fervor appears to have been quite widespread in Catholic Church circles in all parts of the world. In January 1921, in response to a question by British cardinal Francis Aidan Gasquet, High Commissioner Samuel was compelled to explain that land regulations in Palestine gave the Jews no special advantage, as was also proved by land purchase statistics.[6]

Catholic attacks against Zionism continued in 1921. In an article from Paris, the *Osservatore Romano* reported that the French prime minister had stated that Zionism posed a grave danger to Catholic religious and French interests. This time the newspaper produced a new argument, which would be heard many times in the ensuing months: the Zionists wanted to transform Palestine into an amusement center, in gross disregard of the Holy Places' special character. According to its usual habit, the *Osservatore* borrowed from another newspaper, *Al Bashir,* which reported that Mount Carmel and other places were to become resort areas; this was an indication of Zionism's anti-Christian tendencies. It would be naive to believe that the Zionists were interested only in the economic exploitation of Palestine, the newspaper wrote. Not only did they intend to wait for the crops they planted on lands taken from Christians and Arabs to ripen, but they also planned to implement a moral and political program opposed to Christian memories and traditions. Otherwise the Jews would remain strangers in Palestine, unwelcomed by the inhabitants. "To turn the Holy land into an international amusement center—that is its plan and it has two aims: to generate profits and to strip the cradle of Christianity of its Christian character."[7]

The National Catholic News Service, which had not dealt much with the subject, was also mobilized in the Church's fight against Zionism. The *Osservatore*

Romano quoted an item from this agency that pondered the possibility that Zionists would come to dominate Christians in Palestine. Catholic religious institutions, most of them French and Italian, had suffered from the revocation of the special privileges that foreigners had enjoyed (a reference, apparently, to the abrogation of the capitulations), yet the Zionists complained of inadequate support from the Mandate government. The article also noted that Zionism had not succeeded as a national movement among the Jews, both because Palestine could not offer the Jews the material advantages available to them in other lands and because the local Jews (in Palestine) were opposed to the immigration of their fellows.[8] There is an inherent contradiction in this article, however, for if its author truly believed that Zionism had failed, there would be no grounds for his fear that it might come to dominate Palestine.

In March 1921, Colonial Secretary Winston Churchill visited Palestine and reiterated his country's support for Zionism, although in a somewhat-tempered form. For Arabs who hoped his visit would lead to total renunciation of the Balfour Declaration, this was a further disappointment, which was soon followed by violence. The May Day march by Jewish workers through the streets of Jaffa offered Arab extremists a convenient opportunity. At the end of the rioting that then erupted, there were about fifty dead on each side and hundreds of wounded. High Commissioner Samuel responded weakly and even rewarded the attackers by curtailing Jewish immigration. Colonel Richard Meinertzhagen noted in his diary:

> I agree that powerful forces are working against Zionism both in England and in Palestine. Both the pope and the French identified themselves with the anti-Zionist movement. . . . The anti-Zionists have used the occasion to demonstrate the futility and unfairness of the movement and its inevitable failure.[9]

The Palestine Arab Congress sent letters to several heads of states, the pope included, warning of the Bolshevik danger:

> The nation has in vain repeatedly protested against this unfortunate [Balfour] declaration and policy; and now at the time when the fire of Bolshevism is consuming one of our most important cities, and its red flag is openly flaunted in our streets, while its revolutionary publications are being freely and assiduously distributed broadcast [*sic*] in the country, we come again to request that this declaration and policy be abolished before the spirit of Bolshevism is too widely spread.[10]

The British administration shared the view that the Bolsheviks were behind the disturbances, a possibility to which the pope was certainly highly sensitive. It is thus not surprising that against this background he decided to speak out again on the problems of Palestine.

The Pope's Address After the Jaffa Riots (1921)

As the civilian administration in Palestine consolidated, concern within the Catholic Church over the "Zionist danger" increased. Mere allusions to its opposition to Zionism and Barlassina's outspoken protests in Jerusalem no longer were enough for the Vatican. On May 1, 1921, the Jewish workers in Jaffa organized a celebration, and for first time there was a parade in the streets. The Arabs attacked it, and about forty people were killed and many wounded. The *Osservatore Romano* explained that the Bolsheviks had infiltrated into Palestine thanks to the Zionist Organization and they wanted to establish a Communist movement among the Arabs, but the local people revolted. The paper went on to say that the question may be asked whether the Russian Revolution was made in coordination with Zionism or whether Zionism raised a Bolshevik viper in its bosom.[11]

An Italian newspaper wrote that after the aforementioned events in Jaffa, Barlassina submitted a protest to the High Commissioner demanding that the Jewish settlers be disarmed and Zionist immigration be suspended. The German legation asked the Secretariat of State whether this report was true and received a written reply stating that the Vatican was unaware of any protest by Barlassina and that the Holy See had not filed a complaint with the League of Nations.[12]

The pope himself decided to launch a public attack on Zionism in his allocution to the cardinals on June 13, 1921. In this address he said that since his speech on March 10, 1919, his great anxiety regarding the trend of events following the war in Palestine was increasing every day. He lamented the "iniquitous activity of non-Catholic sects which are pleased to glory in the name of Christian, . . . cleverly profiting by the misery in which the inhabitants were plunged after the war." The pope complained that because of a lack of means, he was forced to look on the progressive spiritual ruin of souls for whose salvation men of apostolic zeal have worked, first among them the Franciscans. He went on to say:

> And further, when by means of the Allied troops the Christians returned in possession of the Holy Places, with all Our heart We joined in the general rejoicing of all good men. But with Our joy was also the fear, expressed in the Consistorial Allocution alluded to above, lest as a consequence of that great and glorious event the Jews might attain a position of preponderance and privilege in Palestine. If We are to judge from the present condition of affairs what We feared has come to pass. It is well known, in fact, that the situation of the Christians in Palestine has not only not improved but has even become worse through the new civil ordinances put in force there which tend—if not in the intentions of those responsible for them, certainly, however, in fact—to turn Christianity out of the positions it has occupied up to now and to put Jews in its place. And again We cannot but deplore the intense activity which is being shown by many to take away the sacred character of the Holy Places, transforming them onto pleasure resorts with every worldly attraction. That is worthy of reproof everywhere, but above all in places where at every step the holiest memories of religion are encountered. However, inasmuch as the situation in Palestine is not yet definitely regulated, We now raise Our voice that, when the time comes to establish there a permanent condition of things, to the Catholic Church and to all Christians shall be assured the inalienable rights they hold. Certainly We have no desire that any damage shall be done to the rights of the Jewish element; what We mean is that they must in no way be put above the just rights of the Christians. And to this end We warmly urge all the Governments of Christian nations, even if not Catholic, to bring vigilant pressure to bear on the League of Nations which, it is commonly said, is to consider and adjudicate on the English Mandate in Palestine.[13]

For many years, this speech was the foundation for the Vatican policy on Zionism. Stripped of the Church's rhetorical style, the pope's arguments can be summarized as follows:

1. The non-Catholic Christians (Protestants) are persuading the Arabs of Palestine to convert.
2. The Jews are ousting the Christians from their positions in Palestine by means of Mandate government regulations.
3. The Jews are turning the Holy Places into pleasure spots.
4. The Great Powers must guarantee the rights of Catholics, although without impairing the rights of the Jews and also without giving the Jews any privileges.

Let us examine these contentions. Protestants of various denominations thought that British rule presented an opportune occasion for them to expand their missionary activities, which they had begun in the nineteenth century. The pope's assertions against the activism of these groups, most of which were radically anti-Zionist, were certainly founded in fact to some extent.[14] The Protestant missions engaged in extensive educational work through which they gained substantial influence over the Arab population, their ample financial means enabling them to overcome the influence of the Catholic Church. Jewish writers, too, attributed to the Protestants a destructive influence on individual morality.[15]

The German legation to the Holy See was especially sensitive to matters pertaining to relations between Catholics and Protestants. Immediately after the pope's address, the German representative reported, on the basis of a talk with the cardinal secretary of state, that the pope had had in mind the English and American Methodists and the profanation of the Calvarium (in the Church of the Holy Sepulcher). Which profanation the German representative meant is not clear, but he may have been referring to the belief of some English-speaking Protestants, such as General Charles Gordon of Khartoum, that the Golgotha was located not in the Church of the Holy Sepulchre but on Skull Hill north of the Damascus Gate.[16] A few days later, the German representative again wrote that the pope's protest was aimed less at Jewish rule in Jerusalem than at those who stood behind the British and that the danger posed by non-Catholics was deemed greater than that from non-Christians.

We do not know to which regulations the pope was referring, for at that time the High Commissioner had just issued new ones, in response to the Jaffa riots, restricting Jewish immigration to Palestine. The Catholic writer H. F. Köck related this passage in the pope's speech to the reorganization of the educational system carried out by the High Commissioner.[17] This claim too is hard to understand, but the Catholics may have felt themselves disadvantaged because of the considerable sums of money allotted by the Mandate government to the Arab educational system, with the result that Catholic institutions had to compete not only with the Protestants but also with the Mandate government. Some support for this explanation can be found in the remarks of Bishop Youssuf Gregorius Hajjar, the head of Palestine's Greek Catholic community. He complained that the schools had been turned into the "mightest organ of propaganda," in which Jews and Protestants, supported by large funds, were working diligently, whereas Catholic missionary work that year had come up against unusual difficulties.[18] In this context we may also note a conversation between Herbert Samuel and Robert de Caix, general secretary to General Henry-Joseph-Eugène Gouraud, commander of the French forces in Syria and Lebanon. De Caix claimed that the French living in Jerusalem were afraid that the country might fall into the hands of the Zionists, fearing that in such an instance the French schools would be burdened with heavy taxes.[19]

The great concern for the educational system was expressed again several months later when the Latin patriarchate propagandized in Bethlehem against the establishment of a government school in this city, on the grounds that the school's objective would be to convert the population to Protestantism and to force it to learn Hebrew.[20] According to A. L. Tibawi, the Latin Catholics opposed the Mandatory government's education laws because they wanted to keep the renown that their educational establishments had developed during the Turkish regime. They also opposed the Mandatory government's supervision of their institutions, for under the Turks they had enjoyed complete freedom. Most of the Latin Catholic pupils, in any event, did not attend government schools, but these schools were attended by the Melkites (Greek Catholics).[21]

The pope may also have meant that the Jews had seized the leading positions in the Mandatory administration. The most prominent such Jew was, of course, Sir Herbert Samuel himself, and we have already seen that his appointment had aroused anxiety in the Vatican. It was also claimed that Jews could more easily take posts in the Mandate government because the Zionist Commission was supplementing their salaries.[22] The Arabs complained time and again that all the good positions in the Mandate government had been given to the Jews, and the Catholic press seized on this grievance.[23] In fact, however, according to an earlier survey, Christians occupied proportionally more administrative posts than their share in the population.[24]

The allegation that the Jews had turned the Holy Places into pleasure resorts apparently referred to Mount Carmel and the urban building plans for Haifa.[25] Some believe that it referred to the plan to build a beach resort on the shores of the Sea of Galilee. The remark encouraging sensuality would seem to point more to the resort, for bathing suits and immodest dress were thought to encourage just that. This all was part of the Vatican's struggle against the modernization that had been introduced by the British rule and the Zionists into a country that until then had been quite underdeveloped and whose inhabitants followed a traditional life style.

Finally was the pope's appeal to the Christian nations to protect the rights of Catholics in the League of Nations deliberations on the future of Palestine. For the first time, in this speech, there was some recognition of the Jews' rights, for the pope declared that he had no desire that any damage should be done to those rights but that in no way should they be put above the just rights of the Christians. Preventing any Jewish advantage over Catholics was the pope's main preoccupation. A Catholic writer sympathetic to the Jews, Michel Riquet, regarded this as the pope's recognition of the Balfour Declaration.[26] But this interpretation seems warranted by neither the wording of the speech nor the atmosphere then prevailing in the Vatican.

The pope's allocution, which was also aimed against British rule in Palestine, caused a number of responses in the Foreign Office in London. One official claimed that it would be easy to contradict the pope's contention that the Catholics' situation had deteriorated since the beginning of British civil administration in 1920.[27] But another official claimed that Zionists' arrogant requests regarding the future of Palestine were to blame for the pope's words.[28]

Reactions to the Pope's Speech

After the pope's oration, the Belgian representative at the Holy See, d'Ursel, had a talk with Gasparri. He afterward reported that the Vatican was disturbed by the British government's positive view of Zionism, at a time when everyone, even many Jews, opposed it. In d'Ursel's view, Zionism benefited primarily lower-class Jews, and their admittance into Palestine would only cause problems. Gasparri explained that the concessions the Jews had received upon entering Palestine followed from the British government's commitment. By that commitment, Sir Herbert Samuel—whose appointment was itself highly significant—would respect freedom of worship but would take whatever measures necessary to enable the Jewish nation to be reborn. The Belgian representative asked Gasparri whether he was worried that the immigration of Jews to Palestine might affect the rights of the Holy See in the Holy Places. Gasparri replied that there was nothing to fear on that account.[29]

Gasparri's reply is interesting, for it reveals that he knew quite well that the Holy See's rights in the Holy Places were not endangered by the Zionists. Rather, his opposition and hostility to Zionism stemmed mainly from the fear that the Jews would obtain predominant rights at the expense of the Arab and Christian inhabitants of Palestine and that by their social patterns the Zionists would disrupt the traditional social order. We can find confirmation for this in the positive attitude that the Vatican then adopted toward a delegation of Arabs from Palestine.

The pope's speech evoked a sharp response in the weekly *Israel*, which said that the claims that the Jews had been granted a privileged position in Palestine—and that they wanted to supplant the Christians and Arabs—were groundless. Nevertheless, it was clear that Palestine must become the national home of the Jewish people, to the benefit of the other inhabitants of the country as well. The weekly said further that the Jewish problem should be kept distinct from Anglo-French rivalry and from the fears aroused by British policy; Zionism was not Britain's ally. As for the regime for the Holy Places, that would have to be decided by the League of Nations.[30] Two weeks later, *Israel* devoted its entire front page to the pope's allocution and reactions to it in the Italian press. Indeed, the weekly's editor thought that the press had attributed to the pope a more extreme anti-Zionist position than he had intended.[31]

The Italian daily *Il Resto del Carlino* wrote that France had enjoyed a privileged status in Palestine through its protectorate over the Christians before World War I but that after the war Britain had used Zionism to oust France as an influential factor in the Middle East. The Arabs, however, wrecked the British dream: The Jaffa riots proved the difficulty of creating a Jewish state in Palestine. In the view of this newspaper, if the Arabs failed to understand the Jews' positive role in Palestine, the Zionist state would have to withdraw its borders considerably or constantly contend with the opposition's demonstrations, which would deprive it of security. Not by chance, wrote the newspaper, had the pope expressed anxiety in his speech; the *Osservatore Romano* had already criticized the Zionist movement and Protestant propaganda in Palestine many times before then, and the pope had merely summarized these arguments. The newspaper believed that the pope's remarks did not so much imply absolute negation of the idea of the reestablishing the Jewish people as they appealed for moderation by the League of Nations.

The *Resto del Carlino* added that in the view of some, the Vatican's protests had been supported by France, for it was not satisfied with the new regime in Palestine, despite the territories in the Levant that it had gained. The paper did not take a stand on the truth of this argument. But if France were truly pulling the strings, it would become evident to all that the Jewish solution to the Palestine problem was the best solution: it would remove Palestine from the conflicts between the various Churches and the Great Powers, would give the fields to Jewish workers, and would leave the Holy Places in the hands of the religious institutions in charge of them. It was not clear to the paper why the Italian press was so ready to accept French imperialism and found it so difficult to understand the Arab game. The Arabs were victims and were tools of unjustified incitement. The Jews could reach an agreement with the Arabs once the latter were no longer subjected to outside agitation and understood that the French and the effendis are inciting them against the Jews only in order to dominate them. For the Arabs, European rule held more dangers than did cooperation with the Jews. French imperialism was more dangerous to Italy, its commerce, and its freedom than was the peaceful project of Jews' rebirth in Palestine.[32]

The Egyptian newspaper *La Bourse Egyptienne* stated that the pope's comment about the disecration of the Holy Places apparently referred to the fact that Jerusalem had become a modern city, comfortable and safe, with streetlights and even cinemas. It added that Zionist and Catholic circles alike felt that the pope's speech was a victory for Barlassina, who had become the representative of the protest in Palestine against the appointment of a Jew as High Commissioner.[33]

An anti-Jewish tone was apparent in the commentary of the Swiss newspaper *L'Echo,* in Lausanne, which wrote:

> England serves Jewish nationalism, which under the name of Zionism aspires to rebuild a Jewish state and to bring the dispersed Jews back to the ancient homeland. The English High Commissioner in Palestine, Sir Herbert Samuel, is a Jew. People call him "king of the Jews," and as much as he can he favors his coreligionists, who enjoy all possible benefits thanks to his official post. The Jews have the upper hand in Jerusalem; they occupy all the positions in the administration and hold all the important posts.

The newspaper went on to say that Jerusalem had become quite modernized since the British conquest, which in its view was not a welcome change. What was more, immigrants had arrived from Russia, Bolsheviks who had caused disturbances in Jaffa; the Arabs, who were the majority, had watched their land being taken from them by the Jewish immigrants. The situation was indeed a cause for concern among Catholics because of the Protestant propaganda and the Zionists' schemes, but the final word had yet to be said, and there was still time for England to change course.[34]

In Rome, the secretary of the Italian Zionist Federation, Dante Lattes, arranged to meet with a high-ranking official in the Vatican, with whom he spoke about the possibility of contacts between the Vatican and the Zionist Organization.[35] Lattes had received word from London that Sokolow was ready to go to Rome immediately upon receipt of a written invitation for an audience with the pope.[36]

The pope's speech and his position on Zionism also had reverberations in Spain, whose government evinced special interest in the Holy Places. The Spanish newspaper *Mundo* wrote on June 20 that dance halls would soon be set up near the Church of the Holy Sepulchre and that the Christians and Muslims in Palestine had become the victims of Sir Herbert Samuel and his intolerant Jewish Sanhedrin. *Mundo* also wrote that the Jews intended to expel all other peoples from the land of the Revelation, as they had done after the Exodus from Egypt, and that Vladimir Evgeneviç Jabotinsky, "an ex-prisoner, professional criminal and Bolshevik of Russian origin, leader of the Zionist left in Palestine," had announced that all the Christian and Muslim sites should be destroyed. Jerusalem was in danger of losing its Christian character, and Jabotinsky, as a businessman, would hand over the Church of the Holy Sepulchre to an American film company. The paper further lamented the fact that despite the pope's appeals, Christian countries were viewing the events in Palestine with total indifference.[37]

The heading "Zionism and Palestine" became almost a regular feature in *Osservatore Romano*. On June 23, the newspaper examined "the most interesting and most dangerous political event: 'Zionism,' " relying for its report on the anti-Zionist study by the Catholic writer C. Crispolti.[38] He claimed that both Barlassina and the pope were unduly optimistic. In 1917, when the Balfour Declaration was issued, France and Italy were not concerned about the future of Palestine. The Latins did not then understand the danger that one enemy of Christianity would be replaced by another, more real and greater than the traditional enemy: Judaism. The British government, which was controlled by the Jewish international, altered the term "national home" and consented to establish a Jewish national center in Palestine. According to the draft mandate proposed by Britain on February 22, 1921, a Jewish agency cooperating with the Mandatory government would be formed that would encourage immigration and facilitate the acquisition of citizenship by Jews. Crispolti went on to say that a minority should not rule over the majority and that the riots should be seen against this background. The League of Nations must not overlook the rights of the Christians. The Latin nations must insist on revisions in the draft submitted by Britain, for otherwise the Holy Land would be lost to Christians, and an attempt would be made, with the Great Powers' consent, to erase two thousand years of (Christian) history and to place a new and heavier burden on the land of Jesus.[39]

Jacques Maritain, however, was at this time already an exceptional voice in this Catholic chorus, and many years later, during the World War II, he continued to support the Jews. He warned against the cultivation of anti-Semitic sentiments and wrote: "One need not [accept] that the Jewish problem will serve as an objective to which the public's dissatisfaction would be diverted."[40]

The Christian–Muslim Delegation to Europe

The Arab leadership in Palestine believed that the policy announced in the Balfour Declaration could still be changed. It therefore decided to send a delegation to London to explain the Arab position, with the aim of having the declaration re-tracted. The Arab leaders wanted Christians to have broad representation in this delegation and sought to include outstanding religious figures such as Greek Cath-olic Bishop Hajjar, who, however, did not take part. The participation of clerical figures was intended to underscore the religious element in the opposition to Zion-ism and to present it as a struggle to safeguard the sacredness of the land. The delegation was headed by Mussa Kazim el-Husseini, the former mayor of Jerusalem who had been dismissed by the British because of his participation in the 1920 riots.[41] The delegation left Palestine on July 19 and, en route to London, stopped off in Rome, where it was received by the pope.

The members of the delegation were in Rome from July 25 to July 28, 1921, and upon their arrival were received by Gasparri. He asked them about the purpose of their visit, and they started to explain their position. But the secretary of state cut them short and said that unlike the interests of the Catholic Church in Palestine, this problem had no bearing on the Vatican. That, at least, is what the Vatican reported after the meeting to Cecil Dormer, the British chargé d'affaires at the Holy See. Gasparri did, however, refer the members of the delegation to the pope's ad-dress, particularly his call to the League of Nations to examine the mandate and to ensure that the Jews did not receive a privileged position, which they did not de-serve. The members of the delegation remarked that the pope's speech had not been submitted for publication in Palestine, and then they asked to be received by the pope. The cardinal replied that the pontiff was very busy but that he could arrange a meeting, provided that it would be brief, would not concern matters other than the speech, and would not be made public. After the members of the delegation accepted these conditions, the pope met with them for a few minutes in the after-noon.[42]

The head of the delegation handed the pope a memorandum that spelled out the Arabs' claims concerning the Holy Places, over which they demanded the right of custody. Despite the promise not to make any part of the meeting public, the state-ment they had presented to the pope was published in the Haifa-based Arab news-paper *al-Karmil*.[43] After the audience, the secretary of the delegation, Shibli el-Jamal, a Protestant from Jerusalem, stated that the pope had asked for support in the League of Nations debates from the Catholic countries (France, Spain, Portugal, and Italy).[44]

The members of the delegation declared in Rome that the Palestinian people were enthusiastic about the pope's protests against Zionist policy and recognized the voice of Benedict XV as the only one raised against the policy of the Jews, whom many governments were helping. The delegation demanded that the Balfour

Declaration be renounced and that a national government be established that would be accountable to a parliament elected by the Palestinian people, that is, by Muslims, Christians, and those Jews who had been in Palestine before the war.[45]

But a year later, when Sir Herbert Samuel proposed to establish a legislative council consisting of the High Commissioner and twenty-two members, the Palestinian Arab Executive opposed it because it did not contain a clear majority of Arabs over all others.[46]

The meeting between the delegation and the pope was discussed at the Foreign Office in London, which felt that there were insufficient grounds for a British protest to the Vatican. This was also the position of Colonial Secretary Churchill.[47] The delegation proceeded from Rome to London, where it held a series of talks. Shibli el-Jamal was received on September 1 by the German embassy, where he said that the pope had expressed his full support for the Arab cause and promised to write to all governments that "the Holy Land cannot be allowed to fall into the hands either of the Jews or the Protestants, to both of whom he objected to the same degree." The pope had told this to Jamal privately, assuming that he was a Catholic, although in fact he was a Protestant.[48]

In Palestine, Barlassina claimed that while the Mandate government had forbidden publication of the pope's speech in its entirety, the press had published inaccurate extracts. In his pastoral letter, Barlassina therefore included the full text of the pope's address and added a public protest in which he said:

> Our pain is all the sharper because the discrimination against Catholics is plain enough. The censor arbitrarily prohibited us from publishing the pure words of the pope, even without any commentary, while at the same time the Zionist press was permitted to publish disgraceful comments against the pope and to assail his authority in terms that constitute vulgar defamation.

Barlassina also responded to an article that appeared on June 30, 1921, in the Jewish newspaper *Pinkas,* which claimed that priests "sacred to God" were delivering (nationalist) sermons in the churches, were creating a national movement, were encouraging murder and robbery, and were concluding a pact with both Satan and the pope. Barlassina asserted that no Catholic priest had called for violence in a church or anywhere else.[49] The patriarch's response was picked up by the Italian Catholic newspaper *Il Corriere d'Italia.*[50]

Around this time Chaim Weizmann received a letter from the political secretary of the Zionist Organization, Leonard Stein, who was then in Jerusalem, with further confirmation of the Vatican secretary of state's "uncompromising hostility towards Zionism." Stein had met a most reliable person, whose name was not mentioned, who had recently met with Gasparri, from whom he had heard the following arguments:

1. The Zionists are not religious and are even antireligious, and therefore Zionism cannot be regarded as the fulfillment of prophecy. Zionism has no connection with the promised return of the Jews to the Holy Land.
2. Zionist immigration will sweep the Christians out of Palestine and destroy its Christian character.
3. The possibility that a Jewish government might be formed was unbearable.

4. The cardinal referred with surprising bitterness to the uncalled-for atten-
dance of Sir Herbert Samuel at the special memorial worship service held
by the Latin patriarch for his deceased predecessor.[51]

Weizmann apparently gave Foreign Office officials a copy of the letter, one of
whom suggested that the four points be conveyed to the British representative at
the Vatican without indicating their source.[52] Eric Forbes-Adam commented that the
Vatican would never accept modernization of the Holy Land in any form.[53]

Storrs's Vatican Visit

As discussed in Part I, Ronald Storrs, the governor of the district of Jerusalem,
visited the Vatican in August 1921. One of the topics that came up during his
meeting with the pope on August 25 was the Jews' status in Palestine. Details of
the conversation are known from the report that Storrs wrote after the meeting. The
pope first inquired about the High Commissioner's health and then stated that a year
ago the High Commissioner had declared his intention of acting with complete
impartiality, but to His Holiness's surprise and disappointment, there were signs
that the impartiality of the Palestine government had its limits. Storrs asked the
pope to be more specific, and he replied that the preponderant influence of the Jews
was clear, that in all committees of importance the Jews had the majority and were
consequently able to influence political decisions. Storrs said that he did not understand to what committees His Holiness could be alluding. Indeed, in all the
governmental and municipal committees over which the central government had
any control, the Jews were in proportion to their numbers in the population, which
were known to be a minority. If the pope were alluding to the Zionist Commission,
that was a purely Jewish institution. If the pope could indicate any special instance
in which Jews were unduly favored in any such committees, he (Storrs) would not
fail to inform the High Commissioner.[54]

About that meeting Storrs wrote in his book:

> The relations of the Palestine Government with the Palestine representative of the
> Holy See up to 1922, though correct, could hardly be called cordial, and bristled
> with misunderstandings. . . . About midsummer of that year . . . I was received by
> the new Pope Pius XI, in a private audience lasting half an hour.[55]

Cecil Dormer, the British chargé d'affaires, reported from Rome that the Vatican was well aware of Barlassina's shortcomings and the difficulty of dealing with
him. The French, for their part, were trying to have a Frenchman appointed as
auxiliary, as in the past. Dormer repeated his explanation of the Vatican's feelings
about Zionism, which he felt were the result of the fact that certain Zionists having
openly boasted of their aims and having said that they quite expected to have to
wait one hundred years before they were in a majority and could take control of
Palestine. To a large extent, Dormer identified with the Vatican's attitude toward
Zionism. He also wrote that the suggestion by the Pro-Jerusalem Society that a
promenade be built on top of the wall of the Old City had caused new troubles at
the Vatican.[56]

As mentioned, on September 16, several days after his meeting with the pope, and on the eve of his return to Jerusalem, Storrs met with Gasparri in the cardinal's village. Beginning the conversation with talk about the French religious protectorate, Gasparri then moved on to the Jewish Question. He said that His Majesty's government was fortunate that the Jews in England were well-to-do and orderly, in contrast with the bulk of the Jews in Romania, Poland, and Hungary. In Hungary, they made up 5 percent of the population, but 40 to 50 percent of those in the liberal professions.[57] This fact made him skeptical when he saw that the key official posts in Palestine were so quickly given to the Zionist Jews. Gasparri did not deny that the Vatican was worried by Zionism, but he was persuaded of the goodwill and good intentions of the British government. The cardinal further remarked that it was not the immigration of considerable numbers of Jews to Palestine that caused his misgivings so much as the possibility that they might one day control the administration. Gasparri listened attentively to Storrs's explanations of various matters that had been subjects of complaint either by the patriarch or by the press. Dormer described Storr's visit as most helpful.[58]

We do not know whether Storrs convinced the pope or the cardinal secretary of state, but the same arguments against Zionism, which indirectly were also arguments against the British administration, were aired time and again by the Vatican after these meetings, as were the complaints about important official posts in Palestine being handed over to Jews and about cinemas and prostitutes in Jerusalem. These complaints seem to have sprung from general anti-Semitic feelings and the distorted information sent to the Vatican by its representatives and priests in Palestine.

The Twelfth Zionist Congress

At the Twelfth Zionist Congress, held in Carlsbad (Karlovy Vary), Czechoslovakia, on September 11 to 14, 1921, Sokolow brought up the subject of the Holy Places and, among other things, pointed out:

> The same is true of the sacredness of Palestine, which latterly is being used again as an argument against Zionism. It is a fact that we have never lost sight of, that Palestine is sacred to the great religions of mankind. . . . The inviolable rights of conscience and religious liberty must reign in Jerusalem, the city of God; for Jerusalem is more than a city, it is a principle, that of peace. . . . To us, every stone, every grain of sand in Palestine is sacred, and we want to see the sanctuaries of that country preserved and protected. We made a declaration to this effect some time ago to the venerable head of the Catholic Church, to which he was agreeable, and he gave full expression of his cordial acceptance. From the beginning it has been our greatest anxiety lest other elements might intrude, and do their best to spoil the good work that had been commenced in the spirit of fullest responsibility. Nevertheless, we will not deviate from the hope that the march of events will happily brush aside this misunderstanding also.[59]

The *Zionist Review,* which reported Sokolow's remarks, mentioned the anti-Zionist pronouncements made by the Anglican bishop in Jerusalem on his visit to

London at that time and appealed to the churches to adopt an attitude toward the Jews free of the intolerance of the past.

Sokolow's statement that the pope had acceded to Zionism was undoubtedly based on his recollections of his talk with the pontiff in 1917. However, as we have seen, the Vatican's position had changed drastically since then, but the Zionist leaders, it seems, did not revise their assessments accordingly.

The *Osservatore Romano* devoted a long article to the Zionist Congress, attacking the foundations of Zionism and denying that the pope had acceded to Zionism. The paper wrote that it was naive to think there was general international consent to Zionist aspirations, as these aspirations were nothing if compared with the safeguard of the rights of the people of Palestine. The historical-ethnic principle, which was based on events that had taken place two thousand years ago, could not be accepted, for its acceptance would require changes in every country. The Jews were not a nation but an "ethnic-religious entity" and were citizens and subjects of various countries. The newspaper asked by what right the Jews could establish a reserve nation and benefit from dual citizenship. The proclamations of the Zionist Congress were unable to assuage the Christian conscience, which did not forget that Palestine was the Holy Land where Christ had been sacrificed by the wishes of a people that must bear responsibility for itself and its descendants. "History and world civilization erases all rights, and no claim based on the past two thousand years could be recognized by a state court of law."[60] Here the Jews' "deicide," which for centuries served as the basis of Christian anti-Semitism, was exploited to deny the Jews' rights in the Holy Land.

According to Dormer, the pope's distrust of Zionism was deep and perhaps comparable to that of the Arabs. The liberal press in Italy also came out against Zionism and reinforced the Church's apprehensions. There were political reasons for this as well, as the problem of Zionism was entangled with that of the Cenacle.[61]

Buonaiuti and the Interview with Gasparri

On September 29, 1921, *Il Secolo,* a Milan-based newspaper, published an interview by Ernesto Buonaiuti[62] with a cardinal who was left unnamed, but who, it was hinted, was the papal secretary of state. The interview, which attracted much attention in Italy, included the following comment:

> England, with its open and calculated policy of protection in favor of Zionism, has acted in such a manner that in the most delicate part of the East, the interests of France and Catholicism have come to coincide.
>
> The Holy See has no prejudiced hostility against a Zionist movement which aims exclusively at creating a place of refuge for the poor victims of anti-Semitism. The Zionist representatives, and especially Dr. Sokolow, have never found and will never find the "Portone di Bronzo" closed to them, but the followers of Sir Herbert Samuel, with their occult forms of religious proselitism, cannot and must not aspire to create in Palestine a monopoly which would grievously offend the deepest feelings of the Christian peoples. And England, which covers with its prestige and with its power the partiality of its High Commissioner in the Holy Land, should not forget

that the Holy See also has at its disposal some not ineffectual weapons of retaliation. Imagine, for instance, the effect which would be produced throughout the whole English-speaking world by some act of the Pontiff in favor of an Irish republic.

The threat implicit in the interview alarmed the British, who were already fearful of the Vatican's activity in Ireland. The British chargé d'affaires went to the Vatican and found Gasparri more indignant than ever. The secretary of state said officially that the alleged interview was an entire fabrication and that the statements attributed to him were neither made nor represented in any way his attitude or feelings. The day afterward, Dormer received a note in the cardinal's own handwriting, denying particularly the part referring to Great Britain, "which is not only false but also ridiculous."[63]

The incident did not end there. On October 1, the *Osservatore Romano* published a statement by Buonaiuti declaring that he recognized in the interview a conversation held by him with a person on the staff of *Il Secolo*, in which, however, he did not and could not express—not having been near His Eminence for several months—the thoughts of the cardinal secretary of state. The next day, the Vatican's paper claimed that no such interview with the cardinal had been given; but above all, the paper stressed, the interview did not reflect Gasparri's opinion, and so there were no grounds for ascribing Buonaiuti's views to the cardinal. Gasparri promptly sent the newspaper articles to the British representative.[64]

It is hard to understand why Gasparri went to such lengths to convince the British that he had not given this interview. He had more than once hinted in his conversations that the Vatican was prepared to support a refuge for the Jews on humanitarian grounds but would never support Jewish rule in Palestine. And if he thought it appropriate to deny having threatened England with some intervention on behalf of Ireland, why, such a threat had already been made in 1919 by Cardinal Bourne, who too had linked the problem of Palestine to that of Ireland. Today we are certain that although Buonaiuti did not conduct a special interview with Gasparri—as the two newspapers that published it had claimed—he was a reliable spokesman for Gasparri's views. In his memoirs, Buonaiuti wrote: "Cardinal Gasparri should not have regretted the wide broadcast given to his deepest intentions and dearest plans. But perhaps because of caution and cowardice . . . he did not forgive me for my leak."[65] Buonaiuti was one of the cardinal's closest intimates and, despite Gasparri's denials, certainly knew what the cardinal truly believed. This was also the opinion of Moshe Beilinson, who was in Rome at that time as a journalist and Zionist activist[66] and who published an interview with Buonaiuti.

The interview in *Il Secolo* was echoed in the Zionist press. The *Palestine Weekly* carried a translation of the main part and attributed the interview to Cardinal Achille Ratti, who had just been appointed archbishop of Milan and who some months later would become Pope Pius XI. The weekly stressed that the cardinal would not succeed in frightening Great Britain or those striving to rebuild Palestine:

> The Jews have long been acquainted with such threats and can estimate them at their due worth. The significance of it is quite clear and shows that there are in France some imperialistic appetites which are not satisfied with what they gained from this war. . . . But we have no doubt that the declaration made by the Cardinal cannot be

officially sanctioned by the Holy See. Otherwise it would be an absolute contradiction to what the Pope declared to Mr. Sokolow some three years ago and we may not believe that the Holy Father is given to changing his mind.[67]

The weekly's opinion accurately reflected the view then prevailing among the Zionist leadership, which exaggerated the importance of Sokolow's meeting with the pope in 1917 and remained attached to that assessment despite the consistorial addresses by the pope in March 1919 and June 1921. The blatant anti-Zionist tone of those speeches should have been more of a warning to the Zionist leadership than would an interview in an Italian newspaper from which the Vatican dissociated itself, at least officially.

The monthly *Zionist Review* also devoted a long article to the interview in *Il Secolo* and to the unnamed cardinal threatening England by means of an anti-British combination of France and the Vatican in the Middle East unless England repudiated the Balfour Declaration, and in these critical days of Anglo-Irish negotiations, an anti-British move by the Roman hierarchy in Ireland was hardly in consonance with correct official relations. The disavowed representative of the Vatican was unfortunately supported by the cardinal archbishop of Westminster, Bourne. "We passionately repudiate the implied assumption that . . . the Jews alone are, even in their ancient country, to be tolerated only in so far as they are aiming at finding a refuge for the poor victims of anti-Semitism. . . . Indeed we welcome the invitation to the Vatican . . . extended to Mr. Sokolow," the *Zionist Review* wrote, and it quoted the pronouncement made by Sokolow as president of the Zionist Congress, on the Holy Places of Christendom and Islam.[68]

In October 1921, the *Osservatore Romano* again published a number of anti-Zionist articles, many of them from Paris. One such article dealt with France's position on Zionism. It was thought by some that its negative attitude toward a Jewish rebirth was related to its interests in the East. That indeed was so, but the author of this article believed that there was another reason. The Jewish religion, he wrote, should be differentiated from the political and social power of the Jews all over the world. Jews were entitled to tolerance of and respect for their religion, but not when they were hostile to Christianity because of racism and a desire to dominate. "Today there exist the Jewish problem and the Freemason problem, which possibly are one and the same."[69] This repeats an argument then common among anti-Semites in Europe. Thus, for example, in November 1921, Father Umberto Benigni wrote:

> [We fight the] Israel not of the Pentateuch but of the Talmud, that is, a highly antisocial religious corruption. We fight not against Israel the people, as one of many peoples, but against that one which regards itself, as the "chosen people" to dominate and exploit the world of the "goyim," as the Talmud teaches.[70]

Several days later, the Vatican newspaper ran another article from Paris, declaring that the religious problem must be differentiated from the political problem. The first differentiation between Zionism and religion was made by the Church, which instituted a prayer for the conversion of the Jews.[71] From London, the paper reported the speech by Cardinal Bourne, who asserted that the question of the Holy Places should be kept in mind by all Catholics and that the promise given by Balfour in his declaration must be withdrawn. Cardinal Bourne did not believe that the English people truly wanted to waste money on founding a Jewish state and said, "It would be a grave insult to Christianity if the Holy Land were to pass to the rule of those who had denied Christ."[72]

Also the Anglican bishop in Jerusalem was strongly anti-Zionist. On November 5, 1921, Bishop Rennie MacInnes sent a circular letter in which he stated: "Palestine can live in peace as it is proven by our mixed schools in which Arabs and Christians and Jews study and play to-gether, but [the country] is disturbed by the injust and intolerable demands of the Zionists."[73] Weizmann protested on February 2, 1922, in a letter to Sir John Shuckburgh of the Colonial Office, but the bishop continued his anti-Zionist campaign for many years.

The problem of the relations between the Zionist Organization and the Vatican came up in London at the sixteenth meeting of the Zionist Executive, on November 27, 1921. The meeting was attended by Rabbi Zvi Peretz Chajes of Florence, who tried to explain that the tone of the pope's speech was not as negative as might be surmised from the excerpts that had appeared in the press.[74] It seemed to him that the Vatican would be willing to receive a representative of the Zionist Organization, and the interview in *Il Secolo* hinted, according to Chajes, at an invitation for Sokolow. Weizmann accepted Chajes's view without debate and said that Sokolow should be informed and steps must be taken to avoid the impression that the invitation was being ignored. It was therefore decided at that meeting that Joseph Cowen[75] would inform Sokolow and would ask him to write a letter or issue a statement meant to maintain the Vatican's positive approach. It is hard to understand how the Zionist Executive was able to regard an interview, which was denied, as an invitation to its representative to visit the Vatican, while it totally ignored all the public signals coming from the Vatican itself.

On December 17, 1921, Moshe Beilinson, as we said, published an interview with Buonaiuti on the Catholic Church's attitude toward Zionism. The interview began by Beilinson's asking Buonaiuti his opinion of the value of Zionism. Buonaiuti then replied:

> I have serious doubts as to practicability of the essential Zionist programme. . . . If the Jewish state is to be created on the model of the modern state, . . . it will come into conflict with the principles of Jewish tradition. If, however, it remains loyal to this tradition, will it then not be fragile like an earthenware vessel among vessels made of iron and of bronze? . . . I consider the idea of creating in Palestine a place of refuge for the Jews persecuted by blind, inhuman anti-Semitism as beyond reproach; on the other hand, however, I believe that the Jews have to carry out a higher mission in forming throughout their dispersion a nucleus of constant rejuvenation and social progress, which role they have always played by their dissatisfaction and restlessness.

Asked about his impressions of the Twelfth Zionist Congress in Carlsbad in September 1921, Buonaiuti answered that it seemed to him that Zionism had succeeded in organizing after the war with even greater intensity than before. To another question about the stand of Catholics toward Zionism, he responded:

> The opposition of Catholic circles to the Zionist movement is governed mainly by three motives: in the first instance, . . . Catholicism shares the fears and apprehensions with which existing society views the programme of the reconstitution of the Jewish race, in view of the invincible revolutionary spirit with which the latter appears to many to be imbued. In the second place, Catholicism maintains in its tradition . . . Christ's curse against Jerusalem: "No stone shall remain on your stones." Any attempt to restore Jerusalem to a position of real political value, . . . is regarded as an insult. In the third place Catholic circles are alarmed by the fact that the Zionist movement has placed itself under the protection of England, which is promoting with all means Protestant propaganda in the Near East, and which appears today as the most anti-Catholic people among all European nations.

To disarm the Catholics' suspicions about Zionism, the following measures, in his view, were necessary: (1) to give guarantees that the holy center of Jerusalem would remain outside the attempt at modernization and reconstruction and (2) to withdraw the movement from British tutelage and to weaken the connection between Zionism and British policy in the East. It was also necessary that Christians obtain government posts in Palestine administration. At the end of the interview, Beilinson remarked that Buonaiuti's advice could not be implemented, as England was the Zionists' only friend.[76]

Even if Buonaiuti's suggestions were not practicable, the Zionists should have noted the theological argument he raised (Jesus's curse) and the Catholic fear of Jewish revolutionism. Indeed, the preservation of the specific historical character of the "holy center of Jerusalem" is today the declared aim of the municipality.

The Death of Benedict XV

When Pope Benedict XV died in January 1922, the editor of *Israel* commented: "Although, due to his sudden death, Benedict XV did not yet leave in the history of the Jewish people the impression of deep and humane understanding which Zionism expected of him, we still believe in the sound judgment of the Vatican."[77] The editor mentioned that Sokolow had intended to visit the Vatican again to repeat his promises and to restate the hopes of the Jewish people to achieve its rebirth with deep understanding from the Church.

The *Zionist Review* wrote that in Jewish history Pope Benedict XV would be remembered for various acts of mercy affecting Jews during World War I, and according to this journal, the Jews had especially appreciated his benevolent attitude toward Zionist proposals at the most critical period, at a time when unfriendly intervention of the papacy would have caused serious misgivings in authoritative quarters. "If later the Pope saw fit to express his concern about British policy in the Holy Land, we are inclined to ascribe this to influences of an anti-Jewish and anti-British character which had, we hope, only temporarily risen to the surface at the Vatican."[78]

In Palestine itself, the *Palestine Weekly* published an article full of praise for

Benedict XV. According to this paper, the late pope understood the importance of the Balfour Declaration: "not only a step towards the realisation of the Divine purpose, but . . . he saw in it the means of redemption of a race which had suffered so much at the hands of Christianity."[79] When one reads—in a random but representative cross section of the Zionist press of that period—these encomiums about a pope who in a few years had spoken twice against Zionism, one wonders whether this was blindness or part of an attempt to soften the Vatican's opposition. But as we have said, it seems that the Zionists were still deluding themselves and failed to plumb the deep roots of the Vatican's disapproval of Zionism.

On February 6, 1922, Achille Cardinal Ratti was elected pope and assumed the name Pius XI.

12

Weizmann at the Vatican

Weizmann's First Meeting with Gasparri

In January 1922, the German Foreign Ministry asked its representative at the Holy See to sound out the Vatican's position on Zionist settlement in Palestine and to determine the possibility of improving its stand on Zionism. "Such improvement," the Foreign Ministry noted, "would contribute to the German interest because of the Jews' relationship to German culture."[1] Germany's interest in the Vatican's position did not diminish throughout 1922. In June, Professor Hans Delbrück, a pro-Zionist historian who volunteered to keep a link between the Zionist Organization and the Curia, visited the Vatican, heard its position, and hastened to report what he had heard to the Zionist representative in Berlin, Professor Sobernheim.[2]

Around this time, approval of the draft mandate by the League of Nations became a very real and pressing problem. The Zionist leadership decided to make every effort to ensure a speedy approval without revisions detrimental to Zionism. As part of these efforts, and spurred by information received from Rome according to which the Vatican had supported the Arab riots,[3] Weizmann decided that he should visit Italy and see the pope. In Rome, Dante Lattes and Moshe Beilinson said that once they knew the date of Weizmann's arrival in Italy, they would do what they could to prepare the ground for the visit.[4]

The possibility of a meeting between Weizmann and the pope aroused special interest among friends of Zionism in France, who anxiously awaited a report from Weizmann about it. They were sure the French ambassador at the Vatican would assist Weizmann.[5] France was then acting against Zionism and the British administration in Palestine, and so it is not clear on what ground this hope was based. As with Sokolow's visit in 1917, it was the British legation to the Holy See that arranged a meeting between the Zionist leader and Cardinal Gasparri.[6]

The meeting took place on Sunday, April 2, and although the conversation was "very friendly and even genial," Weizmann was left with no doubt in his mind as to Gasparri's antagonism toward the Zionist movement. The cardinal told Weiz-

Chaim Weizmann, a prominent Zionist leader.

mann that the Holy See had presented a memorandum to the League of Nations, which stated the Vatican's objections to three articles in the draft mandate for Palestine: (1) Article 2, concerning the safeguarding of religious rights; (2) Article 4, concerning recognition of a Jewish Agency; and (3) Article 14, concerning the establishment of a commission for the Holy Places. Gasparri protested against the content of these articles as drafted, particularly Article 14.[7]

Weizmann replied that the problem of the Holy Places and the composition of the commission had nothing at all to do with the Zionist movement, which merely wished that disputes be resolved in a friendly manner for the sake of enduring peace in Palestine. It was in this conversation that Weizmann discovered for the first time that the Vatican's opposition to approval of the mandate, and especially to its Zionist articles, had taken the official form of a memorandum submitted to the League of Nations. Because Weizmann was in contact with the British Foreign Office and had heard nothing there about a Vatican memorandum, he concluded that the British themselves perhaps did not yet know about it. He therefore asked his colleagues in the Zionist Executive in London to find out from the Colonial Office what they knew about the memorandum.[8]

The Times reported the meeting between Weizmann and Gasparri and noted that earlier, Sir Herbert Samuel had been received in a private audience by the late pope.

But

> no practical conclusions seem to have been reached at this meeting, for later the Pope took up a very strong attitude towards the Zionist movement and incidentally towards the British occupation of Palestine. . . . It is considered doubtful whether Dr. Weizmann will be received by the Pope. Meanwhile Dr. Weizmann has already seen the Secretary of the Italian Popular Party, the famous Don Sturzo, and it therefore appears that his visit may help to lessen the animosity between the Jews and the Catholics in Palestine.[9]

The *Bulletin* of the Zionist Organization in London published the same item, as well as Gasparri's dissatisfaction with Article 14. "Notwithstanding this," the *Bulletin* observed, "the Vatican and he [Gasparri] personally were in no way opposed to the creation of a Jewish national home in Palestine, so long as the interests of the other faiths in the country were safeguarded, and the Jews were not given any privileged position."[10]

On the day after the meeting with Gasparri, Weizmann received, through de Salis, an invitation from the cardinal to continue their conversation after Weizmann returned from Capri.[11] Weizmann accepted the invitation, and de Salis wrote to him the following day that he would talk to the Vatican about it, probably meaning that he would set a date for the second meeting.[12]

On April 4, Weizmann delivered a lecture at the Collegio Romano under the aegis of the Istituto per l'Oriente, on the aims of the Zionist movement. According to de Salis, Weizmann said that the program Zionism tended to be the foundation of a true Hebrew state in Palestine, liberal, as far as desired, toward other nationalities and confessions but sovereign in its own territory. According to the weekly *Israel,* Weizmann stressed that the problem was not only practical—to find a solution for that part of the Jewish people that is persecuted—but also one of ideals, spiritual exaltation, moral values, and a right to civic and national life. The Jews were not seeking individual freedom, which they enjoyed in many countries, including Italy, but the freedom of national existence. After Israel was reconstituted, many Jewish communities would continue to live outside the state, but they would be free to unite with the central core of their nation. In any event, they would know that they had a country of their own that preserved the features characteristic of the people's spiritual life.[13]

The *Osservatore Romano* published a somewhat inaccurate summary of Weizmann's lecture, which he later corrected. In an editorial, the Vatican newspaper accused the Jews of wanting to dominate the Arabs of Palestine by force or legal means and of trying to create a homeland where Jews could enjoy the advantages of dual citizenship. The paper also published a commentary on Weizmann's speech which stated that the hospitality given to the Jews in Europe was much more extensive and generous than Weizmann indicated, and consequently there was no historical or social necessity to found a Zionist state to provide protection for the Jews. The editorial claimed that Weizmann had made statements that were not wholly accurate—for example, when he spoke of the desire of the Palestinian Jews to perform manual labor, their peaceful penetration of a country that had not been theirs for two thousand years, or their respect for the freedom and property of

Israel's native inhabitants of other races and religions. The newspaper went on to say that according to Weizmann, about 10 million to 12 million Jews would continue to live outside Palestine in all those countries where they had lived for centuries. The new state thus would be established by only a minority, and its sole purpose would be to allow those Jews who remained in those countries to be better protected, stronger, wealthier, and more able to take the initiative in the positions they have already taken over.[14]

The Zionists believed the Vatican's position to be of considerable importance, especially after relations between the Holy See and Italy had improved, a development that was likely to strengthen the Vatican's opposition to the draft mandate and to increase the difficulties obstructing approval of the mandate that Italy had already presented.[15]

On April 6, 1922, Weizmann's letter from Rome about his visit to the Vatican and the Holy See's memorandum to the British government spelling out the Vatican's objections to the draft mandate was brought to the knowledge of the Zionist Executive in London. The executive, which had not known of this memorandum, decided to investigate the matter at the Colonial Office and the Secretariat of the League of Nations.[16] That same day, Leonard Stein wrote to William Ormsby-Gore at the League of Nations and asked for details about the memorandum of which Gasparri had spoken to Weizmann.[17]

From Capri, Weizmann sent a detailed letter summarizing the Vatican's position on Palestine. In his view, the new pope had not yet had time to immerse himself in the state matters that were entirely in Gasparri's hands.

> It is rumoured in Rome that Gasparri's days [as secretary of state] are counted and that Cerretti, the present Papal nuncio in Paris, will take his place. . . .[18] G.[asparri] gives one the impression of being very rusé, and as far as we are concerned very uninformed and prejudiced. He knows the *Morning Post* and the Arab propaganda literature, thinks that H.M.G. is bought by Rothschild. The general impression from G[asparri]'s talk is that he is much more anti-Protestant, anti-British than anti-Zionist; perhaps because he has less to fear from us than from the British.

Weizmann also wrote that he had seen the first issue of a French periodical published by the Latin patriarchate in Jerusalem, *La Palestine,* and found it "a venomous paper full of untruths."[19]

A few days after Weizmann's meeting with Gasparri, de Salis sent a report to Foreign Secretary Curzon.[20] De Salis said that he had arranged the meeting with Gasparri on Weizmann's request. Weizmann had told him that he anticipated that he might encounter hostility at the Vatican, and de Salis replied that although it would never be easy to induce the Holy See to have much liking for the Zionist policy, it might be possible to remove causes of friction and misunderstanding.

The previous pope, Benedict XV, had defined his views in his allocution on June 13, 1921, and de Salis gave Weizmann an English translation of it before he went to see the cardinal, an act suggesting that de Salis knew that Weizmann was insufficiently acquainted with the Vatican's, and the pope's, public stand on Zionism. Weizmann was anxious to be received by the pope and believed that a failure to arrange for an audience for him would be a sign of hostility on the pope's part.

De Salis took up the matter twice with the secretary of state, and it appeared to him that an audience could be arranged after Weizmann returned from his vacation in Capri. De Salis reported to London that the Vatican had been considering over the last weeks presenting a memorandum that summarized its opposition to the draft mandate proposed to the League of Nations by Balfour on December 7, 1920.

In the meantime, de Salis received the memorandum Weizmann had heard about from Gasparri, and de Salis sent a translation of it to the foreign secretary, although he did not know whether it had also been communicated to the Council of the League of Nations.[21] The memorandum is dated March 6, 1922, but Gasparri added to it in his own handwriting a comment on Weizmann's lecture on April 4, and the British legation received the memorandum only on April 11, 1922.

Gasparri wrote to de Salis:

> The Holy See does not object to the Jews in Palestine receiving civilian rights equal to those of the other nations and religions, but it cannot agree that: (1) The Jews will obtain a privileged position of greater importance than that of other nationalities and religions; (2) that the rights of the Christians will not receive suitable guarantees.

The cardinal also commented that Article 4 of the draft mandate accorded recognition to the alien Zionist Organization as a public body. Furthermore, according to the draft mandate, the Jews were granted privileged status regarding immigration (Article 6) and the acquisition of citizenship (Article 7). In Gasparri's view, the object of the proposed draft was to grant the Jews preference over other nationalities, and thereby it not only impaired the rights that the other nationalities had obtained but also contradicted Article 22 of the Versailles Treaty. The Vatican was therefore opposed to the Zionist plan to establish a Jewish state.[22]

In his letter, Gasparri attached the most importance to the Jews' alleged privileged position and only secondarily touched on Article 14 and the commission for the Holy Places, even though the problem of the Holy Places was then considered by the Vatican to have priority.

The British foreign secretary, Curzon, responded immediately to the memorandum. He cabled his representative at the Vatican that he was "at a loss to understand in what manner the Vatican could regard itself as being entitled to intervene in the matter." In his view, the secretary of state's memorandum "amounts to nothing less than protest against the whole policy which His Majesty's Government has been commissioned by the Powers and the League of Nations to carry out in Palestine."[23]

Weizmann's Second Meeting with Gasparri

Weizmann returned from his holiday and on April 20, accompanied by Lattes, the secretary of the Italian Zionist Federation, was received for a second time by Gasparri.[24] At this meeting, Weizmann pointed out the inaccuracies that had been published in *Osservatore Romano* about his lecture. Weizmann wrote in his memoir:

> The next morning a full report appeared in the *Osservatore Romano* (the organ of the Vatican); not an unfair report in the whole, but with a few pinpricks. For instance, my statement that for the moment we were not buying land in Palestine, as

we have reserves of land sufficient for the next ten years or so, appeared in the *Osservatore* something like this: "Dr. Weizmann stated that the Zionist Organization was in possession of vast reserves of land, and would not need to expropriate the Arabs for another ten years."

When Weizmann complained that his remarks had been distorted, the cardinal smiled and said, "One must bear with the journalists, who sometimes slipped up." Weizmann retorted that he thought far too highly of the Vatican journalists to attribute to them careless mistakes in reporting.[25]

On April 21, the *Osservatore Romano* published a letter by Lattes, who wrote that Weizmann did not speak of a Jewish state in Palestine to which Jews throughout the world would be bound by political links and did not mention dual nationality, both of which he opposed. Nor was it proper to talk of expropriating Arab lands, which in Weizmann's view was unjust and illegal and, in regard to Zionism, unnecessary: all the lands acquired by the Jews had been purchased on the open market.[26]

In his talk with Gasparri, Weizmann tried to determine what was truly behind the Vatican's fear of the Zionist movement:

> It gradually became apparent that His Eminence was concerned with matters which had to do with the British administration rather than the Zionists. . . . His Eminence still suspected that the Zionist Organization was, in some obscure fashion, a branch of the Palestine Government and "could use its influence" if it chose. I spent some minutes trying to make the position clear, but I am not at all sure whether I had any success. . . . At another interview with Cardinal Gasparri, when the talk had been on more general lines, and I had been giving some account of the work we were actually doing and preparing to do in Palestine—agricultural settlement, drainage, afforestation, medical work, education—he indicated that the colonization work and so on caused him no anxiety but added: "*C'est votre université que je crains*" (It is your university that I fear). Which gave me food for thought.[27]

This last remark is most interesting for it reveals some of the real reasons for the Vatican's fears of Zionism. The Catholic Church did not engage in agricultural settlement in Palestine and was not opposed to the Jews doing so. But the Church did have many schools and was highly active throughout the educational system, and, as we have already noted, the pope's comments in 1921 were apparently directed against changes introduced by the High Commissioner in the educational system in Palestine. Furthermore, apart from the problem of the Holy Places, the Vatican's interest in Palestine chiefly concerned moral and ideological values. In addition to the danger from the Protestants, which necessitated constant theological and actual struggle, the Vatican was now presented with a new ideological challenge by the Hebrew University.

As to the preferential position allegedly given to the Jews in Palestine, Weizmann told Gasparri that "the Jews will occupy [in the Holy Land] a position in accordance with their numbers, influence, work, means and energy." "That is a fine phrase," the cardinal remarked, and Weizmann added that the Jews and the Catholic Church would have to live together in Palestine and that they should therefore think how to live in peace. "I desire nothing else," replied Gasparri. Finally,

Weizmann asked whether the representative of the Zionist Organization in Rome might visit the cardinal from time to time to keep him informed of the situation in Palestine. Gasparri responded that this would be a great pleasure for him.[28]

More details about the meeting are provided by the Italian Jewish weekly *Israel*. According to this paper, Weizmann pointed out the inaccuracies in the *Osservatore Romano* report of his lecture and commented that this was an example of the misunderstandings that sometimes are prompted by nonexistent facts. Weizmann emphasized that the Jews wanted to found a national home in Palestine, in the frame of a Palestinian state, in which all peoples would have the place they deserved, with no special privileges for anyone. Gasparri expressed his full satisfaction with these declarations.[29]

Weizmann's second meeting with Gasparri was reported to Foreign Secretary Curzon by de Salis. Gasparri had told de Salis that the meeting with Weizmann had been cordial, like the previous meeting, but that the tone of Weizmann's lecture at the Collegio Romano

> did not seem to correspond with the assurances given to the Vatican respecting the interpretation of the term "national home" and the creation of a Hebrew State in Palestine. . . . The question of the Palestine Mandate had been considered and especially the dispositions of Article 14 which relates to the Holy Places. . . . It had been decided to send a copy of the text to each Cardinal, with a request for observations.[30]

In addition to the reports already mentioned, we have the account presented by Weizmann himself at a meeting of the Zionist Executive in London on May 4, 1922, after his return from Rome. He reported having met twice with Cardinal Gasparri, who apparently had prevented a meeting between him and the pope. Weizmann had heard that this had to do with promises that Samuel had made to the previous pope but had not kept. The *Osservatore Romano* wrote that Samuel had promised to restrict Jewish immigration to Palestine but had not kept his word. This probably refers to regulations limiting Jewish immigration issued by the High Commissioner following the Jaffa riots.

Weizmann reported that Gasparri had been quite friendly but began by claiming that the Jews enjoyed a privileged position in Palestine. Weizmann insisted that the cardinal should give at least one fact proving those alleged privileges. Gasparri complained about three nuns who had been refused entry visas for Palestine; he was surprised to hear that as many as thousand Jews a month were immigrating to Palestine. He also raised the question of Article 14 of the draft mandate and complained that Armenians, Catholics, and other Christians were all put together (in the same subcommission), while they were enemies. In addition, Weizmann had heard from Buonaiuti that Gasparri believed Zionism to be a strong movement and would do everything to combat it. Weizmann added that he was shocked by the parallelism between the Vatican's arguments and those of the Arab delegation.[31]

After returning to London, Weizmann continued his desperate efforts to be received by the pope. He turned to Lattes, who spoke with Gasparri's secretary, but he was told that the pope was too busy and could not see Weizmann. De Salis received a similar reply in writing from the Secretariat of State,[32] and Gasparri delivered yet another negative reply to a friend of Weizmann, N. Kobylinsky.[33] Weizmann even received a letter of recommendation to the pope from the cardinal primate of Hungary, Janos Csernoch, who commented that it was high time to clarify the problems that needed to be dealt with.[34]

Around the same time, Baron Alfredo Porcelli, one of Weizmann's Catholic acquaintances, wrote to him to avoid any illusions about the Vatican:

> I warned you, some 4 years ago, to beware of Rome. . . . [They] are actually intriguing with the greatest foe Zionism possesses, though a disguised one. I will give you a hint. Whenever and wherever in the Press, or at conferences, or at interviews at the Vatican, the word "Christian" is used, substitute the word "Romanists" and you—unless willfully blind to patent facts—will, I hope, perceive that it is not the Christians who join Arabs in opposing Zionism in Palestine—but those who, under the false garb of "Christianity," pretend—for a special object to have dread of the Jews and to agree with the Arabs or more correctly the Moslems. If, instead of being a Jew you were a Christian, you would know that the greatest foes of true Christianity and of the Jews in Palestine are those priest-ridden cults which have churches filled with shrines, images, candles, and priests; those cults which have battered upon Palestine for certainly 50 years, and have plastered it with monasteries, convents, and idolatrous shrines, and swindle tourists and thoughtless visitors. Those are the cults that oppose in every way the desires of the Zionists, though often posing as friends. . . . It is only necessary to read the *Osservatore Romano* and the *Civiltà Cattolica*, *L'Ora*, and similar Papal organs, to see the rancorous hatred for the Jews that underlines all their articles. It necessarily must be so because Rome aims at supremacy. It will not brook rivalry, or tolerate equality. Religious freedom is a mortal sin in its eyes. Buy a copy of Pope Pius X's "Compendio della Dottrina Cristiana"—published in 1906 at the Vatican Press, and read what it says. Another hint. Beware of *The Times*, and other Northcliffe papers. They have sent a special "commissioner" (one of their own staff) to Palestine, and are publishing a series of articles on "The truth about Palestine." . . . You will find that Zionism will fare badly at his hands—for Rome has a finger in that pie, as in all Northcliffe papers. Every day I live I regret more . . . that you ignored my advice. Had you, as I advised, arranged for hordes of Jewish immigrants to enter Palestine—from Mesopotamia, Persia, Arabia, Egypt, and the East generally—(not from Russia or Poland), and so flooded Palestine, matters would have taken a very different aspect by this time. Instead of this you Zionist . . . [concocted] grandiose schemes for a University, which naturally aroused suspicion; for museums, for schools, for this and for that, as though the place already belonged to you, so that, of course, the Romanists took alarm, made friends with the Moslems, and started riots, and agitation—which has checked immigration, and is raising up a hornets' nest. Had I been in your place I should have arranged for bands of Jews to enter Palestine from the East and South—as Pilgrims, not as dwellers; just like the Russians did before the War. . . . Instead of this you gave time for the enemy to bring in fanatical Maltese and Syrians and so-called "Arabs," who now pose as "inhabitants" and pretend to fear the Jews.[35]

Porcelli raised some interesting points: the Catholic's fear of the Jewish university, the Vatican's influence on newspapers such as *The Times*, and the idea of giving priority to the immigration of Jews from the East rather than from Russia. By and large, Porcelli's judgment was undoubtedly sound, as proved by the fact that the *Osservatore Romano* continued its attacks on Zionism. Although it was reacting to criticism from Zionists and although the very choice of "facts" was itself tendentious, the paper did differentiate between news items and commentary. In its commentary on May 4, the newspaper wrote that Zionism had become too extremist even for religious Jews, for whom it was inconceivable that the right to a Zionist state should be based on a majority, reinforced from time to time by new immigrants, against the rights of the local population.[36]

Two days later, the Vatican newspaper took issue with Lattes and argued that his facts contradicted the arguments of the weekly *Israel*. The *Osservatore Romano* stated it had always regarded the view of the Holy See, which deplored aggression against the Jews as well as against other peoples. It claimed that it was presenting objectively the controversy surrounding *The Protocols of the Elders of Zion* and had also published the Jewish denials. The newspaper also argued that there were Jewish influences in the revolutionary movements; although it was necessary to protect Jews from persecution, "it was unacceptable that in Palestine, against justice, a minority should overtake the local population."

Weizmann told Gasparri on April 20 that the Zionists wanted to establish a Jewish national home in the framework of a Palestinian state in which no segment of the population would have more rights than other segments, but the Zionist ambition—the newspaper asserted—was to establish a Jewish state in Palestine. Because of the difficulties involved, however, the plan had been trimmed. The British claimed that there was a Zionist interpretation that extended the meaning of the Balfour Declaration and that there was dissent within the Zionist movement between religious Jews and the Zionists.[37]

Later that month, the *Osservatore Romano* resumed its polemic with *Israel*, which had written that the Vatican was opposing Zionism, even though Zionism was not at all interested in the problem of the Holy Places. The Vatican newspaper, for its part, wrote that Italy feared Zionism because of its inferior position in Palestine and because of the expansion of Great Britain, which used Zionism as a tool (to promote its own interests). The *Osservatore Romano*'s commentary asserted that the Holy See was opposed to Zionism because it disrupted life in Palestine, ignored the rights of the local population, and inverted the principles of national freedom. But the Holy See did not object to Zionism as recently defined, for if those proclamations were genuine, it would entail equality for all the races and religions in Palestine. But in fact the Zionist ideal remained unchanged: Palestine as exclusively Jewish.[38]

Israel, for its part, wondered what the Vatican feared and why its anxiety had intensified after Weizmann's visit, for Weizmann was convinced that he had cleared up the misunderstandings regarding Zionism that had resulted from a lack of accurate information.[39]

Barlassina's Agitation Against Zionism

Early in 1922, Karl Von Bergen, the German ambassador at the Holy See, said that Barlassina "does not miss any opportunity to speak out against the Jewish settlements and openly supports the Arabs. . . . It is also known that he represents the

Monsignor Luigi Barlassina, the Latin patriarch of Jerusalem.

political interests of the Christians and the Arabs." The ambassador felt that the Vatican was hostile to Jewish settlement for spiritual reasons as well as for material reasons related to its friendship with Italy, which was attempting to acquire influence in Palestine, both commercially and as a protector of Catholics.[40]

At the end of April 1922, a few days after Weizmann's visit, Barlassina arrived in Rome. The *Osservatore Romano* published excerpts from the lecture he delivered there:

> Having entered a truly active phase following the well-known Balfour Declaration, Zionism intends, in fact, gradually to expel the present inhabitants of Palestine, in

order to seize the entire country and to erect on it the Zionist kingdom. . . . Zionism has caused damage of the gravest sort to Palestine in that it has utterly altered the way of life there. No longer a patriarchal life, but irreligion, immorality of all sorts, hatred and licentiousness, for the Zionist immigrants, unlike the Jews of Palestine, are not at all religious, and are concerned only with the political and economic realms. One of the most serious troubles Zionism has brought is a lack of public morality: brothels, which had been forbidden under Turkish rule, have been allowed in the period of British rule. . . . In the Holy City of Jerusalem alone there are five hundred prostitutes! It should be added that several of the new colonies live by the principles of pure communism, and they observe practices and have a way of life which are best not mentioned at all. . . .

After the war, thanks to dollars and pounds sterling, Zionism exploited the poverty in which Palestine was sunk because of the war; today it is assisted by the local administration, which is headed by Herbert Samuel, a Zionist and high commissioner who hands over the representation of the interests of Palestine exclusively to the Zionist Commission. . . . Thus have they aroused the opposition and animosity of the native inhabitants, mainly the Arabs, and the anger of the Catholics. . . . The constant battle of Zionism, cold and merciless, is waged not only against the Moslems and Christians, but also against the Jews or religious in Palestine against whom means of terror are employed. The efforts of Zionists are aimed at acquiring land; Arabs, Moslems, and the Orthodox, even though politically hostile [to Zionism], allow themselves to be dispossessed because of the great profits, and cannot sell their produce because the Zionists forbid even its export. Having infiltrated all the local offices the Zionists already have a monopoly.[41]

On May 13, 1921, Lord Cecil declared, according to Barlassina, that the instigating element was the Zionist movement. The Greek Orthodox were being favored (by the British), and there was a systematic opposition to Catholic interests. The Protestants, who had ample means for their propaganda, were not hindered because they somehow supported Zionism.

Barlassina sought support for the right of the Catholics, religious rights as well as those related to personal status. The Palestine problem should be discussed among Catholics, and notwithstanding the evildoers who would prevent it, information about what is going on in Palestine should be circulated. The Catholic schools must be given assistance so that they could develop and new schools could be opened everywhere. The Catholic population in Palestine must be made to feel that Catholics throughout the whole world were acting effectively to defend their rights.

Barlassina may have depicted the situation in the blackest terms in order to arouse his audience to action and to raise funds for Catholic institutions in Palestine. His main arguments against Zionism were already familiar by this time: its disruption of the patriarchal way of life and exploitation of the British administration to the detriment of Arabs and Catholics.

De Salis sent a report about Barlassina's lecture to Foreign Secretary Curzon and attached a clipping from *L'Italie* that stated that for an hour and a quarter Barlassina explained, complete with facts and figures, the acts of dispossession, the wrecking of morality, and the de-Catholicization being carried out by the Zionists in Palestine. The newspaper reported Barlassina as saying:

The avowed aim of Zionism is the resettlement of the Jewish people on the land of its forefathers and the expulsion of all other nationalities. Under the pretext of establishing a Jewish national home, Zionism is actually seeking to take the conquest of Palestine. With the help of the British authorities—Sir Herbert Samuel, the high commissioner, and almost all the high officials are active Zionists—the Zionist leaders are in effect the lords of Palestine. They determine the law and impose their will on the whole population—Christian, Moslem, and Jewish—while the religious Jews themselves suffer at the hands of their coreligionists. The Zionists have not only the authorities on their hands, but also much money, and they are buying up the lands of the poor local Moslems. . . . They are opening schools, and sometimes they also corrupt conscience. The Zionists intend to gradually dislodge the Arabs and the Christians and to settle in their place. The Zionists organized the immigration to Palestine of Russian Jews who are almost all Bolsheviks. It is said that this immigration has ceased, but that is untrue, and only those who are not Jews are being refused entry visas. It was also said that this immigration is beneficial for the local population, which regards it as a source of wealth for the country. That too is untrue. The Zionists and Sir Herbert Samuel himself are seen without sympathy by the Arabs and Christians, and the Palestinians' hostility toward the Zionists is indisputable; Zionism's activity is deadly for morality. From the day they began to lord over Palestine, immoral acts in the land that soaked up the blood of Christ, have reached worrisome proportions. They have even permitted prostitution houses to be opened in Jerusalem, Jaffa, Nazareth, and Haifa, and venereal diseases are spreading. . . . The Zionists are systematically hindering the Catholics, and if there is a dispute between a Catholic and a Greek Orthodox, the latter always wins. . . . The Catholics, who have their own schools, have to pay taxes for the maintenance of non-Catholic schools. Heavy taxes are levied on Catholic property. If that is not enough, the intolerable situation of the Palestinian Catholics is rounded out by Protestant propaganda through their schools, clinics, and subsidies.

Lastly, Barlassina appealed for Palestine to be saved from a yoke a hundred times worse than that of the Turks. "A new strong crusade is needed by means of pen, action, and money. Zionism must be fought to rescue the land of the Savior."[42]

According to another newspaper, Barlassina said: "Palestine is under an oppressive domination a thousand times more violent than Turkish rule. Only corruption and immorality reign in the sacred land. The whole Zionist movement, directed by a few fanatics, is waging war against both Catholic and Arab elements."[43] In his report, de Salis remarked that to the best of his knowledge, Barlassina

owned his appointment [as patriarch] to the influence with Propaganda [Fide] of the French orders, which are strongly represented in Palestine. These elements, over and above the general anxiety felt here with regard to Zionism, are opposed to British influence in the East. The Franciscans, I gather, were not pleased at the lecture. Many of them attended and remarked that their work was not once mentioned though for seven centuries they have borne the burden of defending the interests of the Church, while the Patriarchate is an institution of the 19th century.[44]

The German ambassador at the Vatican, Karl von Bergen, reported a conversation between an embassy official and Barlassina. The patriarch said that the Arabs were unable to understand why nothing was being done to protect the Holy Places. The Zionists' plot was gradually to expel the present inhabitants of Palestine, in order to seize the whole country and turn it into the state of Zion. Barlassina also spoke about the Jewish immigrants' immorality. Some of the Jewish settlers were living by Marxist ideology in unmarried love. Some of the new immigrants from Russia had been accustomed to bathe in the nude in the Black Sea. "That might be fine there, but they were now doing the same in the Sea of Galilee . . . causing much indignation among the more conservative inhabitants."[45]

After a few days in Rome, Barlassina continued on to London, where, according to the press, the mission assigned him by the Vatican was to conduct talks with the British government on the problem of Zionism in Palestine.[46] It seems odd, however, that the Vatican would have assigned Barlassina a special mission to the British government, for it knew quite well that the British did not regard him as a friend. The Foreign Office read the news items about the patriarch's mission and was surprised that de Salis had not reported it. De Salis had protested to Gasparri about Barlassina's lecture but had heard nothing of the mission on which the patriarch had supposedly been sent.[47]

Several days later, de Salis reported that the Vatican had told him that it had not sent Barlassina to London. Rather, he had asked permission to travel there to present certain claims, and the Vatican did not object.[48] On June 4, de Salis sent a cable stating that Barlassina had been asked by the Vatican to return to Rome immediately.[49] British Foreign Office officials expressed their satisfaction at the Vatican's prompt recall of "that gentleman."[50] Indeed, the Vatican may initially have wanted to send Barlassina to London on the eve of the approval of the mandate, to alert public opinion there to the "Zionist danger." However, once that had been done, Gasparri apparently preferred to dissociate himself somewhat from Barlassina and to claim that the patriarch had not been on an official mission. This may have been true formally, but the fact that Barlassina continued to serve as Latin patriarch of Jerusalem for many years afterward would seem to indicate that Gasparri and the pope had full confidence in him.

In London, Barlassina was not received in British government circles, which would have nothing to do with him, but he did obtain an interview in the influential *Times*, which had earlier published a series of anti-Zionist articles. In this interview, Barlassina stated:

> Since the advent of Zionism, however, they [Latins] have experienced many practical difficulties which have given serious cause for alarm. . . . What do the Zionists really seek in Palestine? Their well-known object is the establishment of a Jewish kingdom. That is the object of political Zionism, a policy upon which even the Orthodox Jews of Palestine look with apprehension. These Zionists come from Russia, from Hungary and other countries, and are Bolsheviks, Communists or Socialists. . . . All these Jews are animated by political as opposed to spiritual ideals. It is sometimes said that the Bolsheviks and political element [are] not numerous. To that I answer, "Go to Palestine and see." And even were it true that they are not numerous, they have great influence, witness the terrible riots which have resulted from their action. . . . Since the advent of Sir Herbert Samuel the influence of the Zionists had become almost absolute. The idea of Sir Herbert has been to create an autonomous Jewish body which should be at the same time politico-religious and Zionist. . . . The Zionist organization in Jerusalem calls itself the "Council of the

Jews of Jerusalem," and the Zionist organization of Palestine calls itself the "National Council of the Jews of Palestine." As a matter of fact the orthodox Jews took no part in the elections for the said councils, as they refuse to recognize their authority. . . . Legally they [Arabs] are allowed to buy and keep land; but in fact they do not enjoy full liberty in this respect. For instance when the Greek Patriarchate was about to sell a large quantity of land a schedule was prepared by the Commission appointed by the Palestine Government in which many of the lots were so large that it was impossible for the inhabitants of Palestine to purchase them. The first five lots, moreover, were not to be divided, but had to be sold together, and the Zionist Committee bought them for about £350,000. Obviously such prices are beyond the means of individual Arab purchasers. . . . Are the peasants free from anxiety as to the sale of their crops? No, because as it was the case last year, they were not allowed to export their super-abundant crops till the market was flooded by crops from other districts. . . . Therefore they prefer to sell their land rather than risk again incurring such a great loss. . . . I deeply regret to say that there can be no question but the moral condition of the country has gravely declined since the influence of Zionism made itself felt. I could give you many terrible details of how the Holy City and the Holy Land have been desecrated in various ways.

Barlassina concluded the interview by claiming that the government was indirectly preventing the Latins from enjoying the rights of their personal status, that in juridical matters the Jews were clearly being favored,[51] and that overall, the British government did not have adequate knowledge of what was occurring in Palestine.[52]

13

The Vatican's Opposition
to the Mandate

The Fight for Approval of the Mandate

While Zionist diplomatic activity concentrated on removing the obstacles to approval of the mandate by the Council of the League of Nations in Geneva, the Vatican was stepping up its efforts to thwart approval or, at the least, to obtain substantial revision of the Zionist articles. The Vatican's opposition of the Zionist idea and to the draft mandate proposed by Britain was increasingly significant, especially when it became clear that the Vatican was using its influence with a number of Catholic countries in addition to France and Italy, including Spain, Poland, Brazil, and Belgium. That at least was the impression received by officials in the British Foreign Office.[1]

Weizmann was in Geneva in connection with the convening there of the Council of the League of Nations. Decisions by the Council had to be reached unanimously, and on May 11 he heard from Balfour that Brazil, a Catholic country on the Council and under the Vatican's influence, was likely to object to approval of the mandate.[2] On the same day, Gasparri cabled the Belgian foreign minister that he was surprised to have learned that the British government was to submit the mandate on Palestine to the Council for approval on that very day. He therefore asked that the debate be postponed, for he had some important comments on the subject.[3] The Belgian foreign minister replied that the debate had been postponed and that he was sure the Council would give serious consideration to any comments Gasparri might present.[4]

Four days later, on May 15, Gasparri sent a note to the secretary general of the League of Nations similar to the one he had sent to de Salis on April 6, in which he raised his objections to a number of articles in the draft mandate.[5] This letter is one of the most important documents on the Vatican's position on Zionism, and we shall consider it in some detail. We begin by presenting some major passages:

> The Holy See is not opposed to the Jews in Palestine having civil rights equal to those possessed by other nationals and creeds, but it cannot agree to:

1. The Jews' being given a privileged and preponderant position in Palestine vis-à-vis [the Catholics in general and other nationalties and] other confessions.

2. The religious rights of Christians [especially the Catholics] being inadequately safeguarded.

On the first point . . . the proposed draft . . . conveys the impression of wishing to set up an absolute preponderance—economic, administrative, and political—in favour of the Jewish element to the detriment of the other nationalities [and religions]. The articles of the draft:

a. recognize as a public legal institution that Jewish agency, which is no other than the powerful Zionist Organization (Article 4);

b. this Jewish agency is set up side by side with the Palestine administration, and very large powers are even given it in all questions relative "to the development of the country";

c. the immigration (Article 6), and naturalization (Article 7) of Jews are favored; care is taken to provide them with the means of becoming a compact community, including grants of undeveloped State land (Article 6). They are also given preferences in the construction of public works (Article 11).

Thus the project, aiming as it does at an absolute Jewish preponderance over all the other peoples [and the religions] of Palestine, and moreover apparently constituting a grave breach of the existing rights of other nationalities, does not appear to be in consonance with Article 22 of the Treaty of Versailles, which established the nature and purpose of each Mandate.

The letter goes on to deal with the problem of the commission for the Holy Places, which we discussed earlier. Several days later, on June 4, the Vatican sent to the Council of the League of Nations a memorandum that differed slightly from Gasparri's May 15 note. This memorandum received immediate and broad publicity. In it, the Holy See stressed first that it did not oppose the decision to grant Britain the mandate for Palestine. On each of the articles bearing on the Jews, it emphasized the Catholics as victims of discrimination and mentioned the term *religions,* expressions I have placed in square brackets in the preceding quotation. But where it differed most from Gasparri's letter was on the commission for the Holy Places.[6]

Walter Zander, who relied solely on this second memorandum, remarked that the tone of the letter is very different from that of the pope's allocution in 1921, *Causa Nobis.*[7] The Holy See said that it did not oppose granting the mandate to Britain, but Gasparri expressed concern for the future of Palestine's non-Jewish population. To my mind, there was no divergence here from the line established by Benedict XV, for after beginning with praise for Britain, the Vatican argued that the draft of the mandate gave the Jews a privileged position and then specified the realms in which this preference was most pronounced. Gasparri thus opposed all the Zionist articles of the draft mandate, without which the dream of a Jewish national home might never have been realized.

As a consequence of these pressures from the Vatican, the approval so eagerly desired was not obtained at the May meeting of the Council, and so the decision on the mandate was postponed to the July meeting. Weizmann commented that "our enemies—especially the Vatican and the Orthodox Jews, are working very hard against us."[8] Weizmann received at least some satisfaction from Balfour's statements to the Council: referring to the Balfour Declaration, he insisted that those who either hoped or feared that it would in any way be modified were mistaken. Concluding his remarks, Balfour expressed his surprise that there could be any fears for Christian interests resulting from the British mandate in Palestine and that it was not credible that any of the Holy Places should suffer by being transferred from Muslim to Christian rule.[9] Weizmann was convinced that the most important consideration in the Italian government's attitude was the Vatican's role.[10]

But it seems that the game being played by the Great Powers was more complex than that. Certainly it was convenient for France and the other Catholic powers to present themselves to the British as the defenders of Catholic interests and as acting on behalf of so esteemed a spiritual figure as the pope, but once the Vatican removed its objections, the real interest of those countries was bared. Despite the veil of religion, what they actually wanted was to underscore their presence in Palestine and, accordingly, fought for amendments to Article 14 with the aim of ensuring themselves a place on the still-to-be-constituted commission for the Holy Places. This was done by France, Italy, Belgium, and Spain. Nonetheless, at this time the Vatican appeared to be the principal organizer of France's, Belgium's, Spain's, and Brazil's opposition to approval of the mandate. British Foreign Office officials, at least, thought that to be the case. After their defeat at the May session of the Council, Lancelot Oliphant wrote that "all opposition regarding the approval of the Mandate is to be attributed to the same action of the Vatican."[11] The British therefore began to think that they ought to reach an understanding with the Vatican,[12] and so the foreign secretary decided to summon de Salis to London for consultations.[13]

Weizmann sent a report on the Vatican's activity to the Zionist Executive in London.[14] Although the Vatican's opposition focused mainly on the composition of the commission for the Holy Places, it in fact took the form of a general protest against British policy in Palestine. Officials at the Colonial Office[15] seemed to have trouble understanding this, especially John Shuckburgh, who was furious at the Vatican's interference.[16]

Italian Foreign Ministry officials often revealed to British and Zionist representatives details of the Vatican's opposition to approval of the mandate. This disclosure of Vatican pressure was an attempt on their part to dissociate themselves from responsibility for Italy's hostile stand. On May 12, 1922, Marquis Alberto Theodoli di Sambuci, the chairman of the Mandate Commission of the League of Nations, told Weizmann in Geneva that he had recently seen Gasparri, who remarked that he had realized that the Zionist movement was not a negligible entity but a force to be reckoned with and added: "I must stop them" ("Il faut que je le freine").[17]

Vito Catastini, an Italian diplomat in the Secretariat of the League of Nations, told a member of the British delegation in Geneva that the Vatican's opposition was serious and that it seemed that every priest in France and Italy had been instructed to take part in the crusade against the Zionists and to do all he could to prevent the development of Jewish hegemony anywhere in the world.[18]

In another letter, Weizmann said that he was "greatly impressed by the indefatigable efforts which the Vatican is making to thwart and obstruct us in every possible way." He did not believe that

> the Vatican policy in this matter necessarily corresponds to the views of the Roman Catholic world at large. For instance in Venice at Easter the Cardinal Archbishop went out of his way to preach a sermon in favor of Zionism, at [the main Cathedral of] St. Mark. On the other hand, so far as the Curia is concerned, there is no doubt that we have to contend with an implacable hostility.[19]

The Vatican intensified its activity as the July 1922 session of the Council—at which the draft mandate for Palestine was to be approved—drew near. As Weizmann explained in a letter to Nahum Sokolow, the Vatican was seeking a delay in approval of the mandate and a thorough revision of the policy toward Palestine. The Vatican objected not only to Article 14, which dealt with the commission for the Holy Places, but also the Zionist provisions of the mandate. Weizmann had no doubt that the Arab agitation was to a great extent encouraged by the Vatican. The Latin patriarch had made inflamatory speeches and had become a great source of anti-Zionist propaganda. Weizmann, however, was "not prepared to admit that the attitude of Gasparri or the Latin Patriarch is identical with the attitude of the Catholic world. . . . America can do more than anybody else to exercise a certain amount of influence on the Vatican. America at present is the greatest source of income to Rome." Weizmann thought that if the Knights of Columbus were made aware of the situation and of how the Vatican's agents were trying to thwart Zionist policy—which he said was also the United States' policy—it would be possible to get "Rome to see some reason."[20]

Despite the lobbying and the mobilization of forces on behalf of approval of the mandate, Weizmann had to acknowledge that "the Vatican is moving Heaven and Earth against us, and the old fight between Judaism and Paganism has been renewed with vigour."[21] Indeed, Weizmann maintained that the French and the Italians would consent to debate on the mandate in the Council of the League of Nations were it not for the Vatican's obdurate hostility.[22]

Dante Lattes, the secretary of the Italian Zionist Federation, wrote to Weizmann that Beilinson had heard it said in the Italian Foreign Ministry that the Vatican was taking a forceful stand in opposition to a Jewish nation and that Barlassina had gone to London on a "war mission."[23] Barlassina's arrival in London had already been reported to the Zionist Executive by members who had heard about the patriarch's travel plans while they were in Geneva.[24] Lattes himself heard from Theodoli in Rome that the Vatican had begun direct talks with Britain about approval of the mandate. Theodoli thought that the Vatican was not opposed to the mandate as such but had put forward demands from the Catholic point of view, with respect especially to Article 14. He said that someone in London was conducting the negotiations on behalf of the Vatican, but not Barlassina, who had no authority to speak in the name of the Holy See, even though the Vatican did not deny his remarks.[25]

Lattes cautioned Weizmann about de Salis, who was not considered objective in presenting the Zionist arguments to the Vatican. He proposed to get a declaration from Agudath Israel in order to stop the Vatican's hostile propaganda. Lattes also recommended that the Zionist Organization issue a formal statement refuting the

Vatican's anti-Zionist arguments. Such a statement, he said, should include the Holy Places, the alleged dispossession of the Arabs, the alleged decline in morality, Agudath Israel, and the claim that British policy was dependent on Jewish American bankers.[26]

The Vatican's Objections to the Mandate's "Zionist" Articles

On June 30, 1922, the *Osservatore Romano* published the official text of Gasparri's May 15 memorandum to the League of Nations on the Palestine problem. According to the newspaper, Zionism was unacceptable as a ruling element because it would disrupt the social peace in Palestine and trample the rights of the native population. The League of Nations, the paper wrote, attached great importance to the Vatican's memorandum, which faithfully expressed the views of Catholics around the world. Catholic public opinion has been alerted. "To this end a Catholic international may be established, which would unite all Catholics in the world in the defense of the Holy Places and against Bolshevik Judaism in Palestine." Karl von Bergen, reporting on this article, added:

> The Curia sees in the Balfour Act a privilege for the Jewish element, which is incompatible with the meaning of the Holy Land for Christianity. Therefore it [the Curia] looks for an alteration of the Balfour Act in order to obtain equality and corresponding representation for all nationalities and religions in Palestine.[27]

The idea of a Catholic international was expressed at that time on other occasions as well. Charles Loiseau, who unofficially represented France at the Holy See between 1914 and 1919, wrote that "the only permanent feature of the Church's policy is that it is international.[28] In his purported interview with Gasparri, Buonaiuti raised the idea of the "White International" and put the following words in Gasparri's mouth: "Catholicism is the true White International, with rules of discipline and modes of supervision."[29]

Around this time, Gasparri repeated his objections and sent a copy of the June 4 memorandum to the British government as well. The memorandum was attached to his letter to de Salis, in which he stated that the Vatican's demands were reasonable and concerned the establishment of peace among peoples. Gasparri noted in his letter that the pope himself was grateful for de Salis's support of this policy of peace.[30]

As the crucial debate in the Council of the League of Nations neared, the Zionist leadership continued its efforts to blunt the Vatican's opposition to the draft mandate proposed by Britain. A report prepared by the Zionist Executive stated that it was evident at the meetings of the Council in May that the Vatican had taken steps to encourage the Catholic countries represented on the Council, including Brazil, to block approval. It was at last decided that the Council would hold a special meeting on July 15, 1922, to discuss the mandate. The Zionist Executive therefore asked Yehuda Nissan Wilensky, an envoy of the fund-raising campaign of the Keren Hayesod to Latin America, to persist in his attempts to persuade the Brazilian government to instruct its representative on the Council to vote in favor of approval.[31]

In Palestine, the *Palestine Weekly* pointed out that every responsible Zionist leader had insisted that Zionism had no direct interest in the Holy Places and was prepared to leave their settlement in the hands of the interested Powers. Consequently, the reports spread by the Latin patriarch of Jerusalem, Barlassina, about the Zionists' intentions and the attitude of the Palestine administration were unjustified and malicious. Referring to the patriarch's public statements in Rome, the weekly expressed its surprise that such mischevious sentiments, couched in such a vulgar tone, should issue from such a responsible ecclesiastical dignity. The weekly attributed to the current pope the ideas expressed in the Buonaiuti interview, although there was no proof that the interview had been given by Cardinal Ratti while he was archbishop of Milan. The weekly went on to say that the claims made by the Latin patriarch in his Rome lecture—that the Latins possessed the same rights as the Jewish agency did—were simply wrong. The interests of the Jews in Palestine, as recognized by all the Great Powers, were primarily national and only indirectly religious, whereas those of the Roman Church were exclusively religious.[32]

Weizmann was in Paris in June and asked Angelo Donati, a wealthy Italian Jew residing there, to contact Nuncio Bonaventura Cerretti, the Vatican's representative, in order to obtain a precise explanation of the Holy See's demands.[33] On June 17, Weizmann met with Cerretti, who disavowed Barlassina, saying, "He is too impulsive and going rather quickly." The nuncio spoke with considerable contempt of the Arabs and almost indicated that "one uses them if necessary." Weizmann received the impression that if the Vatican were "satisfied on the Holy Places Commission, it would not press the other matter [Zionism]." Cerretti was certain that once the matter of the mandate was settled satisfactorily, there would be a "detente," and he would arrange for Weizmann an audience with the pope. Weizmann also gathered that Cerretti was trying hard to influence the Spanish ambassador to the League of Nations Council.[34]

Sir Eric Drummond, the secretary general of the League of Nations, also reported to the Foreign Office that the Vatican's attacks on British policy regarding the Jewish nation were meant primarily "to have something to bargain with as regards the Holy Places," to which the Vatican attached the greatest importance. Drummond believed that any arrangement for the Holy Places concluded with the Vatican would have a number of beneficial consequences:

1. Catholic opinion would be more favorable to the Zionist movement.
2. The alliance between the Arabs and some Catholic forces in Palestine would be broken.
3. The Anti-Jewish movement, arising again throughout the world, would be stopped short.
4. The Vatican would adopt a favorable view of the mandate, whereas its hostility to the mandate, if continued and if reinforced by the Orthodox Church, would be most serious.[35]

In an attempt to apply last-minute pressure on the Vatican, and trusting his feeling that anti-Zionism was not acceptable to the Catholic world, Weizmann urged Bernard Rosenblatt, an American Zionist, to persuade the Convention of the Zionist Organization of America to issue a strong resolution of protest against the attacks on Zionism. "A word should be spoken to the Vatican firmly but peacefully, expressing the determination of building up Palestine, but in reverence to the Christian interests."[36]

On June 21, the Zionist movement suffered a serious setback in Britain when the House of Lords debated a motion that "the Mandate for Palestine in its present form is unacceptable, because it directly violates the pledges made by H. M.'s Government to the people of Palestine. . . . and is . . . opposed to the sentiments and wishes of the great majority of the people of Palestine."[37] It was clear to Weizmann that the Vatican and the Arabs were trying to have the whole policy of the National Home and the Balfour Declaration annulled, and he was worried that the Vatican might be "capable of arraying all the Catholic Powers against England."[38] Italy, for its part, was presenting exaggerated demands in league with the Vatican; together, they used the Vatican's propaganda to win concessions from the British. Italy's stand and the decision in the House of Lords, in turn, might encourage France to press further, and then the easiest way for the British to secure the smooth passage of the mandate would be to whittle down the Zionist policy as expressed in the mandate.[39]

In another letter, Weizmann wrote that the Vatican was the leader of all the dark forces, which it was trying to organize into an anti-Jewish and anti-Zionist campaign assuming the dimensions of the Dreyfus case. "Legends are created of our domination on Palestine, of our sinister desires to oust the Arabs and to establish from Palestine a dominion."[40]

The claim that the Jews in Palestine were Bolsheviks from Russia had been voiced previously in Catholic papers. But Weizmann treated the accusation seriously and emphasized that no Jew would ever dream of treating the Holy Places with anything but reverence.[41]

On July 1, the British government sent a note to the secretary general of the League of Nations in reply to Gasparri's letter of May 15. In reference to the status of the Zionist Organization, according to Article 4 of the draft mandate, the note pointed out that the British colonial secretary had already announced that this special status did not include any administrative functions; rather, it referred to measures to be taken with regard to the Jewish population in Palestine and to enable the Zionist Organization to assist in the country's general development, but it did not give it any part in the government. The immigration of Jews and their settlement on the land, including state lands, was an integral part of the establishment of a national home for the Jewish people in Palestine, with which the Mandate government had been charged. Indeed, the acquisition of Palestinian citizenship by Jews settled in Palestine, according to Article 7 of the mandate, was designed to prevent such preferential discrimination of which Cardinal Gasparri had written. In the cardinal's opinion, Article 11 was proof that the Jews were given a privileged status, as compared with that of the other nationalities and religions, but the British government regarded the possibility of participation by the Jewish agency in public works, services, and development of natural resources merely as a legitimate recognition of the special situation created in Palestine as a result of giving the mandatory role to Britain. It was evidence of the will and readiness of the Jewish people to contribute from its own wealth and with its own efforts to the development of the country for the benefit of all its inhabitants.[42]

The New British Policy in Palestine

On July 1, 1922, Colonial Secretary Winston Churchill published a White Paper defining a new nine-point British policy toward Palestine, which included reaffirmation of the Balfour Declaration, the founding of a Jewish nation "as of right and not of suffrance," the equality of all citizens and the fostering of gradual self-government, the exclusion of the Zionist Executive from the country's government, the promise that Jewish immigration would not exceed the country's economic capacity, and the promise that all religious communities would have the right to appeal to the League of Nations. The Zionists accepted these principles, but the Arabs of Palestine rejected them, because they fell short of giving the people of Palestine full control of their own affairs.[43]

In the meantime, on July 4, a debate on Palestine was held in the British House of Commons at which Churchill offered a vigorous defense of the White Paper policy. He demanded a vote of confidence, and the government's policy was approved by a decisive majority, an important victory for the supporters of Zionism.[44]

July was a month of feverish activity by the British government and the Zionist leadership, aimed at winning approval for the mandate in the Council of the League of Nations, which was about to convene in London. The British did their utmost to eliminate the obstacle of the Vatican's opposition. They cabled de Salis the text of the new version of Article 14, which took into account the Vatican's objections. Gasparri stated that the new draft of Article 14 seemed quite satisfactory and mentioned France's latest attempt to raise the issue of the liturgical honors.[45] On the basis of de Salis's report, the British Foreign Office felt that at long last the problem of Article 14 had been resolved and that the Vatican would cease opposing the mandate.[46]

Earlier, in the middle of June, the British prime minister had suggested to Churchill that Samuel see the pope and try to dissuade him from continuing his opposition to the mandate for Palestine.[47] Samuel was in fact received by the pope on July 6 for a lengthy audience during which the pope was most friendly. He had read the British government's reply to the League of Nations, and it seemed to him generally satisfactory. In the course of the conversation, the pope said that he well understood the Jewish people's special interest in Palestine; when he lived in Milan, he had studied Hebrew and so had been in close touch with the grand rabbi, for whom he had much regard. He did not think it at all probable that the Jews would become a majority in Palestine. In any case, it was essential that no section of the population receive privileges to the detriment of others. Samuel replied that this was far from the British government's intention, as had been clearly stated in the declaration of policy statement that had recently been published (on July 1). With respect to the Holy Places, there was no point at which Christian interests and Jewish interests conflicted; the only thing that Jews desired with respect to the Christian Holy Places was not to be concerned with any of the questions relating to them.

As we have said, Samuel was received cordially by the pope and had no reason to suppose that the Vatican would persist in opposing approval of the mandate. But as soon became apparent, it stood fast by its opposition. It may be that the pope and his secretary of state did not want to reveal their cards, perhaps had not yet had time to examine the new version of Article 14, or did not want to cloud the meeting with Samuel with disputations about drafts and versions of drafts. It is also possible that Article 14 was a veil for the Vatican's much deeper opposition to Zionism.

It is not at all clear who, in the game being played by the powers, was acting and who was being acted upon. The Vatican encouraged the Catholic countries to oppose the draft mandate, and so they did. Because they wanted above all to defend their presence in Palestine, they continued to oppose Article 14 even when it seemed to be acceptable to the pope.

In any event, on July 10, the French prime minister, Raymond Poincaré, wrote to the British prime minister that France would support the mandate but would propose its own version of Article 14. Poincaré also said that the plan put forward by Samuel had not won the pope's consent.[48] As Charles Hardinge of Penshurst, the British ambassador in Paris, explained, Poincaré tried to secure the chairmanship of the commission for the Holy Places for France and, through that position, to renew the liturgical honors.[49] A more striking example of the exploitation of religious matters for political ends would be hard to find. In truth, the British Foreign Office might already have been aware that France intended to insist on taking the chairmanship of the commission, for Weizmann had written to the assistant colonial secretary about that in the middle of June.

After meeting with the pope, Samuel, accompanied by de Salis, met with Gasparri and told him that the Zionists had no share in the administration of Palestine, as had been made quite clear in the declaration recently published. Gasparri agreed that this was so but repeated that he thought it important that this be made known to all the world.[50] Samuel said that the mandatory system contemplated a gradual progress toward autonomy; as mentioned, the British government had published two documents on July 1, in which it declared publicly that the Zionists would have no part in the country's administration: Churchill's White Paper and the letter to the League of Nations. Samuel gave Gasparri full details about the new British White Paper.

After his meetings at the Vatican, Samuel met with Angelo Sereni, the chairman of the Jewish community in Rome, and with the chief rabbi, Angelo Sacerdoti. Lattes and Beilinson were not in Rome at the time. Samuel said that he had cleared up a few of the pope's prejudices and that the pontiff would no longer be fundamentally opposed to the mandate. Asked by Sereni if he was optimistic, Samuel replied that he was confident the mandate would be approved. He did not want to talk about his meeting with Gasparri, and the Vatican also did not discuss it.

An editorial in *Corriere d'Italia,* the newspaper of the (Catholic) Popular party, emphasized that it was impossible to break the silence of the official circles at the Vatican but nonetheless analyzed the Vatican's open and systematic opposition to Zionism. In the view of the newspaper, the main reason for it was the wish to preserve the status and prestige of the Catholic Church in the East, with the aim of drawing Orthodox Christians to the pope.[51] The article made no mention of Weizmann's conversation with Gasparri, nor did it explain how opposition to Zionism would induce Orthodox Christians to join the Catholic Church.

The Vatican's hostility toward Zionism was echoed by other Italian newspapers as well. *La Voce Republicana* wrote that Gasparri, "who for some time has been relentlessly and unsuccessfully pursuing the ghost of Zionism manifesting itself in Palestine," was unlikely to succeed. The Reform Socialist paper *Ora Nuova* was of the opinion that the energies the Holy See was expending in opposing Zionism could better be channeled elsewhere and that the anti-Semitic crusade in the West would prove more dangerous to its promoters than to the Jews.[52]

Attacks against Zionism also began coming from the Anglican Church. The Anglican newspaper in England, the *Church Times,* wrote that the Bolshevik Jews were perfectly capable of causing damage to the Holy Places.

Weizmann was worried by all the anti-Jewish propaganda. He feared that after the mandate has been ratified, the Arabs might attempt a general uprising in Palestine, tamper with the Holy Places, and lay all this at the door of the Jews. In his view, articles of this sort were liable give the Arabs ideas of this kind. Weizmann cabled his friends in the Zionist Commission in Jerusalem to ask that they see that no Jew, whether a resident or a visitor, go into the area of the Holy Places, Christian or Muslim. "An anti-Semitic crusade has been initiated," wrote Weizmann, and he sought to convey his fears to Sir Wyndham Deeds and Samuel.[53]

Tensions mounted as the time approached for the debate on the mandate in the Council of the League of Nations. "If the mandate does not go through this time," wrote Weizmann,

> it never will. The Catholics have been chiefly responsible for uniting the Muslims and the Christians against us, because what the Vatican really wishes to have is something which amounts to power in Palestine, and it has been using various Catholic members of the League, such as Spain, Brazil, Italy, Belgium and France, in order to achieve its object, and this is really the inner meaning of its attacks against us.[54]

We do not know what led Weizmann to suspect that the Vatican was interested in temporal rule in Palestine, but this was a farsighted conjecture. The pope's desire to be once again sovereign over a territory of his own, however small, had come clearly to the fore in the matter of Rome, which had been removed from the Church's rule in 1870 to become the capital of Italy. The Roman Question had not yet been resolved at this time, and World War I again underscored the problems the Vatican had as a consequence of its not having a territory over which it was sovereign. One such problem, for example, was the departure from Rome of the legations to the Holy See of countries with which Italy was at war.[55] Despite the difficulties in realizing this wish for sovereignty in the Holy Land, we cannot rule out the possibility that there were some in the Vatican who dreamed of Church rule there.

In this context, we might mention the rumor spread by the German press in 1916 that the kaiser had promised to establish a papal state in Palestine that would include Jerusalem, the Holy Places, and Jaffa port, to be governed by a cardinal viceroy.[56] At the Vatican in 1917, Sokolow had been told by Pacelli, and later by Gasparri, that the Holy See would be asking for the central region in Palestine, a clear allusion to its territorial ambitions. It may also be recalled that in describing the future of Palestine to the Belgian representative in December 1917 and February 1918, Gasparri spoke as if the central portion of the country—from Nazareth and the Sea of Galilee in the north to Hebron in the south—was to be a "Holy Places state." The fears about the Vatican's territorial ambitions thus seem to have been grounded in reality, and indeed some believe that to this day the Vatican has yet not abandoned its designs on Palestine, or at least on Jerusalem (or part of it).

In any case, the draft mandate was finally approved on July 22, 1922, by the Council of the League of Nations. All the Vatican's attempts to prevent its approval proved to be of no avail. Although the Vatican concurred in most of the Palestinian Arabs' arguments against Zionism, it is hard to accept Weizmann's view that the Vatican incited them against Zionism. The Vatican and the Arabs were indeed anti-Zionist, each for its own reasons, and apparently each influenced the other. In fact, I believe that the outcry against Zionism by the Arab residents of Palestine, some of whom were Christians, was what caused the Vatican to take a stronger stand against Zionism. The pope did try to avoid statements that were too extreme and even recognized that the Jews had certain rights in Palestine, but the Vatican's fundamentally anti-Zionist position had crystallized, and it adhered consistently to it for many years to come.

In the view of an Italian scholar, S. Marchese, the Vatican's anti-Zionism had another cause as well—the special international position in which the Vatican found itself as a result of the unresolved Roman Question. Having no territory of its own, the Vatican found itself outside the League of Nations and consequently had no influence on the important decisions about the world order being made in the wake of World War I. It therefore wanted above all to raise its voice against the injustice that it had suffered. The Vatican had to prove that the pope needed a state and wanted to be allowed to join the League of Nations in order to collaborate in making peace.[57]

Pope Benedict XV expressed publicly his ambitions concerning the League of Nations in an encyclical on May 28, 1920, in which he presented the Holy See's candidacy for membership in the League of Nations. Palestine was an excellent field for action for him, for it could not be claimed that he had no right to interfere in this issue, which, though political, also had profound religious ramifications. Accordingly, while urging the Church's admission to the League of Nations, the Catholic press in that period referred to the problem of Palestine and the religious interests of the Catholic world related to it.[58]

The Covert Activity of Reverend Bandack

In addition to extensive open diplomatic activity by the British government and the Zionists to reduce the Vatican's antagonism, and especially Barlassina's enmity, the Zionists also tried to work in covert ways. In the middle of May 1922, David Eder, the head of the Zionist Commission in Palestine, wrote to the Zionist Executive in London that a Catholic priest from Bethlehem, Father Salvatore Bandack, had approached him and was prepared to go to Rome and England to counter Barlassina's venomous propaganda. As was later learned, Bandack was attached to the Latin patriarchate in Jerusalem, and his uncle, Suleiman Bandack, was head of the Latin *millet* (national group) in the city. Eder understood that his journey would have to be financed but feared lest this be found out and be seen as meddling in the internal disputes of another religious community. He also thought that Bandack might in the end work against the Zionist in Rome or become hostile to Zionism if promoted to a higher station.[59]

Two weeks later, Eder wrote to Weizmann about the matter, adding that Bandack would be leaving for London in a matter of days to meet with Cardinal Bourne and General Arthur Money,[60] who had written to the priest that he supported "spiritual Zionism." Bandack intended to explain to him and others that Catholics and other Christians had no reason to fear the Zionist movement, whereas exclusive Arab rule in Palestine was likely to lead to the demise of the Christian communities. Bandack accordingly viewed a Christian–Muslim alliance as a danger and believed that a strong Jewish movement offered a chance to counterbalance radical Muslim demands.

From England, Bandack was to continue to Rome, where he was to meet with Dutch cardinal Wilhelm van Rossum, prefect of the Congregation of Propaganda Fide, who dealt directly with Palestine problems.[61] Bandack knew Van Rossum well and thought that through him he could refute the Latin patriarch's arguments and show how dangerous the anti-British propaganda was to Catholics. He also hoped to see Gasparri and the pope, through the cardinal's intervention. In his letter, Eder added that the patriarch's personality should not be a matter of concern for the Zionists. Bandack would be setting out with a power of attorney by the Catholic committee that had been formed in Jerusalem, as proof to the Vatican that he represented an important group.

Bandack impressed Eder as energetic and highly intelligent. Although he was unable to assess the extent to which Bandack sided with the Jews, Eder had no doubt about the importance of the priest's mission. (The fact that the priest had personal aspirations and hatreds could be of use to the Zionists.) Eder gave him £100 for travel expenses to England and promised that Weizmann would provide the financial assistance necessary for his stay there, which might be as long as six months. Weizmann would also prepare letters of introduction for him to Italian Foreign Minister Carlo Schanzer, to Lord Balfour, and to Churchill, if he thought it appropriate. The whole matter was being kept secret because the Latin patriarch's spies kept a close watch on Bandack, and the slightest leak would arouse the fury of the Vatican.[62] But it is hard to understand how Bandack intended to keep his contacts with the Zionists secret and at the same time receive letters of introduction from Weizmann to government ministers in Italy and Britain.

Bandack arrived in London in June 1922 and shortly thereafter wrote a letter to Weizmann outlining his plans. He wrote that it was essential to his mission's success that no link between him and Weizmann be disclosed, for otherwise he would be seen as a mere tool in the hands of the Zionists, and his words would lose all value. In Rome, too, he intended to operate on his own without the help of the British embassy, as he was aware of the Vatican's sensitivity. He meant to use his own personal acquaintances, including a number of cardinals, in order to get a clear and accurate picture of the situation. "Allow me to act with your full trust," wrote

Bandack, "and I am confident you will be satisfied by my efforts." He thought that the support he had from Catholics in Jerusalem would not allow the Vatican to turn a deaf ear to him. As a priest contacting the Holy See directly, without the support of the civil administration, he believed he would be given a hearing and did not fear that he would be suspected of being a tool of some policy. For these reasons, he did not want a letter from the British Foreign Office to de Salis, although he would not have refused such a letter had it been offered to him. In London he planned to meet with Milles of the Foreign Office to learn the British government's position. Finally, he expressed his hope that Weizmann would allow him to act freely "for the supreme benefit of the campaign."[63]

Bandack arrived in Rome where he contacted Moshe Beilinson of the local Zionist Federation, who cabled Weizmann about him. Weizmann replied that he was a friend and should be received as such.[64]

Bandack wrote to Weizmann from Rome that the Supreme Muslim Council had decided at its meetings on June 23 to 26 to send a Christian delegation to the Vatican, which would make the case for the Arabs' basic demands. At the same time, a Muslim delegation was to be sent to Mecca. The Christian delegation was to conduct propaganda against the proposed Jewish nation, the Balfour Declaration, and the policy of the Mandate government. There were two Catholics on the delegation, one from the Haifa district and one from Jerusalem. The Supreme Muslim Council decided at that same time to dismiss its president, Aref Pasha Dajani, who was also head of the Muslim–Christian Association in Jerusalem. The delegation would go to Rome even if the League of Nations approved the mandate. A Muslim sheikh, who was traveling to Germany on business, also joined the delegation, and the Greek Orthodox decided to send a representative as well.

Bandack's brother John was chosen by the Catholics to be a member of the delegation, but Jamal al-Hussayni, the secretary of the Muslim council, informed him that all travel expenses would have to be borne by the delegation members themselves. The Catholic delegate from the Haifa district, Fuad Ben Sa'id, of the Greek Catholic community there, agreed to travel at his own expense. Bandack did not think that Eder would agree to finance his brother's trip, and he had a long talk about the delegation with Lattes, who said that he would write to Weizmann about it directly. Bandack explained that his brother's participation could help the delegation and could even contribute to the common cause, for John had the advantage of being able to explain in Italian the great damage likely to ensue from the Holy See's approach to the Palestine issue. With John's help and the power of attorney he himself would receive not only from the Catholics but also from all the Arabs, "we could win totally and easily; be certain that the other members of the delegation will be in our hands."

Bandack therefore asked Weizmann to finance the trip and, at the same time, waited for the power of attorney from the Catholic committee in Jerusalem, which was on its way to him. He would soon send telegrams to the pope, Gasparri, Van Rossum, and de Salis in which he would put forward his demands. He prepared a small pamphlet in which he tried to detract from the prestige of Barlassina and the Arab government in Transjordan, from a point of view that was likely to be of special interest to the Vatican. But because he described Barlassina as an "Italian clerk" and thereby also indirectly attacked Italian policy, Lattes thought it would be difficult to get the pamphlet printed in Italy, and so Bandack asked Weizmann whether it could be printed in London.[65]

The power of attorney from the Latin community in Jerusalem was sent by Bandack's uncle, Suleiman Bandack, on July 19 and included a demand that the patriarchate be headed by a bishop selected from the local Arabs and that the other administrative posts in the patriarchate be filled also by local priests. These demands were aimed at improving the situation of the local Church, which had deteriorated since Barlassina had been appointed patriarch.[66] Telegrams were sent from Jerusalem simultaneously to the pope, Gasparri, and Van Rossum, saying that Bandack had been charged with explaining to the Holy See the dangerous political and religious situation in Palestine that Barlassina had created.[67]

Probably to ensure secrecy, the correspondence between Weizmann and Bandack was conducted through Lattes, who wrote to Weizmann that Bandack thought it would be best to try to delay the delegation's arrival.[68] The last letter from Bandack to Weizmann that has reached us is a long and detailed missive dated August 22, 1922. Bandack wrote that he tried to be received by de Salis but was informed that de Salis could not see him. He in fact was pleased by that, for even without the intervention of the British representative, the Vatican suspected that he was a tool of British policy, a suspicion that Barlassina tried to reinforce.

Bandack stated that as soon as he arrived in Rome, he tried to refute Barlassina's virulent accusations concerning the situation in Palestine and the "Zionist danger." In certain circles, where Barlassina was known from before he had been made patriarch, it had long been felt that he had gone too far. Bandack noted that Barlassina had used Zionism as a pretext to try to wrest Palestine from Britain's hands, and he, Bandack, spared no effort to tarnish Barlassina's credibility and to clarify matters in the finest detail. He added, in praise of Zionism, that if it did not exist, it would have had to be invented, for it was capable of lifting Palestine out of its wretchedness. In any event, he had been asked about Zionism and about the difficult plight of the native inhabitants, and so he used the opportunity to correct Barlassina's lies. He also said that two days after his talk with the editor of *Osservatore Romano*, Count Giuseppe Dalla Torre, an article was published expressing a readiness to accept economic Zionism. Dalla Torre and the editor of *Civiltà Cattolica* told him that the articles about Palestine until then had been written under Barlassina's influence, which seems to have been the case in all of the Italian press, most of which had no independent knowledge of the question.

The cables from the Catholic committee in Jerusalem reached their destinations on July 26. Bandack received the power of attorney and delivered the Arabic original to the archives of the Congregatio de Propaganda Fide, which was headed by Cardinal Van Rossum. On August 3, Bandack paid an official visit to the cardinal, with whom he had met earlier and who in the meantime had received the telegram from Jerusalem. Van Rossum felt uncomfortable with Bandack and said that he had already spoken to the pope about the power of attorney. He showed Bandack a letter from the pope instructing him as a matter of principle not to accept the power of attorney, which could set a dangerous precedent for the freedom of the various Churches throughout the world.

In any case, the cardinal listened to the priest, who went over the points mentioned in the letter of accreditation and described Barlassina as a ridiculous adventurer and troublemaker who was harming the interests of the religion and the land and sullying the honor of the Holy See. The cardinal was impressed by Bandack's remarks, and though he was unable to recognize him as a representative of the Catholics in Palestine, he accepted his accreditation and asked him to set down his claims in writing. He also assured him that if any decisions were reached, he would notify Bandack within a few months. Because the cardinal had to leave for Switzerland on the very next day, he asked Bandack to contact his secretary, Archbishop Pietro Fumasoni-Biondi, who was well versed in the situation but supported Barlassina. The secretary knew of the telegrams and of the priest's mission, from Monsignor Giuseppe Pizzardo, the assistant secretary of state. Fumasoni-Biondi had turned to another priest, who was in Rome en route from the patriarchate of Jerusalem to the apostolic delegation in Persia, to let the rumor leak to the Holy See that Bandack had been sent by the British government.

On August 4, Bandack met with Fumasoni-Biondi and presented him with a detailed report for distribution to the twenty-two cardinals of the Congregatio de Propaganda Fide. The secretary of the congregation, who tried to persuade Bandack to leave Rome, was himself received by the pope that afternoon and gave him Bandack's report.

On August 5, Bandack met with Gasparri, who refused to recognize the accreditation that had been sent from Jerusalem but nonetheless had a long conversation with him. The priest told Gasparri that the decisive failure of the Vatican's policy, as manifested in the approval of the mandate by the Great Powers, had done little to enhance the Holy See's prestige. Gasparri replied that the Vatican had obtained what it wanted. As for Zionism, it was without doubt a great danger for the future of Palestine because the Jews were capable of raising enormous sums of money. Bandack responded that when the Zionists invested their money for the benefit of Palestine, the country's Arab Muslim inhabitants would be the first to welcome Zionism. The Muslim riots in Palestine had been caused by a misunderstanding, for the Muslims believed that the Zionists would take from them the little they had. But once the Zionists brought in capital, they would benefit the country rather than harm it, as Barlassina had told the world. Bandack also brought up specific points in Barlassina's speech in order to refute them. Gasparri asked Bandack if he knew the High Commissioner and the governor of Jerusalem personally and added that the pope was very interested in the Holy Land. He ended the conversation with wishes for peace and happiness for Palestine, which he had visited in 1907 before becoming a cardinal.

On the afternoon of August 9, Bandack was received by the pope during the latter's walk in the Vatican gardens. The talk lasted forty-five minutes, and apart from the fact that the pope sighed deeply and bestowed his apostolic blessing, we know nothing of what they said. Several days later, on August 13, the pope received Cardinal Cacci Porcelli, who had been appointed secretary of the Congregation for the Eastern Churches.

Earlier, on August 3, the pope had ordered Barlassina to return to Jerusalem, despite the telegrams that had arrived from there. He sent Monsignor Respitti, the

Vatican chief of protocol, to Palestine to investigate the reasons for the Catholic unrest in the Holy Land and to determine whether it was being encouraged by the British government. Bandack was sure that Barlassina would be called back from Palestine, even if not immediately, because after his speech on May 12 the British government had asked the Vatican to recall him to Rome, and the Holy See had refused. According to Bandack, before he returned to Jerusalem, Barlassina received explicit instructions from Cardinal Van Rossum, in the name of the pope, to refrain from becoming involved in political controversies and to engage only in his religious occupations.

As a result of Bandack's brother's efforts, the departure of the Supreme Muslim Council's delegation to Rome was postponed. Monsignor Youssuf Gregorius Hajjar, the Greek Catholic archbishop of Haifa, who was known to be against Zionism, proposed himself as a member of the delegation. Bandack hoped that the Zionist Congress, which had been convening in Carlsbad, would decide on an economic plan to be carried out immediately. In his view, this was the most effective way to quash the anti-Zionist movement in all its forms. Bandack was to return to Palestine on August 23 and intended to continue his correspondence with Weizmann from Jerusalem. He added that he was a Zionist at heart and that he would do all he could for the reestablishment of the kingdom of Israel.[69]

In December 1922, Weizmann was to meet Bandack again in Jerusalem,[70] but we do not know whether the association with him bore any fruit. Today the whole episode looks like an internal Church affair, with Bandack involving the Zionists primarily to extract money from them. There is nothing to ascertain—nor is there evidence from any other source—that Bandack did in fact defend Zionism at the Vatican, as he claimed to Weizmann. His hatred for Barlassina should probably be seen in the context of the endless conflict between the Latins and the Eastern Churches, and among the Latins between the local Arab priests, most of whom were of low rank, and the European clergy, who filled the high positions. (Despite the struggle of the local clergy, the post of the Latin patriarch of Jerusalem continued to be occupied by an Italian, although in January 1988, a Palestinian Arab was nominated to be the Latin patriarch of Jerusalem.) Furthermore, because Barlassina was retained in his post, it must have meant that he was a faithful representative of Gasparri's policy. Despite these reservations concerning the practical benefits the Zionists might have derived from a priest like Bandack, they could have learned a great deal from him about internal problems of the Catholic Church in Palestine, but it is doubtful that they were interested.

The Zionist Movement and the Holy Places

The election of Cardinal Ratti as Pope Pius XI raised hopes in the Zionist Organization, which tried to make clear that it had no interest in the Holy Places. In an official memorandum submitted to the Council of the League of Nations, just before confirmation of the mandate in July 1922, the Zionist Organization wrote:

> With equal emphasis does the Zionist Organization categorically deny that the Jews contemplate, or have ever contemplated, the smallest interference with the religious

traditions and customs of the non-Jewish inhabitants of Palestine, or with the Holy
Places. There has been no attempt at such interference. There will and can be none.
The Jews are not so ignorant as not to be fully conscious of the profound veneration
with which the Holy Land is regarded by adherents of other creeds. . . . The Jews
have from the outset recognized the Christian and Moslem Holy Places as sacrosanct
and inviolable. They indignantly repudiate . . . the suggestion that they desire to
trespass upon them or claim any voice in questions relating to their maintenance or
their custody.[71]

For the Thirteenth Zionist Congress, which was held in Carlsbad in August
1923, the Zionist Executive published a report on the events leading up to the
mandate's approval, in which the following was said:

The opposition of the Vatican, which was largely based on misunderstanding of
Zionist aims, was vigorously developed, and some anxiety was caused by the fact
that the Council of the League of Nations contained a considerable proportion of
Roman Catholic Powers. . . . Meanwhile, Article 14 of the Mandate, which was
the concrete subject of discussion, was recast, and between May and July 1922, the
British Government made every effort to mold it into a form acceptable to all the
interested parties. It need hardly be added that with these discussions the Zionist
Organization had no concern. The Organization has repeatedly disinterested itself in
the problem of the Christian and Moslem Holy Places, and neither has nor claims to
have any voice in its solution.[72]

Secular observers well acquainted with Vatican affairs, such as Professor A. C.
Jemolo, wrote at that time that Pope Pius XI's election was largely due to Cardinal
Gasparri, who was immediately reappointed secretary of state. On the problem of
the Holy Places and the new pope, Jemolo wrote:

The pope will thus not be able, without damage to his reputation, to retreat from the
position on the Holy Places taken by Benedict XV or withdraw support for the moral
rights of the "Christian people." The problem is very delicate. All the Jews of
Europe and America are solidly united behind the Zionist core. An anti-Zionist position by the pope will lead to a worsening of anti-Catholic and anti-Vatican hostility
wherever there beats a Semitic heart. Simultaneously, by providing an excuse, even
if unintentionally, for a renewal of anti-Semitism, which is present now more than
ever in the territory of the former Habsburg kingdom, in Poland, Romania, and in a
great portion of Germany, the pope does a disservice to the cause of peace. But if
the Holy See succeeds in carrying out what appears to be its policy, which until now
had been hindered by the British, it will be able to conclude direct agreements with
the Zionist Organization, which until now has revealed neither fanaticism nor disregard for the rights of others. If it succeeds in finding a common denominator
between the moral interest of the Christian people and the need to reestablish a
national home for the dispersed Jews, the Holy See will achieve a success of the
first order that will be of great benefit to its reputation throughout the Mediterranean
region and in all countries where the Semitic problem is crucial and permanent.[73]

These hopes soon proved to have been unrealistic. Several months later, on
December 11, 1922, Pope Pius XI spoke out in a consistorial address on the problem of the Holy Places:

To mention some of the most serious—great sorrow is still caused Us by the trend
of affairs in Palestine, that Holy Land, cradle of our faith, bathed with the sweat and

the Blood of the Divine Redeemer. You know well, Venerable Brethren, all that was done in defence of the rights of the Holy Places by Our revered Predecessor Benedict XV, one of the gravest records of whose Pontificate remains in the memorable Allocution pronounced in the Consistory of June 13 of last year. Now, inasmuch as it seems that the representatives of the Powers at the League of Nations are soon going to consider the Question of Palestine again, We make Our own both the protest and the purpose of Our Predecessor:—"That when time comes to establish there a permanent condition of things, to the Catholic Church and to all Christians shall be assured the inalienable rights they hold."

And indeed, considering how manifestly the rights of the Catholic Church prevail there, We must desire in conformity with the duty which derives from our Apostolic Ministry, that they be assured not only in front of Jews and infidels, but also before non-Catholics, to whatever sect or nation they may belong.[74]

The Vatican persisted in its opposition to Zionism for many years in this matter, with the problem of the Holy Places serving as a major pretext for its position.

Afterword

We have examined the Vatican's position on political Zionism, the factors that influenced it, the changes and developments it underwent in the first quarter of the twentieth century, and the interrelations between the Vatican's stand and the policy of the Great Powers.

As we have seen, from the very beginning of political Zionism, the pope did not conceal his opposition to this movement. The theological element in the Vatican's antagonism was apparent as early as January 1904, when near the end of his short life Theodor Herzl met with Pope Pius X and his secretary of state, Rafael Cardinal Merry del Val.

The Vatican's supreme interest in the Holy Land was the safeguarding of the rights of the Catholics in the Holy Places, often in opposition to the Greek Orthodox Church. But neither was political rivalry among the Great Powers absent from this arena. France, for historical reasons, had for centuries offered its protectorate to Catholics throughout the Ottoman Empire, and czarist Russia extended its protectorate to the Greek Orthodox. In any case, the pope felt obliged to ward off "the danger" of Jewish domination of the Holy Places. To no avail, Herzl explained that the places sacred to Christianity would be accorded extraterritorial status, but Cardinal Merry del Val replied that these places were not to be separated from the Holy Land as a whole.

The Zionist leadership imagined that it had mitigated the Vatican's hostility when Sokolow was received by Pope Benedict XV in May 1917. "We shall be good neighbors," the pope said to Sokolow. He used the word *neighbors* probably because he was confident that Jewish settlement would be outside an internationally protected area that would include not only Jerusalem but also Bethlehem, Nazareth, Tiberias, and Jericho. Indeed, at that time, the Vatican was ready to soften its objections to Zionist aspirations if its demands related to the Holy Places were accepted. On this subject, it assumed that it had to deal with the Great Powers and not with the Jews.

This was the period of World War I, and the Ottoman Empire was on the verge of collapse. On the basis of secret information that it had about the Sykes–Picot agreements, the Vatican was convinced that the central portion of the Holy Land would become an international zone, and it felt that Catholics' rights would be best protected in that way. Certain rumors even pointed to a vague wish by the Vatican for temporal rule of its own in Jerusalem and other parts of Palestine. The pope also continued to hope that the Holy See would be invited to participate in the Peace Conference and be able to apply its full political and religious weight to the new arrangements in the world order that would be made in the wake of World War I.

But the Balfour Declaration and the conquest of Jerusalem by General Allenby at the end of 1917 awakened anxieties in the Vatican. In Gasparri's view, the establishment of a Jewish state would endanger the Holy Places and would upset the feelings of Christians. The Vatican feared further that in Palestine, Protestant Britain would side with the Greek Orthodox and would ultimately transfer the civil administration to the Jews. Not long after, the Vatican was given another cause for concern: the appearance in Palestine of Jewish pioneers, whom they pictured as Bolsheviks threatening the traditional way of life in that land.

In 1919, the Vatican began vigorously to oppose the tendency, which it believed was emerging, to give the Zionists in Palestine privileged status and preferential rights as compared with those of the Christians. This theme recurred in the speeches of Pope Benedict XV.

The change in the Vatican's position, or perhaps the return to the original position of Pius X in 1904, took place in the aftermath of a number of events and other changes. Enlightened British rule did away with the European consuls' jurisdiction over their subjects, which had actually been terminated earlier when the capitulations were abolished. The influence of foreign parties, such as consuls and Church heads, in Palestine's affairs was, perforce, diminished. The Vatican feared that its extensive school system would be harmed and that the British would support the Catholics' chief rivals, the Greek Orthodox, who for centuries had held many of the Holy Places, and the Protestants, who, although latecomers to the scene, had extremely large purses. Furthermore, the Vatican's hope of being invited to the Peace Conference was dashed when it became public knowledge that Catholic Italy had set the Vatican's nonparticipation in the conference as its condition for joining the war in 1915.

France, for centuries the "eldest daughter of the Church," renewed its diplomatic relations with the Vatican only in 1921. In any event, the Vatican was reluctant to rely again on France to defend the interests of Catholics, for it understood that Britain, which ruled Palestine, would not accept French intervention even under the guise of a protectorate of the Catholic religion.

But above all, the Vatican was disturbed by the privileged status that the Zionists had won on the basis of the Balfour Declaration. The Sanremo Conference (1920) and the appointment of a Jew, Sir Herbert Samuel, as the first High Commissioner of Palestine could not but reinforce the Vatican's fears. These assumed more importance in 1922, on the eve of approval of the mandate for Palestine by the Council of the League of Nations, when Cardinal Secretary of State Gasparri and Pope Pius XI fought a vigorous battle against the draft mandate's "Zionist" articles.

The essence of the policy that guided the Vatican for decades to come was spelled out in an official letter sent by Gasparri to the League of Nations on May 15, 1922, which was slightly modified in a memorandum on June 4. According to this letter, the Holy See was not opposed to conferring on Britain the mandate for Palestine but sought a revision of some of its articles, because they accorded the Jews a privileged position over the Catholics and because, in the view of the Holy See, the rights of Christians were not adequately protected. The Vatican ultimately gave up, however, for it realized it had no other choice.

Some believe that the Vatican's persistent diplomatic struggle against Zionism stemmed from a desire to demonstrate to the Great Powers that even though the Vatican had been refused participation in the deliberations of the League of Nations, its views had to be taken into account in the resolution of international problems. On no other international issue could the Vatican put forward such a well-established claim of a right to interfere as in the affairs of the Holy Land.

The Vatican's position on Zionism was undoubtedly influenced by the battle waged against Zionism by the Arabs of Palestine, and vice versa. The Vatican adopted most of the arguments of the Arabs, some of whom it counted among its faithful, and the Arabs, for their part, were encouraged by the Vatican's support. The individual who acted as an intermediary between the two sides was Barlassina, the Latin patriarch of Jerusalem, who excelled in his hatred of Jews and who served in his post throughout the years of the British mandate.

The arguments against the Zionists that the Vatican advanced in the early 1920s can be summarized as follows:

1. The Zionists were not religious and were even antireligious. Therefore, they were not fulfilling biblical prophecy and had nothing to do with the promised return to the Holy Land.
2. Zionist immigration would sweep the Christians out of Palestine and would destroy the country's Christian character.
3. The possibility that a Jewish government would be formed was intolerable.
4. The Jews were causing radical changes in the traditional life-style of the local population, and the accelerated modernization they were inducing was often damaging to moral values.

Among the factors that influenced the Vatican, we should also mention the anti-Semitic prejudices and propaganda of *The Protocols of the Elders of Zion* sort. But in truth, in that period such views were widespread not only in the Vatican but also in secular circles in Europe and the United States.

We also studied the episode of Reverend Bandack, for it demonstrates that the Zionist leaders also tried to find covert ways to soften the Vatican's opposition, although, as it turned out, to no avail. Nevertheless, it should not be assumed that the Catholic Church is monolithic. Indeed, there were Catholic supporters of Zionism in all parts of the world. But my research was restricted to the attitude of the Holy See as the central government of the Church toward the Zionist undertaking. I tried to uncover the historical roots of the Vatican's position on Zionism, which hardly changed from the period we considered until the establishment of the state of Israel. In our own time, there have been far-reaching changes in the Middle East: Israel was established; the Church revised its attitude toward the Jews for the better in its declaration of 1965; and there have been official contacts between a number of popes and leaders of Israel. Nonetheless, the Vatican is still a long way from normal relations with Israel. The Vatican does not have diplomatic relations with Israel and continues to be influenced in no small measure by the arguments of the Arabs. We can only hope that progress toward peace in the Middle East will also lead to the normalization of relations between Israel and the Holy See, despite the theological difficulty that the Church has not yet resolved.

Notes

PREFACE

1. S. Minerbi, "Il Vaticano e la Palestina durante la prima guerra mondiale," *Clio*, July–September 1967, pp. 424–44.

INTRODUCTION

1. S. Minerbi, "The Italian Activity to Recover the 'Cenacolo,'" *Risorgimento* 1, no. 2 (1980): 181–209.

CHAPTER 1

1. There is no clear definition of a "holy place"; one must rely on the list compiled by the Mandatory government. See L. G. A. Cust, *The Status Quo in the Holy Places* (London, 1929). For a description of the Christian churches in Palestine, see S. P. Colbi, *Christianity in the Holy Land, Past and Present* (Tel Aviv, 1968). See also R. Simon, "The Struggle over the Places Holy to Christianity in Palestine During the Ottoman Period, 1516–1583" (in Hebrew), *Cathedra* 17 (September 1981): 107–26.

2. On the religious protectorate, see A. Bertola, "Il protettorato religioso in Oriente e l'accordo del 4.12.1926 fra la S. Sede e la Francia," *Oriente Moderno*, October 1928, pp. 437–54, November 1928, pp. 501–11. On the capitulations, see N. Sousa, *The Capitulatory Regime of Turkey* (London, 1933); L. A. Missir, *Églises et état en Turquie et au Proche-Orient* (Brussels, 1973); and G. Pélissié du Rausas, *Le régime des capitulations dans l'Empire Ottoman* (Paris, 1910–11).

3. On the problem of the Holy Places from a Catholic point of view, see B. Collin, *Les Lieux saints* (Paris, 1962); A. Gassi, *Contributo allo soluzione della questione dei Luoghi Santi* (Jerusalem, 1935). A French translation of the firman of 1852 is in S. Sayegh, *Le Status Quo des Lieux saints, nature juridique et portée internationale* (Rome, 1971). For the Israeli position, see Y. Engelard, "The Legal Status of the Holy Places," and S. Berkowitz, "Proposals for a Settlement of the Status of the Holy Places Within the Framework of a Peace Agreement," both in *Jerusalem—Legal Aspects* (in Hebrew) (Jerusalem, 1980); and W. Zander, *Israel and the Holy Places of Christendom* (London, 1971).

4. See H. E. Cardinale, *The Holy See and the International Order* (Gerrards Cross, England, 1976), p. 83. Ever since the Lateran Treaty between Italy and the Holy See in 1929, the pope has been the sovereign of Vatican City. Thus the pope's temporal rule over a territory was renewed, after its cessation in 1870 after the Italian conquest of Rome.

5. That organizational format existed until 1967, with some modifications having been introduced since then.

6. On the structure of the Catholic Church, see G. Noel, *The Anatomy of the Catholic Church* (New York, 1980); S. Negro, *L'Ordinamento della Chiesa Cattolica* (Milan, 1940); and R. A. Graham, *Vatican Diplomacy* (Princeton, N.J., 1959).

7. On the Eastern Churches, see J. Hajjar, *Les Chrétiens au Proche-Orient* (Paris, 1962); A Simonet, *L'Orient chrétien au seuil de l'unité* (Namur, Belgium, 1962); J. G. Clarke, *L'Enjeu chrétien au Proche-Orient* (Paris, 1965); and L. Missir, *Rome et les églises d'Orient* (Brussels, 1976).

8. See J. Parkes, *A History of Palestine: From 135 A.D. to Modern Times* (London, 1949), p. 239.

9. See J. Meyendorff, *The Orthodox Church* (London, 1962).

10. Colbi, *Christianity in the Holy Land*, p. 87; Parkes, *History of Palestine*, pp. 228–29.

11. The order was founded in Italy by St. Francis (ca. 1182–1226). The Franciscans are also called "minori," to emphasize their humility. Five popes came from their ranks. In 1944, the order numbered 25,000 monks and had 2,000 monasteries. See A. O. Issa, *Les Minorités chrétiennes de Palestine* (Jerusalem, 1977), p. 169.

12. According to Pope Pius X's bull of November 17, 1912, the posts were distributed thus: the custos, an Italian; his deputy (*vicaire*), a Frenchman; the procurator (*procureur*), a Spaniard; and the two members of the council (*discretes*), one an Italian and the other a Frenchman or German. Today this rule is not necessarily implemented.

13. Parkes, *History of Palestine*, pp. 234–36.

14. Y. Ben Arieh, *A City Reflected in Its Times. New Jerusalem—The Beginnings* (in Hebrew) (Jerusalem, 1979), pp. 379–80.

15. Ibid., p. 394.

16. R. Bachi, *The Population of Israel* (Jerusalem, 1977), p. 373.

17. M. Harel, "The Jewish Presence in Jerusalem Throughout the Ages," in *Jerusalem* (New York, 1974), p. 147.

18. A. O'Hare McCormick, *Vatican Journal, 1921–1954* (New York, 1957), pp. 14, 17.

19. L. Salvatorelli, *La politica della Santa Sede dopo la guerra* (Milan, 1937), pp. 10–11.

20. I. Garzia, *La Questione Romana durante la I Guerra Mondiale* (Naples, 1981), p. 13. The Fondo per il Culto was a department of the Italian Ministry of the Interior.

21. M. Toscano, *Il Patto di Londra* (Bologna, 1934).

22. W. E. Addis and T. Arnold, *A Catholic Dictionary* (London, 1951).

23. C. Loiseau, "Ma mission auprès du Vatican," *Revue d'histoire diplomatique* (April–June 1960): 100.

24. Relations between Britain and the Vatican were established by Lord H. H. Asquith on November 9, 1914. See Cmd. 736. On December 18, 1919, in reply to the contention that the British representation at the Vatican was illegal, Harmsworth (Viscount Northcliffe) said that it was not out of keeping with any existing laws. Replying to a query in Parliament on November 11, 1920, the prime minister announced that the government had decided to make the "special mission" a regular one and to continue its diplomatic representation at the Vatican, which had proved fruitful. See letter from Jones, the prime minister's private sec-

retary, to Prime Minister Lloyd George, May 9, 1922, PRO, FO 371/7671, E 8227/8227/22. See also Graham, *Vatican Diplomacy,* p. 78. Only on January 16, 1982, did the British legation become an embassy.

25. Garzia, *La Questione Romana,* p. 16.

26. See Addis and Arnold, *Catholic Dictionary,* p. 102.

27. See the apologetic article by Calisse, "Il Cardinale Pietro Gasparri," *Nuova Antologia,* March 16, 1933. The city hall, church, and power station of Ussita were built with the help of his generosity and funds.

28. Sir A. Randall, *Vatican Assignment* (London, 1956), p. 61.

29. Salvatorelli, *La politica della Santa Sede dopo la guerra,* pp. 9–10.

30. J. D. Gregory, *On the Edge of Diplomacy, 1902–1928* (London, 1928), p. 89.

31. On the Italian effort to get free of the French religious protectorate, see S. Minerbi, "L'Italie contre le protectorat religieux français," in *L'Italie et la Palestine 1914–1920* (Paris, 1970), pp. 152–73.

32. Sir Herbert Louis Samuel (1870–1963) was a member of the British government from 1909 to 1916. In 1920, he was appointed as the first High Commissioner in Palestine, where he served until 1925. In 1931, he again became a member of the government. See H. L. Samuel, *Memoirs* (London, 1945), p. 142.

33. Ibid., p. 141.

34. Sir Edward Grey (later Viscount Falloden) was Britain's foreign secretary from 1905 to 1916. The first meeting at which the plan was discussed took place on November 9, 1914. See I. Friedman, *The Question of Palestine, 1914–1918* (New York, 1973), p. 11.

35. Samuel, *Memoirs,* p. 143.

36. Samuel's memorandum is quoted in full in A. Bowle, *Viscount Samuel* (London, 1957), p. 172.

37. T. Herzl, *The Jewish State* (New York, 1946), p. 96; the details appear in Part II of this book.

38. David Lloyd George, later Earl Lloyd George of Dwyfor (1863–1945), was chancellor of the exchequer in 1908, minister of munitions from 1915 to 1916, and prime minister from 1916 to 1922.

39. Herbert H. Asquith was prime minister from 1908 to 1916.

40. See Samuel, *Memoirs,* p. 143. Asquith's letter is also quoted in M. Gilbert, *Exile and Return* (Jerusalem, 1978), p. 83.

41. See Barrow's memorandum in PRO, Cabinet Papers 17/11, quoted in Gilbert, *Exile and Return,* p. 83.

42. Lewis Harcourt (1863–1933) was colonial secretary from 1910 to 1915.

43. See Gilbert, *Exile and Return,* who quotes Harcourt's memorandum (p. 84).

44. See J. Nevakivi, *Britain, France and the Arab Middle East, 1914–20* (London, 1968), p. 19. The committee was appointed in April 1915 and was chaired by Sir Maurice de Bunsen, assistant undersecretary of state at the Foreign Office, formerly minister in the British embassy in Vienna. Sykes too was on the committee.

45. Quoted in L. Stein, *The Balfour Declaration* (London, 1961), p. 247.

46. Sir Mark Sykes (1879–1919), M.P., worked in the War Office from 1915 to 1916, was attached to the Foreign Office as chief adviser on Near Eastern policy in 1916, was deputy to the cabinet secretary from 1916 to 1917 and was acting adviser on Arabian and Palestine affairs in the Foreign Office from 1917 to 1919.

47. See Stein, *Balfour Declaration,* p. 249.

48. Ibid., p. 254. According to Nevakivi, Sykes said on that day that he would like to keep the area to the south of Haifa, not Acre (*Britain, France, and the Arab Middle East,* p. 34).

49. Quoted in R. Adelson, *Mark Sykes, Portrait of an Amateur* (London, 1975), pp. 201.

50. Quoted in Stein, *Balfour Declaration,* pp. 233–34.

51. Comment by Hugh O'Beirne, February 28, 1916, PRO, FO 371/2671/35433, quoted in Friedman, *Question of Palestine,* p. 53.

52. Stein, *Balfour Declaration,* p. 224.

53. C. J. Smith, *The Russian Struggle for Power 1914–1917,* p. 419, quoted in Y. Herzog, *Israel in the Middle East: An Introduction* (Jerusalem, 1975), p. 66.

54. Buchanan (Starograd) to Grey, no. 371, March 15, 1916, PRO, FO 371/28171/42608, quoted in Friedman, *Question of Palestine,* p. 59.

55. Buchanan to Foreign Office (London), March 14, 1916, PRO, FO 371/2767/938, quoted in Friedman, *Question of Palestine,* p. 114.

56. Buchanan to Foreign Office (London), March 16, 1916, PRO, FO 371/2767/938, quoted in Friedman, *Question of Palestine,* p. 116.

57. It seems that an envoy from the Holy See gave Orlando the main points of the secret agreement as early as the spring of 1916. See M. Toscano, "Colloqui con Gafenco," in *Pagine di storia diplomatica contemporanea* (Milan, 1963), vol. 2, p. 288.

58. See the map in Nevakivi, *Britain, France, and the Arab Middle East,* p. 38. The agreement stated, "The brown zone includes: Palestine without Haifa and Acre," and Article 3 said, "A condominium will be established in the brown zone; its nature would be determined after consultations with Russia and in agreement with the other allied powers, and the Sheriff of Mecca."

59. Stein, *Balfour Declaration,* p. 261.

60. R. Poincaré, *Au service de la France* (Paris, 1930), vol. 6, p. 118.

CHAPTER 2

1. Lord Beaverbrook, "Men and Power, 1917–1918," p. xxxv, quoted in J. Kimche, *The Unromantics* (London, 1968), p. 29.

2. R. Adelson, *The Formation of British Policy Towards the Middle East, 1914–1918* (Ann Arbor, Mich., 1972), pp. 341–42.

3. I. Friedman, *The Question of Palestine, 1914–1918* (New York, 1973), p. 124.

4. Memorandum on meetings held on February 8, 9, and 10, 1917, CZA LG/90/1, quoted in Friedman, *Question of Palestine,* p. 132.

5. Protocol of the meeting of the committee on the territorial demands included in the peace conditions, April 17, 18, 19, and 23, 1917, CAB 21/77, quoted in Adelson, *Formation of British Policy,* pp. 341–42.

6. S. Minerbi, *L'Italie et la Palestine 1914–1920* (Paris, 1970), p. 28.

7. Cabinet meeting of April 25, 1917 (war cabinet, PRO, CAB 23/3).

8. The "secret consistory" is a meeting of cardinals with the pope for discussion of Church affairs and decision making.

9. L. Salvatorelli, *La politica della Santa Sede dopo la guerra* (Milan, 1937), p. 14.

10. See "Motu proprio 'Dei Providentia' de sacra congregatione pro ecclesia orientale," *Acta Apostolicae Sedis* (1917): 529–31.

11. The new office had no territorial authority. When in 1918 a new custos of the Holy Land and a new Latin patriarch of Jerusalem were to be nominated, this was handled by the Congregatio pro Propaganda Fide, as it concerned the Latins. The situation changed in 1938, when the department's responsibilities were broadened, and all matters concerning institutions and believers, both Latin and Eastern, in Palestine and other countries, were transferred to the Congregatio pro Ecclesia Orientali. See *La Sacra Congregazione per le Chiese Orien-*

tali nel cinquantesimo della fondazione (1917–1967) (Rome, 1967), and *Oriente Cattolico* (Vatican City, 1974), p. 12.

12. Proclamation read from the steps of David's Tower, quoted in W. T. Massey, *How Jerusalem Was Won* (London, 1919) p. 286.

13. Lord Arthur James Balfour (1848–1930) was prime minister from 1902–1905, foreign secretary from 1916 to 1919, and lord president of the State Council from 1919–1922.

14. Sir A. Randall, *Vatican Assignment* (London, 1956), p. 12.

15. Draft of de Salis's cable to Balfour, no. 66, December 12, 1917, PRO, FO 308/16, quoting *Osservatore Romano* of that date.

16. Draft of de Salis's cable to Balfour, no. 80, December 16, 1917, PRO, FO 380/16. The newspaper *Il Messagero* published an interview with Monsignor Louis-Marie-Olivier Duchesne, who was then in Rome at the French embassy. He declared that Italy was the power best suited to fill an important role in Palestine, for it had proven experience in controlling a complex and complicated area, having already resolved the problem of the dual presence of both the pope and the Italian government in Rome. De Salis added that this remark did little to increase Duchesne's meager support in the Vatican.

17. Draft of de Salis's report to Balfour, no. 87, December 25, 1917, PRO, FO 380/16. The next day, de Salis cabled the Foreign Office, asking on behalf of Colonel Clutterbuck that Captain Birch keep his meetings in Rome secret (ibid., cable no. 69, December 26, 1917).

18. Van den Heuvel to Foreign Minister de Broqueville (Le Havre), December 12, 1917, no. 132, ABRE, St. Siège 1917. Also quoted in R. Aubert, "Les démarches du Cardinal Mercier en vue de l'octroi à la Belgique d'un mandat sur la Palestine," *Bulletin de la classe des lettres et sciences morales et politiques*, 5th ser., vol. 65 (1975–79): 170. Jules Van den Heuvel (1854–1926) was minister of justice from 1899 to 1906 and minister plenipotentiary to the Holy See from 1915 to 1918.

19. Ministry for Foreign Affairs (Le Havre) to Van Den Heuvel (Rome), no. 666, ABRE, St. Siège 1918.

20. Unsigned, handwritten memorandum, April 6, 1919, AAE, E 312.2, Paquet 27. The Sykes–Goût meeting is also mentioned by J. Nevakivi, *Britain, France and the Arab Middle East, 1914–20* (London, 1968), p. 64. Sykes returned from Paris satisfied that "the French Government was not animated by any desire of colonial domination or annexation in Arab lands." See R. Adelson, *Mark Sykes, Portrait of an Amateur* (London, 1975), p. 254.

21. Draft of de Salis's cable to Balfour, no. 70, December 28, 1917, PRO, FO 380/16.

22. On the relations between France and the Vatican during that period, and especially on the objection of Camille Barrère, the French ambassador in Rome, to the nomination of a French ambassador to the Holy See after the death of Pius X, see P. Charles-Roux, *Souvenirs diplomatiques Rome–Quirinal (Fevrier 1916–Fevrier 1918)* (Paris, 1958), pp. 59–61. He stated: "In order to mend somewhat this oversight, the French Ministry for Foreign Affairs decided to send a talented writer to the representation in Rome, Charles Loiseau, an expert in two kinds of problems: those of the Churches, and of the southern Slavs."

23. Quoted in C. Loiseau, *Politique romaine et sentiment français* (Paris, 1923), pp. 73–74, H. F. Köck, *Der Vatikan und Palästina* (Vienna, 1973). Köck noted that unlike the other church bells in Rome, those of St. Peter did not chime for the liberation of Jerusalem because the pope found it inappropriate to Vatican neutrality.

24. F. Scaduto, in *Per la liberazione di Gerusalemme: Giudizi ed impressioni originali raccolte dell'Agenzia Volta* (Rome, 1917), p. 26.

25. See *Israel* (Florence) January 1916.

26. See L. Stein, *The Balfour Declaration* (London, 1961), p. 406; also Part II of this book.

27. See the opinion of the former secretary of state, Cardinal Rafael Merry del Val, in 1915, in I. Garzia, *La Questione Romana durante la I Guerra Mondiale* (Naples, 1981), p. 117.

28. *Le Pape et Jerusalem: Solution de la question italienne et de la question orientale* (Paris, 1861), quoted in W. Zander, *Israel and the Holy Places of Christendom* (London, 1971), pp. 31–32.

29. A. Pini-Tronati, "Jules Van den Heuvel, ambasciatore presso la S. Sede (Lettere del 1916)," *Risorgimento* 15, no. 1 (1972): 3; letter from Van den Heuvel to the minister of foreign affairs, January 4, 1916.

30. Bethsaida, located not far from the Sea of Galilee, is mentioned in the New Testament as the site of one of Jesus's miracles. See B. Pixner, "Putting Bethsaida–Julias on the Map." *Christian News from Israel* 37, no. 4 (1982): 165–70.

31. Van Den Heuvel (Rome) to Foreign Minister Hymans, February 4, 1918, no. 45/16, ABRE, St. Siège 1918.

32. AAE, vol. 38, Feuille 165–68, quoted in S. Marchese, *La Francia ed il problema dei rapporti con la Santa Sede (1914–1924)* (Naples, 1969), p. 165.

33. Ibid.

34. Baron de Gaiffer to Hymans, March 9, 1918, quoted in Aubert, "Les Démarches du Cardinal Mercier," p. 208.

35. See B. Collin, *Le Problème juridique des Lieux saints* (Paris, 1956), p. 23.

36. See A. Bertola, "Il protettorato religioso in Oriente e l'accordo del 4.12.1926 fra S. Sede e la Francia," *Oriente Moderno,* October 1928, p. 444. The Capitulations Treaty of 1604 deals specifically with the Holy Places. According to it, the priests of Jerusalem were free there to come and go as they pleased. See S. Sayegh, *Le status quo des Lieux saints, nature juridique et portée internationale* (Rome, 1971), p. 148.

37. See B. Collin, *Les Lieux saints* (Paris, 1962), p. 70.

38. See Minerbi, *L'Italie et la Palestine,* pp. 153–73.

39. The letter was published in the press a few months later. See Collin, *Le Problème juridique,* pp. 64–65.

40. See Sayegh, *Status quo des Lieux saints,* p. 169.

41. D'Agostino to the War Office (Rome), August 1918, ASME file 184.

42. Cable from Castellani, of the Custodia Terrae Sanctae, to Father Cimino, general head of the Franciscan order in Rome, January 4, 1918. See also the letter of Monti, the Italian representative, to Foreign Minister Sonnino, January 9, 1918, ASME file 185.

43. Quoted in T. E. Hachey, *Anglo-Vatican Relations, 1914–1939* (Boston, 1972), p. 21.

44. Draft of a secret report from de Salis to Balfour, no. 6, January 12, 1918, PRO, FO 380/20.

45. Monti to Sonnino, March 18, 1918, ASME file 185.

46. Manzoni to Sonnino, March 25, 1918, ASME file 185.

47. Draft of a report by de Salis to Balfour, no. 39, April 22, 1918, PRO, FO 380/20.

48. Van Zuylen (Rome) to Hymans (Brussels), January 14, 1918, no. 10/4, ABRE, St. Siège 1919–20.

49. De Salis to Balfour, March 10, 1919, PRO, FO 371/4179.

50. Protocol of a conversation between C. R. (Charles-Roux) and M. H. (Herzog), March 7, 1919, about Amette's visit to the Vatican, AAE 262, Serie Z, St. Siège.

51. Minutes to de Salis cable of March 10, 1919, PRO, FO 371/4179.

52. Protocol of the meetings, May 22, 1919, AAE, E 312-2.

53. Gaisford to the Foreign Office, August 2, 1919, PRO, FO 608/118.

54. Curzon to Balfour, August 2, 1919, PRO, FO 608/118.

55. Translation of Gasparri's letter, July 30, 1919, PRO, FO 608/118.

CHAPTER 3

1. Cable from Imperiali (London) to Ministry of Foreign Affairs (Rome), January 3, 1919, no. 38/25, ASME file 185. Guglielmo Imperiali di Francavilla, the Italian ambassador in London, heard this from Angelo Levi Bianchini. See S. Minerbi, *Angelo Levi Bianchini e la sua opera nel Levante, 1918–1920* (Milan, 1967), pp. 35–36. At a British cabinet meeting in December 1918, it was also said, "Pledges concerning the Holy Land should be effectively fulfilled." See H. N. Howard, *The King–Crane Commission* (Beirut, 1963), p. 8.

2. See Howard, *King–Crane Commission,* p. 18.

3. Quoted in ibid., pp. 12–13. The same idea is expressed elsewhere in the memorandum in a different fashion: "The Christian, Jewish and Moslem Holy Places in Palestine, like the waterway in the zone of the straits, constitute a world interest of such importance that it should take precedence, in case of conflict, over political aspirations of the local inhabitants" (ibid., p. 18).

4. Francis Bourne (1861–1935) was appointed archbishop of Westminster in 1903 and became a cardinal in 1911. He was exceedingly influential and proved to be highly patriotic during World War I. Bourne was active primarily in matters related to the rights of Palestinian Arabs and Catholic demands concerning education.

5. Cables from Soragna (Jerusalem), January 18, 1919, no. 291/18, and January 23, 1919, no. 369/212, ASME file 1575.

6. E. Oldmeadow, *Francis Cardinal Bourne* (London, 1944), vol. 2, pp. 173, 148.

7. See p. 131.

8. Oldmeadow, *Francis Cardinal Bourne,* p. 174.

9. Cable from Soragna (Jerusalem), January 25, 1919, ASME file 1575.

10. Cable from de Salis to Foreign Office, no. 38, March 21, 1919, PRO, FO 608/118; copy also found in WO 106/189. Anti-Zionist minute by S. K. On Cardinal Amette's visit to Rome, see p. 26.

11. *The American Jewish Year Book 5680,* September 1919–September 1920 (Philadelphia, 1919), vol. 21, p. 262.

12. Draft of cable from Balfour (Paris) to de Salis (Rome), April 2, 1919, PRO, FO 608/118.

13. Cable from de Salis to Balfour, no. 43, April 4, 1919, PRO, FO 608/118, E 6440.

14. Van Zuylen to Foreign Minister Hymans, April 6, 1919, no. 65/33, ABRE, St. Siège 1919–20. A translation from *Osservatore Romano,* April 5, 1919, was attached, which included a corrected version of the interview in the *Petit Parisien.* In this version, Gasparri said that he preferred to see Jerusalem under international rather than Zionist rule.

15. For details on the visit and on the disagreement between France and Italy, see S. Minerbi, *L'Italie et la Palestine 1914–1920* (Paris, 1970), pp. 187–93.

16. Louis Dubois (1856–1929) was appointed archbishop of Paris in 1920. He dealt mainly with strengthening cultural ties and with relations with foreigners in Paris and played an important role in bridging the differences of view between the state and the Church in France.

17. Tuozzi to Foreign Minister, January 13, 1920, ASME file 1566.

18. H. F. Köck, *Der Vatikan und Palästina* (Vienna, 1973), p. 44.

19. De Robeck, the British High Commissioner in Constantinople, to Curzon (London), no. 363, February 17, 1920, PRO, FO 371/5221, E 2308/1965/44. See also the confidential

report by British intelligence in Constantinople to Curzon, March 14, 1920, PRO, FO 371/5166, E 2306/262/44.

20. Lord Derby (Paris) to Curzon (London), March 20, 1920, PRO, FO 371/5221, E 1965/44, includes the main points in the cardinal's interview given that day in Bucharest to the *Journal des débats*.

21. Sir Oswald Arthur Scott (1893–1960) was an official in the Foreign Office from 1919 to 1921. See D. Ingrams, *Palestine Papers, 1917–1922,* (London, 1972), p. 188.

22. This commission's report is dealt with extensively later. See Howard, *King–Crane Commission,* p. 218.

23. Quoted in ibid., p. 352.

24. Letter from Gasparri (Vatican) to de Salis (Vatican), February 19, 1920, PRO, FO 371/5191, E 589/44.

25. See A. Giannini, *L'ultima fase della Questione Orientale (1913–1923)* (Rome, 1933), p. 288.

26. BD, 1st ser., vol. 8, 1920 (London, 1958), no. 15, p. 171.

27. De Salis (Vatican) to Foreign Office (London), July 3, 1920, PRO, FO 371/5205, E 7911/1136/44.

28. H. L. Samuel, *Memoirs* (London, 1945), pp. 153–54.

29. Report from Samuel, on a conversation with the pope and Gasparri, to Curzon, June 26, 1920, ISA, Herbert Samuel Archives; also in FO 371/5205, E 7570/1136/44.

30. De Salis (Vatican) to Curzon (London), no. 83, July 3, 1920, PRO, FO 371/5205, E 7911/1136/44.

31. Young to Vansittart, July 26, 1920, PRO, FO 371/5191, E 8890/588/44.

32. See Great Britain, *Treaty of Peace with Turkey,* Sèvres, August 10, 1920, art. 95.

33. *Les Lieux saints de la Palestine, memoire des Latins à la Conférence de la Paix, 1919* (Jerusalem, 1922); W. Zander, *Israel and the Holy Places of Christendom* (London, 1971), p. 181.

34. "Memorandum; Greeks and Franciscans in the Holy Places," *Nea Sion* (1919); Zander, *Israel and the Holy Places,* p. 186.

35. Osborne to Father Robinson (Rome), September 24, 1920, PRO, FO 371/5191, E 11696/589/44. D'Arcy Osborne was deputy head of the Eastern Department at the Foreign Office. See Sir G. Rendel, *The Sword and the Olive, 1913–1954* (London, 1957), p. 49.

36. S. Sayegh, *Le Status Quo des Lieux saints, nature juridique et portée internationale* (Rome, 1971), p. 280.

37. See R. Tritonj, "La questione dei Luoghi Santi," in *L'Italia e il Levante* (Rome 1934), p. 114.

38. Manzoni to foreign minister Sonnino, March 15, 1918, ASME file 185.

39. Manzoni to Sonnino, December 11, 1917, ASME file 185.

40. Monti to Sonnino, January 2, 1918; cable from Negrotto (Cairo) to Sonnino, March 2, 1918, ASME file 185.

41. Diotallevi to Cimino, March 6, 1918, ASME file 185.

42. Monti to Sonnino, August 10, 1918, ASME file 185.

43. "Latin Patriarch on Zionism. Moral Decadence in the Holy Land," *The Times* (London), May 31, 1922, p. 9.

44. "Inclitum Fratrum Minorum Conditorem," in Sayegh, *Status Quo des Lieux saints,* pp. 223–24. The pope addresses believers in various types of letters; a brief is a letter on matters of discipline, less formal than a papal bull.

45. R. Storrs, *Orientations* (London, 1937), p. 298.

46. De Salis to Curzon, August 11, 1922, PRO, CO 41914/733/31, E 8070/582/65.

47. De Salis to Curzon, February 5, 1920, PRO, FO 371/5191, E 588/588/44. Monsi-

gnor Bonaventura Cerretti served in 1917 in the Secretariat of State as secretary for special ecclesiastical affairs. He held talks with Italian Prime Minister Vittorio Orlando during the Paris Peace Conference (1919) and was later appointed nuncio in Paris.

48. Notes by Scott, February 26, 1920, PRO, FO 371/5191, E 588/588/44.

49. De Salis to Foreign Office, March 11, 1920, PRO, FO 371/5191, E 1504/588/44.

50. Notes by Sir John Tilley, May 29, 1920, PRO, FO 371/5191, E 5376/588/44.

51. Memorandum by the patriarch of Jerusalem, undated, with Tilley's notes, May 29. 1920, PRO, FO 371/5191, E 5376/588/44.

52. Samuel to Tilley, June 2, 1920, PRO, FO 371/5191, E 5793/588/44.

53. Cable from de Salis (Vatican) to Curzon (London), no. 30, July 22, 1920, PRO, FO 371/5191, E 8782/588/44.

54. Notes by A. C., July 20, 1920, relating to de Salis's cable.

55. See BD, vol. 7, February 17, 1920, no. 11, p. 109, quoted in L. Stein, *The Balfour Declaration* (London, 1961), p. 656. See also E. Bovis, *The Jerusalem Question, 1917–1968* (Stanford, Calif., 1971), p. 7.

56. De Salis (Vatican) to Curzon, February 21, 1920, PRO, FO 371/5181, E 589/44. Marquis George Nathaniel Curzon of Kedleston was secretary of state for foreign affairs from 1919 to 1924. See *Who Was Who* (London, 1929), p. 256.

57. Francesco Saverio Nitti was the Italian minister of finance from 1917–1919 and prime minister from 1919–1920. See *Enciclopedia Italiana* (Milan, 1934), Vol. 24, p. 858.

58. BD, vol. 8, April 24, 1920, no. 15, p. 170.

59. Report by Samuel (Rome) to Curzon (London), June 26, 1920, PRO, FO 371/5205, E 7570/1136/44; ISA, Samuel Archives. On the meeting with the pope, see also Samuel, *Memoirs,* pp. 153–54

60. Doulcet, chargé d'affaires at the Vatican, to Foreign Minister Millerand, AAE, St. Siège, E 312.2, June 27, 1920.

61. Letter from Preziosi, Italian chargé d'affaires (London), to the British Foreign Office, June 1, 1920, PRO, FO 371/5244, E 5208/4164/44.

62. Memorandum from Gasparri (Vatican) to de Salis (Vatican), PRO, FO 371/5244, E 7911/1136/44 (also in FO 406/44), received in Rome, July 3, 1920, attached to de Salis's letter to the Foreign Office, no. 82, July 3, 1920.

63. De Salis (Vatican) to Curzon (London), no. 82, July 3, 1920, De Salis also quoted the article by Lambelin, *Le Correspondant,* May 25, 1920. PRO, FO 371/5244, E 7911/1136/44.

64. Sir Hubert Winthrop Young was assistant to the political officer in Mesopotamia from 1915 to 1917, an official in the Foreign Office from 1919 to 1921, and assistant secretary, Colonial Office Middle East Department, from 1921 to 1927. See Ingrams, *Palestine Papers,* p. 189.

65. Comments on the file containing report no. 82 by de Salis, PRO, FO 371/5244, E 7910/4164/44. The first comment, July 10, 1920, and the last, July 21, 1920, are Curzon's.

66. De Salis (Vatican) to Foreign Office, no. 24, July 12, 1920, PRO, FO 371/5205, E 8323/1136/44.

67. Draft from Foreign Office to de Salis (Vatican), July 24, 1920, PRO, FO 371/5244, E 7910/4164/44.

CHAPTER 4

1. Cable from Curzon to de Salis, August 6, 1920, BD, vol. 13, no. 299, p. 331.

2. Cable from de Salis, August 15, 1920, BD, vol. 13, no. 311, p. 341.

3. Doulcet to foreign minister (Paris), November 15, 1920, AAE, E 316.1, St. Siège.

4. Quoted in T. E. Hachey, *Anglo-Vatican Relations, 1914–1939* (Boston, 1972), p. 22.

5. Samuel to Curzon, October 27, 1920, PRO, FO 371/5191, E 14067.

6. Comments, November 26, 1920, and the text of the interpellation (PRO, FO 371/5191, E 15008).

7. Quoted in Hachey, *Anglo-Vatican Relations*, p. 22.

8. Cable from de Salis (Vatican) to Foreign Office, no. 51, December 20, 1920, PRO, FO 371/5191, E 15916/589/44.

9. Cable from Foreign Office to Samuel (Jerusalem), no. 319, December 22, 1920, PRO, FO 371/6381, E 57/57/88. De Salis sent the Foreign Office a copy of Gasparri's letter, dated December 20, 1920, and his reply expressing British protest against the cardinal's decision.

10. Cable from Foreign Office de Salis (Vatican), no. 42, December 23, 1920, PRO, FO 371/6381, E 57/57/88.

11. Cable from Samuel (Jerusalem) to Foreign Office, no. 444, December 21, 1920, PRO, FO 371/5192, E 15976/589/44. A portion of Samuel's letter, dated December 21, 1920, is also quoted by S. Sayegh: "It is in the view of H. M. Government undesirable that the privileges referred to should be continued" (*Le status quo des Lieux Saints, nature juridique et portée internationale* [Rome, 1971], p. 169).

12. Samuel (Jerusalem) to Foreign Office, December 21, 1920, PRO, FO 371/6281, E 490/57/88.

13. De Salis (Vatican) to Curzon (London), no. 8, January 16, 1921, PRO, FO 371/6381, E 1122/57/88.

14. Comments by Forbes-Adam, January 16, 1921, PRO, FO 371/6381, E 1122/57/88. Sir Eric Graham Forbes-Adam (1888–1925) was an official in the Foreign Office and a friend of Weizmann. He attended the Peace Conference (1918–19) and the Sanremo Conference (1920).

15. Letter from Gasparri (Vatican) to Roger Thynne, the British chargé d'affaires (Vatican), October 16, 1920, PRO, FO 371/5124, E 13184/85/44, enclosed with Thynne's letter to Curzon, no. 123, October 20, 1920.

16. Comments to Gasparri's letter, October 16, 1920, PRO, FO 371/5124, E 13184/85/44.

17. Deeds (Jerusalem) to Curzon (London), no. 141, November 18, 1920, PRO, FO 371/5124, E 13184/85/44. Brigadier General Sir Wyndham Deeds was the chief secretary to the Palestine Government from 1920 to 1923.

18. De Salis (Vatican) to Foreign Office, no. 150, December 29, 1920, PRO, FO 371/6382, E 58/58/88.

19. For the complete text of the pope's speech, see *Osservatore Romano*, June 13, 1921; also, *Oriente Moderno*, no. 1 (1921): 81; *Acta Apostolicae Sedis*, June 18, 1921, pp. 281–84; *The Tablet* (London), June 25, 1921, pp. 821–22. Scott believed that the last sentence quoted from the pope's speech alluded to the plan to build a funicular to the top of Mount Carmel (comments to de Salis's cable, PRO, FO 371/6375, E 7189/35/88).

20. Dormer (Vatican) to Forbes-Adam (London), September 7, 1921, PRO, FO 337/6376, E 10315/85/68.

21. See R. Storrs, *Orientations* (London, 1937), pp. 311–12; C. R. Ashbee, ed, *Jerusalem 1918–1920. Records of the Pro-Jerusalem Council During the Period of the British Military Administration* (London, 1921), p. 19.

22. Y. de la Brière, "Les Raisons nationales et internationales de renouer avec le Vatican," *Études*, July 5, 1917, pp. 42–120, quoted in Marchese, *La Francia il problema dei rapporti con la Santa Sede* (Naples, 1969), p. 169.

23. A. De Monzie, "Rome sans Canosse" (1918), quoted in Marchese, *Francia*, p. 170.

24. Draft of instructions to the French chargé d'affaires at the Holy See, March 12, 1920, AAE, series 7, St. Siège 1918–20, vol. 13.

25. De Salis (Vatican) to Foreign Office, November 13, 1920, PRO, FO 372/4802, E 11452/10042/22.

26. Aristide Briand (1862–1932), a socialist, eleven times the prime minister of France, received the Nobel Peace Prize in 1926, and was foreign minister from 1915 to 1917.

27. Lord Hardinge (Paris) to Foreign Office (London), February 19, 1921, PRO, FO 371/6465, E 2236/1/44. Lord Hardinge of Penshurst was the British ambassador in Paris from 1920 to 1923.

28. L. Salvatorelli, *La politica della Santa Sede dopo la guerra* (Milan, 1937), p. 58.

29. De Salis (Vatican) to Foreign Office, June 30, 1921, PRO, FO 371/6381, E 7598/57/88. Charles Jonnart (1857–1927) had been governor of Algiers from 1900 to 1911.

30. De Salis (Vatican) to Curzon (London), no. 17, June 19, 1921, PRO, FO 371/6381, E 6719/57/88.

31. Lord Derby (Paris) to Foreign Office, September 8, 1920, PRO, FO 371/5122, E 11190/85/44. The French claimed that in September 1920 the Italians had a hundred troops and three officers in Palestine. According to Italian documents, however, between 1919 and 1921, there were only fifty *carabinieri* still in Jerusalem, left there to guard the Holy Sepulchre, and they too were removed at the end of February 1921. See S. Minerbi, *L'Italie et la Palestine 1914–1920* (Paris, 1970), p. 221.

32. Comments by A. D. Cooper, a Foreign Office official, June 24, 1921, PRO, FO 371/6381, E 6710/57/88. French and Italian forces had joined General Allenby in 1917 when he entered Jerusalem.

33. Comments to a letter from de Salis (Vatican) to Curzon (London), June 30, 1921, PRO, FO 371/6381, E 7598/57/88.

34. Dormer (Vatican) to Foreign Office, June 24, 1921, PRO, FO 371/6375, E 7594/35/88.

35. Col. Meinertzhagen (Cairo) to Foreign Office, March 2, 1920, PRO, FO 371/5200, E 920/44, quoted in R. Meinertzhagen, *Middle East Diary, 1917–1956* (London, 1959), p. 70. Col. Richard Meinertzhagen (1878–1967) participated in the conquest of Palestine and was a member of the British delegation to the Paris Peace Conference. From 1919 to 1920, he was the chief political officer in Palestine; he was military adviser to the Middle East Department of the Colonial Office from 1921 to 1924.

36. Comment by Mong, July 4, 1921, FO 371/6375.

37. Lord Hardinge (Paris) to Foreign Office, August 8, 1921, PRO, FO 371/6984, E 8386/809/17.

38. *Le Temps,* August 4, 1921.

39. Alexandre Millerand (1859–1943) was several times war minister and prime minister of France and was president from 1920 to 1924.

40. See Salvatorelli, *La politica della Santa Sede dopo la guerra,* pp. 53–54. Lord Hardinge (Paris) to Curzon (London), no. 2270, August 8, 1921, PRO, FO 371/6984, E 8476/809/17. Enclosed with the letter was a clipping from *Journal Officiel,* August 7, 1921, containing the full texts of both speeches.

41. Letter from Gasparri (Vatican) to the British legation, September 13, 1920, PRO, FO 371/5123, E 11689/85/44, enclosed with letter from de Salis (Vatican) to Curzon (London), no. 117, August 17, 1920. Forbes-Adam remarked that prima facie the Vatican's claim was totally groundless.

42. Bulletin of the Italian Ministry for Foreign Affairs press office, November 1, 1920, ASME file 1467.

43. Samuel to Foreign Office, October 12, 1920, PRO, FO 371/5191, E 12614/589/44.

44. Foreign Office to Samuel, October 19, 1920; cable from Samuel to Foreign Office, no. 367, November 12, 1920, PRO, FO 371/5191, E 12614/589/44.

45. Protocol no. 17 of the meeting of the interministerial committee that convened in London on December 17, 1920, PRO, FO 371/6390, E 656/656/88. Mentioned in the protocol are Samuel's cables to Foreign Office, no. 367, November 12, 1920, and no. 414, December 8, 1920.

46. Protocol of the meeting of the interministerial committee, December 17, 1920, PRO, FO 371/6390, E 656/656/88. The meeting was attended by Sir John Tilley, assistant secretary, Foreign Office, and chair; M. F. Headlam, Treasury; Major R. Marss, India Office; P. N. Waggett; Major Money Sheman, War Office; Captain J. D. Macindoe, War Office; Major H. W. Young, Foreign Office; J. Murray, Egyptian Department, Foreign Office; H. W. Malkin, Foreign Office; E. G. Forbes-Adam, Foreign Office; A. W. Lidderdale, Foreign Office; and O. A. Scott, Foreign Office (secretary).

47. Great Britain, Parliament Papers by Command, Cmd. 1176, *Draft Mandates for Mesopotamia and Palestine As Submitted for the Approval of the League of Nations, December 1920* (London, 1921); Cmd. 1500, *Final Drafts of the Mandates for Mesopotamia and Palestine for the Approval of the Council of the League of Nations, August 1921* (London, 1921).

48. See B. Collin, *Les Lieux saints* (Paris, 1948), p. 132.

49. See Y. de la Brière, *L'Organisation internationale du monde contemporain et la papauté souveraine,* première série, 1885–1924 (Paris, 1930).

50. Foreign Office memorandum, April 19, 1921, PRO, FO 371/6388, E 4632/598/88.

51. Comments by Forbes-Adam, April 19, 1921, PRO, FO 371/6388, E 4632/598/88.

52. Cable from Shuckburgh (London) to High Commissioner (Jerusalem), May 20, 1921, PRO, FO 371/6388, E 5879/589/88.

53. Shuckburgh to deputy foreign secretary, May 21, 1921, FO 371/6389, E 5879/598/88; comments by Oliphant, May 23, 1921, FO 371/6389, E 5879/598/88.

54. L. Oliphant to Sir Milne Cheetham, May 25, 1921, FO 371/6389, E 5879/598/88.

55. Samuel to deputy foreign secretary, June 6, 1921, FO 371/6389, E 6458/598/88.

56. High Commissioner (Constantinople), June 29, 1921, FO 371/6389, E 5232/5232/21.

57. *Acta Apostolicae Sedis,* June 18, 1921, pp. 281–84; *The Tablet,* June 25, 1921, pp. 821–22.

58. De Salis (Vatican) to Foreign Office, June 14, 1921, PRO, FO 371/6375, E 6874/35/88.

59. Comments by Scott on de Salis's letter, May 20, 1921, FO 371/6375, E 7189/35/88.

60. De Salis (Vatican) to Foreign Office, June 21, 1921, PRO, FO 371/6389, E 7121/598/88.

61. Osborne (London) to de Salis (Vatican), no. 141, July 26, 1921, PRO, FO 371/6389, E 8481/598/88; Shuckburgh (London) to Osborne (London), July 23, 1921.

62. H. L. Samuel, *Memoirs* (London, 1945), p. 161.

63. Colonial secretary to Foreign Office, August 16, 1921, PRO, FO 371/6397, with a copy of a cable from Jerusalem, August 15, 1921. Scott commented, "His visit could be most useful" (August 18, 1921).

64. Dormer (Vatican) to Curzon (London), August 27, 1921, PRO, CO 733/11/45708, E 10038/9382/88.

65. R. Storrs, *Orientations* (London, 1937), pp. 432–33.

66. Storrs's memorandum, August 25, 1921, enclosed with Dormer's letter to Curzon

(London), August 27, 1921. The memorandum was forwarded from the Foreign Office to the Colonial Office. Storrs personally forwarded a copy to Young in the Colonial Office. See CO, 733/11/44783. Another copy is in FO 371/6397.

67. On Italy's efforts to obtain the Cenacolo, see S. Minerbi, "The Italian Activity to Recover the 'Cenacolo,'" *Risorgimento* 1, no. 2 (1980): 181–209.

CHAPTER 5

1. R. Storrs, *Orientations* (London, 1937), p. 451.

2. Memorandum by Storrs (Rome), September 23, 1921, PRO, FO 371/6387 E 11714/9382/88.

3. Storrs, *Orientations,* p. 344.

4. Cable from Lord Hardinge (Paris), no. 51, January 31, 1922, PRO, CO 7369/33/502, commenting on a cable from Constantinople, no. 58, January 28, 1922. *L'Echo de Paris* of that day wrote that although France had been forced at Sanremo to relinquish the rights of providing protection for the Holy Places in Palestine, it was still the protector of Catholics throughout the Ottoman Empire.

5. Cable from Foreign Office to Graham (Rome), no. 32, February 1, 1922. Sir Ronald Graham was adviser to the minister of interior in Egypt from 1910 to 1916, assistant undersecretary in the Foreign Office, permanent undersecretary in 1919, and ambassador to Rome from 1920 to 1923.

6. Cable from Graham (Rome) to Foreign Office, no. 72, February 13, 1922, PRO, CO 7339, E 733/33/508.

7. Cable from de Salis (Vatican) to Foreign Office, February 1, 1922, PRO, CO 7369/33/505, E 1027/900/44.

8. De Salis (Vatican) to Lord Hardinge (Paris), February 5, 1922, PRO, CO 7349, E 733/33/501. In a cable on the following day, de Salis asked for the precise text of the Sanremo agreement.

9. Cable from Jonnart (Rome) to Ministry for Foreign Affairs (Paris), February 26, 1922, AAE, St. Siège, vol. 18.

10. "L'Hostilité Vaticane se manifeste en Orient," *L'Homme Libre,* August 2, 1923.

11. See B. Collin, *Les Lieux saints* (Paris, 1948), pp. 147–50. See also "Accord entre le St. Siège et la France, 4.12.1926," *Oriente Moderno,* February 1927, pp. 62–63.

12. "L'Inviato apostolico di Terrasanta," *Il Tempo,* October 12, 1920.

13. Cable from Foreign Minister (Paris) to Doulcet (Rome), October 16, 1920, AAE, E 312/2, St. Siège, vol. 9.

14. Doulcet (Rome) to Foreign Minister Leygues (Paris), October 19, 1920, AAE, E 312/2, St. Siège, vol. 9.

15. Doulcet to foreign minister, October 26, 1920, AAE, E 312/2, St. Siège, vol. 9.

16. Samuel (Jerusalem) to W. Tyrell (London), January 27, 1921, PRO, FO 371/6393, E 2749/2749/88, received March 2, 1921. The British government had first proposed appointing an English auxiliary bishop when the post became vacant in 1919.

17. Memorandum by Storrs (Rome), September 23, 1921, PRO, FO 371/6397, E 11714/9382/88, circulated by the Colonial Office (London), October 24, 1921.

18. Dormer (Vatican) to Curzon (London), no. 98, restricted, September 17, 1921, PRO, FO 371/6397, E 10714/9382/88.

19. Memorandum by Storrs (Rome), September 23, 1921.

20. Cable from Villarey (Jerusalem) to Ministry for Foreign Affairs (Rome), August 18, 1921, no. 4743, ASME, Siria 1921, file 1568. Monsignor Ruggero Rossetti would have ended the conflict between the Franciscans and the patriarchate. Many years later, a similar

arrangement was twice put into effect, and a Franciscan who had served in the custodia was appointed as the Latin patriarch.

21. Foreign Minister Della Torretta (Pietro Tomasi Della Torretta dei Principi di Lampedusa) to Monti (Rome), August 21, 1921, no. 51732, ASME, Siria 1921, file 1568.

22. Monti (Rome) to Foreign Minister Della Torretta (Rome), September 16, 1921, ASME, Siria 1921, file 1568. Monti's comments were forwarded to the consul general in Jerusalem in Lago's cable (Rome), no. 59275, September 28, 1921.

23. Sir Herbert Samuel (Jerusalem) to Colonial Secretary Churchill (London), no. 375, October 14, 1921, PRO, FO 371/6376, E 12120/35/88. After this memorandum was received, the Colonial Office asked the Foreign Office what steps the Vatican was about to take (PRO, FO 371/6376, E 12120/35/88).

24. Dormer (Vatican) to Foreign Office, November 17, 1921, PRO, FO 371/6372, E 12816/35/88.

25. Churchill (London) to Samuel (Jerusalem), no. 655, December 5, 1921, PRO, FO 371/6376, E 13408/35/88. Comments by Oliphant, who headed the Eastern Department in the Foreign Office, November 2, 1921. Oliphant's view was accepted, and Curzon asked Churchill, who passed the question on to the High Commissioner.

26. Colonial Office to Foreign Office, December 6, 1921, PRO, FO 371/6376, E 13408/35/88.

27. De Salis (Vatican) to Curzon (London), August 11, 1922, PRO, CO 4194/733/31, E 8070/582/65.

28. De Salis (Vatican) to Foreign Office (London), September 8, 1922, PRO, FO 371/7791, E 9131/582/65.

29. Top-secret report from Tritonj (Jerusalem) to minister for foreign affairs (Rome), no. 1443/246, ASME, Siria 1921, file 1568.

30. Top-secret letter from Tritonj (Jerusalem) to Foreign Office (Rome), no. 1523, November 18, 1921, ASME, Siria 1921, file 1568.

31. Samuel (Jerusalem) to Churchill (London), October 1, 1921, PRO, FO 371/6389, E 12001/598/88.

32. Curzon to undersecretary of state for the colonies, November 7, 1921, PRO, FO 371/6389, E 12001/598/88.

33. Shuckburgh to Cabinet Secretary, November 15, 1921, PRO, FO 371/6389, E 12001/598/88.

34. Karl Ludwig Diego Von Bergen (Rome) to Ministry for Foreign Affairs (Berlin), on his talk with Gasparri, AA, Palästina-Zionismus, N 902, Rom/Vat 157/1. Bergen was appointed director for political affairs in the Foreign Ministry in 1919 and was sent as ambassador to the Holy See in 1933. Drummond was Lord Balfour's private secretary, participated in the British delegation to the Peace Conference (1918–19), and in 1919 became the first secretary general of the League of Nations.

35. H. A. L. Fisher, acting secretary of the British government (London), to the secretary general of the League of Nations (Geneva), January 3, 1922, PRO, FO 371/7785, E 673/178/65.

36. Letter to Masterton-Smith, January 17, 1922, PRO, CO 2697/733/33. Sir James Edward Masterton-Smith (1878–1938) was assistant secretary in the Ministry of Munitions from 1917 to 1918, assistant secretary in the War Office and Air Ministry from 1919 to 1920, and permanent undersecretary of state for the colonies from 1921 to 1924.

37. Harmsworth (Geneva) to cabinet secretary (London), January 15, 1921, PRO, FO 371/7785, E 651/178/65.

38. Foreign Office (London) to Colonial Office (London), January 18, 1922, PRO, FO 371/7785, E 651/178/65.

39. See *Enciclopedia Cattolica* (Vatican City, 1949), vol. 2, pp. 1288–93.

40. See S. P. McKnight, *The Papacy: A New Appraisal* (London, 1953), p. 201.

41. For a detailed discussion of Weizmann's visit to the Vatican, see Chapter 12.

42. Bulletin of the Zionist Organization, April 25, 1922, CZA KH 1/28 A 1.

43. Gasparri to de Salis (Vatican), April 6, 1922, ISA, Secretariat of Mandatory government.

44. De Salis (Vatican) to Foreign Office, no. 17, April 21, 1922, PRO, FO 371/7772, E 4545/65/65.

45. De Salis (Vatican) to Curzon (London), April 25, 1922, ISA, Secretariat of Mandatory government.

46. Mémoire adressé à la Société des Nations par l'Union Catholique d'Études Internationales" (1921), in B. Collin, *Le Problème juridique des Lieux saints* (Paris, 1956), pp. 223–29.

47. Foreign Office to De Salis (Vatican), no. 10, May 8, 1922, PRO, FO 371/7773.

48. H. F. Köck, *Der Vatikan und Palästina* (Vienna, 1973), p. 71. The person who Gasparri had in mind was Jules Van den Heuvel, a Catholic politician, former member of the Belgian government, and Belgium's minister to the Holy See from 1915 to 1918.

49. The ambassador in Paris to Foreign Minister Jaspar, May 2, 1922, ABRE, file 114477. Cerretti, the nuncio in Paris, came to the Belgian embassy and said that he had handed a letter to French Prime Minister Poincaré requesting a postponement of the appointment of a president or, alternatively, the appointment of Van den Heuvel. Nicotra, the nuncio in Brussels, asked the Belgian government to persuade the Council of the League of Nations to accept the Holy See's request. See his letter to Belgian Prime Minister Theunis, ABRE, file 114477. Theunis promised the nuncio that he would act in accord with his request. See Theunis to Foreign Minister Jaspar, May 3, 1922, ABRE, file 114477.

50. Ambassador De Martino (London) to Ministry for Foreign Affairs (Rome) April 30, 1922, ASME, file 1457.

51. De Salis (Vatican), on a talk with the French ambassador (Rome), May 9, 1922, PRO, FO 371/7785. See also aide-mémoire, May 9, 1922, ABRE, file 114477. France supported the Holy See's stand, and so did Belgium, Italy, and Spain. See Melot, the Belgian representative at the League of Nations, to foreign minister, telegrams of May 8, 1922, and May 12, 1922, ABRE, file 114477.

52. Hymans (Geneva) to minister for foreign affairs (Brussels), May 15, 1922, ABRE, file 114477.

53. Ministry for Foreign Affairs (Brussels) to Nuncio Nicotra (Brussels), May 20, 1922, ABRE, file 114477.

CHAPTER 6

1. Comment by Dormer, November 17, 1921, as quoted by Ormsby-Gore, May 30, 1923, PRO, CO 733/54.

2. De Salis (Vatican) to Curzon (London), May 18, 1922, PRO, CO 25079/733/30, E 5249/65/65. Also in FO 371/7773.

3. See H. F. Köck, *Der Vatikan und Palästina* (Vienna, 1973), p. 42.

4. Ibid.

5. See *Oriente Moderno*, no. 1 (1921): 405.

6. See *Acta Apostolicae Sedis*, June 18, 1921, pp. 281–84; *The Tablet* (London), June 25, 1921, p. 821.

7. R. Storrs, *Orientations* (London, 1937), p. 326.

8. *Osservatore Romano*, May 13, 1922.

9. De Salis (Vatican) to Curzon (London), May 18, 1922, PRO, CO 25079/733/30, E 5249/65/65. Also in FO 371/7773.

10. See *The Times* (London), May 15, 1922.

11. *Israel*, May 25, 1922, quoting *Il Tempo*.

12. Cable from Cora (London) to Ministry for Foreign Affairs (Rome), no. 3639, May 29, 1922, ASME file 1572.

13. Cable from Schanzer (Rome) to Italian Embassy (London), no. 1291, June 1, 1922, ASME file 1572.

14. Protocol of forty-first meeting of Zionist Executive in London, May 18, 1922, CZA Z4/4020.

15. E. Bovis, *The Jerusalem Question, 1917–1968* (Stanford, Calif., 1971), p. 10.

16. Letter from Gasparri to the Council of the League of Nations, May 15, 1922, PRO, CO 26443/733/34; see Société des Nations, Mandat pour la Palestine, Note du Secretaire General, C.322. 1922, VI, Geneva, May 23, 1922, PRO, FO 371/7776.

17. Aide-mémoire, June 4, 1922, PRO, FO 371/7777. This memorandum was widely publicized; see *Osservatore Romano*, June 30, 1922; *The Tablet*, July 8, 1922; and *The Palestine Weekly*, June 30, 1922); excerpts from the note were also published in *Oriente Moderno* 2 (1922): 142–43, and in W. Zander, *Israel and the Holy Places of Christendom* (London, 1971), pp. 64–65.

18. Letter from Gasparri (Vatican) to de Salis (Vatican), May 24, 1922, PRO, CO 25-79/733/30, E 5495/65/65, enclosed with de Salis's letter to Curzon, May 25, 1922; also in FO 371/7773.

19. Protocol of forty-first meeting of Zionist Executive in London, May 18, 1922, CZA Z4/4020. Marius Moutet (1876–1968) was a socialist member of the Chamber of Deputies who later served as colonial minister from 1936 to 1938. Léon Blum (1872 to 1950), a socialist, Jew, and member of the Chamber of Deputies since 1919, supported Zionism and joined the Jewish Agency when it was established in 1929; he was prime minister from 1937 to 1938 and again in 1938. Raymond Poincaré (1860–1934) was president of the republic from 1913 to 1920 and prime minister from January 1922 to June 1924.

20. Weizmann (London) to Sokolow (New York), confidential, April 25, 1922, WA.

21. Letter from Tufton, of the Government Secretariat, to Oliphant, June 2, 1922, PRO, FO 371/7776, E 5678/78/65, containing a report of a conversation with Da Gama, the Brazilian ambassador in London, who also represented Brazil on the Council of the League of Nations.

22. Carnegie's comments, June 7, 1922, PRO, FO 371/7776, E 5678/78/65.

23. Drummond to Foreign Office (London), June 9, 1922, PRO, CO 28865/733/34/434.

24. Memorandum by Forbes-Adam (London), June 14, 1922, PRO, FO 371/7776, E 6067/78/65, on the meeting between representatives of the Foreign and Colonial Offices de Salis and Drummond, about the Vatican's fears concerning the Holy Places.

25. Dormer (Vatican) to Foreign Office (London), June 4, 1922, PRO, FO 371/7785, E 6318/178/65. Gasparri also spoke to the Belgian representative about the French counterproposal, the Vatican's wish to see Belgium on the commission, and the Vatican's preference for a rotating chairmanship; see Ambassador Beyens (Rome) to Foreign Minister Jaspar, June 23, 1922, ABRE file 114477.

26. Great Britain, Mandate for Palestine, *Letter from the Secretary of the Cabinet to the Secretary-General of the League of Nations of July 1, 1922, Enclosing a Note in Reply to Cardinal Gasparri's Letter of May 15, 1922, Addressed to the Secretary-General of the League of Nations*, Cmd. 1708 (London, 1922).

27. De Salis to Balfour, July 6, 1922, PRO, FO 371/7777, E 6840/78/65.

28. Samuel (Rome) to Churchill, July 6, 1922, PRO, FO 371/7777, E 7079/78/65, also in ISA, Samuel Archive.

29. Weizmann to Motzkin (Paris), July 5, 1922, in *The Letters and Papers of Chaim Weizmann*, ed. B. Wasserstein (Jersualem, 1978), vol. 11, no. 146, p. 135 (hereafter cited as Weizmann, *Letters*).

30. Weizmann (London) to Shuckburgh (London), June 18, 1922, WA.

31. Weizmann (Paris) to his wife, Vera (London), June 15, 1922 (Weizmann, *Letters*, vol. 11, no. 120, p. 116). He was probably referring to de Monzie, Blum, and Moutet.

32. French Ambassador de Saint-Aulaire to Balfour, July 13, 1922, PRO, FO 371/7777, E 6966/78/65.

33. Colonial Office, July 17, 1922, PRO, FO 371/7777, E 7055/78/65.

34. *Daily Telegraph,* July 24, 1922, quoted in B. Collin, *Les Lieux saints* (Paris, 1948), pp. 136–37.

35. League of Nations, *Official Journal,* no. 8 (August 1922): 817–25.

36. De Salis to Foreign Office, July 22, 1922, PRO, FO 371/7786, E 7356/178/65.

37. C. Weizmann, *Trial and Error* (Philadelphia, 1949), vol. 2, pp. 292–93.

38. Foreign Office memorandum, August 3, 1922, PRO, FO 371/7786, E 7871/178/56.

39. De Salis to Curzon, August 4, 1922, PRO, FO 371/7786, E 7971/178/65; also in CO 400998/733/131.

CHAPTER 7

1. All quotations in preceding two paragraphs from Balfour to de Saint-Aulaire (London), August 5, 1922, PRO, FO 371/7777, E 7055/78/65.

2. Sir Cecil B. Hurst's comments, August 10, 1922, PRO, FO 311/7779, E 8045/78/65, also in CO 4340/733/31.

3. The memorandum is published in full in B. Collin, *Le Problème juridique des Lieux saints* (Paris, 1956), pp. 230–32. It was cabled by de Salis, August 18, 1922, PRO, FO 371/7786, E 8343/178/65; also in CO 42439/733/31.

4. Balfour to de Saint-Aulaire, August 18, 1922, PRO, CO 41244/733/31, E 7055/78/65.

5. See E. Bovis, *The Jerusalem Question 1917–1968* (Stanford, Calif., 1971); X. Z. Blum, *The Juridical Status of Jerusalem* (Jerusalem, 1974), p. 31.

6. B. Collin, *Les Lieux saints* (Paris, 1948), p. 139.

7. Colonial Office cable, no. 38280/22, PRO, FO 371/7786, E 8380/178/65.

8. Memorandum from Colonial Office to Cabinet, August 30, 1922, PRO, FO 371/7786, E 8668/178/65.

9. Memorandum submitted by Lord Balfour to the Council of the League of Nations on August 31, 1922.

10. *Osservatore Romano,* September 6, 1922, quoted in Collin, *Lieux saints,* p. 141; see also A. Giannini, *L'ultima fase della Questione Orientale (1913–1923)* (Rome, 1933), p. 332; W. Zander, *Israel and the Holy Places of Christendom* (London, 1971), p. 67.

11. Memorandum by Forbes-Adam (London) on his talk with the Italian ambassador, September 4, 1922, PRO, FO 371/7786, E 9042/178/65.

12. De Salis (Vatican) to Foreign Office, no. 10, September 15, 1922. PRO, FO 371/7786, E 9462/178/65.

13. Cable from Italian government, through its ambassador in London, to Foreign Office, September 19, 1922, PRO, FO 371/7786, E 9581/178/65. See also De Martino (London) to Colonial Office, September 18, 1922, PRO, CO 48291/733/31.

14. De Salis (Vatican) to Curzon (London), no. 129, August 19, 1922, PRO, FO 371/7786, E 9924/178/65, also in ISA CO 48659/733/31. De Salis reported on Dormer's meeting with the pope. He himself may have been ill on those days.

15. Dormer to Curzon (London), no. 133, September 22, 1922, PRO, FO 371/7786; also in CO 48659/733/31 and mentioned by H. F. Köck, *Der Vatikan und Palästina* (Vienna, 1973), p. 83. Gasparri's letter is included in a collection of documents that the British government handed over to the Secretariat of the League of Nations with the request that they be distributed among all the members. See Société des Nations, *Commission des Lieux saints,* Communiqué aux membres du Conseil, Note du Secrétaire Général. No. 1/24687/4406 C. 781/1922, vol. 6, Geneva, December 22, 1922. As noted, similar contentions were aired a few days earlier in the Vatican daily, *Osservatore Romano,* September 6, 1922.

16. Dormer (Vatican) to Curzon (London), no. 134, September 26, 1922, PRO, FO 371/7786, E 10201/178/65; also in CO 49851/733/31.

17. Minutes, PRO, FO 371/7786, quoted in W. Zander, "On the Settlement of Disputes About the Christian Holy Places," *Israel Law Review* 8, no. 3 (1973): 331–66.

18. Oliphant (London) to deputy colonial secretary (London), September 27, 1922, PRO, FO 48391/722/31, E 9581/178/65.

19. Dormer (Vatican) to Foreign Office, no. 138, October 5, 1922, PRO, FO 371/7787, E 1086/178/65.

20. Oliphant (London) to deputy colonial secretary (London), August 30, 1922, PRO, CO 48659/733/31, E 9825/178/65.

21. Young of Colonial Office (London) to deputy foreign minister (London), October 6, 1922, PRO, FO 371/7787, E 10617/178/65; also in CO 48659/733/31.

22. League of Nations, *Official Journal,* November, 1922, pp. 1150–52, quoted extensively in Collin, *Le Problème juridique des Lieux saints,* p. 239; see also Köck, *Vatikan und Palästina,* p. 86; Zander, *Israel and the Holy Places of Christendom,* pp. 68–69.

23. Köck, *Vatikan und Palästina,* p. 87.

24. Société des Nations, Communiqué, December 22, 1922. See also Lloyd George (London) to Gasparri (Vatican), October 13, 1922, PRO, CO 52126/733/31, E 10617/178/65; also in CO 2168/733/65.

25. See Report for the year 1923, in T. E. Hachey, *Anglo-Vatican Relations, 1914–1939* (Boston, 1972), p. 44. Francis Aidan Gasquet (1846–1929), a British Benedictine monk, was nominated cardinal in 1914 and librarian and archivist of the Church in 1919.

26. Sir O. Russel (Vatican) to Foreign Office, June 6, 1924, PRO, FO 371/9010, E 6080/1411/65.

27. Dormer (Vatican) to Foreign Office, August 14, 1924, PRO, FO 371/10087, E 7082/71/65, reporting Reverend Keane's appointment. News of the appointment was also received the next day from the Mandate government in Jerusalem (PRO, FO 371/10087, E 7594/71/65).

28. Dormer to Foreign Office, April 16, 1925, PRO, FO 371/10889, E 4242/4242/65.

29. Colonial Office to Foreign Office, April 16, 1926, PRO, FO 371/11478, E 2442/2442/65.

30. S. Sayegh, *Le Status quo des Lieux saints, nature juridique et portée internationale* (Rome, 1971), pp. 225–27. The arrangement is mentioned in a letter of the Congregation de Propaganda Fide, April 12, 1923. See Gasparri to the patriarch, February 23, 1929. From 1929 to 1948, the apostolic delegation in Palestine was part of the delegation in Cairo; the independent delegation in Jerusalem was set up later.

31. Sir E. Howard (Madrid) to Foreign Office, no. 685, October 13, 1922, PRO, FO 371/7787, E 11222/178/65.

32. Dormer (Vatican) to Foreign Office, October 30, 1922, PRO, FO 371/7787, E 11222/178/65.

33. Wingfield (Madrid) to foreign secretary (London), November 8, 1922, PRO, FO 371/7787, E 11222/178/65.

34. Dormer (Vatican) to Curzon (London), October 30, 1922, PRO, FO 371/7787, E 11222/178/65. Also in ISA, CO 55907/733/31.

35. See the text of the mandate.

36. The Belgian ambassador (London) to Foreign Office, no. 4084, November 11, 1922, PRO, FO 371/7787, E 12576/178/65.

37. Wingfield (Madrid) to Foreign Office, no. 741, November 8, 1922, PRO, FO 371/7787, E 12677/178/65.

38. Collin, *Lieux saints*, p. 146.

39. See *Acta Apostolicae Sedis* (1922), pp. 610–11; also De Salis (Vatican) to Foreign Office, no. 32R, December 12, 1922, PRO FO 371/7787, E 13938/178/65.

40. See Société des Nations, Communiqué, December 22, 1922.

41. Colonial Office report, May 6, 1924, PRO, FO 371/10112, E 4300/4300/65; see also A. Hyamson, *Palestine Under the Mandate* (Westport, Conn., 1976), p. 194.

42. See Zander, *Israel and the Holy Places of Christendom*, p. 70. Zander also cited a confidential memorandum by L. G. A. Cust, "The Status Quo in the Holy Places," published by the government of Palestine in 1929. See also J. Stoyanovsky, *The Mandate for Palestine* (London, 1928), p. 302.

CHAPTER 8

1. J. Isaac, *L'Enseignment du mépris* (Paris, 1962).

2. Of the many works published on this subject, especially after Vatican II and the 1965 statement on the Jews, *Nostra Aetate*, see, for example, C. Mannucci, *Antisemitismo e ideologia cristiana sugli Ebrei* (Milan, 1982).

3. *Osservatore Romano*, September 3, 1987.

4. *The Diaries of Theodor Herzl*, ed. M. Lowenthal (New York, 1956), p. 7. For the most part, I follow Patai's version, although in some places I have used my own translation from the German of Theodor Herzl, *Tagebücher, 1895–1904* (Berlin, 1922–23).

5. Sir F. Piggot, *Extraterritoriality* (1907), quoted in W. R. Fishel, *The End of Extraterritoriality in China* (Berkeley and Los Angeles, 1952), p. 2.

6. T. Herzl, *The Jewish State, An Attempt at a Modern Solution of the Jewish Question* (New York, 1946), p. 30.

7. Diary entry of May 7, 1896, in *Diaries of Theodor Herzl*, p. 127.

8. Entry of May 19, 1896, in *Diaries of Theodor Herzl*, p. 132.

9. *Civiltà Cattolica*, May 1, 1897, pp. 258–70, quoted in E. Feldblum, *The American Catholic Press and the Jewish State, 1917–1959* (New York, 1977), p. 15.

10. Entry of September 4, 1897, in *The Complete Diaries of Theodor Herzl*, ed. R. Patai (New York, 1960), p. 587 (hereafter cited as Herzl, *Diaries*.)

11. Entry of September 9, 1897, in Herzl, *Diaries*, p. 589. The item was reported in the *Daily News*.

12. September 23, 1897, in Herzl, *Diaries*, p. 592.

13. *Jewish Chronicle*, August 17, 1897, p. 21.

14. Entry of February 8, 1899, in Herzl, *Diaries*, pp. 785ff.

15. Quoted in A. Bein, *Theodor Herzl* (in Hebrew) (Jerusalem, 1977), p. 225.

16. Ibid., p. 254.

17. *Civiltà Cattolica,* September 1899, p. 749.

18. Entry of December 29, 1899, in Herzl, *Diaries,* p. 899.

19. Herzl to Ravenna, September 10, 1903; see U. Nahon, "Le lettere di T. Herzl a Felice Ravenna," *La Rassegna Mensile di Israel,* 26, no. 6 (June 1960).

20. Entry of January 23, 1904, in Herzl, *Diaries,* pp. 1591–95.

21. This remark is entered in Italian in Herzl's diaries.

22. According to Catholic doctrine, the Jews live in darkness, and on the day they see the light, they will convert.

23. Entry of January 26, 1904, in Herzl, *Diaries,* pp. 1601–5.

24. Entry of January 27, 1904, in Herzl, *Diaries,* p. 1606.

25. *Die Welt,* April 1, 1904, quoted in D. Vital, *Zionism: The Formative Years* (Oxford, 1982), p. 339.

26. L. Stein, *The Balfour Declaration* (London, 1961), p. 410.

27. W. Laquer, *A History of Zionism* (New York, 1977), pp. 174–78.

28. Stein, *Balfour Declaration,* p. 410.

29. I. Friedman, *The Question of Palestine, 1914–1918* (New York, 1973), p. 155.

30. See *Wiener Morgenzeitung,* November 30, 1925.

31. V. Weizmann, *The Impossible Takes Longer, the Memoirs of Vera Weizmann,* ed. D. Tutaev (London, 1967), p. 61.

32. Notes of a meeting held on Thursday, February 8, 1917, at the residence of Sir Mark Sykes, CZA Z4/728; see also Friedman, *Question of Palestine,* p. 132.

33. Sokolow (Rome) to Weizmann (London), May 2, 1917, CZA A 18/W.

34. Sokolow to Weizmann, May 12, 1917, CZA A 18/15.

35. Entry of April 24, 1917, in S. Tolkowsky, *Zionist Political Diary, 1915–1919* (in Hebrew) (Jerusalem, 1981), p. 47.

36. Sokolow (Rome) to Weizmann, April 24, 1917, CZA A 18/W. I wish to thank Dr. Dvorah Barzilai for calling my attention to these letters, and the staff of the Central Zionist Archive in Jerusalem for sparing no effort in making them available to me. I also thank Dr. Salman Dermeik for the translation from Russian and Mr. Shmuel Susser for its revision.

37. Sykes to Graham, April 15, 1917, PRO, FO 371/3052, quoted in R. Sander, *The High Walls of Jerusalem* (New York, 1983), p. 502.

38. Sykes to Sokolow, April 14, 1917, CZA 18/W, cited in Stein, *Balfour Declaration,* p. 405.

39. Sokolow (Rome) to Weizmann (London), April 24, 1919, CZA A 18/W.

40. Sokolow (Rome) to Weizmann (London), April 29, 1917, CZA A 18/W; excerpts from the letter appear in Stein, *Balfour Declaration,* p. 406.

41. Ibid.

42. Menachem Mendel Beilis (1874–1934) was the victim of a blood-libel charge in Russia in 1911. His trial took place in Kiev in 1913, and he was found not guilty. Bernard Malamud's novel *The Fixer* is based on this case.

43. See *Israel,* May 4, 1916; *La Croix,* December 4, 1917.

44. Sokolow (Rome) to Weizmann, May 1, 1917 CZA A 18/W; see also excerpts in Stein, *Balfour Declaration,* p. 406.

45. See Tolkowsky, *Zionist Political Diary,* p. 47.

46. See Chapter 2, note 16.

47. Sokolow stated that the meeting had taken place on May 10 (*History of Zionism* [London, 1918], p. 53); G. M. Gelber claimed that it had taken place on May 6 (*Hatzarat Balfour wetoldotea* [*The Balfour Declaration and Its History*] [Jerusalem, 1938], p. 87). The record in French, in Sokolow's handwriting, which was probably written immediately after the meeting, in undated. According to a brief item in *Osservatore Romano,* May 5, 1917,

in a section reporting the pope's audiences, the meeting had been held on May 4. This is also Stein's view (*Balfour Declaration,* p. 407).

48. Aide-mémoire in French, in Sokolow's handwriting, untitled, undated, CZA Z4/728; published in full in S. Minerbi, *L'Italie et la Palestine 1914–1920* (Paris, 1970), p. 63. See also the typewritten memorandum in Italian, CZA A18/25. Stein relies exclusively on the Italian version (*Balfour Declaration,* pp. 407ff). The French aide-mémoire was published in an Italian translation; see U. Nahon, "Herzl e Sokolow in Vaticano," *Scritti sull' Ebraismo in memoria di G. Bedarida* (Florence, 1966).

49. F. Sokolow, *My Father, Nahum Sokolow* (in Hebrew) (Jerusalem, 1970), p. 148.

50. Tolkowsky, *Zionist Political Diary,* p. 71. An abridged version is found in Sokolow's draft, mentioned in footnote 47. A slightly different version appears in Weizmann's cable to De Haas (New York), May 10, 1917, in Weizmann, *Letters,* vol. 7, no. 382, p. 406.

51. Draft of a cable, in English, in Sokolow's handwriting, to Weizmann, undated, CZA Z4/728.

52. Stein, *Balfour Declaration,* pp. 409–10. The pope addresses believers in an encyclical when important events take place or when he wishes to clarify an important religious issue.

53. H. Rumbold (Bern) to the Foreign Office; attached to his dispatch is a report by Edelmann, the American vice-consul in Geneva, no. 237630, December 10, 1917, PRO, FO 371/3054.

54. C. Loiseau, "Une Mission diplomatique près du Saint Siège, 1914–1919," *La Revue des Deux Mondes,* May 1, 1956, pp. 54–73.

55. Friedman, *Question of Palestine,* p. 155.

56. Ibid.

57. Zionist Organization, *Zionism During the War. A Record of Zionist Political Activity, 1914–1921* (London, 1921), p. 11.

58. The pope said: "I wish for liberty for all people, and I'm sorrowfully aware that one of the weakest peoples is being persecuted."

59. It may be noted in this context that the first rumors of the secret Sykes–Picot agreement reached Italy's Prime Minister Orlando through the Vatican.

60. Weizmann (London) to Sokolow (Rome), May 1, 1917 (Weizmann, *Letters,* vol. 8, no. 365, p. 391).

61. Ibid., p. 392.

62. See Tolkowsky, *Zionist Political Diary,* p. 62. Felix Pinkus was a member of the Jüdisches Korrespondenz Bureau in Zurich. Matias Erzberger (1875–1932) was a leader of the Catholic Center party.

63. Ibid., p. 95.

64. Ibid., p. 97.

65. *Journal de Genève,* April 25, 1917, quoted in *Israel,* May 31, 1917.

66. Weizmann, May 4, 1917 (Weizmann, *Letters,* vol. 7, no. 370, p. 395).

67. Sokolow (Rome) to Weizmann (London), May 12, 1917, CZA A 18, also quoted in Weizmann, *Letters,* vol.7, footnote to no. 365, p. 393.

68. Weizmann to Sokolow, in French, CZA Z4/728.

69. Cable from Weizmann to Sokolow (Rome), PRO, FO 380/15.

70. Draft of report from de Salis (Rome) to Balfour, no. 20, June 22, 1917, PRO. Florian Sokolow wrote that upon a request by Sokolow, Gasparri sent instructions to his representative in Constantinople, Monsignor Dolci, and this intervention led to the cancellation of the expulsion order, "thus saving Tel Aviv from destruction" (*My Father,* p. 151). As we have seen, the British documents contradict this version. Some nine thousand Jews from Jaffa–Tel Aviv had already been expelled to the north on April 9, 1917, that is, before

Weizmann sent his cable. See I. Friedman, *Germany, Turkey and Zionism, 1897–1918* (Oxford, 1977), p. 349. P. E. Lapide, who tried to lionize Pacelli, cited Florian Sokolow's version uncritically (*The Last Three Popes and the Jews* [London, 1967], p. 84).

71. Memorandum in Sokolow's handwriting, May 8, 1917, National Library, Jerusalem, manuscripts division.

72. Note by De Martino, May 6, 1917, ASME file 186, quoted in Minerbi, *L'Italie et la Palestine*, p. 57.

73. Ibid., p. 59.

74. See Herzl, *Tagebücher.*

75. See J. Wenkert, "Les Archives de Herzl," in *Theodor Herzl* (Jerusalem, 1960), p. 87.

CHAPTER 9

1. See C. Loiseau, "Ma mission auprès du Vatican (1913–1918)," *Revue d'histoire diplomatique* (April–June 1960).

2. Quoted in C. Loiseau, *Politique romaine et sentiment français* (Paris, 1923), p. 74; also quoted H. F. Köck, *Der Vatikan und Palästina* (Vienna, 1973), who noted that unlike the other church bells in Rome, those of St. Peter were not rung on the occasion of Jerusalem's liberation, for the pope thought it unbefitting to the Vatican's neutrality.

3. I. Friedman, *Germany, Turkey and Zionism, 1897–1918* (Oxford, 1977), p. 390.

4. "La parola del Cardinale Vicario," *Osservatore Romano*, December 13, 1917.

5. *Jewish Chronicle*, December 14, 1917.

6. *The Times* (London), quoted in the *Jewish Chronicle*, December 14, 1917.

7. *Il Tempo*, December 15, 1917, quoted in *Israel*, January 10, 1918.

8. J. Katz, *Bonim hofshim veyehudim (Freemasons and Jews)* (Jerusalem, 1968), pp. 142ff; M. T. Pichetto, *Alle radici dell'odio, Preziosi e Benigni antisemiti* (Milan, 1983), p. 35.

9. Van Den Heuvel (Vatican) to Foreign Minister Hymans, December 18, 1917, ABRE, quoted in R. Aubert, "Les Démarches du Cardinal Mercier en vue de l'octroi à la Belgique d'un mandat sur la Palestine," *Bulletin de la classe des lettres et sciences morales et politiques*, 5th ser., vol. 65 (1975–79): 170.

10. Quoted in Friedman, *Germany, Turkey and Zionism*, p. 380.

11. See *Papers Relating to the Foreign Relations of the U.S., The Lansing Papers, 1914–1920* (Washington, D.C., 1940), vol. 2, p. 71.

12. Meeting in the prime minister's office, PRO, war cabinet, 261, October 31, 1917, quoted in J. Kimche, *The Unromantics* (London, 1968), p. 42.

13. Draft of a cable from de Salis to Balfour, no. 70, December 28, 1917, PRO, FO 380/16.

14. *La Croix*, December 27, 1917, quoted in S. Marchese, *La Francia il problema dei rapporti con la Santa Sede* (Naples, 1968), p. 162.

15. *Il Resto del Carlino*, July 15, 1918.

16. *Jewish Chronicle*, May 25, 1917, quoted in "Zionist Declarations on the Subject of the Holy Places," September 28, 1926, WA.

17. Zionist Organization, *Great Britain, Palestine and the Jews* (London, 1917).

18. *Jewish Chronicle*, May 10, 1918.

19. Sykes (Rome) to Sokolow, November 5, 1918; see L. Stein, *The Balfour Declaration* (London, 1961), p. 282.

20. Ibid.

21. Cable from Soragna, December 1, 1918, ASME, file 153/20813.

22. Letter by Gibbons, November 10, 1918, published on November 24, 1918, quoted in E. Feldblum, *The American Catholic Press and the Jewish State, 1917–1959* (New York, 1977), p. 19.

23. Van den Heuvel (Rome), December 26, 1918, ABRE, St. Siège 1918.

24. Van Zuylen (Rome) to Foreign Minister Hymans, no. 10/4, January 14, 1919, ABRE file 11414.

25. E. Oldmeadow, *Francis Cardinal Bourne* (London, 1944), vol. 2, pp. 166–67.

26. Bourne (Jerusalem) to prime minister and Balfour (London), January 25, 1919, FO 371/4179, quoted in D. Ingrams, *Palestine Papers, 1917–1922* (London, 1972), pp. 60–61.

27. Balfour to prime minister, January 19, 1919, FO 371/4179.

28. Francis Cardinal Bourne, *Occasional Sermons* (London, 1930), p. 126. The sermon was delivered in 1925.

29. Quoted in Oldmeadow, *Francis Cardinal Bourne,* p. 173.

30. See Y. Porat, *The Emergence of the Palestinian-Arab National Movement, 1918–1929* (London, 1974), p. 32.

31. Ibid., p. 35.

32. Ibid., p. 42.

33. Ibid., p. 58.

34. Ibid., pp. 59–60.

35. Turkish propaganda (ibid., p. 37).

36. Ibid., p. 32.

37. Nablus protest, January 1920 (ibid., p. 50).

38. Manifesto, 1920 (ibid).

39. Memorandum to the Peace Conference, February 3, 1919 (ibid., p. 54).

40. See D. Tsimhoni, "The Arab Christians and the Palestinian Arab National Movement During the Formative Stage," in G. Ben-Dor, ed., *The Palestinians and the Middle East Conflict* (Ramat Gan, Israel, 1978), p. 83.

41. G. Rossi, "Come nacque e maturò l'idea di una grande università palestinese," *Corriere d'Italia,* September 22, 1923.

42. G. Frumkin, *Dereh shofet biyerushalaym* (*The Behavior of a Judge in Jerusalem*) (Tel Aviv, 1945), pp. 218–21.

43. *La Croix,* June 13, 1919.

44. F. E. Manuel, *The Realities of American–Palestine Relations* (Washington, D.C., 1949), p. 222.

45. *Jewish Chronicle,* March 7, 1919.

46. Ibid.

47. Quoted in Stein, *Balfour Declaration,* p. 409.

48. Second conversation with Cardinal Gasparri, March 7, 1919, AAE, St. Siège, June 1918–September 1920, vol. 13/Z, pp. 54–55.

49. J. Boubée, "Les Juifs en Hongrie," *Etudes,* November 5, 1920, pp. 317–36; November 20, 1920, pp. 433–53; January 1921, pp. 52–65.

CHAPTER 10

1. De Salis to Lord Derby (Paris), no. 28, March 2, 1919, PRO, FO 608/118, E 3408; cable no. 25, PRO, FO 371/4179.

2. See E. Feldblum, *The American Catholic Press and the Jewish State, 1917–1959* (New York, 1977), pp. 24–25. Barlassina sent a report to the pope, which is quoted in P. E. Lapide, *The Last Three Popes and the Jews* (London, 1967), p. 270.

3. Cable from De Salis, no. 28, March 2, 1919, PRO, FO 608/118, E 3408.

4. Comments by L. M. and A. T. of the delegation in Paris. Sir Louis Mallet (1864–1936) was at the time head of the political section of the British delegation to the Peace Conference. On the eve of World War I, he was ambassador in Constantinople and in April 1918 became assistant to the undersecretary at the Foreign Office.

5. Cable to de Salis, March 5, 1919, PRO, FO 371/4179.

6. Foreign Office to de Salis, no. 28, March 12, 1919, PRO, FO 371/4179.

7. *Osservatore Romano,* March 14, 1919; also *Acta Apostolicae Sedis,* March 12, 1919, pp. 100–101; the English translation is in *The Tablet,* March 22, 1919, pp. 353–54.

8. See *Osservatore Romano,* March 21, 1919; also *Acta Apostolicae Sedis,* March 12, 1919, p. 108.

9. Pierre van Zuylen (Rome) to Foreign Minister Hymans, March 16, 1919, no. 57/26, ABRE, St. Siège 1919–20.

10. The view that Germany had considerable influence over the Zionists was also shared by General Clayton.

11. Van Zuylen to Foreign Minister Hymans, March 16, 1919, no. 57/26 ABRE, St. Siège 1919–20.

12. *Jewish Chronicle,* March 14, 1919.

13. See L. C., "L'eterno errore," *Osservatore Romano,* March 17, 1919.

14. "Dove sta il torto?" *Osservatore Romano,* March 19, 1919.

15. *Civiltà Cattolica,* March 1919, quoted in C. Klein, "Vatican and Zionism, 1897–1967," *Christian Attitudes on Jews and Judaism* 36–37 (June–August 1974), pp. 11–12.

16. P. Molajoni, "Il programma della S. Sede per la Palestina," *Il Giornale d'Italia,* March 17, 1919.

17. Memorandum to the foreign minister (Rome), with a clipping from *La Tribuna* (March 17, 1919) containing the text of the pope's speech. In the margins: "I have asked for, but not yet received, the text of the letter the Pope probably sent the powers concerning Palestine, Biancheri" (ASME). We do not know what letter is being referred to.

18. Cable from de Salis, no. 34, March 12, 1919, PRO, FO 371/4179/39684.

19. Monti to Foreign Minister Sonnino, March 29, 1919, ASME file 1571.

20. Cable from de Salis, no. 35, March 13, 1919, PRO, FO 371/4179; see minute by S. K., March 15, 1919.

21. De Salis to the Foreign Office, no. 38, March 21, 1919, PRO, FO 371/4179.

22. Minute by M. D. P., March 22, 1919, PRO, FO 371/4179.

23. Minute by S. K., March 24, 1919, PRO, FO 371/4179.

24. Van Zuylen (Rome) to Foreign Minister Hymans (Brussels), April 6, 1919, no. 65/33, ABRE, St. Siège 1919–20.

25. Cable from de Salis to Balfour, no. 43, April 5, 1919, PRO, FO 608/118 E 6440; *Osservatore Romano,* April 5, 1919, according to which the cardinal said he preferred an internationalized Jerusalem to Zionist rule there.

26. Charles Crane continued his anti-Zionist activity for a long time. In 1922, he met the pope, who also supported Palestinian Arabs joining the anti-Zionist front. Crane told United States Ambassador William Dodd that he was going to meet the pope "about a sort of pact with the Islamic world whereby the followers of Mohammed may be protected against the Jews who are taking Palestine." See W. E. Dodd, Jr., and M. Dodd, *Ambassador Dodd's Diary* (New York, 1941), p. 42. In 1933, Crane went as far as to express support of Hitler; see M. Kaufman, "George Antonius ve'arzot ha-brit," *Iyunim beyahadut zemanenu* (Jerusalem, 1984), p. 35.

27. Quoted in H. N. Howard, *The King–Crane Commission* (Beirut, 1963), pp. 351–52.

28. "L'Oriente ed il miraggio di Sion" *Osservatore Romano,* April 10, 1919.

29. Monti to Sforza, the undersecretary for foreign affairs, October 17, 1919, ASME file 1564. Cable from Sforza to the Italian delegation in Paris and London, no. 4124104, October 23, 1919, ASME file 1564.

30. Report by Lt. Col. (Capitano di Fregata) Tonta, the captain of *Il Quarto,* to the minister of the navy (Rome), December 20, 1919, ASME file 1564.

31. Top-secret report from Negrotto (Cairo) to the Ministry for Foreign Affairs (Rome), November 14, 1919, ASME file 1564.

32. *Israel,* February 26, 1920, quoting *Jüdische Presszentrale* (Zurich).

33. Lord Derby (Paris) to Curzon (London), February 20, 1920, PRO, FO 371/5221, E 1965/1965/44.

34. Cardinal Dubois's lecture, May 28, 1920, published in *La Croix,* October 10–11, 1920, quoted in S. Marchese, *La Francia il problema dei rapporti con la Santa Sede* (Naples, 1968), p. 265.

35. Earl of Derby (Paris) to Curzon (London), July 27, 1920, PRO, FO 406/44.

36. This was also the opinion of the Italian consul general in Jerusalem (see Tuozzi on Jerusalem, June 26, 1919, ASME file 1565).

37. Article by Christianus in *Documentation Catholique* 3 (January–June 1920): 151–53. Barlassina too later commented on the sale of land to Jews, in his lecture in Rome on May 1922.

38. M. Asaf, *Hayahasim beyn haaravim vehaveyhudim beEretz-Yisrael, 1860–1948 (The Relations Between Arabs and Jews in Eretz-Israel, 1860–1948)* (Tel Aviv, 1970), p. 86.

39. *La Croix,* July 24, 1920, quoted in Marchese, *Francia,* p. 263.

40. Reuters dispatch (Rome), April 26, 1920; quoted in *Israel,* May 6, 1920.

41. See H. L. Samuel, *Memoirs* (London, 1945), p. 153.

42. De Salis (Vatican) to Curzon, July 3, 1920, PRO, FO 406/44.

43. Chargé d'affaires Doulcet (Vatican) to Foreign Minister Millerand, June 27, 1920, AAE 312–2.

44. "La Palestina e il Sionismo," *Osservatore Romano,* June 16, 1920.

45. "Occorre Provvedere," *Osservatore Romano,* June 16, 1920.

46. See R. Lambelin, *Protocoles des sages de Sion* (Paris, 1921).

47. See G. Spadolini, *Il cardinale Gasparri e la questione romana* (Florence, 1972), p. 163. These are Gasparri's memoirs; he wrote: "The article bears the name of Father de Floch, but it is actually mine from beginning to end."

48. *Osservatore Romano,* June 23, 1920.

49. Quoted in *Israel,* July 8, 1920.

50. Ibid. The paper reported that Samuel was joined in his visit to the pope by his secretary, Lord Edward Hay, and by the British minister to the Holy See, de Salis.

51. Ibid.

52. Paternò (Damascus) to Ministry for Foreign Affairs (Rome), June 14, 1920, ASME, Siria/9, file 1567.

53. Tuozzi (Jerusalem) to Ministry for Foreign Affairs (Rome), August 7, 1920, ASME file 1566.

54. Excerpts from the pastoral letter are enclosed with Samuel's (Jerusalem) dispatch to Curzon (London), August 13, 1920, PRO, FO 406/44. It is also mentioned in *Israel,* July 7, 1921, and in C. Crispolti, "Il pericolo della nazione ebraica in Palestina," *Rassegna Italiana del Mediterraneo,* no. 4 (April–May 1921): 103–5.

55. Tuozzi (Jerusalem) to Ministry for Foreign Affairs (Rome), Top Secret, October 4, 1920, no. 1103/176, ASME file 1457.

56. *Osservatore Romano,* October 9, 1920.

57. *Civiltà Cattolica,* no. 1690, November 20, 1920.

58. *Civiltà Cattolica*, no. 1691, December 4, 1920.

59. *Civiltà Cattolica*, no. 1692, December 18, 1920.

60. *Osservatore Romano*, October 15, 1920.

61. Bulletin of the press officer, October 11, 1920, ASME file 1457.

62. *Zionist Review* 4 (April–May 1921): 99.

63. Minutes of the meetings of the Zionist Executive, CZA Z4/4020. The Franciscans' demands for a change in the status quo of the Holy Places were presented to the Peace Conference in 1919. The reference here is probably to the claim to the Cenacle, the hall of the Last Supper on Mount Zion in Jerusalem.

CHAPTER 11

1. See M. T. Pichetto, *Alle radici dell'odio, Preziosi e Benigni antisemiti* (Milan, 1983), pp. 42–55; N. Cohn, *Warrant for Genocide* (London, 1967).

2. E. Caviglia, "Il sionismo e la Palestina negli articoli dell' *Osservatore Romano* e della *Civiltà Cattolica* (1919–1923)," *Clio*, January–March 1981, p. 83.

3. *Osservatore Romano*, October 15, 1920.

4. *Osservatore Romano*, May 30–31, 1921.

5. See article by J. Boubée, S.J., in *Messager du Coeur de Jesus* (October 1920), quoted in *Documentation Catholique* 4 (1920): 307.

6. Samuel (Jerusalem) to Foreign Office (London), January 6, 1921, PRO, FO 371/6374, E1576/35/88. Samuel's reply came after a note from the prime minister's office on December 20, 1920, conveying Cardinal Gasquet's anxiety over Jewish land purchases in Palestine.

7. *Osservatore Romano*, February 25, 1921.

8. *Osservatore Romano*, May 1, 1921.

9. Entry of July 5, 1921, in R. Meinertzhagen, *Middle East Diary, 1917–1956* (London, 1959), p. 101.

10. Copy in CO 733/16-23918, quoted in A. Klieman, *Foundations of British Policy in the Arab World—The Cairo Conference of 1921* (Baltimore, 1970), p. 181.

11. "La genesi dei gravi disordini," *Osservatore Romano*, May 8, 1921.

12. *Il Messaggero*, May 28, 1921; reply of the Secretariat of State to the German legation, no. 902, June 23, 1921, AA Palästina-Zionismus, Rom/Vat. 157/1.

13. "Allocutio 'Causa Nobis'," *Osservatore Romano*, June 25, 1921; *Acta Apostolicae Sedis*, June 18, 1921, pp. 281–83; *Oriente Moderno* 1 (1921): 81–82; see the English translation in *The Tablet*, June 25, 1921, pp. 821–22.

14. J. L. Grabill, *Protestant Diplomacy and the Near East, Missionary Influence on American Policy, 1810–1927* (Minneapolis, 1971), pp. 178, 307. We may recall Rev. Bliss among the pro-Arab missionaries.

15. Esco Foundation for Palestine. *Palestine, a Study of Jewish, Arab, and British Policies* (New Haven, Conn., 1947), vol. 1, pp. 540–41.

16. Letter by German representative (Rome), no. 902, June 14, 1921, AA Palästina-Zionismus, Rom/Vat. 157/1. On Calvary, see W. E. Addis and T. Arnold, *A Catholic Dictionary* (London, 1951).

17. H. F. Köck, *Der Vatikan und Palästina* (Vienna, 1973), p. 58.

18. Bishop Hajjar to Les Missions Catholiques. The letter was published in the American Catholic periodical *Ave Maria*, on May 21, 1921, p. 665, and is quoted in E. Feldblum, *The American Catholic Press and the Jewish State, 1917–1959* (New York, 1977), p. 26. The Greek-Catholic (or Melkite) community was one of the largest Christian denominations in Palestine. It was headed at that time by an archbishop residing in Haifa. More recently, Greek

Catholic Bishop Capucci was imprisoned in Israel for criminal activities on behalf of the Palestine Liberation Organization.

19. Samuel (Jerusalem) to Curzon (London), October 12, 1920. Several months later, Weizmann complained to Curzon about a newspaper interview given by de Caix (Weizmann to Curzon, February 24, 1921, PRO FO 371/6393).

20. Report by the Colonial Office about the situation in Palestine, no. 42528/1921, August 29, 1921, 337/6376, E 9807/35/86.

21. A. L. Tibawi, *Arab Education in Mandatory Palestine, a Study of Three Decades of British Administration* (London, 1956), pp. 150–51, 188.

22. Y. Porat, also noted this belief among the Arabs (*The Emergence of the Palestinian-Arab National Movement, 1918–1929* [London, 1974], p. 36). The chief administrator in Palestine from 1918 to 1919, General Arthur Money, had said that the Zionist Commission would supplement the pay of Jewish administrative employees, to encourage them to enter government service.

23. For example, the anti-Zionist Giulio de Rossi wrote: "More than half the posts in the [Palestinian] bureaucracy are occupied by Zionists, and the highest, best paid positions are entirely in Zionist hands" (*Corriere d'Italia,* December 20, 1922). David Eder, the chairman of the Zionist Commission, asserted, by contrast, that of 360 senior officials, only 50 were Jews (*Palestine Weekly,* June 30, 1922).

24. Esco Foundation, *Palestine,* vol. 1, p. 302. In 1924, Christians made up 10 percent of the population but held 30 percent of the posts. Jews, who made up 15 percent of the population, held 20 percent of the posts. Excluding railway services, 45 percent of administration employees were Christians, and 30 percent were Jews.

25. The pope probably wanted to condemn the Zionist company Hacarmel, which he thought intended to turn Mount Carmel, a site holy to Christians, into a resort and entertainment center see *Oriente Moderno,* no. 1 (1921): 82. The Foreign Office, too, understood the pope's speech as referring to Mount Carmel, especially to the plan to construct a funicular. The Foreign Office officials felt that any new promises to the pope should come from the Colonial Office; see FO 371/6375, E 6874/35/88, Scott's comment on the text of the pope's speech cabled from Rome by de Salis, no. 18, June 14, 1921.

26. See M. Riquet, S.J., *Un Chrétien face à Israel* (Paris, 1975), p. 221.

27. Scott's comments to de Salis's cable, no. 18, June 14, 1921, PRO, FO 371/6375, E 6874/35/88.

28. Mong's comment to Dormer (Vatican), June 24, 1921, PRO, FO 371/6375, E 7594/35/88: "It is not Zionism, as it was first announced, which alarms them, but what may lie behind it. The more active Zionists in Palestine have done the mischief, not only by their activities, but by their foolish boasting of what is to come."

29. Letter from d'Ursel (Rome) to the foreign minister (Brussels), June 21, 1921, ABRE, St. Siège 1919–20, Classement B/230, file 132156.

30. *Israel,* June 23, 1921, quoted in *Oriente Moderno* 1 (1921): 90.

31. *Israel,* July 7, 1921.

32. *Il Resto Del Carlino,* quoted in *Israel,* July 7, 1921.

33. Ibid.

34. *L'Echo,* June 25, 1921.

35. Lattes (Rome) to the Zionist Organization (London), June 24, 1921, CZA Z4/699.

36. Landman (London) to Lattes (Rome), June 28, 1921, CZA Z4/699.

37. Wingfield (Madrid) to Foreign Office, June 28, 1921, PRO, FO 371/6375, E 7617/35/88. Sir Charles John Fitz Roy Rhis Wingfield (1877–1960) was a counselor in the British embassy in Madrid from 1919 and served as chargé d'affaires in 1920, 1921, and 1922.

38. See C. Crispolti, "Il pericolo della nazione ebraica in Palestina," *Rassegna Italiana del Mediterraneo*, no. 4 (April–May 1921). Crispolti wrote for *Il Corriere d'Italia*, the Popular (Catholic) party's newspaper.

39. "Sionismo e Palestina," *Osservatore Romano*, June 23, 1921.

40. *Documentation Catholique*, July 30, 1921, pp. 80–81, quoted in S. Marchese, *La Francia il problema dei rapporti con la Santa Sede* (Naples, 1968), p. 263.

41. See Porat, *Emergence of the Palestinian-Arab National Movement*, p. 138. *Osservatore Romano*, June 18, 1921, reported from Paris that the delegation had been sent and included Msgr. Hajjar, who in fact was not a member.

42. De Salis (Vatican) to Foreign Office, no. 25, July 29, 1921, PRO FO 371/6386, E 8767/8364/88; see also Klieman, *Foundations of British Policy in the Arab World*, p. 192.

43. *Al-Karmil* (Haifa), August 10, 1921, quoted in *Oriente Moderno* 1 (1921): 224. The British minister to the Holy See did not take part in the talks, for he had received no authorization from his government to do so, as was explained in reply to interpellation in the British Parliament on August 10, 1921; see *The Times*, August 11, 1921.

44. See *Ha'aretz*, August 17, 1921, quoted in M. Asaf, *Hit'orerut ha'aravim b'eretz yisrael uvrihatam (The Awakening of the Arabs in Eretz-Israel and Their Flight)* (Tel Aviv, 1967), p. 99.

45. *Corriere d'Italia*, August 14, 1921, quoted in *Oriente Moderno* 1 (1921): 224.

46. Royal Institute of International Affairs, *Great Britain and Palestine, 1915–1945* (London, 1946), p. 41.

47. Young, of the Colonial Office (London), to the undersecretary at the Foreign Office, August 10, 1921, PRO FO 371/6396, E 9154/8364/88.

48. Sthamer (London) to Ministry for Foreign Affairs (Berlin), no. 902, September 1, 1921, AA Palästina-Zionismus, Rom/Vat 157/1, no. 69; see also AA III/Palästina Politik 5, bd. I; also quoted in B. Yisraeli, *Hareich haghermani v'eretz yisrael* (Ramat Gan, Israel, 1974), p. 73.

49. Quoted in *Oriente Moderno* 1 (1921): 22.

50. *Corriere d'Italia*, August 1, 1921. The passage is quoted in letter from Dormer (Vatican) to the Foreign Office, August 10, 1921, FO 337/6376.

51. Young (London) to Lindsay, August 24, 1921, FO 337/6376, with Stein's letter to Weizmann, August 6, 1921, attached. Sir Ronald Lindsay was a minister in the embassy in Paris from 1920 to 1921, undersecretary at the Foreign Office from 1922 to 1924, and ambassador to Constantinople, Berlin, and Washington.

52. Comment by Scott, August 26, 1921, FO 337/6376.

53. Comment by Forbes-Adam, August 26, 1921, FO 337/6376.

54. Storrs memorandum, August 25, 1921, CO 733/11/45708, E 10038/9382/88, attached to Dormer's letter to Curzon, August 27, 1921.

55. R. Storrs, *Orientations* (London, 1937), p. 432.

56. Dormer (Vatican) to Forbes-Adam (London), September 7, 1921, FO 371/6376, E 10315/35/88. Barlassina claimed that the walk would intrude on his privacy.

57. The claim about the Jews' exaggerated power in Hungary was raised also a year before in the meeting of Gasparri with Cardinal Amette. See on the same subject J. Boubée, "Les juifs en Hongrie," *Etudes*, October–December 1920 and January–March 1921.

58. Dormer (Vatican) to Curzon (London), restricted, no. 98, September 17, 1921, FO 371/6397, E 10714/9382/88; a copy is in CO 733/11/50054. I have supplemented Storr's August 25 report with excerpts from a memorandum by him from September 25, 1921, FO 371/6397, E 11714/938218, distributed by the Colonial Office (London) on October 24, 1921.

59. *Zionist Review* 5, no. 7 (November 1921): 105–6; see also *Oriente Moderno* 1 (1921): 354.

60. "Dopo il Congresso Sionistico," *Osservatore Romano*, September 29, 1921.

61. Dormer (Vatican) to Forbes-Adam (London), September 7, 1921, PRO, FO 337/ 6376, E 10315/85/88. On the Cenacle, see S. Minerbi, "The Italian Activity to Recover the 'Cenacolo,' " *Risorgimento* 1, no. 2 (1980): 181–209.

62. Prof. Ernesto Buonaiuti was a Catholic priest and a professor of philosophy at the Pontifical University in Rome and later a professor of Christian history at the University of Rome. He was the editor of the *Rivista di Teologia* and was close to Gasparri. Years later, he left the priesthood. The full text of the interview in Italian appears in E. Buonaiuti, *Pellegrino di Roma, la generazione dell'esodo* (Rome, 1945); cited also in P. Scoppola, *La Chiesa e il fascismo, documenti e interpretazioni* (Bari, Italy, 1971), pp. 46–51.

63. Dormer (Vatican) to Foreign Office, no. 105, September 29, 1921, completed September 30, PRO, CO 50635/733/11, E 10968/10850/88; attached to the letter is a translation of the interview as published in *Il Messagero*, September 29, 1921, and a translation of Gasparri's letter of September 30, 1921.

64. Dormer (Vatican) to Foreign Office, no. 108, PRO, CO 50135/733/11, E 11196/ 10850/88; attached was Gasparri's letter to Dormer, dated October 3, 1921, and a translation of the articles from *Osservatore Romano*, October 11–12, 1921.

65. Buonaiuti, *Pellegrino di Roma*, p. 199.

66. Dr. Moshe Beilinson (1889–1936), a Russian-born physician, resided in Italy from 1917 to 1924, where he did journalistic and public work for the Zionist movement. He immigrated to Palestine in 1924 and became a member of the editorial staff of the Histadrut newspaper *Davar* and one of its leading columnists.

67. *Palestine Weekly,* October 7, 1921.

68. "Zionism and Christendom," *Zionist Review* 5, no. 7 (November 1921): 105–6.

69. "La Questione israelita e i cattolici francesi," *Osservatore Romano*, October 9, 1921.

70. Fer, "Azione di difesa sociale," *Fede e Ragione*, November 6, 1921. Fer was the pen name of Rev. Benigni (Pichetto, *Alle radici*, p. 119).

71. "La preghiera per i giudei," *Osservatore Romano*, October 13, 1921.

72. "Sionismo e Palestina," *Osservatore Romano*, October 15, 1921.

73. C. Esclapon, "Anglican Bishop McInness in Jerusalem" (in Italian) (Master's thesis, University of Florence, 1989), p. 35.

74. Minutes of meetings of the Zionist Executive, no. 16, November 24, 1921, CZA Z4/4040. Rabbi Zvi Peretz Chayes (1876–1927), Judaic scholar and Zionist leader, was a professor at the Rabbinical Seminary in Florence from 1902, from 1912 was the chief rabbi of Trieste, and from 1918 until his death was the chief rabbi of Vienna. He was chairman of the Zionist Executive from 1921 to 1925.

75. Joseph Cowen (1868–1932), Herzl's aide, was one of the founders of the Zionist Federation in England and Ireland, a member of the Zionist Commission in 1918, and a member of the Zionist Executive from 1921 to 1925.

76. English translation of Beilinson's article from the *Wiener Morgenzeitung*, December 17, 1921, WA. Stein sent the translation to Forbes-Adam in the Foreign Office with a covering letter, dated January 9, 1922 (FO 371/7773, E 370/65/65). The article is in CZA Z4/2136.

77. *Israel,* January 26, 1922.

78. *Zionist Review* 6 (1922): 54.

79. *Palestine Weekly,* February 3, 1922, pp. 6–7.

CHAPTER 12

1. Ministry for Foreign Affairs (Berlin) to Bergen (Rome), January 20, 1922, AA Politik 6, Vatikan, L 300650.

2. Delbrück (Berlin) to Bergen (Rome), July 14, 1922, AA Politik 6, Vatikan, L 330706.

3. Lattes (Rome) to the Zionist Organization (London), February 5, 1922, CZA Z4/ 2136.

4. Chajes (Florence) to Weizmann (London), February 14, 1922, WA; Lattes (Rome) to the Zionist Organization (London), March 2, 1922, CZA Z4/2136; also KH1/28a1. Lattes consulted Sereni, the president of the Unione delle Comunità Israelitiche Italiane, who was prepared to accompany Weizmann on his visit to the pope if necessary.

5. De Monzie (Paris) to Weizmann (London), March 27, 1922, WA. Anatole de Monzie (1876–1947), a member of the French senate from 1920 to 1929, had expressed support for Zionism. The French president, Millerand, received Weizmann on March 22, 1922, and heard his assurances concerning the Holy Places in Palestine. See Weizmann, *Letters,* vol. 11, footnote to no. 72, p. 96.

6. De Salis (Rome) to Weizmann (Rome), March 30, 1922, WA.

7. Draft of a Foreign Office report on the Vatican's position regarding the Zionist movement, written by Carnegie, April 6, 1922, FO 371/7773, E 3737/65/65. The report is based on Weizmann's letter from Rome about his meeting with Gasparri. The Colonial Office forwarded the contents of Weizmann's conversation to the Mandate government (Shuckburgh to Deeds [Jerusalem], PRO, CO 16424/733/30, April 13, 1922).

8. Excerpt from letter by Weizmann (Rome) to the Zionist Executive (London), April 3, 1922, WA. The next day, Weizmann wrote to Lichtheim and asked him to obtain the contents of the memorandum. He himself was about to take a week's vacation in Capri, at the Hotel Quisisana (Weizmann [Rome] to Lichtheim [London], in German, April 4, 1922, WA). It appears from this letter that the preceding excerpt is from a letter to Cowen, April 13, 1922, which has since been published; see Weizmann, *Letters,* vol. 11, no. 80, p. 76.

9. *The Times* (London), April 4, 1922, quoted in Zionist Organization, *Bulletin,* April 4, 1922, CZA KH1/28-1.

10. Lattes joined Weizmann in his meeting with Gasparri (Zionist Organization, *Bulletin,* April 4, 1922).

11. De Salis (Vatican) to Weizmann (Rome), April 3, 1922, WA.

12. De Salis (Vatican) to Weizmann (Rome), April 4, 1922, WA.

13. *Israel,* April 6, 1922. The Istituto per l'Oriente was headed by G. Colonna di Cesarò, a member of the Chamber of Deputies who supported Zionism; see S. Minerbi, *L'Italie et la Palestine 1914–1920* (Paris, 1970), pp. 47–52.

14. See "Il Sionismo in una conferenza del prof. Weizmann," *Osservatore Romano,* quoted in *Israel,* April 27, 1922.

15. Stein (London) to Colonel Kisch (Paris), April 5, 1922, WA.

16. Minutes of the thirty-fourth meeting of the Zionist-Executive, CZA Z4/4020.

17. Stein (London) to Ormsby-Gore (London), April 6, 1922, WA. Harlech William George Arthur Ormsby-Gore (1885–1946) was an intelligence officer from 1916 to 1917; assistant secretary in the war cabinet from 1917 to 1918; assistant political officer to the Zionist Commission in 1918; member of the Permanent Mandate Commission from 1921 to 1922; and colonial secretary from 1926 to 1938.

18. As in the case of Barlassina, the Zionists deluded themselves that the anti-Zionist Gasparri would soon be replaced. He continued as secretary of state until 1931.

19. Weizmann (Capri) to the Zionist Executive (London), April 10, 1922, CZA Z4/ 16145; see also Weizmann, *Letters,* vol. 11, no. 84, p. 80. Weizmann told Graham, the

British ambassador in Rome, that he was astonished by Gasparri's question concerning financial benefits offered to Rothschild by the British government to ensure Jewish support for the British mandate (Graham [Rome] to Curzon [London], confidential, April 29, 1922, PRO, FO 371/7773).

20. De Salis (Vatican) to Curzon (London), no. 58, April 13, 1922, PRO, CO 733/30; also in PRO, FO 371/7773, E 4091. A few days earlier, de Salis wrote to Weizmann that there was no possibility of holding talks in the Vatican before April 16, 1922 (de Salis [Vatican] to Weizmann [Rome], April 6, 1922, WA).

21. Memorandum to the Council of the League of Nations, in Gasparri's letter, May 31, 1922, PRO, CO 733/34.

22. Letter from Gasparri to de Salis, April 6, 1922, PRO, CO 16829/733/30, E 4091.

23. Curzon to de Salis, no. 10, May 8, 1922, PRO, FO 371/7773, E 4545/65/65.

24. Jewish Correspondence Bureau, *Bulletin,* April 22, 1922, CZA KH1/28A-1.

25. C. Weizmann, *Trial and Error* (Philadelphia, 1949), vol. 2, p. 285.

26. "Sionismo e Palestina," *Osservatore Romano,* April 21, 1922.

27. Weizmann, *Trial and Error,* vol. 2, pp. 285–86. He wrote that this meeting had taken place after his April 4 lecture. Because he first met with Gasparri on April 2, before the lecture, it is clear that he is referring here to his second meeting with the cardinal, on April 20.

28. Jewish Correspondence Bureau, *Bulletin,* April 27, 1922, CZA KH 1/28A-1.

29. *Israel,* April 27, 1922.

30. De Salis (Vatican) to Curzon (London), confidential, no. 67, April 25, 1922, ISA, Secretariat of the Mandatory government, 2/147; see also PRO, FO 371/7773, E 4441. The letter was forwarded by the colonial secretary to High Commissioner Samuel.

31. Weizmann was referring to the Christian–Muslim Arab delegation that had visited Rome and London the previous year to explain the Palestinian Arabs' plight. Weizmann repeated the rumors that Gasparri would soon resign and would be replaced by Cardinal Cerretti from Paris, whom he planned to meet. Commenting on the British legation to the Holy See, Weizmann said that he believed de Salis had little influence, whereas his secretary, Dormer, was more Catholic than the pope and unfriendly toward Zionism (Minutes of the 34th Meeting of the Executive, CZA Z4/4020).

32. Lattes (Rome) to Weizmann (Geneva), May 14, 1922, CZA Z4/4121. De Salis applied to the Secretariat of State on May 9, 1922.

33. Kobylinsky (Rome) to Weizmann (Geneva). Kobylinsky was a Jewish physician who had settled in Italy and had fought on the Italian side in World War I. He was married to Beilinson's sister and was a personal friend of Weizmann. On a number of occasions, he introduced Weizmann to his wide network of acquaintances in government circles in Rome. In 1933 he delivered a personal letter from Weizmann to Mussolini. See S. Minerbi, "Gli ultimi due incontri Weizmann–Mussolini, 1933–1934," *Storia Contemporanea* 5, no. 3 (1974): 439; Weizmann, *Letters,* vol. 11, no. 250, p. 212.

34. The recommendation was presented by Prof. Adolf Strusz of Budapest, who wrote to Weizmann about it on May 13, 1922, WA.

35. Col. (res.) Alfredo Porcelli (Hove) to Weizmann (London), April 4, 1922, WA. Baron Porcelli was a Catholic who had become a British subject and was a supporter of Zionism.

36. *Osservatore Romano,* May 4, 1922.

37. *Osservatore Romano,* May 6, 1922.

38. *Osservatore Romano,* May 13, 1922.

39. *Israel,* May 25, 1922.

40. Von Bergen (Rome) to Ministry of Foreign Affairs (Berlin), July 2, 1922, quoted in P.E. Lapide, *The Last Three Popes and the Jews* (London, 1967), p. 262.

41. *Osservatore Romano,* May 13, 1922, attached to PRO, CO 25079/733/30, and the letter from de Salis (Vatican) to Curzon (London), May 18, 1922, FO 371/7773, E 5249/65/ 65. As reported in the paper, the lecture was delivered in the Istituto di San Giuseppe and was attended by Cardinals Giorgi, Ranuzzi de Bianchi, Laurenti, and Cattan, Melkite archbishop of Beirut. Giorgi visited Palestine a few years later, in 1924.

42. *L'Italie,* May 13, 1922, attached to de Salis's report, May 18, 1922, FO 371/7773, E 5249/65/65.

43. *The Times,* May 13, 1922, quoted in Weizmann, *Letters,* vol. 11, no. 101, p. 96.

44. De Salis to Curzon, May 18, 1922, FO 371/7773, E 5249/65/65. Since the revival of the Latin Patriarchate of Jerusalem in the mid-nineteenth century, relations between it and the Franciscans, who felt their premier status had been eclipsed by the new arrival, were strained.

45. Letter by von Bergen, May 4, 1922, AA, Stellung der Kuria Zum Zionismus, Pol. II (3.20–3.36) Politik 6 Vatikan, L 1015, IIa, 32019, quoted in Lapide, *The Last Three Popes and the Jews,* p. 262.

46. See *Il Tempo,* quoted in *Israel,* May 25, 1922.

47. Report on query in Parliament, May 23, 1922, PRO, FO 371/7773, E 5333/65/65.

48. De Salis (Vatican) to Foreign Office, June 1, 1922, PRO, FO 371/7773, E 5619/65/ 65. On Barlassina's visit to London, see pp. 68–69.

49. Cable from de Salis (Vatican), no. 23, June 4, 1922, PRO, FO 371/7773, E 5655/ 65/65.

50. Comments by Carnegie, June 7, 1922, PRO, FO 371/7773, E 5655/65/65.

51. As we have seen, all partiality by the courts had been denied. Still, after the capitulations were canceled, first by the Turks and then by the British, the jurisdiction over many Catholics passed from the European consuls to the secular judicial authorities of the Mandate government.

52. "Latin Patriarch on Zionism. Moral Decadence in the Holy Land," *The Times,* May 31, 1922, p. 9.

CHAPTER 13

1. London (Geneva) to Foreign Office, May 13, 1922, ISA, PRO, CO 23608/733/30; see also letter from Balfour to Sir Maurice Hankey, the cabinet secretary, May 13, 1922, PRO, CO 733/30/435, quoted in Weizmann, *Letters,* vol. 11, footnote to no. 98, p. 94. See another letter from Balfour to Hankey, CAB 24/136, quoted in D. Ingrams, *Palestine Papers, 1917–1922* (London, 1972), p. 168.

2. Weizmann (Geneva) to his wife, Vera (London), May 11, 1922, in Weizmann, *Letters,* vol. 11, no. 96, p. 92.

3. Cable from Gasparri (Rome), May 11, 1922, ABRE file 114477.

4. Draft of Belgian foreign minister's reply to Gasparri, no date, probably May 12, 1922, ABRE file 114477.

5. Note from Gasparri to the Council of the League of Nations (Geneva), May 15, 1922, PRO, CO 733/34. See pp. 69–70.

6. *Osservatore Romano,* June 30, 1922. The full text is in B. Collin, *Recueil de documents concernant Jerusalem et les Lieux saints* (Jerusalem, 1982), pp. 9–11. Gasparri's letter was published in the *Morning Post* and copied from there by *The Palestine Weekly;* see also E. Farhat, *Gerusalemme nei documenti pontifici* (Vatican City, 1987), pp. 205–7.

7. W. Zander *Israel and the Holy Places of Christendom* (London, 1971), p. 64.

8. Weizmann (Geneva) to his wife (London), May 12, 1922, in Weizmann, *Letters,* vol. 11, no. 97, p. 93.

9. Balfour's speech in the Council of the League of Nations, May 17, 1922. Council of Minister's Meeting, League of Nations, *Official Journal,* June 1922, pp. 546–48.

10. Weizmann (Geneva) to Sullam (Venice), May 17, 1922, Weizmann, *Letters,* vol. 11, no. 100, p. 95.

11. Comments by Oliphant, PRO, FO 371/7773, E 5333/65/65.

12. Ibid.

13. Comments by Carnegie, May 31, 1922, PRO, FO 371/7773, E 5495/65/65.

14. Minutes of the forty-first meeting of the Zionist Executive in London, May 18, 1922, CZA Z4/4020.

15. Notes for the British representative on the Council of the League of Nations from Middle East Department, PRO, CO 23245/733/34.

16. Cowen, in the minutes of the forty-first meeting of the Zionist Executive, May 18, 1922, CZA Z4/4020.

17. See letter from Stein, in Weizmann's name, to Shuckburgh of the Colonial Office, June 12, 1922, WA. As we mentioned, Weizmann heard something similar from Buonaiuti.

18. Observations on Palestine Affairs in their relations to the Council of the League of Nations at Geneva, May 22, 1922, PRO, CO 24280.

19. Weizmann (London) to Porcelli, May 23, 1922, in Weizmann, *Letters,* vol. 11, no. 101, p. 96.

20. Weizmann (London) to Sokolow (New York), confidential, May 24, 1922, WA; published in Weizmann, *Letters,* vol. 11, no. 102, p. 97.

21. Weizmann (London) to Deeds (Jerusalem), June 2, 1922, WA; published in Weizmann, *Letters*, vol. 11, no. 106, p. 103.

22. Weizmann (London) to Sokolow (New York), confidential, May 25, 1922, WA.

23. Lattes (Rome) to Weizmann (London), June 4, 1922, WA.

24. Minutes of the forty-first meeting of the Zionist Executive, May 18, 1922, CZA Z4/4020.

25. Lattes (Rome) to Weizmann (London), June 2, 1922, WA.

26. Lattes (Rome) to Weizmann (London), May 28, 1922, WA; also in CZA Z4/16081.

27. Von Bergen (Rome) to Ministry for Foreign Affairs (Berlin), no. L 300680, July 4, 1922, AA, IIa, Vatikan 590; partially quoted in P.E. Lapide, *The Last Three Popes and the Jews* (London, 1967), p. 334.

28. C. Loiseau, *Politique romaine et sentiment français* (Paris, 1923), p. 2.

29. E. Buonaiuti, *Pellegrino di Roma, la generazione dell'esodo* (Rome, 1945), p. 199.

30. Gasparri (Vatican) to de Salis (Vatican), June 4, 1922, PRO, CO 733/34, with a memorandum of that date enclosed.

31. Memorandum from the Zionist Executive (London) to Wilensky, June 9, 1922; see also Weizmann, *Letters,* vol. 11, no. 132, p. 125.

32. *Palestine Weekly,* June 9, 1922.

33. Donati (Paris) to Weizmann (Paris), June 13, 1922, WA.

34. Weizmann (London) to Shuckburgh (London), June 18, 1922, CZA Z4/16145; see also Weizmann, *Letters,* vol. 11, no. 123, p. 119.

35. Memorandum by Sir Eric Drummond, June 16, 1922, PRO, CO 28865/733/34.

36. Weizmann (London) to Rosenblatt (London), June 20, 1922, in Weizmann, *Letters,* vol. 11, no. 125, p. 121.

37. Ibid.

38. Weizmann (London) to Deeds (Jerusalem), June 29, 1922, in Weizmann, *Letters,* vol. 11, no. 134, p. 127.

39. Weizmann (London) to David Eder (Jerusalem), June 29, 1922; in Weizmann, *Letters,* vol. 11, no. 135, p. 128.

40. Weizmann to Scott (Manchester), June 30, 1922, CZA Z4/16145.

41. Weizmann (London) to Eder (Jerusalem), July 4, 1922, in Weizmann, *Letters*, vol. 11, no. 142, p. 133.

42. *Letter from the Secretary to the Cabinet to the Secretary of the League of Nations of July 1, 1922, Enclosing a Note in Reply to Cardinal Gasparri's Letter of May 15, 1922. Addressed to the Secretary-General of the League of Nations*, Cmd. 1708 (London, 1922).

43. See A. Klieman, *Foundations of British Policy in the Arab World—The Cairo Conference of 1921* (Baltimore, 1970), p. 203. The principles of the new policy are included in the British document, Cmd. 1700, *Palestine, Correspondence with the Palestine Arab Delegation and the Zionist Organization* (London, 1922); see also E. Friesel, *Ha-mediniyut ha-ziyonit l'ahar hazharat Balfour, 1917–1922* (Tel Aviv, 1977), pp. 286–308.

44. Weizmann, *Letters*, vol. 11, footnote to no. 144, p. 135.

45. Shuckburgh to Lindsay, June 16, 1922, PRO, FO 371/7774, ISA. The Colonial Office consulted de Salis, who promised to see that the High Commissioner would be received at the Vatican without being rebuked.

46. De Salis (Vatican) to Foreign Office, July 3, 1922, PRO, FO 371/7777, E 6625/78/65.

47. Foreign Office to Graham (Rome), no. 185, July 5, 1922. PRO, FO 371/7777, E 6625/78/65.

48. Poincaré (Paris) to Lord Hardinge, July 10, 1922, PRO, FO 371/7777 E6886/78/65.

49. Hardinge to Balfour, July 10, 1922, PRO, FO 371/7777, E 6625/78/65.

50. Samuel to Churchill, July 6, 1922, PRO FO 371/7777, E 6840/78/65.

51. Isaac Sciaky (Rome) on behalf of the Italian Zionist Federation, to Weizmann (London), July 7, 1922, WA. Sciaky also cabled Weizmann that day that Samuel had visited the "priest" (the *galah*) and the "king" (the *melekh*) (ibid).

52. Newspapers quoted in *Israel*, July 6, 1922.

53. *Church Times*, June 30, 1922. The newspaper wrote: "The Zionist experiment is fast becoming not only a danger to world peace but a peril to the Jews themselves. . . . We feel today, especially after our experience of Russian Bolshevism, that there are in modern Jewry elements full of danger to our religion and social order." The article condemned Samuel's appointment on the ground that he was a Jew and warned: "Any insulting action in regard to pilgrims or the Holy Places of which Oriental Bolsheviks are perfectly capable, may produce a European crisis. . . . In the Holy Land Christianity and Islam also have interests and rights, and in the land the Bolshevik must have no place." See Weizmann (London) to David Eder (Jerusalem), July 4, 1922, in Weizmann, *Letters*, vol. 11, no. 141, pp. 132–33. Eder was then head of the Zionist Commission in Palestine.

54. Weizmann (London) to Julius Simon (New York), July 16, 1922, WA; see also Weizmann, *Letters*, vol. 11, no. 158, p. 144. Julius Simon (1875–1969) was a German-born American Jew; he resigned from the Zionist Executive in 1921 and joined the Brandeis group.

55. See I. Garzia, *La Questione Romana durante la I Guerra Mondiale* (Naples, 1981), p. 59.

56. See *Israel*, January 1916; J. Macabe, *The Papacy in Politics Today* (London, 1951), p. 21, who wrote that Germany probably promised the new pope temporal rule.

57. S. Marchese *La Francia il problema dei rapporti con la Santa Sede* (Naples, 1968), p. 343.

58. Ibid., p. 257.

59. Eder (Jerusalem) to Stein (London), May 16, 1922, WA; a copy was sent to Weizmann on May 31, 1922.

60. Sir Arthur Money, a general with the British army in Palestine from 1918 to 1919,

served as chief administrator of O.E.T.A. (Occupied Enemy Territory Administration), South.

61. Weizmann met Cardinal Van Rossum during his April 1922 visit to Rome, but we have no details of their conversation.

62. Eder (Jerusalem) to Weizmann (London), May 31, 1922, WA.

63. Bandack (London), in French, to Weizmann (London), June 30, 1922, WA; also in CZA Z4/16020. Probably he referred to Eric Milles, of the Colonial Office.

64. Beilinson (Rome) to Weizmann (London), July 10, 1922, and Weizmann's cable to Beilinson, July 11, 1922, in Weizmann, *Letters*, vol. 11, no. 153, p. 140.

65. Bandack (Rome), in French, to Weizmann (London), July 14, 1922, WA. He also wrote that Barlassina was received that day by the pope. Barlassina had probably completed his visit to England.

66. Letter of Authorization, July 17, 1922, approved by Suleiman Bandack on July 19, 1922, WA. The document we have is an Italian translation of the Arabic original.

67. A copy of a cable in French, on a Palestine postal service form, signed by Yakoub Alour, Francis Salib, Shukri Karmi, and Bandack, WA.

68. Lattes (Rome) to Weizmann (London), July 28, 1922, WA; also in CZA Z4/16081.

69. Bandack (Rome) to Weizmann (London), August 22, 1922, WA. At the end of the letter, Bandack wrote that he was left without money as a result of dental treatment he received from a swindler dentist who extorted £ 47 from him and presented him with an inflated bill for £ 600.

70. Weizmann (Jerusalem) to his wife (London), December 4–6, 1922, in Weizmann, *Letters,* vol. 11, no. 255, p. 218.

71. "The Mandate for Palestine—Memorandum Submitted to the Council of the League of Nations by the Zionist Organization, July 1922," p. 30, WA.

72. *Report of the Executive of the Zionist Organization to the XIIIth Zionist Congress* (London, 1923), pp. 8–9.

73. A. C. Jemolo, "Pio XI e la nuova situazione politica del papato," *Nuova Antologia* (1922): 378.

74. *Acta Apostolocae Sedis* 14, no. 17 (1922): 610–11; *The Tablet,* December 23, 1922.

Bibliography

Abbreviations

AA	Auswärtiges Amt, Bonn
AAE	Archives du Ministère des Affaires Etrangères, Paris
ABRE	Archives du Ministère des Relations Extérieures, Brussels
ASME	Archivio Storico del Ministero degli Affari Esteri, Rome
BD	*Documents on British Foreign Policy*
CO	Colonial Office
CZA	Central Zionist Archives, Jerusalem
DDI	*Documenti Diplomatici Italiani*
FO	Foreign Office
ISA	Israel State Archives, Jerusalem
PRO	Public Record Office, London
WA	Weizmann Archives, Rehovot (Israel)
WO	War Office

ARCHIVES

ARCHIVES DU MINISTÈRE DES AFFAIRES ETRANGÈRES
St. Siège

E 312.2; Paquet 27	1918–20; Vol. 13; Serie Z
E 312.2; Vol. 9	1918–20; Vol. 17
E 316.1	Serie Z-262

ARCHIVES DU MINISTÈRE DES RELATIONS EXTÉRIEURES
St. Siège 1918; St. Siège 1919–20; Dossier 11414; Dossier 114477; Classement B/160

ARCHIVIO STORICO DEL MINISTERO DEGLI AFFARI ESTERI
Pacco 184; Pacco 185; Pacco 186; Pacco 1457; Pacco 1467; Pacco 1564; Pacco 1566; Pacco 1567 (Siria/9); Pacco 1568 (Siria, 1921); Pacco 1572; Pacco 1575

AUSWÄRTIGES AMT
Palästina/Zionismus-N 902-Rom/Vat 157/1
III/Palästina Politik 5, Bd. I
Politik 6, Vatikan

CENTRAL ZIONIST ARCHIVES
1/28 A (Keren Hayesod, KH); LG/90/1; Z4/699; Z4/728; Z4/2136; Z4/4020; Z4/4124; Z4/16020; Z4/16081; Z4/16145; A18/25; A18/W; A18/15

ISRAEL STATE ARCHIVES
Archives of Sir Herbert Samuel
Copies of documents from the Public Record Office
Secretariat of the Mandatory government

PUBLIC RECORD OFFICE
War Cabinet Papers
CAB 17/11; CAB 21/77; CAB 23/3; CAB 24/136
Foreign Office Files (FO)
General Correspondence, Political: FO 371/2767; FO 371/3052; FO 371/4179; FO 371/4902; FO 371/5122; FO 371/5123; FO 371/5124; FO 371/5166; FO 371/5191; FO 371/5192; FO 371/5200; FO 371/5205; FO 371/5221; FO 371/5244; FO 371/6372; FO 371/6374; FO 371/6375; FO 371/6376; FO 371/6381; FO 371/6382; FO 371/6388; FO 371/6389; FO 371/6390; FO 371/6393; FO 371/6396; FO 371/6397; FO 371/6465; FO 371/6984; FO 371/7671; FO 371/7772; FO 371/7773; FO 371/7776; FO 371/7777; FO 371/7779; FO 371/7785; FO 371/7786; FO 371/7787; FO 371/7791; FO 371/7795; FO 371/9010; FO 371/10087; FO 371/10112; FO 371/10889; FO 371/11478
Confidential prints, Iraq: FO 406/44
Peace Conference, Paris (1919): FO 608/118
Holy See: FO 380/15; FO 380/16; FO 380/20
War Office (WO)
WO 106/189
Colonial Office (CO)
Original correspondence, 1921: CO 733/11; CO 733/16; ; CO 733/30; CO 733/31; CO 733/33; CO 733/34; CO 733/54; CO 733/65; CO 7339; CO 7349; CO 7369/33

WEIZMANN ARCHIVES
Letters from and to Weizmann

OFFICIAL PUBLICATIONS

GREAT BRITAIN
Cust, L. G. A. *The Status Quo in the Holy Places.* London: His Majesty's Stationery Office, 1929.
Documents on British Foreign Policy, 1919–1939, 1st ser., vols. 4, 7, 8, and 13. London: His (Her) Majesty's Stationery Office, 1952, 1958, 1963 (BD).
Parliament Papers by Command:
Cmd. 736. *Dispatch to Sir Henry Howard Containing Instructions Respecting His Mission*

to the Vatican Presented to Both Houses of Parliament by Command of His Majesty. London: His Majesty's Stationery Office, January 1915.

Cmd. 964. *Treaty of Peace with Turkey, Sèvres, August 10, 1920.* London: His Majesty's Stationery Office, 1920.

Cmd. 1176. *Draft Mandates for Mesopotamia and Palestine As Submitted for the Approval of the League of Nations, December 1920.* London: His Majesty's Stationery Office, 1921.

Cmd. 1500. *Final Drafts of the Mandates for Mesopotamia and Palestine for the Approval of the Council of the League of Nations, August 1921.* London: His Majesty's Stationery Office, 1921.

Cmd. 1700. *Palestine, Correspondence with the Palestine Arab Delegation and the Zionist Organization.* London: His Majesty's Stationery Office, 1922.

Cmd. 1708. *Letter from the Secretary to the Cabinet to the Secretary of the League of Nations of July 1, 1922, Enclosing a Note in Reply to Cardinal Gasparri's Letter of May 15, 1922, Addressed to the Secretary General of the League of Nations.* London: His Majesty's Stationery Office, 1922.

ZIONIST ORGANIZATIONS

Great-Britain, Palestine and the Jews. London, 1917.

The Mandate for Palestine—Memorandum Submitted to the Council of the League of Nations, July 1922.

Report of the Executive of the Zionist Organization to the Thirteenth Zionist Congress. London, 1922.

Zionism During the War, a Record of Zionist Political Activity, 1914–1921. London, 1921.

NATIONAL SOCIETIES

Commission des Lieux saints. Communiqué aux membres du conseil. Note du secrétaire général, n. 1/24687/4406; c 781/1922. Vol. 6. Geneva, December 22, 1922.

Mandat pour la Palestine. Note du secrétaire général c 322.1922. Vol. 6. Geneva, May 23, 1922.

Official Journal, 1922.

UNITED STATES

Papers Relating to the Foreign Relations of the U.S., The Lansing Papers, 1914–1920. Vol. 2. Washington, D.C.: Government Printing Office, 1940.

BOOKS

Addis, W. E., and T. Arnold. *A Catholic Dictionary.* London: Routledge and Kegan Paul, 1951.

Adelson, R. *The Formation of British Policy Towards the Middle East, 1914–1918.* Ann Arbor, Mich.: University Microfilms, 1972.

Adelson, R. *Mark Sykes—Portrait of an Amateur.* London: Jonathan Cape, 1975.

The American Jewish Yearbook, 5680. September 1919–September 1920. Vol. 21. Philadelphia: Jewish Publication Society, 1919.

Asaf, M. *Hayahasim beyn haaravim vehayehudim beEretz-Yisrael (1860–1948) (The Relations Between Arabs and Jews in Eretz-Israel [1860–1948]).* Tel Aviv: Tarbut vehinuch, 1970.

Asaf, M. *Hitorerut haaravim beEretz-Yisrael ubrihatam (The Awakening of the Arabs in Eretz-Israel and Their Flight).* Tel Aviv: Mifalei Tarbut vehinuch, 1967.

Ashbee, C. R. *Jerusalem 1918–20, Records of the Pro-Jerusalem Council During the Period of the British Military Administration 1918–1920*. London: Murray, 1921.

Bachi, R. *The Population of Israel*. Jerusalem: Hebrew University, 1977.

Beaverbrook, W. M. *Men & Power, 1917–1918*. London: Collins, 1956.

Bein, A. *Teodor Herzl* (in Hebrew). Jerusalem: Hasifrià Hazionit, 1977.

Ben Arieh Y. *Ir bereì tekufà, Yerushalaym hehadashà bereshità (A City Reflected in Its Times. New Jerusalem—The Beginnings)*. Jerusalem: Yad Ben-Zvi, 1979.

Blum, X. Z. *The Juridical Status of Jerusalem*. Jerusalem: Davis Institute, 1974.

Bourne, F. *Occasional Sermons*. London: Sheed & Ward, 1930.

Bovis, E. *The Jerusalem Question, 1917–1968*. Stanford, Calif.: Hoover Institution Press, 1971.

Bowle, A. *Viscount Samuel*. London: Gollancz, 1957.

Brière, Y., de la. *L'Organisation internationale du monde contemporain et la papauté souveraine*, 1st ser. (1885–1924). Paris: Spes, 1930.

Buonaiuti, E. *Pellegrino di Roma, la generazione dell'esodo*. Rome: Darsena, 1945.

Cardinale, H. E. *The Holy See and the International Order*. Gerrards Cross, England: Colin Smith, 1976.

Charles-Roux, P. *Souvenirs diplomatiques Rome–Quirinale (Fevrier 1916–Fevrier 1919)*. Paris: Fayard, 1958.

Chouraqui, A. *Theodore Herzl, inventeur de l'Etat d'Israel, 1860–1904*. Paris: Club des Editeurs, 1960.

Clarke, J. G. *L'Enjeu chrétien au Proche-Orient*. Paris: Centurion, 1965.

Coen, A. *Israel wehaolam haaravì (Israel and the Arab World)*. Merhavia, Israel: Sifriat Hapoalim, 1964.

Cohn, N. *Warrant for Genocide. The Myth of the Jewish World Conspiracy and the Protocols of the Elders of Zion*. London: Eyre and Spottiswood, 1967.

Colbi, S. P. *Christianity in the Holy Land—Past and Present*. Tel Aviv: Am Hassefer, 1969.

Collin, B. *Les Lieux saints*. Paris: Les Éditions Internationales, 1948.

Collin, B. *Les Lieux saints*. Paris: PUF, 1962.

Collin, B. *Le problème juridique des Lieux saints*. Paris: Sirey, 1956.

Collin, B. *Recueil de documents concernant Jerusalem et les Lieux saints*. Jerusalem: Franciscan Printing Press, 1982.

Dodd, W. E., Jr., and M. Dodd. *Ambassador Dodd's Diary*. New York: Harcourt Brace, 1941.

Enciclopedia Cattolica. Vatican City, 1949.

Esco Foundation for Palestine. *Palestine, a Study of Jewish, Arab and British Policies*. Vol. 1. New Haven, Conn.: Yale University Press, 1947.

Farhat, E. *Gerusalemme nei documenti pontifici*. Vatican City: Libreria Editrice Vaticana, 1987.

Feldblum, E. *The American Catholic Press and the Jewish State, 1917–1959*. New York: Ktav, 1977.

Fishel, W. R. *The End of Extraterritoriality in China*. Berkeley: University of California Press, 1952.

Friedman, I. *Germany—Turkey and Zionism, 1897–1918*. New York: Oxford University Press, 1977.

Friedman, I. *The Question of Palestine, 1914–1918*. New York: Schocken, 1973.

Friesel, E. *Hamediniut hazionit leahar hatzarat Balfour, 1917–1922 (The Zionist Policy After the Balfour Declaration, 1917–1922)*. Tel Aviv: Tel Aviv University, Hakibbutz Hameuhad, 1977.

Frumkin, G. *Dereh shofet biyerushalaym (The Behavior of a Judge in Jerusalem)*. Tel Aviv: Dvir, 1945.

Garzia, I. *La Questione Romana durante la I Guerra Mondiale*. Naples: ESI, 1981.

Gassi, A. *Contributo alla soluzione della questione dei Luoghi Santi*. Jerusalem: Tip. dei Francescani, 1935.

Gelber, G. M. *Hatzarat Balfour wetoldotea (The Balfour Declaration and Its History)*. Jerusalem: Haanhalà hazionit, 1938.

Giannini A. *L'ultima fase della questione orientale, 1913–1923*. Rome: Istituto per l'Oriente, 1933.

Gilbert, M. *Exile and Return*. Jerusalem: Steimatzky, 1978.

Grabill, J. L. *Protestant Diplomacy and the Near East: Missionary Influence on American Policy, 1810–1927*. Minneapolis: University of Minnesota Press, 1971.

Gregory, J. D. *On the Edge of Diplomacy, 1902–1928*. London: Hutchison, 1928.

Hachey, T. E. *Anglo-Vatican Relations, 1914–1939; Confidential Annual Reports of the British Ministers to the Holy See*. Boston: Hall, 1972.

Hajjar, J. *Les Chrétiens au Proche-Orient*. Paris: Seuil, 1962.

Herzl, T. *The Complete Diaries of Theodor Herzl*. Edited by R. Patai. New York: Herzl Press and T. Yoseloff, 1960.

Herzl, T. *The Diaries of Theodor Herzl*. Edited by M. Lowenthal. New York: Dial Press, 1956; London: Gollancz, 1958.

Herzl, T. *The Jewish State, an Attempt at a Modern Solution of the Jewish Question*. New York: American Zionist Emergency Council, 1946.

Herzl, T. *Tagebücher, 1895–1904*. Berlin: Judischer Verlag, 1922–23.

Herzog, Y. *Israel and the Middle East, an Introduction*. Jerusalem: Hebrew University, Davis Institute, 1975.

Howard, H. *The King–Crane Commission*. Beirut: Khayats, 1963.

Hyamson, A. *Palestine Under the Mandate, 1920–1948*. Westport, Conn.: Greenwood Press, 1976.

Ingrams, D. *Palestine Papers, 1917–1922, Seeds of Conflicts*. London: Murray, 1972.

Isaac, J. *L'enseignement du mépris*. Paris: Fasquelle, 1962.

Yisraeli, B. *HaReich haghermanì veEretz-Yisrael (The German Reich and Eretz–Israel)*. Ramat-Gan, Israel: Universitat Bar Ilan, 1970.

Issa, A. O. *Les Minorités chrétiennes de Palestine*. Jerusalem: Franciscan Printing Press, 1977.

Katz, Y. *Bonim hofshiim weyehudim (Freemasons and Jews)*. Jerusalem: Mosad Bialik, 1967.

Kimche, J. *The Unromantics: The Great Powers and the Balfour Declaration*. London: Weidenfeld & Nicolson, 1968.

Klieman, A. *Foundations of British Policy in the Arab World: The Cairo Conference of 1921*. Baltimore: Johns Hopkins University Press, 1970.

Köck, H. F. *Der Vatikan und Palästina*. Vienna: Herold, 1973.

Lambelin, R. *Protocoles de sages de Sion*. Paris: Grasset, 1921.

Lapide, P. *The Last Three Popes and the Jews*. London: Souvenir Press, 1967.

Laquer, W. *A History of Zionism*. New York: Holt, Rinehart and Winston, 1972.

Lattes, D. *Il Sionismo*. 2 vols. Rome: Paolo Cremonese, 1928.

Les Lieux saints et la Palestine: Mémoire des Latins à la Conférence de la Paix en 1919. Jerusalem: Imprimerie des Frères Franciscains, 1922.

Loiseau, C. *Politique romaine et sentiment français*. Paris: Grasset, 1923.

Mannucci, C. *Antisemitismo e ideologia cristiana sugli Ebrei*. Milan: Unicopli, 1982.

Manuel, F. E. *The Realities of American–Palestine Relations*. Washington, D.C.: Public Affairs Press, 1949.

Marchese, S. *La Francia ed il problema dei rapporti con la Santa Sede (1914–1924).* Naples: Edizioni Scientifiche Italiane, 1969.

Massey, W. T. *How Jerusalem Was Won.* London: Constable, 1919.

McCabe, J. *The Papacy in Politics Today,* London: Watts, 1951.

McCormick, A. O'Hare. *Vatican Journal, 1921–1954.* Edited by M. T. Sheehan. New York: Farrar, Straus, and Cudahy, 1957.

McKnight, S. P. *The Papacy. A New Appraisal.* London: McGraw-Hill, 1953.

Meinertzhagen, R. *Middle East Diary, 1917–1956.* London: Cresset Press, 1959.

Meyendorff, J. *The Orthodox Church.* London: Darton, Longman & Todd, 1962.

Mills, E. *Census of Palestine, 1931.* Vol. 1. Alexandria, Egypt: Printed for the Government of Palestine by Whitehead Morris, 1933.

Minerbi, S. *Angelo Levi Bianchini e la sua opera nel Levante, 1918–1920.* Milan: Fondazione Sally Mayer, 1967.

Minerbi, S. *L'Italie et la Palestine, 1914–1920.* Paris: PUF, 1970.

Missir, L. A. *Eglise et état en Turquie et au Proche-Orient.* Brussels: Dembla, 1973.

Missir, L. *Rome et les églises d'Orient.* Brussels: La Pensée Universelle, 1976.

Monzie, A. de. *Rome sans Canosse.* 1918.

Negro, S. *L'Ordinamento della Chiesa Cattolica.* Milan: Bompiani, 1940.

Nevakivi, J. *Britain, France and the Arab Middle East, 1914–1920.* London: Athlone, 1969.

Noel, G. *The Anatomy of the Catholic Church.* New York: Doubleday, 1980.

Oldmeadow, E. *Francis Cardinal Bourne.* London: Burns Oats Washbourne, 1944.

Le Pape et Jerusalem. Solution de la question italienne et de la question orientale. Paris: E. Dentu, 1861.

Parkes, J. *A History of Palestine from 135 A.D. to Modern Times.* London: Gollancz, 1949.

Pélissié du Rausas, G. *Le Régime des capitulations dans l'Empire Ottoman.* Paris: Arthur Rousseau, 1910–11.

Per la liberazione di Gerusalemme, Giudizi ed impressioni originali raccolti dall'Agenzia Volta. Rome: Tipog. Centenari, 1917.

Pichetto, M. T. *Alle radici dell'odio. Preziosi e Benigni antisemiti.* Milan: Franco Angeli, 1983.

Poincaré, R. *Au service de la France.* Vol. 6. Paris: Plon, 1930.

Porat, Y. *The Emergence of the Palestinian–Arab National Movement, 1918–1929.* London: Cass, 1974.

Randall, A. *Vatican Assignment.* London: Heinemann, 1956.

Rendel, G. *The Sword and the Olive, 1913–1954.* London: Murray, 1957.

Rhodes, A. *The Vatican in the Age of the Dictators, 1922–1945.* London: Hodder and Stoughton, 1973.

Riquet, M. *Un Chrétien face à Israel.* Paris: Laffont, 1975.

Royal Institute of International Affairs. *Great Britain and Palestine, 1915–1945.* London and New York: Royal Institute of International Affairs, 1974.

Sacra Congregazione per le Chiese Orientali. *Oriente Cattolico.* Vatican City, 1974.

La Sacra Congregazione per le Chiese Orientali nel cinquantesimo della fondazione (1917–1967). Rome, 1967.

Salvatorelli, L. *La politica della Santa Sede dopo la guerra.* Milan: ISPI, 1937.

Samuel, H. *Memoirs.* London: Cresset Press, 1945.

Sanders, R. *The High Walls of Jerusalem: A History of the Balfour Declaration and the Birth of the British Mandate for Palestine.* New York: Holt, Rinehart and Winston, 1983.

Sayegh, S. *Le statu quo des Lieux saints. Nature juridique et portée internationale.* Rome: Pontificia Università Lateranense, 1971.

Scoppola, P. *La Chiesa e il fascismo, documenti e interpretazioni.* Bari, Italy: Laterza, 1979.

Simonet, A. *L'Orient chrétien au seuil de l'unité.* Namur, Belgium: 1962.

Sokolow, F. *Aví Nahum Sokolow (My Father, Nahum Sokolow)*. Jerusalem: Hasifria Hazionit, 1970.

Sokolow, N. *History of Zionism, 1600–1918*. London: Longman, 1919.

Sousa, N. *The Capitulatory Regime of Turkey*. London: 1933.

Spadolini, G. *Il cardinale Gasparri e la questione romana*. Florence: Le Monnier, 1972.

Stein, L. *The Balfour Declaration*. London: Valentine & Mitchell, 1961.

Storrs, R. *Orientations*, London: Nicholson & Watson, 1937.

Stoyanovsky, J. *The Mandate for Palestine*. London: Longman Group, 1928.

Sykes, C. *Two Studies in Virtue*. London: Collins, 1953.

Tibawi, A. L. *Arab Education in Mandatory Palestine, a Study of Three Decades of British Administration*. London: Luzac, 1956.

Tolkowsky, S. *Yoman zioní mediní, 1915–1919 (Zionist Political Diary, 1915–1919)*. Jerusalem: Hasifria Hazionit, 1980.

Toscano, M. *Il patto di London*. Bologna: Zanichelli, 1934.

Vital, D. *Zionism: The Formative Years*, Oxford: Clarendon Press, 1982.

Weizmann, C. *The Letters and Papers of Chaim Weizmann*. Vols. 7, 8, 9. Edited by M. Weisgal. Jerusalem: Israel University Press, 1975–77.

Weizmann, C. *Trial and Error*. Philadelphia: Jewish Publication Society, 1949.

Weizmann, V. *The Impossible Takes Longer, the Memoirs of Vera Weizmann*. Edited by D. Tutaev. London: Hamish Hamilton, 1967.

Zander W. *Israel and the Holy Places of Christendom*. London: Weidenfeld & Nicolson, 1971.

ARTICLES

Aubert, R. H. "Les Démarches du cardinal Mercier en vue de l'octroi à la Belgique d'un mandat sur la Palestine." *Bulletin de la classe des lettres et sciences morales et politiques*, 5th ser., vol. 65 (1979).

Berkowitz, S. "Hazaot leesder maamadam shel hamekomot hakedoshim bemisgeret hesder shalom" (Proposals for an Arrangement of the Holy Places' Status in the Framework of a Peace Treaty). In Ora Ahimeir, ed., *Yerushalaym, hebetim mishpatiim (Jerusalem, Legal Aspects)*. Jerusalem: Mahon Yerushalaym lemehkar, 1980.

Bertola, A. "Il protettorato religioso in Oriente e l'accordo del 4.12.1926 fra la S. Sede e la Francia." *Oriente Moderno*, October 1928, pp. 437–54; November 1928, pp. 501–11.

Boubée, O. "Les Juifs en Hongrie." *Etudes* 165 (October–December 1920), (January–March 1921).

Brière, Y. de la. "Les Raisons nationales et internationales de renouer avec le Vatican." *Etudes*, 5, no. 7 (1917).

Calisse. "Il Cardinale Pietro Gasparri." *Nuova Antologia* 16, no. 3 (1933).

Caviglia, E. "Il Sionismo e la Palestina negli articoli dell'*Osservatore Romano* e della *Civiltà Cattolica* (1919–1923)." *Clio*, January–March 1981, pp. 79–89.

Crispolti, C. "Il pericolo della nazione ebraica in Palestina." *Rassegna Italiana del Mediterraneo* 4 (April–May 1921).

Engelard, Y. "Maamadam hamishpati shel hamekomot hakedoshim" (The Juridical Status of the Holy Places). In Ora Ahimeir, ed., *Yerushalaym, hebetim mishpatiim*. Jerusalem: Mahon Yerushalaym lemehkar, 1980.

Harel, M. "The Jewish Presence in Jerusalem Throughout the Ages." In *Jerusalem*. New York: John Day, 1974.

Jemolo, A. C., "Pio XI e la nuova situazione politica del papato." *Nuova Antologia*, 1922.

Kaufman, M. "George Antonius weharzot habrit" (George Antonius and the United States). In G. Wigoder, ed., *Yunim beyahadut zemanenu mugashim le Moshè Davis (Contemporary Jewry—Studies in Honor of Moshe Davis)*. Jerusalem: Institute of Contemporary Jewry. Hebrew University, 1984.

Klein, C. "Vatican and Zionism, 1897–1967." *Christian Attitudes on Jews and Judaism* 36–37 (June–August, 1974).

Loiseau, C. "Ma Mission auprès du Vatican (1913–1918)." *Revue d'histoire diplomatique*, April–June 1960.

Loiseau, I. "Une Mission diplomatique près du Saint Siège, 1914–1919." *La Revue des deux mondes* 1, no. 5 (1956).

"Memorandum; Greeks and Franciscans in the Holy Places." *Nea Sion*, 1920.

Minerbi, S. "Gli ultimi due incontri Weizmann–Mussolini (1933–1934)." *Storia Contemporanea* 5, no. 3 (1974).

Minerbi, S. "The Italian Activity to Recover the 'Cenacolo.'" *Risorgimento* 1, no. 2 (1980), 181–209.

Minerbi, S. "Il Vaticano e la Palestina durante la prima guerra mondiale." *Clio*, July–September 1967, pp. 424–44.

Molajoni, P. "Il programma della S. Sede per la Palestina." *Il Giornale d'Italia* 17, no. 3 (1919).

Nahon, U. "Herzl e Sokolow in Vaticano." In *Scritti sull'Ebraismo in memoria di G. Bedarida*. Florence: Giuntina, 1966.

Nahon, U. "Le Lettere di T. Herzl a Felice Ravenna." *La Rassegna mensile di Israel* 16, no. 6 (1950).

Pini-Tronati, A. "Jules Van den Heuvel, ambasciatore presso la S. Sede (Lettere del 1916)." *Risorgimento* 15, no. 1 (1972).

Pixner, B. "Putting Bethsaida–Julias on the Map." *Christians News from Israel*, 37, no. 4 (1982).

Rossi, G. "Come nacque e maturò l'idea di una grande Università Palestinese." *Il Corriere d'Italia* 22, no. 9 (1923).

Simon, R. "Hamaavak al hamekomot hakedoshim lanazrut beEretz–Yisrael betekufà haottomanit, 1516–1583" (The Struggle for the Christian Holy Places in Palestine During the Ottoman Period, 1516–1583). *Kathedra* 17 (September 1981): 107–26.

Toscano M. "Colloqui con Gafenco." In *Pagine di storia diplomatica contemporanea*. Milan: Giuffrè, 1963.

Tritonj, R. "La questione dei Luoghi Santi." In *L'Italia e il Levante*. Rome, 1934.

Tsimhoni. D. "The Arab Christians and the Palestinian Arab National Movement During the Formative Stage." In *The Palestinians and the Middle East Conflict*. Ramat-Gan, Israel: Turtledove, 1978.

Wenkert, J. "Les Archives de Herzl." In *Theodore Herzl*. Jerusalem, 1960.

Zander, W. "On the Settlement of Disputes About the Christian Holy Places." *Israel Law Review* 8, no. 3 (1973).

NEWSPAPERS AND PERIODICALS

Acta Apostolicae Sedis (Vatican City), 1917–21.

Civiltà Cattolica (Rome) 1887–89, 1919–21.

Il Corriere d'Italia (Frankfurt), 1923.

La Croix (Paris), 1917–20.

The Daily Telegraph (London), 1927.

La Documentation Catholique (Paris), 1920–22.

L'Echo (Lausanne), 1921.

Fede e Ragione (Florence), 1922.
Il Giornale d'Italia (Rome), 1919.
Haaretz (Tel Aviv), 1921.
L'Homme Libre (St. Etienne), 1923.
Israel (Florence), 1916–22.
L'Italie (Rome), 1922.
The Jewish Chronicle (London), 1897, 1917–19.
Le Journal des Débats (Paris), 1920.
Le Journal de Genève (Geneva), 1917.
Jüdische Presszentrale (Zurich), 1921.
Il Messaggero (Rome), 1921.
Morning Post (London), 1920.
Oriente Moderno (Rome), 1921–26.

L'Osservatore Romano (Vatican City), 1917–22.
The Palestine Weekly (Jerusalem), 1922.
La Rassegna mensile di Israel (Città di Castrello), 1950.
Il Resto del Carlino (Bologna), 1918–21.
Risorgimento (Brussels), 1972, 1980.
The Tablet (London), 1922.
Il Tempo (Rome), 1920.
Le Temps (Paris), 1921.
The Times (London), 1922.
La Tribuna (Rome), 1919.
Die Welt (Vienna), 1904.
The Zionist Review (London), 1920–22.

Index